D0556277

AFRICAN EXPRESSIVE CULTURES

Patrick McNaughton, editor

ASSOCIATE EDITORS

Catherine M. Cole

Barbara G. Hoffman

Eileen Julien

Kassim Koné

D. A. Masolo

Elisha Renne

Zoë Strother

HIP HOP AFRICA

New African Music in a Globalizing World

EDITED BY ERIC CHARRY

INDIANA UNIVERSITY PRESS
BLOOMINGTON AND INDIANAPOLIS

This book is a publication of

Indiana University Press
601 North Morton Street
Bloomington, Indiana 47404-3797 USA

iupress.indiana.edu

Telephone orders   800-842-6796
Fax orders   812-855-7931

∞ The paper used in this publication meets the minimum
requirements of the American National Standard for
Information Sciences—Permanence of Paper for Printed
Library Materials, ANSI Z39.48-1992.

Manufactured in the United States of America

Library of Congress Cataloging-in-Publication Data

Hip hop Africa : new African music in a globalizing world /
edited by Eric Charry.
     pages cm. — (African expressive cultures)
   Includes bibliographical references and index.
   Includes discography, videography, and webography.
   ISBN 978-0-253-00307-2 (cloth : alkaline paper) — ISBN
978-0-253-00575-5 (paperback : alkaline paper) — ISBN 978-
0-253-00582-3 (ebook) 1. Rap (Music)—Africa—History and
criticism. 2. Popular music—Africa—History and criticism. 3.
Hip hop—Africa. 4. Music and youth—Africa. 5. Music and
globalization—Africa. 6. Popular music—Social aspects—
Africa. I. Charry, Eric S., editor. II. Series: African expressive
cultures.
   ML3531.H565 2012
   782.421649096—dc23
                                                    2011052793

1 2 3 4 5 17 16 15 14 13 12

For our parents and our children

CONTENTS

PREFACE
ERIC CHARRY

This book has its origins in a roundtable entitled "New Music, New Research: Youth, Western Africa, and the Outside World," which was part of the 2003 African Studies Association annual meeting in Boston, whose theme was "Youthful Africa in the 21st Century." The enthusiastic reception suggested that we expand our scope into the resulting book. Here thirteen authors carefully look at and listen to what young Africans are doing in the realm of music. They are an international group of scholars from Ghana, Nigeria, Kenya, South Africa, Germany, and the United States. Nine countries are examined: Senegal and Mali in the Muslim western sahel and savanna; Côte d'Ivoire, Ghana, and Nigeria along the southern coast of West Africa; Kenya and Tanzania on the Swahili coast in the east; Malawi in the heart of central Africa; and South Africa, with the most significant multiracial and white minority communities and racially polarized past. The Mediterranean Arab-tinged Muslim north is unfortunately missing here.

The approaches herein are diverse, including focusing on single artists or pieces (Tang, Reed), broad overviews (Charry, Watkins, Collins, Seebode), a balance between the two approaches (Shipley, Fenn, Schulz, Shonekan, Kidula, Perullo), and intensive participatory ethnography (Polak). While the bulk of the contributions here cover hip hop and are responsible for the title of the book, the inclusion of reggae and ragga (Reed, Fenn, Seebode), gospel music (Kidula, Collins), and especially drumming (Polak) adds a unique comparative dimension. The variety of approaches and musics make for a rich story of how recent generations of Africans are making sense of the world around them.

The countries covered in this book are in many ways representative of Africa, although, to be sure, they each have their own identities. The most populous country (Nigeria) and the country with the biggest economy (South Africa) in Africa are covered here. The countries with strong international reputations for hip hop are here (Senegal, Tanzania) as is Malawi, which has a minimal presence. Kenya, where politics and rap have been closely intertwined; Côte d'Ivoire, where a reggae song sent an artist into exile; Ghana, with its close ties to the United States and the UK; and Mali, where drumming traditions thrive in an urban environment, are all present.

The following table shows some statistics that may be helpful in grasping the economic and demographic standing of these countries, both within Africa and also compared to the United States and France (I have added Algeria to represent North Africa). African nations have some of the youngest populations in the world, in part because of the short life expectancy. The third youngest median population in the world is represented here: Mali (the first two are Uganda and Niger). Four of the twelve countries with the highest HIV/AIDS infection rates in the world are represented here (South Africa, Malawi, Kenya, Tanzania); the other eight are neighboring countries. Access to the internet is extremely low in Africa, especially compared with the most prosperous nations of the world.

As our sources come from a variety of media, readers may need to search through the bibliography, discography (including separate sections for Tanzania and Malawi), and videography to find a particular citation. Online articles and radio interviews and documentaries are placed in the bibliography. Indiana University Press's website for the book contains links to supplemental sources.

We would like to thank Indiana University Press editor Dee Mortensen for helping to bring this book to fruition, Magee McIlvaine for his photos on the front cover, and the artists for their permission to print their lyrics in this volume. All authors' royalties earned from the sales of this book will be donated to a nongovernmental organization working to improve the lives of young Africans through music or dance (see the book website at www.iupress.indiana.edu/a/hiphop for details).

Population and other statistics of countries discussed in this volume

Country	Population in millions (2011)	Median age (2011)	GDP per capita (2010)	% Christian	% Muslim	% Adult HIV/ AIDS rate (2009)	Internet users in millions* (2009)
Algeria	34.9	27.6	$7,400		99	0.1	4.7
Côte d'Ivoire	21.5	19.6	$1,800	32.8	38.6	3.4	.97
Ghana	24.7	21.4	$1,600	68.8	15.9	1.8	1.3
Kenya	41.0	18.9	$1,600	78	10	6.3	4.0
Malawi	15.8	17.2	$900	79.9	12.8	11	.72
Mali	14.1	16.3	$1,200	1	90	1.0	.25
Nigeria	155.2	19.2	$2,400	40	50	3.6	44.0
Senegal	12.6	18.0	$1,900	5	94	0.9	.92
South Africa	49.0	25.0	$10,700	79.7	1.5	17.8	4.42
Tanzania	42.7	18.5	$1,500	30	35**	5.6	.68
USA	313.2	36.9	$47,400	78.5	0.6	0.6	239.9
France	65.1	39.9	$33,300	85–90	5–10	0.4	44.6

Sources: http://www.cia.gov/library/publications/the-world-factbook/.
*http://data.worldbank.org/indicator/IT.NET.USER.
**Mainland Tanzania; Zanzibar is 99 percent Muslim.

HIP HOP AFRICA

A Capsule History of African Rap

ERIC CHARRY

The notion that rap has arrived home, in Africa, common in much rhetoric both inside and outside Africa, demands investigation. African rap artists get little international respect. Representing the inspirational homeland, Africans can find a small audience abroad, but there is hardly any competing in the international marketplace in that role. Some Africans, young and old, vigorously object to some of the surface values purveyed in commercial hip hop culture, such as the pursuit and display of high price consumer goods, glorification or romanticizing of street violence and vulgar language, and public degradation of women. If rap has come home, something that could be said of any artistic form created by peoples of African descent around the world that has been embraced within Africa, it has been primarily young people, part of an African hip hop generation, who embraced this distant relation.

After an incubation period in the 1980s, marked by imitation of its American source, African rappers came into their own in the 1990s. African hip hop has reached a maturity and urgency illustrated by a recent intense and remarkable flurry of documentary films from across the continent—Morocco, Senegal, Burkina Faso, Ghana, South Africa, Tanzania, Kenya, Uganda, and Equatorial Guinea (see the videography)—each in their own way making compelling cases for how the genre has become one of the most relevant cultural forms of expression for African youth. The presence of African hip hop videos on YouTube is equally remarkable and overwhelming. MP3 audio recordings can be found easily enough, but still, one has to search hard to find CDs on the international market, one sure sign of a lack of record label and hence economic support.

What follows is a preliminary history of rap in Africa.

Out of New York

The story of the growth of rap and hip hop in the United States is well known, and there are hundreds of books and theses and many magazines, films, and websites seriously documenting the genre.[1] It originated in the streets of New York in the 1970s, born out of those specific historical circumstances that threw

Caribbean immigrants in with local African American urban culture, marked by concerns of neighborhood security and pride, which often erupted into gang turf battles. Rap emerged as a grassroots party music associated with neighborhood DJs (disc jockeys or record spinners) and then MCs (masters of ceremonies or rappers).[2] It was part of a broader New York borough youth culture (e.g., Bronx, Brooklyn, Queens) that came to be known as hip hop, which included break dancing and graffiti. Semiprivate and public events throughout the mid- and late 1970s were more or less confined within this geographically limited culture. Commercial recordings, which could disseminate the music and dance beyond its borders of origin, were not being made, and MCs and DJs were not yet performing for a broader public.

In the late 1970s, rap and hip hop moved outward on two fronts: recordings and live events. Break dancers doing their moves (usually to recorded music) on Manhattan sidewalks for passersby became more common, although the first major newspaper report to take it seriously did not come until 1981 when hip hop had already gone commercial (Banes 1981). While graffiti had beleaguered the streets and subway trains in New York City for at least a decade (the general public did not necessarily see it as "art"), graffiti taggers (writers) began to gain attention as artists. In 1979 street and subway train graffiti taggers "Fab Five" Freddy Brathwaite (from Brooklyn) and Lee Quiñones (from Manhattan's Lower East Side), both only 19 years old, landed an art show in Italy. Brathwaite had been hanging out in downtown Manhattan, and he became hip hop's ambassador to the predominantly white world of trendy art galleries and music and dance clubs. By the end of 1980 he was immortalized in the downtown white new wave group Blondie's "Rapture," a pseudo-rap that went to number one on the pop singles chart early the next year. Brathwaite's entrepreneurial work bore fruit by 1982 with the making of *Wild Style,* a film he helped conceive and in which he appeared (the first film to document rap and hip hop culture), Friday rap nights at the Roxy, a dance club in the Chelsea neighborhood of Manhattan, and a legendary hip hop tour of England and France. Brathwaite was the obvious choice as co-host for American MTV's first regular show dedicated to rap in 1988.

Rap recordings—the primary means of disseminating the genre abroad—became a viable commercial product as the New Jersey–based Sugarhill label released "Rappers Delight" by the Sugarhill Gang, which broke into the top ten of the Black Singles chart in late 1979 and the Pop Top 40 by early 1980. The pantheon of pioneer rap artists (those who would later be called old school) and labels would very quickly establish themselves on the commercial market. The earliest stars included Harlem MC Kurtis Blow, whose "The Breaks" (1980) was the first rap single to be certified gold (500,000 copies sold), DJ Grandmaster Flash (born in Barbados, raised in the Bronx) and the Furious Five ("The Message," 1982), Bronx DJ, community organizer, and Zulu nation founder Afrika Bambaataa ("Planet Rock," 1982), and Queens natives Run-D.M.C. ("It's Like That," 1983), whose 1986 album

Raising Hell was the first rap album to hit number one on the R&B chart, to break into the top ten of the pop album chart, and to be certified platinum (1 million copies sold).[3]

Wild Style was a small budget independently produced film. A series of more lavish Hollywood-produced films were distributed widely and were among the first wave of videos to expose Africans to break dancing and rap performance. The first major exposure was a brief scene featuring dancing by the Bronx-based Rock Steady Crew in the hit film *Flashdance,* released in the United States in April 1983. The first films devoted exclusively to the new culture included *Breakin'* (May 1984, with Ice T), *Beat Street* (June 1984, with Afrika Bambaataa, Kool Herc, Melle Mel, Kool Moe D, Rock Steady Crew, and New York City Breakers), *Breakin' 2: Electric Boogaloo* (December 1984, with Ice T), and *Krush Groove* (October 1985, with Run-D.M.C., Kurtis Blow, and LL Cool J). Through video cassette copies, these films made their way to Africa and were some of the most important models there for the development of hip hop culture, especially dancing.

Beyond audio and video recordings, foreign tours of American hip hop practitioners, beginning when Kurtis Blow had a support slot on Blondie's 1980 British tour (Terrell 1999: 46), were one important means of spreading the genre. Tours to Europe became more common throughout the 1980s, and Africa became a destination by the end of the decade.

African Origins?

While rap historians point to the spoken word artistry of public figures such as boxer Muhammad Ali in the 1960s and musical artists like the Last Poets and Gil Scott-Heron in the early 1970s as progenitors, it is important to distinguish between the commercial genre known as rap (and its accompanying hip hop culture) and more deeply rooted noncommercial oral traditions, including those which laid the artistic groundwork for the birth of the genre. Using this same reasoning, one must make a similar distinction in Africa. American rap was the source for African rap, and it was not necessarily the deep historical and cultural connections that caused Africans to embrace American rap. On the one hand, it was initially only an elite Westernized segment of African youth that embraced rap, and on the other hand, rap has been embraced around the world by peoples that have few, if any, kind of connections with Africa or African Americans. Rap was a youth music, which was perhaps its most attractive quality. Furthermore, it was a malleable form and could be shaped to fit local circumstances.

The myriad traditions of public speaking, poetry, storytelling, epic recitation, chanting, and percussion performance in Africa that resemble in one way or another some stylistic element of modern-day rap (some of which are described in the chapters that follow) may indeed have laid the groundwork centuries ago when they moved across the Atlantic. But African rap did not emerge from these homegrown traditions. Most first-generation African rappers had little relationship with the traditional performance genres of their home countries and were often more culturally allied with the United States. Rap as the expressive genre of choice for the children of the post-independence generation of Africans did not emerge out of any traditions on African soil, but rather began as a direct imitation and appropriation of imported American rap. African rap did not gain a voice of its own until rappers began to shed some American influences, which entailed rapping in their local tongues about local issues. Second- and third-generation African rappers completing the loop and making organic connections with deep-rooted traditions is one of the most fascinating recent developments, adding a degree of linguistic and cultural sophistication that moves the genre to a whole new level.

The historical connection and at least partial origins in Africa for African American ways of speaking, moving, and making music are not in dispute here. After centuries of living on American soil, however, African Americans have created their own signature cultures and expressive genres, such as blues, gospel, jazz, and rhythm and blues, all of which were unknown in Africa until imported from the United States (either directly or indirectly). So it was with rap. And so it is with so many musics in the African diaspora, such as reggae, ragga, and rumba.

There were several routes through which rap made its way to Africa. In the 1980s, rap was rarely played in the African mass media, such as radio and television (with some exceptions), but rather it had to be physically imported in the form of audio and video cassettes and vinyl records. Because there was no significant market yet, it was literally brought over in bits and pieces by Africans traveling abroad. The two primary routes were via New York and Paris. In the mid-1980s New York began receiving significant numbers of African travelers and immigrants. Paris, by contrast, already had a thriving, though not always welcome, African community due to its French colonial past and the need for imported menial labor. As a result, France became a crucial first link in the chain that brought rap to Africa— or at least to Francophone Africa. The emergence of an original French rap scene in the early 1990s preceded that of Africa by just a few years.

The French Connection

Rap and hip hop quickly took root abroad, but with a stark contrast. Hip hop developed on its home turf in New York as a relatively unmediated local form of entertainment and expression for urban working-class and marginalized youth—part of what is known as street culture. Abroad, however, it was typically the mass media (radio, TV, newspapers), recorded objects (audio and video cassettes, vinyl singles, and LPs), and occasional tours that introduced the various elements of hip hop to young people. Furthermore, initial adherents (at least in Europe and Africa) typically came from a socioeconomic elite, those who had better access to, and stronger interest in, foreign imports.

The way in which rap took root in France is instructive not only because it became the second largest market (after the United States) for the genre, but also because it was a major conduit to Africa via its sizable African population—immigrants and their children—living and working there. France's first and most successful rap star, MC Solaar, was born in Senegal to parents from Chad and raised in France.

The year 1982 was pivotal. In November the New York City Rap Tour reached Paris.[4] Produced by two Frenchmen in New York—Jean Karakos (head of the French Celluloid label) and Bernard Zekri (New York correspondent with the French newspaper *Actuel*)—under the sponsorship of the European station Radio 1, the tour featured the cream of the crop: Fab Five Freddy; deejays Afrika Bambaataa and Grandmixer D.S.T. (and the Infinity Rappers); dance groups Rock Steady Crew and Double Dutch Girls; and graffiti artists Futura 2000, Phase 2, Ramelzee, and Dondi. To coincide with the tour arrival, *Liberation* published an article on Afrika Bambaataa (Thibaudat 1982) and a first-person account of the New York hip hop scene by Rock Steady Crew member Mr. Freeze (Zekri 1982) alerting the French public to the new culture; tour members appeared on Alain Manéval's TV show *Megahertz*.[5]

The tour did not arrive in a vacuum. A small fan base had already been established by local radio shows and a small club scene. Two key deejays were largely responsible for the popularization of rap in France at the time: Sidney Duteil and Dee Nasty. The child of immigrants from Guadeloupe in the French Caribbean, DJ Sidney was born and raised in the northwestern Parisian suburb of Argenteuil.[6] He obsessively collected American records from the few import record stores operating in Paris (later making trips to London), and his deejaying at the club L'Emeraude beginning about 1978 attracted a crowd, including a younger Daniel Efferne, who as Dee Nasty would produce the first album of French rap and host a radio show on Radio Nova that would help launch many careers. A regular at the club was a radio announcer, Clémentine Célarié, who recommended Sidney to her boss, Marie-France Brière, resulting in him being hired about 1982 to host a show on the state Radio France affiliate Radio 7, which aired 10 p.m. to midnight Monday through Friday. DJ Sidney played the latest music available from the United States, including rap. As his show could only be picked up in the vicinity of Paris, people would record his shows and give cassette tapes to their friends.

When the Rap Tour was in Paris in November 1982, Sidney hosted Afrika Bambaataa on his radio show. During the show, at the radio station studio, Futura 2000 put on graffiti exhibitions and Mister Freeze taught people how to break dance, quickly attracting a crowd. The popularity of Sidney's show led to him hosting a TV show at the national station TF1 in 1984. Called *H.I.P.H.O.P.*, it was the first French television show hosted by a black person, and it was the first regular national TV show in the world dedicated to hip hop.[7] In 1987 an artistic director for the show, Sophie Bramly, would be tapped by MTV to create their first rap show, in London, called *Yo!* This became the model for the first national rap TV show in the United States, *Yo! MTV Raps*, beginning in 1988.

Broadcast every Sunday afternoon just after the U.S. television series *Starsky and Hutch* and lasting less than a year, *H.I.P.H.O.P.* was crucial to the growth of rap in France. According to Marie-France Brière, the executive at Radio 7 and then TF1 who hired DJ Sidney for both his radio and TV shows, "Seven years later I understood that it [the show] was important when MC Solaar said to me that it was because of *HIPHOP* that he decided to go into music" (Brière in Peigne-Giuly 1996). The presence of Afrika Bambaataa (who established a French branch of his Zulu Nation) on Sidney's radio and TV shows gave them credibility: "He [Bambaataa] was a DJ and an MC. So [on the TV show], he selected some records, he mixed a little, and performed. It was just his presence. . . . He didn't really need to do anything more. And he helped give the show authenticity, like FUTURA 2000. FUTURA 2000 would come and do these big graff pieces" (Sidney Duteil in Spady, Alim, and Meghelli 2006: 287).

Perhaps the starkest contrast with the United States can be illustrated by what happened when *H.I.P.H.O.P.* ended. In an ironic process, rap went from Parisian clubs, radio, and TV to the streets or, rather, the suburbs (*banlieues*) of Paris, home to low-income immigrants and others. As Zekri noted, "Trendy Paris was burying rap . . . but no one told the banlieues" (Zekri 1994: 88; Cannon 1997: 153). Bramly, who would become director of new media for the global conglomerate Universal Music in 1999, said, "After that [the end of the TV show], it was gone. Everyone was fed up with rap. And it went back in the suburbs" (Bramly in Spady, Alim, and Meghelli 2006: 310).

DJ Sidney had a direct impact on African rap beyond his work in France. He toured Francophone West Africa with a show that included the Paris City Breakers, who had danced on his TV show. Modeled on the New York City Breakers, the three-member Paris crew included Solo, whose Malian immigrant parents sent him to Bamako for summers while he was growing up in France. Seeing the Rap Tour on TV had a major impact on Solo: "And I saw that on TV and I saw the Rocksteady Crew and I was like, 'What the fuck is this shit?!?! I gotta know how to dance like that, that's the new shit in America, I gotta know, I gotta know, I gotta know!'" (Solo in Spady, Alim, and Meghelli 2006: 337).[8] Sidney's account of his African tours gives some insight into what was happening there in the mid-1980s.

> M[eghelli]: But, when you arrived in Africa, you saw that people had video-cassettes of the show?
> S[idney]: Yeah, because there are always Africans traveling between France and Africa. So, some young folks had brought back with them some video-cassettes so others could see what was going on in France. . . . I became famous there, because of that . . . and also, because of RFO—a TV station—that re-airs shows in Africa. Quite a while afterwards, some TF1 shows were stocked up,

and then re-aired. So, six months later, they would see the shows that were already aired here.[9]

M: But were there Hip Hop dancers there already when you arrived?

S: Yeah, definitely. They were dancing just like we had been doing on the show. They created the Abidjan City Breakers [in Côte d'Ivoire]. The dancers were real good, they were even on the same level as me. They had that same Hip Hop spirit: the track suits, all fresh and fly, they had their shirts with their names on them. . . . Later on, when we went back to Africa, we brought more stuff with us. I gave them basketball shoes. . . . You get there with the newest gear, and you leave with nothing. (Spady, Alim, and Meghelli 2006: 289)

Break dance crews became important forces in Africa in the mid-1980s. Abidjan City Breakers released one of the earliest rap albums in Africa. Bamako City Breakers, Dakar City Breakers, and Cape Town City Breakers were pioneers in raising the profile of the new American style of dancing.[10]

Sidney was not the only one spreading the rap word in France. In 1981 Dee Nasty had a weekly radio show playing rap on a small independent neighborhood station broadcasting to some of the Parisian districts and banlieues that would become flashpoints for hip hop culture (18th, 19th, and Saint Denis).[11] His account of the immediate impact of the 1982 Rap Tour is vivid:

From one day to the next, there were some news reports about the famous tour. It was on a show called *Megahertz* on FR3. . . . The next day, in all the housing projects around France, people were break-dancing on cardboard boxes, trying to do the same thing they had seen in the footage aired on the show. And, people just took to it, immediately. For everyone, it was like we were waiting for something powerful like that. Since Soul music, there had been nothing conscious, nothing with a voice. And this was something positive, but also political at the same time, and that belonged to us, the youth, whether that be the Arabs, the Blacks. Everyone felt that it related to them, and that took on that importance. (Dee Nasty in Spady, Alim, and Meghelli 2006: 314–15)

In 1983 Dee Nasty had a show on the independent radio station Carbone 14. He met another radio host, Bad Benny, from the station RDH, and soon they began to rap in French on the radio. The move to rapping in a local language was fundamental and would be done over and over again around the world: "First off, we were like, 'The only way that Rap music will ever work in France is if it's in French.' . . . Everyone was rapping in English. But we said, 'No, the only way for this art to progress is to rap in French'" (Dee Nasty in Spady, Alim, and Meghelli 2006: 316).

It may have been Afrika Bambaataa who first spread this message.

S[pady]: When I talk to members of the Hip Hop community in France they claim that it was you who encouraged them to use their own language. What actually happened?

B[ambaataa]: Yes, that happened back in the early 1980s, like 1982 or 1983. . . . Everybody tried to rap like Americans. I told them in France, "No, rap in your own language and speak from your own social awareness. Rap about your own problems that are happening in your own country and whatever and talk about what you want to talk about." . . . And this is what happened. Now, France is really the second biggest Hip Hop place in the world. (Spady, Alim, and Meghelli 2006: 264)[12]

In 1984 Dee Nasty self-produced the first French rap album, *Paname City Rappin'*, on his own Funkazilla label.[13] The title track illustrated another tendency in early rap around the world: it was an adaptation of an American rap song, in this case Melle Mel's "New York, New York." That same year Dee Nasty met Lionel D., who was also rapping in French. These three—Dee Nasty, Lionel D., and Bad Benny—were the pioneers who demonstrated the potential of rapping in French. Lionel D. was on his way to becoming France's first rap star, but personal issues got in the way. In the late 1980s, Dee Nasty's weekly show on Radio Nova became a proving ground for French rap, with many emcees debuting, including MC Solaar (Cannon 1997: 157).[14]

The release in 1990 of *Rapattitude,* a compilation of the new scene on the new Labelle Noire, signaled that French rap had matured and was sufficiently original to gain recording contracts and challenge the omnipresence of American rap. Very few French rap recordings had been released until then.[15] *Rapline,* a weekly television show dedicated to hip hop, debuted in 1990, running for five years. And MC Solaar released his first single that year, "Bouge de la," which went to number 22 on the French pop singles chart in 1991.

Claude M'Baraly (MC Solaar), born in Senegal in 1969 of parents from Chad, grew up in France and went on to become France's first superstar of rap. He raps exclusively in French, and his style is marked by a laid-back cool sound that draws on jazz and brilliant manipulation of the French language. MC Solaar's first album (*Qui sème le vent récolte le tempo,* 1991) was certified platinum (300,000) and his second album (*Prose Combat,* 1994) was certified double platinum (600,000) in France within a few years of their release. These were decent numbers for an American rap group at the time, but extraordinary for France or a non-American rapper. His third album (*Paradisiaque,* 1997) hit number 1 on the French album charts. Solaar's jazz leanings included recording "Un ange en danger" with American bass player Ron Carter on *Stolen Moments: Red Hot + Cool,* an album featuring jazz and rap collaborations.[16] Solaar's support for the Senegalese group Positive Black Soul was crucial for their move into the international market.

A further observation contrasting French and American hip hop concerns race and ethnicity. In France the population known as *noir* (black) is comprised of two broad communities: Caribbean (called Antillaise), from former colonies and departments such as Haiti, Martinique, and Guadeloupe; and African (meaning sub-Saharan). The other relevant minority community is called Arab or Beur (in the slang known as *verlan* in which syllables in a word are reversed), referring to those from North Africa, also known as the Maghreb (west of Egypt). Within these communities, there are strong affiliations based on place of origin, language, and ethnicity (in the case of Africa). Until recently, the French government did not keep population statistics on the ethnic or racial composition of the country. Recent estimates put the black population anywhere from 3 to 5 million, in a country of more than 61 million people (Kimmelman 2008; Ndiaye 2008: 59).

As many have noted (e.g., Cannon 1997: 161–62; Prévos 2002: 5–6), hip hop in France is multiethnic, involving children of minorities from sub-Saharan Africa, the Caribbean, and North Africa, as well as whites. The group 113, which began recording in the late 1990s, represents precisely these three French minority communities: Mokobe Traore, Yohann Duport (AP), and Abdelkrim Brahmi (Rim'K) have family origins in Mali, Guadeloupe, and Algeria, respectively. Although French rappers are predominantly black and Arab, it is more common there than in the United States to see broader types of integration.[17]

Into New York and Back

One of the oldest, most robust, and sophisticated rap scenes in Africa is in Senegal. The first African rap group to gain a major international recording contract was Positive Black Soul from Senegal. When *The Source,* the first major American hip hop magazine, celebrated its 100th issue in 1998, it featured articles on hip hop around the world, including France, Italy, and Cuba. The only African country represented was Senegal.[18]

There is a good reason for Senegal's high profile and public presence in African rap: Senegalese had both routes to rap—Paris and New York—wide open. Positive Black Soul's third CD, *New York/Paris/Dakar* (2002), recorded in Dakar and New York, with guests from the United States and France, acknowledges this triangle. Paris was not just a given because of its French colonial past; there were especially close political and cultural ties between Senegal and France. Senegal's first president, the poet and negritude philosopher Léopold Senghor, was the only sub-Saharan African ever elected to the elite 40-member French Academy, which is the official authority on the French language. Senegal is also the geographically nearest sub-Saharan African nation to France. And it is home to the Paris-Dakar rally, an annual road race begun in 1979.

By the mid-1980s, New York became a major destination—what one Senegalese official called a suburb—for both short- and long-term traders looking to expand their markets. Beginning about 1983 young male Senegalese merchants began hawking wares on the streets of New York, forming a pioneering wave of immigrants. In early 1985 the police estimated that there were about 300 Senegalese vendors working the streets of Manhattan, primarily in the commercial midtown area. Later that year the *New York Times* (1985) began reporting on this phenomenon.

In 1987 a *Times* reporter in Dakar interviewed a man who had spent two years in New York selling on the street, sending $35 to $45 home every month, planning his next trip back (Brooke 1987). Even in such a large city of immigrants like New York, the sudden presence of Senegalese in midtown was news. Less visible were the growing numbers of West African immigrants working as taxi drivers taking the late night shifts in neighborhoods that were considered too dangerous by the Yellow Cab service (Noel 2000).

The timing of the Senegalese influx can be attributed to a number of contributing factors: the ending of exit visa requirements for Senegalese citizens in 1981; a severe drought that devastated peanut farmers from 1973 to 1985; structural adjustment programs beginning in 1984, intensifying rural poverty; a new and cheap direct flight from Dakar to New York ($600 in 1987 on Air Afrique); France joining other Common Market nations in 1986 in imposing visa restrictions on visitors from Africa; the French franc (and the Senegalese currency, which is tied to it) depreciating by half against the U.S. dollar between 1981 and 1985 making U.S.-earned dollars more valuable back home (the franc regained its value in the second half of the decade); and a venerable tradition of long-distance trading. From 1980 to 1987, the number of nonimmigrant visas granted each year to Senegalese quadrupled from 1,177 to 4,369, despite a refusal rate that went from 3 to 32 percent due to pressure from New York officials complaining about Senegalese overstaying their visas. Between 1985 and 1987 alone, the number of applications for nonresident visas jumped from 300 to 800 a month. By 1997 it was estimated that there were 10,000 to 20,000 Senegalese living in New York City (Brooke 1987, 1988; Perry 1997). A recent estimate puts the current number at 30,000, with the majority undocumented (Kane 2011: 77).[19]

That the flow of goods from New York to Dakar was wide open was confirmed in a 1987 *New York Times* article in which the information director of the Senegalese government described two kinds of traders he personally encountered on an Air Afrique flight to New York:

> The traders told him they planned to spend the day in New York shops, mostly buying electronic goods and cosmetics for black people, and then return to Dakar in the evening. "New York has become a commercial suburb of Dakar," the information director said. "You cross the big lake, make your purchases, and then come home the same day."
>
> The second type of vendor, more familiar to New Yorkers, is Dakar's 'banabana,' or street peddler. (Brooke 1987)

No doubt the extensive traffic in goods that went back and forth in that decade between New York, the world center of rap, and Dakar included all the accoutrements and paraphernalia of hip hop culture.

Both founding members of Positive Black Soul confirmed the importance of this route, as did Faada Freddy of the Senegalese group Daara J.

S[pady]: How did you first hear rap music?

D[idier Awadi]: I had a lot of friends of mine who used to travel a lot to New York and they'd bring rap records back. The first thing I heard was Kurtis Blow and "Rappers Delight" by the Sugarhill Gang. . . . You could find all of this in Senegal. Senegalese are big travelers. (Spady, Alim, and Meghelli 2006: 648).

S[pady]: How did your brother learn the hardcore style of rapping in West Africa? Was he watching madd videos?

A[madou Barry]: Yeah, a lot. We had friends that used to work at Air Afrique. They used to bring things over from the States.

(Spady, Alim, and Meghelli 2006: 641).

[Marlon Regis:] How'd you get in touch with hip-hop, way back in the late 1980s being way over there in Senegal, Africa?

[Faada Freddy:] We had some friends—middle-class friends—that used to get stuff coming from all over like the United States. Because their parents were rich and used to travel, those boys used to tell their parents "bring me this, bring me that." They brought back rap tapes. (Regis 2005)

Amadou Barry's father was a pilot for Air Afrique and so probably had even more direct access than other Senegalese.

But even though they moved goods back and forth, this generation of traveling peddlers and immigrant workers was not the one to take up rap as its music of choice. Indeed, there was occasional animosity between African immigrants and the African Americans among whom they lived.[20] The musical heroes of this immigrant generation were the 1980s generation of world music stars, some of whom sang about the predicaments of African immigrants, such as Salif Keita ("Nous pas bouger" on *Ko-Yan*, 1989) and Youssou N'Dour ("Immigrés" on *Immigrés*, 1989). By the summer of 1988, the first major solo U.S. tour of Senegalese Youssou N'Dour and Malian Salif Keita, who both were embarking on solo international careers under the auspices of new world music label support, could fill the 2,800-seat Beacon Street Theater on the upper west side of Manhattan at $20 a ticket to a crowd that was largely West African.[21]

Senegalese probably had the most direct access to New York street culture in the 1980s. Other Africans also had access, especially Ghanaians (Shipley, this volume), but perhaps not as widespread and regular.

Rap in Africa: The First Decade

One of the most fundamental challenges across the continent was how to create something original that spoke to young people. The basic components to be addressed by artists included the musical foundation, language, lyrics, vocal style (the flow), and overall message. The pioneering Ghanaian hiplife producer Panji Anoff voiced a common concern: "If hiplife was going to be about translating America into Africa, then I wanted no part of it. My idea was always to translate Africa into something global" (in *Living the Hiplife*, Shipley 2007). African rap spans the full continuum between these poles.

A key to understanding this challenge and appreciating the various solutions is that hip hop was initially embraced in Africa by secondary school–educated (and some college-educated), well-traveled, and relatively privileged youth. They represented a different kind of Africa than the stereotypes that the rest of the world was used to seeing, one that was more culturally allied with trends in the United States and Europe than the more deeply rooted traditions that were closer to home. Their compatriots often viewed them as leaving their own cultures behind in favor of foreign imports. Some were able to move beyond fascination and emulation to fully grasp the possibilities of the genre and shape it for their own communities, reaching into their own home cultures. Others, to be sure, never moved beyond the wannabe stage.

The 1980s were an incubation period for rap and hip hop in Africa, bubbling well beneath the surface of the regional stars and their music that defined broader popular tastes. Very few commercial African rap recordings were made in this decade, most likely because rappers were still trying to absorb the genre and producers did not yet see a market for their work. The sequence throughout the decade and into the 1990s was simple and widespread: direct imitation, substituting their own English language lyrics, and localizing it by rapping in African languages (or at least letting go of the American accents) about issues of relevance to their communities. It was not until the early and mid-1990s that African genres had emerged as rappers, deejays, and producers began to localize the music.[22]

Rap neither arrived nor developed uniformly throughout Africa, in part because the mass media was not involved at first. Happenstance, such as individual travelers bringing back news from France or the United States, was the order of the day. Occasional visits or tours to Africa, such as DJ Sidney's mid-1980s tour with the Paris City Breakers or Malcolm McLaren's 1983 visit to South Africa, exposed youth to the new genre and inspired them.[23]

The first commercial recordings of African rap may be from Nigeria: Lagos nightclub and radio DJ Ronnie Ekundayo's "The Way I Feel," from his 1981 LP of the same name, and Dizzy K Falola's "Saturday Night Raps," from his 1982 album *Excuse Me Baby.*[24] These are the first two recordings listed in Ikonne's (2009a) extraordinary online survey of the first decade of Nigerian rap, profiling nineteen vinyl albums released between 1981 and 1992 that have at least one track with rapping or strong hip hop inflections. Most are clearly under the influence of American disco, funk, or old school New York rap, both lyrically and musically, with the increasing presence of synthesizers and drum machines as the decade wears on. "Pump," a 1982 collaboration between Nigerian Mambo Kristo and American Gloria Hart (called Mams and Hart), contains a percussion break that features what sounds like a large Yoruba dundun (talking drum), perhaps the first example of using an African instrument in the genre.[25] Timi Gawi's 1984 "Boxing Rapping Show" features guitars, keyboard, and bass played in a Nigerian style, rather than

American. I. C. Rock's 1985 "Advice/Oge Chi Ka Nma" is distinguished by its social message and rapping partially in Igbo. Rick Asikpo's 1986 "Beat Jam" features what sounds like a bell pattern (perhaps played on a drum machine) and tenor saxophone, which conjures up the afrobeat sound created by Nigerian Fela Kuti. Ikonne points to the 1991 recording "Which One You Dey" by Emphasis (rappers Terry and Mouth MC and singer Junior) as

> represent[ing] homegrown Nigerian hip-hop finally finding its own voice. Unlike most of their predecessors, Emphasis didn't rely on barely-rhymed doggerel aping the rhythms and cadences of American old-school rap records, but instead presented a lucid narrative complete with plot, characterization, and humor, delivered with a relaxed flow in pidgin English—the true language of Nigeria's streets. (Ikonne 2009a)

Nigerian rap achieving its own voice by 1991 is consistent with what was going on in Tanzania, Senegal, and South Africa.

Outside Nigeria, early recordings include that of Abidjan City Breakers from Côte d'Ivoire, who released an album in 1986. The influence of late 1970s funk and disco is apparent, and the genre still seems like a novelty. The first film documentary of an African rap scene may be *African Wave: Prophets of the City* (Bowey 1990), made in South Africa about the time of the group's first album, *Our World,* which was the first South African rap album and among the earliest full-length vinyl albums of rap in Africa. Music video segments throughout the film reveal a firmly rooted and culturally unique scene in Cape Town. A few other countries, such as Senegal and Tanzania, were probably at a similar level of development, but only on the verge of seeing their first local rap cassettes released.

The first edition of the British-based *Rough Guide to World Music* (Broughton et al. 1994), a state-of-the-art country-by-country survey of popular music artists and genres written mostly by journalists and radio show hosts, made no mention of rap in Africa. The 1999 second edition made brief mention in just a single country entry: Senegal. The 2006 third edition, however, could not help but notice: "We have strived in this new edition to chart the changing scene, including coverage, for instance, of African hip-hop, which has swept across the continent in recent years and is the music of choice for young Africans, often in genuinely local forms" (Broughton et al. 2006: xv). In this edition, about half the African countries have entries on rap, ranging from a few sentences to several paragraphs (Senegal has the longest entry).

The most widespread introduction of hip hop culture to Africa came in the form of dance in the early and mid-1980s, being dispersed by the enormous popularity of Michael Jackson and the first wave of American films featuring break dancing, beginning with *Flashdance* in 1983.[26] Early examples of local interest include the start of break dancing competitions about 1982 in Cape Town, South Africa (L. Watkins 2004: 130) and a 1984 festival in Dar es Salaam, Tanzania, showcasing the first generation of hip hop films (Perullo 2007: 253). Young people in Bamako,

Dakar, Abidjan, and Cape Town formed their own "Breakers" troupes modeled on the New York City Breakers or Paris City Breakers.[27]

Bamako City Breakers member Amadou Philippe Konate suggests that three major events beginning about 1983 were responsible for the rise of hip hop culture in Bamako: (1) the popularity of Michael Jackson, especially his performance on the televised *Motown 25th Anniversary Special* in 1983; (2) Sidney's *H.I.P.H.O.P.* show in France (in 1984); and (3) an inspiring performance in Bamako of Abidjan City Breakers.[28] Typical for the first African hip hop generation, Konate knew little about the traditional music of his country. He recognizes the flow of hip hop into Bamako as coming principally from France and the United States, relayed by Dakar and Abidjan, and confirms that initially hip hop was primarily accessible to, and carried by, those from more comfortable socioeconomic classes.

> This is not due to ideology, but rather is explained by the ease of access to the media of the epoque: reserved for those who had the possibility to travel, to view television emissions abroad, to bring back VHS recordings of these emissions and . . . in order to view them one needed a VHS player, an apparatus reserved at the time for an elite. Therefore, rap came by VHS and not the radio! There was only the national radio station, which was not interested in this kind of music.

While dance could be immediately appreciated and imitated, lyrics presented a barrier. In the 1980s, small but growing numbers of youth were listening to rap, and some were directly imitating the language and the fashion. While many subtleties of the semantic aspects of the language must have escaped many—English would have been their second or third language, and the dialect of African American street culture was not taught in schools—the overall linguistic flow could have a more direct impact.[29] In 2007, pioneer Senegalese rapper Aziz Ndiaye could still repeat verbatim some of the classic lines from the 1979 hit "Rappers Delight" that he had memorized two and a half decades earlier. He recalls copying, along with Didier Awadi of Positive Black Soul, the likes of Kurtis Blow, Grandmaster Flash, and Melle Mel (*Democracy in Dakar,* episode 5, 2007). Ndiaye and Awadi were among the first rappers in Dakar (Spady, Alim, and Meghelli 2006: 650).

It is difficult to gauge the impact of rap in Africa in the 1980s before recordings were made, although the genre was slowly developing in live performance for five or ten years before it was commercially recorded. This was also the case in its initial rise in New York, developing at parties and clubs throughout the 1970s. The term *underground* may indeed be appropriate for rap during the 1980s in Africa. I saw no signs of rap or hip hop culture in 1988–90 when I was in the capital cities of Senegal, Mali, and The Gambia, although reggae was present, especially in Anglophone Gambia.[30] But there was a small scene in Dakar, and two of the earliest rap groups there—King MCs and Syndicate, which would soon merge to form Positive

Black Soul—were already active, although not recording (Herson 2000: 17; Lobeck 2002: 21). In Dakar and Bamako, it was the then-current world music generation of Youssou N'Dour, Baaba Maal, Ismael Lo, Salif Keita, and Oumou Sangare who were capturing the attention of everyone, young and old. I do not recall seeing any cassettes of African rap in any of these countries during these years.

The pioneers of the genre began gaining a young audience through live performance rather than recordings. It is no coincidence that when national political systems opened up to multiparty democracies in many countries, rap began to flourish. A key factor was the privatization of radio, which took place in various countries in the 1990s, both broadening the audience and serving as an outlet to stimulate local creativity.[31] As the 1990s began, the popularity of Public Enemy, Los Angeles-based gangsta rap, and then Tupac Shakur were important stimuli. In Francophone countries, MC Solaar's success was key.

Rap in Africa: The 1990s and 2000s

In Tanzania, the first public rap competition was held in Dar es Salaam in 1990, and the following year the first major national rap competition, Yo! Rap Bonanza, was held to find the best rapper in the country.[32] Twenty-year-old Saleh Abry (aka Saleh J) won by rapping partly in Swahili. He released the first Tanzanian rap single in 1991, "Ice Ice Baby," adding lyrics about AIDS to Vanilla Ice's hit. Soon after, he released the album *Swahili Rap*, which was not commercially distributed. It was not until 1995 that the first commercially distributed album of Tanzanian hip hop was released: Mac Mooger's *The Mac-Mooger*.

In Senegal (Tang, this volume), Positive Black Soul started gaining radio airplay in 1990. In 1992 they opened for MC Solaar at the French Cultural Center in Dakar. Solaar was sufficiently impressed to bring them to France for a national competition. A guest appearance on "Swing Yela" on Baaba Maal's 1994 big-budget album *Firin' in Fouta* brought them in contact with British producer Jumbo Van Renen, who in turn produced their first CD album, *Salaam* (1996), on Mango Records, a subsidiary of Island Records (Bob Marley's label), which was a subsidiary of Polygram, one of the six conglomerates that dominated the industry. This was the first African hip hop album to be released on a major international label, a significant milestone.[33] The strength of Senegalese Baaba Maal and Youssou N'Dour on the world music market undoubtedly cleared the path. So, surely, did the fact that PBS co-founder Amadou Barry spent years growing up in France, one step closer to the source, before returning to Senegal.[34]

The first major South African hip hop concert took place in 1990 in Cape Town, featuring Prophets of Da City (POC) and coinciding with the release of their first album (*Our World*), followed two years later by the first album of Black Noise (*Pumpin Loose Da Juice*), the second major group from Cape Town, which was the crucible of South African hip hop (L. Watkins 2004: 131–32). The move of POC to the UK to record their sixth album (*Universal Souljaz*) in 1995 was covered by *Billboard* (Kwaku 1995). In Ghana (Shipley, this volume), the first PANAFEST (Pan-African Theatre Festival) celebrations in 1994 featured a homecoming for rap pioneer Reggie Rockstone, who had already established himself in the UK rapping in English and would soon begin rapping in the Twi language. In Kenya (Kidula, this volume; Rebensdorf 1996), producer Jimmy Gathu inaugurated a television program in 1993 on the Kenyan TV station KTN to popularize rap.

In the 1980s local producers understood that the stage of imitation, rapping in English and using African American accents and slang, had little commercial potential. By the mid-1990s, however, there was a breakthrough, not just in the release of rap recordings across the continent but in recordings that demonstrated that African youth had embraced the genre and made it their own. When the breakout came in 1994 or 1995, African rap had emerged as a mature genre, featuring creative use of mother tongues, smart multilanguage word plays, messages that were relevant to the experience of African youth, original rhythmic flows, and, within a few years, instrumental tracks that drew on local music.[35]

The release of commercial recordings is one important indicator of the status of rap. Two of the most productive and relatively well documented African countries can serve as examples. In Tanzania, the first five years of commercial rap releases, 1995–99, produced twelve albums and one compilation (see discography). The first five years of rap releases in Senegal, 1994–98, produced roughly the same number of albums and two compilations (Nouripour 1998). This level of production in the second half of the 1990s (estimating the combined numbers of the most productive African countries) is probably similar to that of the commercial beginnings in the United States fifteen years earlier (1979–83). The first six years in France (1984–89), by comparison, were relatively fallow (see discography in Bocquet and Pierre-Adolphe 1997: 251–63).[36]

An explosion of releases after this initial period marked a number of African countries. For example, in Tanzania in 2001 alone about 15 albums and more than 100 singles were released (Perullo and Fenn 2003: 49); between 1999 and 2001 several rappers sold over 100,000 copies of their albums (Perullo 2007: 268). Perullo (this volume) estimates about 50 commercial recording studios recently operating in Dar es Salaam for bongo flava artists and perhaps over 100 producers composing and recording bongo flava beats, up from just four producers in the mid 1990s.

Releases of national rap compilations toward the end of the millennium marked a certain maturity for the genre in Africa. These include Senegal (*Senerap: Freestyle*, vol. 1, 1997; vol. 2, 1998), Kenya (*Kenyan: The First Chapter* 1998; *Second Chapter* 1999), Algeria (*Algerap*, 1999; *Wahrap*, 2000), and South Africa (*Kwaito: South African Hip Hop*, 2000). The first continent-wide survey marked the definitive arrival of African rap in the world music market (*Rough Guide to African Rap*, 2004).

Relying on recording industry data alone to assess the impact of rap can be deceptive. In Malawi, the bulk of rap and ragga played on the radio or sold on cassette in Blantyre, the largest city at over half a million people, is of foreign origin. Local rap and ragga, at least until recently, has had little commercial market appeal and functions primarily as a form of local expression in live performance, especially in competitions sponsored by nongovernmental organizations (Fenn, this volume). Malawi stands out in that local rap recordings are minimal, yet the genre has important meaning in the daily lives of its youth population.

In terms of mainstream exposure, African rap was about a decade behind the United States. The first nationally syndicated rap-oriented television show in the United States, *Yo! MTV Raps,* debuted on the seven-year-old private cable channel MTV in 1988. In 1990 a major television network (NBC) debuted the show *Fresh Prince of Bel-Air,* starring rapper Will Smith. But perhaps a more definitive moment of arrival came shortly thereafter when the Fab Five, an astonishing group of five freshman starters on the University of Michigan basketball team, went all the way to the final round of the national collegiate basketball championship tournament during the winter 1991–92 season. Their new-styled oversized baggy uniforms (a sharp contrast to the tight short shorts of the 1980s), youth, and generally brash demeanor announced to a mass American television audience that a hip hop generation was a national phenomenon.[37] Spurred by a second wave of African American–directed hip hop–inflected Hollywood films, such as Spike Lee's *Do the Right Thing* (1989, featuring Public Enemy's "Fight the Power"), John Singleton's *Boyz n the Hood* (1991, with Ice Cube), and Ernest R. Dickerson's *Juice* (1992, with Tupac Shakur), the news traveled quickly, not so much as a novelty or fad (although fashion was a major component) but as a new youth movement based in urban contemporary African American culture.

African recording industry awards for rap came about a decade after the American recording industry began recognizing rap with a Grammy Award category in 1989 (Best Rap Performance by a Duo or Group). Other Grammy categories were established in 1991 (Best Solo Rap Performance) and 1996 (Best Rap Album).[38] The intermittent pan-African Kora awards (based in South Africa), which began in 1996, gave its 1999 Best African Group award to the France-based Congolese rap group Bisso Na Bisso. In 2003 they established Best African Gospel male and female categories. The next year the rap group JJC and 419 (from Nigeria/UK) won the Best African Group award, and Ghanaian rapper Reggie Rockstone won the Best Video award. In 2005 the Best African Hip Hop Group/Artist (won by Koba from Gabon) and Best African Reggae-Ragga categories were established.[39]

National (and subsequently international) hip hop awards and festivals beginning in 2000 marked the mainstreaming of hip hop within Africa. The first annual Ghana Music awards in 2000 had several categories devoted to hiplife (Shipley, this volume). The same year Senegal started its annual Hip Hop Awards. The first annual Festival International de la Culture Hip Hop au Burkina Faso was held in

2000. Now known as the Festival International des Cultures Urbaines or Waga (or Ouaga) Hip Hop, after the capital city in which it is held (Ouagadougou), it has gained a solid international (albeit primarily Francophone) roster of artists.[40]

In the first decade of the 2000s, African hip hop became widely exposed in local and national media. Continental mass media is often skewed toward American or highly commercialized African music videos. In 2005 MTV Networks launched its 100th channel and first pan-African station, the 24-hour English language MTV Base targeted at African youth. In 2006 they met their first-year target of 30 percent African content. In 2008 the MTV Africa Music Awards debuted, with hopes of raising their international profile, although MTV award shows in Europe and Asia have been criticized for leaning too heavily on American and British performers. In 2011 MTV Base reached 10.5 million households (48.5 million viewers), up from 8 million households in 2006. South Africa's Channel O not only broadcasts music videos across the continent but also sponsors music video awards. Private radio stations serve hip hop at the local level, and governmental and nongovernmental organizations alike use hip hop to marshal youth for their various causes.[41]

Collaborations between African and American rappers, though, remain rare. A notable exception was KRS-One being featured on Positive Black Soul's *New York/Paris/Dakar* (2002).[42]

As African rap has matured and second and third generations have emerged, both more critical and more commercial voices have emerged, sometimes in the same time and place.[43] One widespread effect has been to rekindle interest in older local traditions. That is to say, African youth continually search for new ways to make rap relevant and unique, which often means digging through local culture, almost like American deejays would crate-dig—search through crates of obscure vinyl record albums for new sounds. Some of these efforts at connecting with African culture through rap are documented in this volume.[44]

Back in France

Some of the most compelling and commercially successful African rap in the 2000s emanates from France.[45] This perplexing statement points to the increasing difficulty of affixing a single national identity nowadays. One might feel safe in considering rap conceived and produced in Africa as African rap (whether or not it was actually recorded there), even though some artists may have spent significant portions of their life abroad, such as Reggie Rockstone or Amadou Barry. French rappers of African descent (those who grew up and remained in France) may have varied relationships with Africa, ranging from a kind of love or nostalgia for the Africa of their parents, which brings them into close contact with African music, to Africa being just one symbol of their identity among others.[46] Three particularly successful French rappers of the post-MC Solaar generation (in terms of awards, sales, or critical acclaim), whose parents emigrated from Africa, can illustrate. In addition to their personal artistic talent, their appeal also lies with the perspective that comes with having one's feet straddling two continents packaged with the advanced production values and opportunities that come with recording in state-of-the-art studios under multinational patronage.

Serigne Mbaye (also known as Disiz la Peste) was born in France to a Senegalese father and Belgian mother. His third solo album, *Itinéraire d'un enfant bronzé* [Itinerary of a bronzed child], features guest Senegalese and Malian vocalists. "N'Dioukel" is an homage to his father's generation of 1960s Dakar when fashionable young people went out to clubs dancing to the Senegalese variety of salsa, soon to become transformed into mbalax by Youssou N'Dour. The music on the track, performed by a live band, moves imperceptibly from New York–based salsa to Dakar-based mbalax, including Senegalese percussion. Mbaye raps in French about his father's generation, alternating with Pape Djiby Ba, one of the great vocalists who emerged in the 1970s, singing in Wolof. "Santa Yalla" [Praise Allah] is straight up mbalax, with a message that is unusual for rap but common for Senegalese pop singers: affirming one's deep faith in Islam. This mix of rap and a genre (in this case mbalax) which itself was the result of a reshaping of foreign (in this case Cuban) influences, a meeting of generations, is a hallmark of the new music from Africa and children of African immigrants.

Mokobe, whose family name Traore places him in the nobility of traditional Malian society, was born in France to what he calls a Malian-Senegalese father and Malian-Mauritanian mother.[47] His 2007 debut solo album, *Mon Afrique,* made after a decade of working with the French rap group 113, pushes the limit of invited guests in a broad pan-African sweep. Separate tracks, with the music appropriately shaped for each one, feature Malians Salif Keita, Babani Kone, and Amadou and Mariam (who are joined by Ivoirian Tiken Jah Fakoly), Senegalese Youssou N'Dour and Viviane, Guinean Sekouba Bambino Diabate, Nigerian Seun Kuti (son of Fela), Ivoirian Patson, and Congolese Fally Ipupa, among others. His music videos, such as "Safari" shot with Viviane in Senegal, have the look of a Ministry of Tourism production with vivid colors, bright smiling faces, and vibrant street scenes. The video for "Mali Forever" opens with Mokobe meeting with president Amadou Toumani Toure (who knighted him in 2009) and continues with upbeat scenes showing a modernized urban Mali, ending with chanting over jembe drumming and dancing, an activity as Malian as are earlier scenes of the Niger River, or of Salif Keita singing, for that matter.

Abd al Malik was born in France, but spent his early childhood in his parents' native Congo-Brazzaville before moving back to France, where he grew up in Strasbourg. Al Malik does little collaboration with African musicians, but rather is rooted in French popular song traditions rich in harmony, sometimes orchestral, sometimes that of a jazz trio, as in "Gibraltar," based on a piano riff from Nina Simone's "Sinnerman" with a bridge that sounds like John Coltrane's pianist McCoy Tyner in the early 1960s. He tends toward spoken or so-called slam poetry rather than the melodic style of Mbaye or the American-style declaiming of Mokobe. And per-haps distinguishing French rap from its American forebear, al Malik takes his lit-erature and philosophy seriously: "The aesthetic should always serve a moral pur-pose, it's what's called artistic responsibility. The French writer Albert Camus and philosopher Jean-Paul Sartre followed this idea, and I want to do the same" (Abd al Malik in de Blank 2007). What al Malik lacks in overt references to Africa, such as language and music, he makes up for in critical and social perspective as the son of African immigrants.[48]

Because of their base in France and proximity to centers of the music indus-try, performance venues, and capital, these rappers of African origin, and more like them in France, enjoy greater visibility—and record sales—than their African counterparts.

African rappers in the United States are much less numerous and have a much harder time gaining recognition, surely because they are outsiders with little op-portunity to break into such a highly commercialized industry that has little in-terest in immigrant cultures. Sierra Leonean rapper Chosan's "This Is My America," a powerful look at the plight of African immigrants in the United States, seems oddly out of place in the context of American rap, which can appear highly pro-vincial in the face of global currents. Unlike in France, commercially successful American children of African immigrants, such as Akon, Chamillionaire, and Wale, have assimilated enough that their music and public identity bear little trace of Africa.

With this introductory foundation, readers should be able to better appreciate and contextualize some of the stories told in the following chapters. In the con-cluding chapter, which is similarly comparative, I cover some of the broader issues that are raised throughout this volume.

NOTES

1. For recent extensive surveys of this material, see Leach (2008) and Meadows (2010).

2. KRS-One, one of the most outspoken definers of hip hop culture, makes a distinction between a rapper, who has verbal dexterity, and an MC (or emcee), who carries some de-gree of social responsibility. I use the two interchangeably here. Among his many examples is: "An MC is a representative of hip hop culture. A rapper is a representative of corporate interests" (KRS-One in the DVD *The MC: Why We Do It*, 2005). Also listen to KRS-One on "Classic (Better Than I've Ever Been)" (2007, with Kanye West, Nas, and Rakim), and see his section "Emceein" (KRS-One 2009: 115–117).

3. See allmusic.com for *Billboard* magazine chart listings and riaa.org for certified gold and platinum record sales.

4. Information about the New York City Rap Tour comes from Hershkovits (1983), Beckman and Adler (1991), Zekri (1994), Prévos (2002: 2–3), and Chang (2005: 182–84). Writing about French rap is abundant. Some of the excellent surveys include Bazin (1995),

Bocquet and Pierre-Adolphe (1997), Cannon (1997), Prévos (1996, 2001, 2002), Huq (2001), and Meghelli (2004).

5. The summer before the tour, Mister Freeze, whose parents emigrated from France to the Bronx, was in France dancing in public for money (Zekri 1982).

6. Information about DJ Sidney comes from Duka (1984a, 1984b), Peigne-Giuly (1996), Cannon (1997), Bocquet and Pierre-Adolphe (1997), and Spady, Alim, and Meghelli (2006: 272–91).

7. Also in 1984, Ralph McDaniels hosted the daily TV show *Video Music Box* on WYNC channel 31, which regularly broadcast hip hop videos to a New York audience (Newman 2008).

8. Solo credits Rap Tour organizers Zekri and Karakos: "Basically, I can say, to me, they were the people that made Hip Hop worldwide. I don't know if it's true, but from my point of view, these people made it worldwide. Him [Bernard Zekri], Jean Karakos . . . Because they exported that Shit, you know. And before them, it was mainly only in America" (Solo in Spady, Alim, and Meghelli 2006: 348).

9. According to a Radio France International biography of the Senegalese group Daara J, two of the founding members, Faada Freddy and Ndongo D, followed Sidney's TV show (RFI Musique 2003).

10. See Abidjan City Breakers (1986) in the discography. Search "Bamako City Breakers" on youtube.com for a video from 1985. Amadou Barry (aka Doug E. Tee) of Positive Black Soul was a break dancer before he began emceeing, and he spoke positively of Dakar City Breakers (Spady, Alim, and Meghelli 2006: 642). See Lee Watkins (2004: 129, 145) for a reference to Cape Town City Breakers.

11. Information about Dee Nasty comes from Prévos (2002: 2–5), Spady, Alim, and Meghelli (2006), and www.deenasty.com.

12. MC Solaar has confirmed the importance to him of Bambaataa's advice (Meghelli 2004).

13. The first rap single in French was probably made in 1982 by Fab Five Freddy, one of his few rap recordings. Produced in the United States by Zekri for Karakos's Celluloid label, "Change the Beat" featured Freddy rapping first in French and then in English. The "B" side featured Zekri's French girlfriend, simply known as "Beside," rapping over a similar instrumental track. The record was the one used for scratching by DJ Grandmaster D.S.T. on Herbie Hancock's 1983 hit "Rockit" (George et al. 1985: 11; Zekri 1994: 88).

14. Extended broadcasts of Dee Nasty, MC Solaar, Lionel D., and others rapping in the late 1980s on Radio Nova can be found on the internet.

15. Bocquet and Pierre-Adolphe's (1997: 251–63; 239-51 in the reprint edition) comprehensive discography indicates that in the 1980s only four French rap albums (all by Dee Nasty) and twelve singles (called maxis) were produced, and less than ten albums and a handful of compilations were produced each year from 1990 through 1994, at which point the numbers rose to more than 50 in 1996. In 1988 the first collaboration between French and American MCs was released: Marseille-born Philippe Fragione, known variously as Chill or Akehnaton, who would soon form Marseille's most important group, IAM, joined American MC Choice on the single "This is the 'B' Side." The next collaboration was when MC Solaar rapped on "Le bien, le mal" [The good, the bad] on Guru's *Jazzmatazz* album from 1993.

16. MC Solaar and Ron Carter perform together in episode 10 of the 2000 documentary *Jazz* by Ken Burns. French chart positions are available at http://lescharts.com and www.chartsinfrance.net. French album sales certifications are available at www.infodisc .fr/Certif_Album.php. Solaar's DJ Jimmy Jay, who had a share of the composer's royalties, indicated in Bocquet and Pierre-Adolphe (1997: 145) that their first album sold 650,000. Solaar raps about his early years on "Lève-toi et rap" [Get up and rap] from his 2001 album *Cinquième As.*

17. Examples of whites in the scene include Dee Nasty, MC Solaar's DJ Jimmy Jay, and various members of the top groups Suprême NTM, IAM, and Alliance Ethnik. Biracial rappers are also common, including Lionel D., Saliha (on *Rapattitude*), and recent star Serigne Mbaye (Disiz la Peste).

18. Elon D. Johnson, "DKNY: Dakar to New York," *The Source,* January 1998, 118. A directory of musicians and groups in Dakar from 1999 (Dieng et al. 1999) lists more than 100 individual artists and 50 groups who indicate that their musical style is either rap or ragga. Competing magazine *Vibe* published an article on South African hip hop the previous year: Farai Chideya, "Africa's Hip Hop Generation," *Vibe*, August 1997, 67.

19. According to U.S. census figures, the African-born population of metropolitan New York City went from 31,500 to 73,850 between 1990 and 2000 (Logan and Deane 2003: 3–5). Ghanaians, Liberians, and Nigerians predominate in New York, and documented Senegalese immigration to the United States as a whole is comparatively small (Takyi 2009: 246; Capps et al. 2011: 4). These figures do not take account of significant numbers of immigrants who were not counted in the census.

20. See Perry (1997), Noel (2000), and Bouchareb's 2001 film *Little Senegal* for insight into some of these animosities in New York, Stoller (2002) for a rich ethnography of the lives and work of West African immigrants in New York City in the 1990s, and Kane (2011) for an extended study of Senegalese immigrants in the United States. The whole premise of Akon's "Senegal" (released just as a 2- and 3-track with "Smack That," 2006, Universal) could be taken as an admonishment to his African American compatriots: "So don't complain about how they treating you here." See Madichie (2011) for an analysis of this piece from the standpoint of entrepreneurship and place marketing. See Philippe Wamba (1999), the son of an African American mother and African (Congo-Kinshasa) father, for an extraordinary first-hand analysis of relations between African Americans and Africans (I thank Kwame Harrison for referring me to this book).

21. I had the good fortune to attend this concert. For a review, see Jon Pareles, "New Sound Emerging for N'Dour," *New York Times,* July 2, 1988, 14.

22. A similar sequence is described by Tanzanian rapper Mr. II (Seiler and JJ 2005, East Africa [2:55]): imitate the lyrics, imitate the rhythm and flow and put it in the Swahili language, and then "come with our own compositions." Perullo (this volume) discusses some of the musical techniques used by Tanzanian producers.

23. A 2003 Cape Town video lecture by Prophets of Da City members Ready D and Shaheen Ariefdien provides an excellent history of early hip hop in Cape Town; also see Ariefdien and Abrahams (2006), Ariefdien and Burgess (2011), Warner (2011), and Black Noise member Emile Jansen, "History Our Story," http://blacknoise.co.za/site. Ex-Sex Pistols manager Malcolm McLaren's 1983 *Duck Rock* album and videos for "Buffalo Gals" (featuring New York break dancers) and "Double Dutch" (with a South African mbaqanga-based sound) were milestones for dancers and rappers in South Africa (*African*

Wave, Bowey 1990; Ready D and Shaheen Ariefdien 2003). See Hazard (2009) for a brief description of access to hip hop in Zimbabwe in the 1980s by Dumi Right of Zimbabwe Legit.

24. The site africanhiphop.com and the broadcasts of its related africanhiphop.com /radio/ (formerly africanhiphopradio.com) are invaluable sources for early recordings as well as the most recent developments. I have relied on the research done on this site for the earliest recorded examples.

25. It is difficult to identify the instrument in the podcast that accompanies Ikonne (2009a). It may instead be timbales, which were used early on by Kurtis Blow in "The Breaks."

26. Ikonne (2009b) has reprinted nine vinyl and cassette album covers of Nigerian artists whose look or name were clearly modeled on Michael Jackson, including a very close look-alike Moses Jackson.

27. The New York City Breakers were formed in May 1983. Their international fame dates from 1984 when they performed on the TV show *Soul Train,* at the summer Olympics in Los Angeles, and with the Rock Steady Crew in the film *Beat Street* (released in the United States in June 1984). Their manager, Michael Holman, wrote a detailed history of the group, published in 1984.

28. Konate, now a doctor of internal medicine in France, posted to YouTube (search Bamako City Breakers) a mimed performance by him recorded in Bamako in 1985 of Michael Jackson's "Billie Jean." The quotation and information in this paragraph come from email correspondence with him, October 1, 2008.

29. See Tanzanian Kwanza Unit member Rhymson's story about trying to write down the lyrics—incorrectly—to Rakim's "I Got Soul": "I did not understand the meaning of the songs, but I learned the flow and about following the beats" (Perullo 2007: 256).

30. This may be attributed in part to my own interests at the time, which focused on performers of more deeply rooted music, mostly elders and their families.

31. As indicated in the following chapters, privatization and expansion of radio occurred in Mali, Malawi, and Ghana in the 1990s. In 1994 the South African Independent Broadcasting Authority legislated that stations should devote 20 percent of their airtime to local music (Bosch 2003: 221, quoting Gumisai Mutume, "Bringing Local Sounds to Radio," *Inter Press Service,* January 17, 1998).

32. This paragraph is based on Perullo's (2007: 256–263) excellent history.

33. U.S.-born and Zimbabwean-raised brothers Akim and Dumisani ("Dumi Right") Ndlovu moved back to the United States where they recorded and released a promo EP (with four versions of "Doin' Damage in My Native Language") in 1992 as Zimbabwe Legit on the Hollywood Basic label. But the label folded before the album could be properly released. See D. J. Fisher, "Dumi of Zimbabwe Legit Interview," September 18, 2007, www.hiphop-elements.com/article/read/6/7027/1/, and Hazard (2009).

34. According to PBS's Amadou Barry, *Salaam* sold 30,000 copies (Oumano 1999: 30). For more on PBS's early years see Spady, Alim, and Meghelli (2006: 650–54), the documentary *African Portraits: Positive Black Soul* (1996?), and Oumano (1999). PBS recorded early on in N'Dour's recording studio in Dakar (Williamson 2000: 20), and in 1996 they performed and guested on an album with visiting American saxophonist David Murray (1997). For more on Senegalese rap see O. Mbaye (1999), Herson (2000), Lobeck (2002), E. Baker (2002), Benga (2002), Niang (2006), and the film *Democracy in Dakar* (Herson,

McIlvaine, and Moore 2007). See Winders (2006: 150–59) for a snapshot of African rap in France and in Dakar in the late 1990s and early 2000s, especially Awadi's comments about preferring to stay in Senegal rather than emigrate to France (158). Oumano (1999: 30) quotes Amadou Barry: "In '89 we were Senegal's sole hip-hop group. Now, in Dakar alone, we have over 2,000 groups." O. Mbaye (1999) cites a figure of 3,000 rap groups in Senegal from a census taken by the NGO Enda Tiers-monde (although see Dieng et al. [1999] for a much smaller number).

35. This time frame is roughly consistent with what was happening elsewhere (except in France). In 1992 both the U.S. music industry magazine *Billboard* (Sinclair 1992) and the *New York Times* (Bernard 1992) recognized the potential of rap around the world, briefly noting rappers and scenes in Russia, Eastern Europe, China, Korea, Japan, India, Germany, France, England, Mexico, Anglophone Caribbean, South Africa (noting Taps, Prophets of Da City), and West Africa, which simply noted a fondness for American rap in Abidjan and that LL Cool J's concert there in 1988 was the first of its kind on the continent (Kenneth B. Noble, "The Many Accents of Rap around the World: West Africa, a King Yields to a New Messenger," *New York Times*, August 23, 1992, sec. 2, 23). Doug E. Fresh was in Senegal in 1987 or 1988, and Stetsasonic played a major concert in Dakar in 1990 (Eure and Spady 1991: 9-10, 137-39; www.rapindustry.com/daddy-o.htm).

36. Pages 239-251 in the reprint edition. See Androutsopoulos and Scholz (2003: 465–66) for a comparison of the number of rap recordings released in France, Italy, and Spain in the 1990s.

37. See the documentary *The Fab Five,* ESPN Films, 2011.

38. See www.rockonthenet.com/grammy

39. See www.koraawards.org

40. For the Senegal awards, see www.myspace.com/dakarhiphopawards. For a brief history of the Waga festival, see www.afromix.org/html/musique/articles/ouaga-hip-hop .fr.html ("Ouaga HipHop'5"). The festival website (wagahiphop.com) has not been updated since announcing Waga Hip Hop 10 in 2010 (all sites accessed April 17, 2011). The 2003 festival was the subject of a documentary film (*Ouaga Hip Hop*, Malapa 2005), and the 2007 festival has been documented with a single package book, CD, and DVD (Stay Calm! Productions 2007).

41. See Legrand and Paoletta (2005), Coetzer (2006, 2008), www.mtvbase.com (search about, Africa Music Award), http://beta.mnet.co.za/ChannelO, and http://channelo.dstv .com. See Bosch (2003: 185–207) for efforts made by Bush Radio, a community station in Cape Town, South Africa, to reach out to youth with a radio campaign in 2000 called HIV–Hop radio.

42. An early collaboration is Doug E. Fresh's "Africa (Goin' Back Home)" (on *The World's Greatest Entertainer*, 1988), which begins with a Senegalese sabar drum and Wolof speech (the performer is uncredited). In the piece Doug E. Fresh raps about his trip to Senegal (Eure and Spady 1991: 9-10). Senegalese drummer Mbaye Niasse is credited on Fresh's next album (*Doin' What I Gotta Do*, 1992). Kenyan Jean Kidula (this volume) describes her collaboration with Brazilian Sergio Mendes on the piece "Maracatudo" (*Oceano*, 1996).

43. An example of a critical response to first-generation rappers is Rap'adio from Senegal (see Lobeck 2002: 23); an example of an increasing commercialism is Skwatta

Kamp from South Africa (see L. Watkins, this volume). *Democracy in Dakar* (especially episode 6) directly addresses how a changing political environment may lead from youthful critique of the status quo to an acquiescence to play the game.

44. An excellent four-part radio documentary surveys the scenes in West, East, Southern, and North Africa in the mid-2000s (Seiler and JJC 2005). Afropop.org has several radio programs and numerous interviews and articles devoted to African hip hop and gospel (search hip hop, rap, gospel). To help fill in the large gap in coverage of North Africa, see Cestor and Abkari (2008) and the DVD *I Love Hip Hop in Morocco* (Asen and Needleman 2007) for Morocco; Daoudi (2000), Miliani (2000, 2002), and Maluka (2007) for Algeria, which historically has had the most active hip hop scene in North Africa; A. Williams (2010) for Egypt; and Abbas (2005); also see africanhiphop.com. See Nelson (1997) for a snapshot of hip hop in the capital city of Zimbabwe in the mid-1990s, Künzler (2011a) for an analysis of recent developments in South African hip hop, and Künzler (2011b) for a brief history of rap in Mali and Burkina Faso and an examination of issues discussed in rap there.

45. George (1998: 205) suggests that the UK has not produced many significant hip hop MCs because of its pervasive Jamaican dancehall culture, which would be a more attractive expressive form for Caribbean Brits than American hip hop. In the 2000s, however, UK-based rappers with Nigerian roots, such as JJC (Abdul Bello), Ty (Ben Chijioke), and BREIS (Stephen Ovba), have established a significant presence. See Wood (2009) for how the pioneering British hip hop group London Posse drew on Caribbean music for an original identity and Hesmondalgh and Melville (2001) for the varied impacts and repercussions of American hip hop in the UK.

46. See Helenon (2006) for an analysis of some of the varied relationships that rappers of African descent in France may have with Africa.

47. Mokobe's official Facebook page for his fans (Mokobe113Official) contains extensive media about him, including recorded interviews.

48. He has published an English translation of his autobiography in 2009.

PART 1.
RAP STORIES
(GHANA AND SOUTH AFRICA)

The Birth of Ghanaian Hiplife
Urban Style, Black Thought, Proverbial Speech

JESSE WEAVER SHIPLEY

Could it be that you were never told,
Keep your eyes on the road.
—REGGIE ROCKSTONE

Amid the political frustrations and economic transitions of 1980s Ghana, American rap music became the latest African diasporic music to become popular with urban African youth. In Accra clubs, DJs began playing American rappers such as LL Cool J, Heavy D, Public Enemy, and later Tupac Shakur and the Notorious B.I.G. By the early 1990s, at talent shows and small venues, elite youth experimented with rapping over beats and samples, emulating English rap flows. For some, hip hop provided a vision of black agency and economic success, while others derided it as an un-African foreign imitation. Young artists began experimenting with hip hop. Groups like Talking Drums with innovative producer Panji Anoff and Native Funk Lords (NFL) aimed to re-create hip hop in local terms, infusing rap with pidgin lyrics, local beats, and African-oriented imagery. This music moved from a small subculture in schools and clubs onto a main public stage, through the music of Reggie Ossei Rockstone. A Ghanaian rapper based in London, Rockstone returned to Ghana in 1994 and began rapping in Twi over heavy hip hop beats and samples of Ghanaian highlife and Nigerian afrobeat. By the mid-1990s, a new musical genre called hiplife emerged combining rap lyricism and hip hop mixing and beatmaking with older forms of highlife music, traditional storytelling, and formal proverbial oratory. Hiplife gained popularity through dance clubs, radio and television plays, clothing styles, and the circulation of cassettes, videos, CDs, and magazines. Around the open air drinking spots and nightclubs, markets, taxi stands, and compound houses of Accra, hip hop and hiplife clothing styles and bodily forms of expression began to reshape narratives of nationhood and generational change.

It is now widely recognized that hip hop provides a highly adaptable formal structure that has been reinvented by youth around the world in multiple ways. One of the fascinating things about hiplife in Ghana is how, over the course of a few short years, it developed a locally specific musical aesthetic, while continuing to draw on the uneasy balance between rebellious spirit and commercial legitimacy that has come to characterize American hip hop. As with many musical subcultures, hiplife provides a forum for the self-conscious contestation of moral value and legitimate forms of public expression. A central feature of the genre is the ongoing debate about the origins and the significance of foreign and Ghanaian influences in the music and dress of hiplife-oriented youth. To some, hip hop seems foreign, whereas to others it seems familiar; no matter what, it has reshaped Ghanaian public culture. Hiplife has creatively intermingled three main influences: African diasporic popular expression; the legacy of proverb-based Akan-language performance genres; and the rapid development of commercial electronic media in Accra. Hiplife, then, is not characterized by a particular rhythm or lyrical flow but rather by a creative style for mixing diverse African and diasporic performance practices and signs.

This chapter describes the confluence of styles that led to the birth of hiplife in the late 1990s. It shows how the naturalization of this genre relied upon elite youth transformation of American hip hop, privatization of media, and state appropriation of youth taste, in creating this eclectic remix of multiple performance traditions into a locally relevant form.

Embodying Diaspora in Ghanaian Popular Culture

In the decades after independence, black diasporic music provided young Ghanaians with a symbolic language to see themselves as modern and removed from the colonial legacies of older expressive forms. Throughout the 1960s and 1970s, African American soul and rhythm and blues music as well as Afro-Caribbean reggae and dancehall were popular in Ghana and other parts of Africa. American records and magazines circulated widely among the youth. Popular local highlife guitar bands and concert party theater troupes, such as the Jaguar Jokers, covered songs like "I'm Black and I'm Proud" and incorporated soul styles of dance, vocals, and dress into their shows. Nigerian Fela Kuti came to Accra in 1967 and in the early 1970s, developing his afrobeat sound.

The influence of soul, funk, and R&B in Accra culminated in the Soul to Soul Concert in 1971.[1] For youth this concert represented a critique of the authority and cultural icons of the older ruling generation who had been raised under colonial rule and, in the eyes of some, continued to value colonial ways of doing things.[2]

The adoption of African American styles and popular music became, for them, a political and social critique of British colonial forms of cultural capital. Held as a part of the Independence Day festivities, Soul to Soul was a state-sponsored event that provided a celebration of African American popular music, styles of dress, and ideologies of racial identification (e.g., Black Power) and linked them to the political struggles of the Ghanaian nation. The concert marked the rising interest in gospel, rhythm and blues, and soul music in Africa. As one woman who had been in secondary school at the time told me, students saw this concert as a major event facilitating their adoption of African American styles of dress and expression. In school they listened to records of black American music, imitating hairstyles and clothing and setting up groups to imitate the sounds. Many snuck out of their boarding school dormitories, coming from all over the country to attend the massive all-night Soul to Soul Concert at Black Star Square in downtown Accra.

The present generation of Ghanaian leaders, who grew up in the 1960s, defined their political and social differences from their elders partly in terms of soul and R&B music and styles. For many Ghanaians, the music and its associated forms of communication represented Pan-African consciousness. As part of the increasingly global American music industry, soul music also represented Western styles of consumer capitalism and its related forms of commodification.[3]

On 31 December 1981 Flight Lieutenant Jerry John Rawlings staged his second coup d'etat in 19 months, taking over the reins of the government from the democratically elected Dr. Hilla Limann. Rawlings established a socialist government that aimed to discipline and stabilize the country after nearly a decade of military rule and rampant corruption. One of the early dictates of the government was to establish a curfew banning movements from 6 PM to 6 AM. As many musicians recall, this effectively destroyed the vibrant nightlife of Accra, the live music scene, and theatrical and musical groups that toured the country. Many musicians left for the United States, Germany, Holland, England, and Nigeria. This also had the effect of reducing drastically the number of viable recording studios and recorded albums coming out of Ghana, which had been vibrant in the 1970s.

The rise of portable record and tape music systems, as well as the increasing availability of video recording and screening facilities, shifted public entertainment in the 1980s away from live musical and theatrical performances toward the circulation of recorded music. Spinners—mobile DJs who provided music for funerals, outdoorings, parties, and dances—were cheap and easy to hire, further decreasing the shows for live bands and vitality of the live music scene. Highlife music transformed as musicians traveled to Europe and brought back electronic computer and synthesizer music, creating the subgenre known as burger highlife because of the influence of Ghanaian musicians working in Hamburg, Germany. At the same time gospel highlife began to develop out of the influence of African American church music. The governmental tax on the importation of musical instruments and the decrease in the teaching of music in school also crippled the music industry. Since churches were one of the few institutions that were not subject to this tax, the musicians who did not leave often performed in churches and became closely tied to gospel (see Collins 1994 and this volume). In the midst of these changes, African American music remained at the center of what Ghanaians listened to and reinterpreted with local variations.

By the mid-1980s nightlife began to return, though the lack of instruments, the dispersal of bands, and the interest in new electronic sounds reshaped style and music. Babylon Disco, among other clubs and schools, hosted dance competitions focusing on post-disco Michael Jackson–like dancing and fashion. Jackson's singing and dance were the epitome of style for many youth. Others with perhaps a more rebellious sensibility were drawn to break dancing as part of the new hip hop urban cultural movement. As one teenage club-goer at the time recalls, "We thought Michael Jackson, who was all the rage, was really corny. We wanted to be more like the streets, and even more than hip hop and soul music, it was break dancing competitions at first that started to spread." Youth watched copies of films like *Wild Style* (1982) and *Breakin'* (1984) and television shows like *Soul Train*, which featured the latest dance moves and clothing styles. "It was black music. We felt it, but it was also so urban and American, and it made us feel a part of what was happening outside."

Ghanaian Rap

Many hiplife musicians credit Gyedu-Blay Ambolley as the first Ghanaian to use rap in his afrobeat-funk-jazz–infused highlife. Beginning with a 1973 hit single, "Simigwa Do," he used spoken-word lyricism in the Akan language over layered funky beats and horn riffs.[4] Nii Addokwei Moffat, writer for the weekly national entertainment newspaper *Graphic Showbiz*, recalls that in the 1980s there were various isolated experiments with rap by Ghanaian musicians. For example, at a cultural performance held at the State House in 1984, dancer and musical performer Cecilia Adjei "asked why we can't rap in our local dialects. She tried something [in the Dagbane language] and so did I [in the Ga language] and several other artists and people found it to be very interesting and exciting." Eclectic musician Atongo from the north of Ghana also rapped in Hausa at various points in the 1980s, although it never received popular attention.

In the late 1980s, the increasing ease of international travel and expanding access to foreign television, radio, and video facilitated the rapid movement of images, objects, and practices between Ghana and the rest of the world. Through the 1990s the development of cultural tourism brought an increasing number of students and tourists to Ghana to experience African culture. After the return of democratic rule in 1992, many young Ghanaians living abroad returned to seek opportunities in the newly privatizing economy.

One young hiplife artist told me that if a new fashion or product comes out in New York, the next day it is in Accra. CDs, cassettes, and videos are sent by relatives in the United States or Europe, sold by traders who regularly travel abroad, or acquired by elite youth who travel during holidays. Cassettes and music videos began to circulate, and images of African American artists began to appear on T-shirts, paintings, and posters throughout Accra and other urban centers. Young men adopted hip hop styles of dress, African American vernacular phrases, and forms of bodily expression. At first it was mostly elite young men in Accra and Kumasi and in coastal boarding schools listening to these radical foreign-sounding beats with forceful new social messages. Children of Lebanese, Syrian, and Indian merchants as well as those of mixed parentage were drawn to the music as a marker of black American coolness, resonating for the second generation born after independence coming of age in the context of the revolutionary coups of 1979 and 1981. While their older siblings and parents continued to listen to gospel, highlife, soul, and R&B, rap music provided a new defiant sensibility in relation to the radical political changes and economic hopes that they faced.

Students in elite secondary schools such as Accra Academy, Achimota School, and Presec Boys had easier access to American images and products and were more fluent in English than their rural counterparts. School variety shows provided venues for teens to form rap groups. At first they lip-synched to recordings of American rappers. They soon began to copy American lyrical flows and themes and write their own raps in English (Asare Williams interview). As these elite youth began adopting hip hop dress and styles, it became a local marker of cosmopolitanism and status. Ghanaians identified with black diasporic images of capitalist accumulation and success that were increasingly appearing in films and television shows. These styles were understood as status markers and quickly became popular among non-elite urban youth with less direct access to them. Young men in Accra marked their identification with the alternate forms of consumption provided by African American hip hop culture using African American vernacular, wearing baggy pants, oversized chains, basketball sneakers or Timberland boots, sunglasses and goggles, baseball caps, name-brand clothing, and knock-off gear. For poor youth coming to the city to find work, hip hop became a way of differentiating themselves from their rural kinship ties and ideas of traditional culture.

BiBi Menson, program director for Radio Gold, was a part of Accra's early hip hop scene. He remembers how class hierarchies were reflected through popular culture and how they were enacted around the open-air drinking spots around Adabraka and other Accra neighborhoods.

> We were into break dancing, rapping, and all the hip hop culture. . . . Boys from [elite] schools . . . would always be at house parties or clubs; we would get together and talk big things, insulting each other. . . . Then there were the more local boys from down the ghetto, we used them as foot-soldiers. . . . They would easily throw a punch for you. We were the loud mouths, trying to be heard. (Menson interview)

English was seen as the language of cosmopolitanism, and access to hip hop became the purview of elite youth with fluency in English. As Menson recalls,

"Then, you dare not [rap] in the local language. You would be a laughing stock." Local African styles and the use of African languages in many public settings were often looked down upon and seen as outdated or "colo" (colonial) in the context of urban Accra. Reflecting on the negative connotations of traditional culture among certain urban Ghanaians, Menson continued, "I mean it's amazing. In those days you couldn't wear kente cloth [traditional woven cloth]. We had to wait for someone like [American rapper] Heavy D to wear kente caps before we saw it as acceptable to follow our own traditional forms of dress." The irony of the African American legitimization of Ghanaian culture is not lost on local cultural critics, and it emphasizes the transformative power of transnational circuits of authenticity and cultural exchange.

While for older Ghanaians, British English had marked elite status, for Ghanaians born after independence, African American styles and speech became signs of authority. As Menson told me, "Our accents changed. . . . We wanted to sound like black Americans." Hip hop hit a chord with Ghanaian youth through its explicit critiques of American racism, symbols of toughness, and its message of black youth resistance to institutional authority. For Ghanaian audiences, the appeal was not necessarily the specific lyrical content. According to Reggie Rockstone, many youth who were less fluent in English did not even understand the lyrics. Instead, American hip hop appealed to them through its formal stylistic elements. Hip hop street culture expressed defiant forms of bodily expression, new modes of dress, and symbols of male sexual conquest and wealth. This music and style represented the promises of American material success through a particular racial lens. At a time when Ghana was moving away from critiques of neocolonialism in the 1980s and toward an acceptance of Western liberalizing capitalist reforms, these images of black accumulation and consumption became a means for engaging the possibilities and dangers of global free market capitalism. The perceived toughness and worldly success of African American hip hop stars became markers of status for Ghanaian youth. The Notorious B.I.G. and Tupac Shakur's success, wealth, and sudden violent shooting deaths made them particularly popular, though complex, models for Ghanaians to emulate. Tupac represented both the possibilities and dangers of their changing relationship with the institutions of power and desires for worldly success.

Accra clubs such as Globe, Keteke Club, Baby's Inn, and Miracle Mirage and in the nearby port city of Tema, Dzato Krom,[5] She Club, and Felisa, played American rap and hip hop, and hosted lip-synched performances to the likes of Run-D.M.C., MC Hammer, and Heavy D. As several musicians recounted to me, these clubs were the first places many young Ghanaians heard this kind of music. They provided public communal spaces for youth to formulate their musical and social sensibilities. There was a growing underground scene in Accra with groups, rappers, and DJs combining sampling, scratching, mixing, beatboxing, and rap as well as reggae, ragga, and afrobeat. KKD in particular was crucial to introducing contemporary American music into Ghanaian nightlife. Groups included Talking Drums, Native Funk Lords, N' Effect, Funkadelic, Nananom, Keteke, Cy Lover, Root I, Slim Buster, Nana King, Soul Black, General Marcos, Sammy B, CSI Posse, Roy Steel, Gosh MC, Kwame, and Swift. Their names reflected attempts to combine local cultural sensibilities with African American styles. Menson recalls that Joe Davis deejayed at Miracle Mirage and hosted freestyle rap events in English, though he began to call for rap in local African languages. As one music promoter put it, they attempted "at first to directly imitate their favorite American artists in style, music, and lyrics. . . . They were not ready to . . . make the music theirs" (Akoto interview).

DJ Azigiza Jr. was the first to gain a national reputation for rapping in Twi over electronic beats. He became a DJ/presenter for Joy FM, had his own television show highlighting local artists, and represented Ghana at international concerts within the West Africa subregion. Azigiza's public style recalled an older highlife idiom, and as one young artist recalled, he had a "local" sensibility that did not challenge people's taste as later artists would.[6] DJing crews sprung up who would sell mixtapes and beats on cassettes at kiosks and markets around Accra. M.anifest, a rapper later based in Minneapolis, grew up in Madina and recalls, "If you wanted beats to rap over you would go buy them from crews like Prime Cuts." These DJs began to seek out and disseminate new music and creatively use cassette tape players to manipulate the speed and levels of recording.

Talking Drums guided by producer Panji Anoff, as well as Native Funk Lords challenged early views of hip hop rapping in pidgin English over local instrumentation and rhythms. For Panji, hip hop could provide a hybrid formula for bringing Ghanaian and African musical traditions to the global market in new ways: "If hiplife was going to be about translating America into Africa, then I wanted no part of it. My idea was always to translate Africa into something global" (Anoff interview). In 1994 Public Enemy performed an influential concert in Ghana. Talking Drums was the opening act. This concert was seen as hugely influential by many kids who later became involved in hiplife music, as it showcased the best of American hip hop both musically and politically as well as showed the resonances with what was happening in Ghana. Talking Drums' performance was a huge success—moving the crowd with a specific combination of highlife, traditional, and afrobeat music and pidgin rap lyricism—which further pushed musicians and studio engineers to develop their own styles of music. Panji recalls the show: "I remember watching the crowd as they listened to Talking Drums perform. At first they were a bit slow, then they got really worked up. They felt the music; it moved them. I knew we were really onto something, and it was so exciting." Panji and Talking Drums further developed musical combinations of Ghanaian instrumentation and rhythms with pidgin lyrics. However, this was not the direction that popular hiplife took in its first decade. With a few exceptions most hip hop–oriented youth could not play instruments and had no popular or traditional musical training. Instead they were moved by the electronic technologies and lyrical focus of the genre.

Private Radio, New Media, and Ghanaian Returnees

The 1992 constitution of the fledgling Fourth Republic of Ghana provided for the privatization of mass media that had been strictly regulated under PNDC rule. Increasing access to electronic technologies and private media changed the nature of Ghanaian public life and popular culture. Previously, Ghana Broadcasting Corporation's AM broadcast had been the main radio access for Ghanaians, along with BBC and other international broadcasts. Quickly, private FM radio and cheap cassettes took on a national feel taking the place of live music as a primary site of social discourse. Access to hip hop for the Ghanaian masses, then, was largely facilitated by liberalizing government reforms and the relaxation of government restrictions on private media. For several years the government did not issue any licenses for radio frequencies. In 1994 the first private radio station, Radio Eye, went on the air in Accra. It broadcast from an unknown location and its use of the airwaves was seen as a violation of government regulation (Mahama interview). It was quickly and violently shut down by the police. However, it set a precedent, and from 1995 to 1997 a growing number of independent FM stations such as Joy, Choice, Groove FM, Radio Univers, and Radio Gold began legally broadcasting in Accra.

Many of those involved with the new stations and private media companies were Ghanaians who had lived in the United States or Western Europe, acquiring broadcast skills, electronic media knowledge, and interest in African American music. Indeed, in the mid-1990s, many young adults whose families had moved in the 1970s and 1980s to Europe, America, the Middle East or other parts of Africa returned to Ghana. Their cosmopolitan sensibilities and experience of blatant racism in America and Europe entered into national dialogues about culture and development and the definition of foreignness. Public debates on culture and media in national development and the role of the state in regulating these realms have often revolved around fears about the negative influence of foreign images and music on Ghanaian morality. In the first few years, stations played a large percentage of American popular music due to the desires of the younger generation of Ghanaians involved in the industry, the lack of recorded contemporary Ghanaian music, and the availability of foreign recordings. One DJ estimated they were playing 70 to 80 percent American music, partly out of interest but also out of a lack of local programming. Since the live music scene in Ghana had died after the economic and political upheavals of the early 1980s and continued taxation on instruments, the number of viable studios and recordings made by Ghanaian musicians fell significantly. While Ghanaians appreciated the foreign music, many lamented the lack of locally produced recordings. The opening of the airwaves created a new space, at first for access to foreign music and then for new local music. While some were initially resistant, DJs, radio and television presenters, and program managers, such as Azigiza Jnr., BiBi Menson, Twum, DJ Black, Sammy B, Blakofe, Paa Kwesi Holdbrook-Smith, Fifi Banson, Bola Ray, and KOD, linked hiplife to mass circulation through the radio and, by 1997, television. The social connections through old school associations and family connections were crucial to making this music accessible and acceptable.

Rockstone and the Birth of Hiplife Cool

In 1994, Reggie Ossei Rockstone returned to Ghana to perform in the inaugural PANAFEST (Pan-African Theatre Festival) celebrations. Rockstone stayed in Ghana, radically shifting the trajectory of his music and unintentionally shifting the direction of popular music. His hard driving rap and public style revolutionized how Ghanaians thought of hip hop, particularly by popularizing rap in the Akan language. In his early public appearances and music videos shot in Accra, Rockstone had short dreadlocks, Timberland boots, baggy military fatigues, and often went topless bearing his muscular chest. He projected a tough, streetwise persona on stage and on video. For the older generation this appeared as a foreign, morally corrupt, American gangster image. Many people noted that when he spoke English, Rockstone sounded African American. This was especially noticeable because his rap flows in Twi, English, and pidgin demonstrated his codeswitching virtuosity to the astonishment and delight of the youthful Ghanaian audience. Rockstone knew how to reach his audiences: "I looked like the people they saw in the New York videos, but I rapped in Twi, so I was a hero."

This combination of stylistic authenticities gave Rockstone the cultural capital to consolidate the various initial attempts at local rap music. While Rockstone has been dubbed the "Godfather of hiplife" and is usually credited with coining the term *hiplife*, some argue that Panji and his group Talking Drums were the originators of the genre. Although Panji and others had used the term, it was popularized on Rockstone's first EP album in "Tsoo Boi."

> check, check it out for the hiplife,
> it goes on and on for the hiplife.
> *Omo feeli, Omo feeli feeli*

This caught on as a phrase for youth and radio and television presenters to define the local style of rap music.

As a youth in Accra, Rockstone had been known as a break dancer and had been part of the nascent hip hop scene in the 1980s. He left for London after finishing school and studied acting for a time. He began traveling to New York where he would buy the latest hip hop gear to bring back and sell in London at a time when this was new to the British scene. Although he did not have much experience with rap, Rockstone joined PLZ (which at first stood for Party a la Maison and then Parables, Linguistics, and Zlang), an English language hip hop group, with rapper Freddie Funkstone—a Sierra Leonian rapper who had been Rockstone's school friend in Accra—and well-known British DJ Pogo.[7] To gain a sense of authenticity they emphasized African American vernacular and bodily expression and even encouraged the idea that they were from New York. In the early 1990s, they put out several records in London, achieving some success within the small British hip hop scene, which was confined to African and Caribbean youth, and did not yet have mass market appeal. Panji Anoff, Ghanaian-born of German and Ghanaian heritage, had attended school in Britain and worked in music and as PLZ's management. According to Panji, African hip hop in London did not make sense because African music was seen as tribal or primitive. He continues,

> Hiplife really started with PLZ and their success as an American-oriented hip hop group. Considering the [limited] interests of the [British] music industry in hip hop at the time, PLZ had reached the limits of what they could do in Britain. . . . I mean, if they said they wanted to do African music, if they had started rapping in Twi [in Britain], that would have been the end of it. . . . They had traded on their American image in London for legitimacy. . . . So they could not go to New York or orient their music toward Africa. Returning to Ghana was a way to open up new directions for the music. (Anoff interview)

Friends in the music business in Ghana told Rockstone that if he wanted to make money, he should go into established gospel or highlife music. Hip hop was not seen as a style of music that was made locally. Rockstone's image and his American orientation fit in to the negative stereotypes of American rappers that were widely held in Ghana. A breakthrough came one night when Rockstone and Funkstone were free-styling in English to the Fugees' instrumental "Boof Baff" at Accra's Miracle Mirage nightclub, when Rab Bakari, a DJ and engineering student at City College in New York, heard him perform. "I was amazed. I mean, here I was in Africa, and there was this guy who sounded like he was from Brooklyn" (Bakari interview). Later in the evening, Reggie experimented with rapping in Twi, shouting into the mike, "How many of you have ever heard of Twi fucking rap? I'll be the first one." As Rockstone describes it, he began rapping in Twi because "Ghanaians would really feel the music" if it were put in terms that they understood, rather than in African American vernacular, which often they could only partially follow or were copying in a rote fashion (Rockstone interview).

Bakari recalls, "I approached [Reggie and Freddie] and told them I am a DJ. I had left [my records and equipment] in New York but that I could make beats." The next morning they went to Groove Records run by George Brun and began mixing and sampling from African as well as more traditional hip hop beats and loops and putting down lyrics mostly in English. Bakari continued, "In the back of Groove records they had everything, all the latest equipment that I was used to using in New York, including an ASR-10 [Ensoniq's Advanced Sampling Recorder], Tascam mixing board. . . . I started turning out beats." The idiom of hip hop provided an elastic poetic structure within which they could elaborate both socially and musically. This initial session spawned a lasting partnership.

At the end of 1994 and the beginning of 1995, Bakari, Rockstone, and Funkstone joined with others in historic recording sessions at the Combined House of Music (CHM). The CHM sessions were a moment of creative effervescence in which multiple creative figures contributed to the formation of a new musical template. Many young artists came to contribute or just observe and be a part of the scene. Sidney of Nananom, who was also Rockstone's cousin, Root I, Cy Lover, Sammy B, BiBi Menson, and others participated in one way or another. These sessions spawned a creative validation among the small hip hop musical community. Local television stations came and taped Rockstone and Funkstone rapping and did interviews, adding to the recognition of the new music's local validity.[8]

These early sessions defined the parameters of hiplife music. The songs had predominantly English lyrics performed with the authenticity of New York rap. Rockstone's ability to switch languages fluently was groundbreaking. Most people had assumed he was American when he spoke or rapped in English, making the fluidity of his Twi rap and use of Accra street slang all the more effective. The beats Bakari (interview) made were predominantly "hardcore, New York style beats but sampling and drawing on afrobeat and indigenous Ghanaian musical traditions." Panji Anoff and Zap Mallet, a studio engineer and one of the few actual musicians involved, emphasized the need to bring in Ghanaian musical influences and highlife guitar.

Rockstone's first album *MaKaa MaKa* [I said because I said it] was released in 1997 under the name Reggie Rockstone on Kassa Records.[9] His father, Rickie Ossei, was a well-known fashion designer, and Reggie attended Achimota Secondary School, one of the oldest elite boarding schools in Anglophone West Africa. The combination of personal connections through Achimota School's roster of famous alumni and his father's elite network of artists and public personalities gave Rockstone's persona and music legitimacy and access to the rising new radio and media industries. With financial backing from his father, Rockstone formed Kassa Records with Bakari as the technical and practical force. As Bakari explained to me, they crafted their music with the intent of reaching Ghanaian audiences as well as African and African diaspora peoples around the world. But they were struggling to get the formula right: to combine the different linguistic and musical influences in a way that would appeal to multiple audiences. In both the music and the marketing they tried to maintain a balance between the specificity of local music and language idioms and a cosmopolitan, hip hop sensibility accessible to non-Ghanaians. They were aiming at both reaching local youth and breaking into the top ranks of American hip hop artists.

For Rockstone (interview), hip hop became a way to give voice to disenfranchised Ghanaian youth, bridging gaps between African Americans, other Africans in the diaspora, and those on the continent. Bakari feels that the effect of globalization has been to erase local difference and create one global European culture. For him hip hop is an African "counter-hegemonic project" that allows for local diversity among African peoples while drawing on basic shared cultural idioms. As he told me, "The music that Reggie and I were making was a way for us to link Ghana to African peoples in North America, Japan, Europe, and all over Africa by trying to make the music authentically Ghanaian, but also market it to people around the globe."

Rockstone's music addresses the specific daily frustrations and desires of his audience as highlife did for the older generation. His linguistic code-switching—among Twi, pidgin, and African American and Ghanaian vernacular versions of English—reflects the way that many urban youth in Accra communicate. In this sense, his use of language indexes a collectively imagined community of young streetwise hiplifers. The music video for "Nightlife in Accra" from *MaKaa MaKa* was shot by BiBi Menson and reflects a collective sensibility of youth defiance in their celebration of the city life, following Rockstone and a cohort of youth as they dance, drink, and enjoy nightlife in the streets of the capital. Raps by Rockstone and Cy Lover and the chorus by female R&B vocalist Chocolate are in English with an occasional aside in pidgin. Combined with the images, the song projects a sensibility of youth vibrancy and affluence. "Tsoo Boi" was seen as perhaps the most pathbreaking track on the first album with its rapid-fire Twi lyrics intermixed with English words and phrases. The title/chorus refers to the famous Ghanaian political rally cry (which has no literal translation). A future hiplife star, Sidney the Hiplife Ninja, recalls the inspiration he got from hearing Rockstone's first album: "I listened to some of the lyrics. It was so amazing. I thought he was rapping in English, but it was Twi."

Rockstone's second album, *Me Na Me Kae* [It's me that said it] released in 1999, defined the future direction of hiplife in both lyrical content and song format. In the liner notes, Bakari reflects on a version of pan-Africanist hip hop that can connect the African diaspora back to the continent through African-based commercial production and circulation. He also points to the irony that Africa is only seen as a place of past origins and is not linked to diasporic sociality even among people of African descent.

> Often neglected, and not represented in the hip hop community, the African continent now has a champion to build bridges, set foundations, and destroy

all myths, hypocrisies, and misinformation about our people, culture and existence.

Bakari's deployment of highlife and hardcore hip hop in his mixes created crossover appeal and gave the music legitimacy for older listeners who had seen hip hop as a purely American phenomenon. At the same time, their style and music gain authority from their seemingly authentic deployment of African American vernacular and New York hip hop culture. Rockstone's lyrics address the everyday lives of Ghanaian youth by putting them within a global framework. Many of his songs draw heavily on images of global racial inequalities and the necessity of fostering African pride to counter the negative effects of globalization on African peoples.

The titles of both albums point to the high value placed on public speaking in Ghanaian society and the way that hiplife has appropriated that sensibility for youth voices. In Akan society, the largest linguistic and political community in Ghana, elegant public speaking is highly valued for style, flow, and the use of erudite references. The poetics of speech is characterized by indirectness, metaphor, and the use of proverbs (Anyidoho 1983; Yankah 1995; Obeng 1999). Highlife music had drawn on the structure of traditional Ananse moral storytelling. Hiplife quickly incorporated this tradition. This appropriation is especially significant because traditionally youth are not supposed to use proverbs, tell stories, or even speak in many public forums. However, hip hop sensibilities justified youth in taking a place on the public stage and speaking as legitimate national subjects and transnational consumers.

Abraham Ohene-Djan's videos for Rockstone's tracks gave the music a slick, technologically savvy public image. Initially he shot on 16 mm film, directing videos for several Rockstone tracks. His video for "Keep Your Eyes on the Road" established a visual aesthetic for urban youth in Accra. Despite inexperience and low production values in the video industry, Ohene-Djan's work stood out immediately as more in line with international production standards. The videos have remained in circulation on Channel O in South Africa, giving Rockstone international exposure.

Rockstone, ever the self-conscious performer, quickly recognized that in order to be successful with hip hop in Ghana he needed to incorporate familiar styles of speech culture. Many of his songs use a basic storytelling format and detachable hook phrases that easily circulate as proverbs. According to Rockstone, there are three crucial aspects to hiplife in Ghana: humor, danceable rhythms, and storytelling or moral messages. In terms of lyrics, Rockstone has also focused on making his rap flows melodic. In advising a young rapper on how to become successful, Rockstone said, "You have to put melody to the [lyrics]. You can't just talk straight. You have to make the lyrics boogie. If you take out the beat, you should be able to dance just to the rap."

"Plan Ben?" [What's the plan?] and "Eye Mo De Anaa?" [Is it good to y'all?][10] from *Me Na Me Kae* are examples of catchy phrasing that caught on with the public, becoming popular sayings around town. In some of his raps in both in English and Twi, Rockstone uses rapid fire lyrical delivery with vocal force and authority, although the lyrics do not in any way tell a story but rather focus their flow on rhyming, alliteration, dexterity, hyperbole, and self-praise. This type of lyrical style is admired in Rockstone and others for its flow and internal rhythm, in other words, the explicit, reflexive control by the speaker/rapper over verbal form. It is reminiscent of the way in which concert party popular comedians create long lists of introductory titles that go on for minutes (e.g., "My name is Alhaji, Pastor, North America, Mr., Dr., Sister, Brother, President, Minister . . .") or speak in nonsensical English with long names and words.[11] Through verbal mastery, Rockstone poetically mocks the formal and superfluous use of *Abrofuo KeseE* [big English] and highlights the formal elements of language rather than its content.

"Ya Bounce Wo Visa" [They bounced or rejected your visa] is an example of the storytelling aspect of the music. Rapped in Twi, it details two letters written by friends in Ghana to the rapper who is residing "outside" in the West. The letters describes the senders' frustrations at being refused a visa at the British embassy, the humiliating treatment that black applicants often receive at the hands of Western diplomatic officials, and the sadness and pain of being separated from friends and loved ones that is common for highly mobile African youth. It highlights themes of being inside and outside of the nation and the desires and economic necessities of foreign travel that have become one common type of lyric in hiplife.

For "Keep Your Eyes on the Road" Rockstone bought the rights to the highlife track "Kyen Kyen Bi Adi Mawu" [People on all sides are destroying me] by 1970s star Ahlaji K. Frimpong to loop for the beat. Rockstone told me, "We paid him a lot of money at the time. . . . I think he thought we were crazy for giving so much for his song. I don't think he had any idea that the song or hip hop would be so big or that it would get people interested in old-school highlife again." This song is most frequently referenced by foreign music critics, BBC and other radio programs, and local enthusiasts alike as helping to define the genre. According to Rockstone's manager, Paa Kwesi Holdbrook-Smith, many consider this the first hiplife track. However, it also demonstrates the ambiguity of defining the genre. He continued, "While we give Reggie the credit for starting hiplife, he did not really make a hiplife track until the second album with 'Keep Your Eyes on the Road,' when he sampled the highlife song 'Kyen Kyen Bi Adi Mawu,' but the lyrics were in English. So is that hiplife yet or still hip hop?" The song's lyrics address issues of global and local social concern with a direct political agenda:

> Peace to Mr. Kofi Annan whatever the mission,
> Forget the World Cup, check out your condition,
> Economical competition before the dribbling,

The biggest crime in Africa, Skin Bleaching. . .
Jesus Christ was *abibini* [black African] what I believe in,
Make I free my mind this morning, afternoon, and evening.

Rockstone's lyrics make critical connections between common activities, such as skin bleaching and football, and broader global political and economic concerns. He critically engages Africa's position on the margins of the global system. Rockstone's lyrics also establish a new urban geographic imaginary that draws on hip hop's tradition of celebrating urban space. His tracks imagine Ghana from the perspective of the neighborhoods of urban Kumasi and Accra, on the one hand, and toward international spaces in Europe and America, on the other. While these two albums were not huge commercial sellers, they established a language for a new type of music, social style, and cosmopolitan Ghanaian-based electronic media. Through his code switching and ability to bring together multiple social registers, Rockstone symbolizes the daily predicaments of the rising generation of urban Ghanaians. He unites the bravado and pastiche poetics of hip hop with the speech culture and rhythmic sensibility of highlife into a genre that provides new identities and social spaces for youth to inhabit and imagine themselves as modern.

From Global to Local: State Discourses on Cultural Performance and Competing Appropriations of Hip Hop

In 1994, partly in response to anxieties about the influence of foreign—especially American—culture on youth, the National Theatre of Ghana initiated an annual festival called Kiddafest. This program has grown each year and has brought together artists and school children from all ten regions of Ghana, several other African nations (notably Nigeria and South Africa), the United States, and Europe for several days to perform and participate in artistic programs. In the context of a long history of state use of local cultural practices to create the idea of a national culture, the aim was to encourage the youth to become involved in culture and the arts and by association become patriotic and good citizens. The organizers felt music, dance, and drama were good ways "to teach Ghanaian and African moral and social values to youth."[12] The programs focused on fostering what were seen as traditional forms of music, dance, and art, although many of the youth, especially from the urban areas, were not interested in these performances. While attending many of these shows and rehearsals, I saw the audiences making fun of the other kids involved in the traditional dance and drama groups with shouts of "woa bre!" [you're tired!], taunting them for being old-fashioned and uneducated. Most of the youth only wanted to participate in "free-style" hip hop and disco dancing and rap.

At first the organizers were hesitant to include rap in the program. However, they realized the potential of its popularity and decided to allow the kids to rap within certain constraints. As the artistic director of the theater stated, "Rap is an art of the African diaspora and has its origins in Africa." Therefore, they decided to include a rap segment in their youth programming. They stipulated that participants would have to rap in a Ghanaian language and to present "socially relevant and educational messages" in their lyrics. The directors ideally wanted to focus on developing what they saw as modern African arts—grounded in traditional African and Ghanaian forms—but defined by modern idioms of artistic creativity. Although hip hop did not fit within the recognizable possibilities of either traditional or modern artistic forms, it did, nevertheless, attract huge crowds of youth and inculcate them into institutional practices of theater attendance and artistic patronage.

The hip hop segments of Kiddafest quickly became the most popular part of the program. In 1999 there were 65 rap groups performing during the weeklong program with many more youths being turned away. The National Theatre did not let them rap about love or violence (Adjetey Sowah interview), but rather prescribed themes which they saw as educational, such as abstinence, AIDS awareness, and the importance of education. These performances became a launching point for many hip hop groups, such as Buk Bak, Tic Tac, Nananom, Terry Bonchaka, Chicago, and Ex-Doe. They rapped mostly in Twi, although other Ghanaian and African languages such as Ewe, Ga, Fante, and Hausa were used. To back up their vocals the young artists used cassettes of prerecorded synthesizer dance beats, which they would make themselves or get from a private recording studio. During the program, the National Theatre and its surrounding space in downtown Accra was transformed by thousands of youth. The crowds were different demographically than those coming to the National Theatre to see *Key Soap Concert Party*. The youth listening to hip hop initially tended to be more educated and to have elite affiliations.

The boys paid meticulous attention to their clothing, dressing in urban, African American–inspired styles, and the girls were wearing tight jeans and revealing tops; many kids from Accra and the surrounding schools came to see and be seen. Most of them came to see the rap groups and were uninterested in the many other dance and theater performances. Kwesi, a sixteen-year-old boy dressed in baggy jeans, white Reebok sneakers, an oversized T-shirt with a picture of Tupac on it, and motorcycle goggles, summed up many youths' initial relationship to hip hop when he said that he loved American rappers, especially Tupac, because he wanted to be tough like them, and he admired how wealthy they were.

Hip hop engages class, ethnic, and urban/rural difference within Ghana. Many people from poorer areas of Accra and from rural areas were intimidated by the conspicuous display put on by the urban kids, though at the same time it is through these more cosmopolitan boys and girls that marginalized people gain access to partially translated foreign symbols and practices. Some, coming from remote parts, such as Wa and Bolgatanga, were not native speakers of Twi and had never been to a city such as Accra. Some were shocked that kids in Accra were allowed to behave so wildly. As one youth from the Upper East Region explained to me, if they behaved and dressed in such a disrespectful manner back home they would be insulted and beaten by their elders. Another girl from the Ashanti Region attending Kiddafest as a part of a traditional dance group who performed *adowa* and *kete* dances told me that she felt hip hop was a foreign activity that was not a part of Ghanaian culture and it was a bad influence on African youth. She was certainly in the minority, as most youth from the rural areas were awed by the displays of cosmopolitanism. Another boy from the North said that he was so impressed that he could not wait to go home and tell all his friends about the people, styles, buildings, and ways of life in Accra. In these events at the National Theatre we can see that the state lags behind and struggles to control publics that are increasingly shaped by private mass media circulations that evade official, centralized ideas of culture.

The National Theatre organizers attempted to fulfill their mandate of reviving and inspiring traditional African cultural forms while attracting audiences. In the process, their programming pointed at the ways that hip hop became creatively integrated into the gamut of Ghanaian expressive cultural practices. Innovative young artists began to draw upon idioms of storytelling, proverbial speech, and traditional indirect speech culture in creating a new type of critical public voice. These youth referenced and drew upon older traditions while distancing themselves from established genres and past speech acts to facilitate creativity. Hiplife is engaged in contesting ideas of the traditional and the modern. In the process, the genre itself has been reshaped. Similarly, highlife music was still seen as unconventional and modern until the early 1980s, although now it is considered by many Ghanaians to be the embodiment of tradition. These popular forms, then, must be understood as involved in the sociocultural production of historical narratives about tradition and modernity and ultimately national belonging.[13]

For many urbanites in the older generation as well as rural traditional elites, American rap and its influence on Ghanaian youth was explicitly negative. Reflecting these sentiments, one older radio executive from a well-known family privately expressed to me frustration at the proliferation of Western culture and its threat to African sensibilities.

> [T]he way these kids are running around Accra showing no respect to African traditions and their elders, it's disgraceful. My nephew was shown lip-synching and dancing to a rap song on television, broadcast from the National Theatre, and his mother [the interviewee's sister-in-law] almost died of embarrassment when people who had seen the program called to tell her that her son was jumping around on television. (interview, December 2004)

Reflecting the views of many middle-aged Ghanaians, a member of the National Commission on Culture explained to me, "Rap is not a Ghanaian tradition; it encourages kids to ignore their own communities and proper Ghanaian values of respect." Indeed, in line with state-centered notions of national culture from colonialism through Nkrumah and into the Rawlings era, cultural institutions were focused on fostering what were seen as cultural, national, and pan-African traditions as a basis for national consciousness and economic development. Rap music created generational debates about what constitutes African culture.[14]

Retraditionalization of Next Generation Hiplife: 'Typical' Twi, Electronic Beats, and the New Styles

Following Rockstone's success, a series of albums and hit singles by young rappers in 1999 filled the airwaves, giving hiplife new public legitimacy. Rap events at the National Theatre, secondary schools, clubs, and cheap outdoor venues such as the Trade Fair Centre attracted massive followings of fans and aspiring artists. Highlife's legacy of using storytelling, proverbs, and humorous moral messages and Rockstone's success in synchronizing this with a hip hop aesthetic inspired aspiring young rappers. Rockstone's music received critical acclaim and heavy radio play, even though none of the albums sold well. It influenced a generation of youth into believing in Ghanaian hip hop and paved the way for the creative expansion and marketing of the music by younger artists. Non-elite younger kids born in the late 1970s and 1980s who had less firsthand international experience began to fashion this music to suit particularly Ghanaian sensibilities.[15]

By 1999 hiplife was regularly played by radio DJs, with the radio stations Joy, VIBE, and Groove leading the way in garnering a hiplife audience. In 2000, events production company Charter House sponsored the first annual Ghana Music Awards with several categories devoted to hiplife. Hiplife was moving away from more mainstream global forms toward a more specifically Ghanaian form of cosmopolitanism. The new market share that the genre was commanding gave artists and producers the impetus to experiment with creative combinations of styles. Many of the young artists had attended elite secondary schools, although they also were more closely connected with regions where traditional language use and performance traditions had influenced them. Reflecting a social system that relies on patronage networks, aspiring rappers often would approach established artists, producers, and radio presenters to find patronage and an entry into the music business. The programs at the National Theatre helped young artists enter into the music business. Others looked to established artists and producers for mentors and guidance.

As Paa Kwesi Holdbrook-Smith (interview) recalls, the ways in which youth looked to established producers and musicians to help them be successful reflects local ideas of patronage: "There was always a group of young rappers trying to get featured on one of [Reggie's] tracks or coming around to get advice and support. Most of the artists now recording albums at one point came through Reggie's house. It reflects how people do things here in traditional society. There is a proverb that says, 'If you climb a big tree you deserve a push.' That is how things get done in Ghana."

As Rockstone's mixing of hip hop beats and Twi lyrics gained public acceptance, artists began to elaborate and experiment with the stylistic potential of hiplife, combining a variety of influences within this generic formula. The use of electronic beats and sampling were favored over live instrumentation; *kpanlogo, jamma, adaha* (or other traditional rhythms), reggae, and hardcore hip hop beats were looped and used as the basis for lyrical experiments; artists interwove traditional clothing styles such as kente cloth versus hip hop clothing and jewelry; naming, proverbial, and storytelling structures were mixed with hip hop slang; harmonic highlife choruses framed rap lyrics in various combinations of English, pidgin, Twi, Ewe, Ga, and Hausa.[16]

The second group of important rap artists following the pioneers include Obrafour, Lord Kenya, Akyeame, Sidney from Nananom, VIP, Ex-Doe, Chicago, Sass Squad, Buk Bak, and Tic Tac.[17] Artists increasingly experimented with lyrics using Twi, Ga, pidgin, and sometimes Ewe and Hausa languages, and integrated rap flows and hip hop beats with electronic versions of highlife dance music. Many of the newer artists had attended elite secondary schools. But increasingly, uneducated youth saw hiplife music as a possible way to fulfill elusive dreams of financial and social success. Significantly, with the development of sophisticated local language lyricism, public discourse about hiplife shifted to include it as Ghanaian music rather than foreign. In comparing language use, Rockstone explained to me, "Man, I started rapping in Twi, but these cats today, they're deep. I mean, they really go into the traditional proverbs, the deep indigenous culture from the villages. I use more street Twi, the way the kids talk in the streets of Accra." Rockstone and the earlier groups had been associated with cosmopolitan elites, on the one hand, and African American foreign popular culture, on the other, with the aim of linking Ghanaian sensibilities to a global hip hop community. But the younger generation focused on making music for a Ghanaian market. And while Rockstone was interested in using diasporic cultural forms to reimagine Ghanaian urban life, new artists increasingly used hiplife as a way to explore traditional expressive forms in new ways.

Many artists used names that drew on traditional figures of authority.[18] For example, the group Akyeame, made up of Okyeame Quophi and Okyeame Quaom, uses the iconic figure of the Okyeame (pl. Akyeame), who is the spokesperson or linguist in the chiefly courts of the Ashanti. Other uses of traditional figures include Nananom [ancestors], made up of three performers who described themselves as the chief, the linguist, and the queen mother in the stage performances, Obrafour [court executioner], Abrewa Nana [old wise woman], Kontihene [a kind

of chief], and Motia [magical dwarf]. Others use names to imagine broader diasporic connections sometimes through specific hip hop and reggae icons with artists including 50 Cedis, Black Prophet, Black Rasta, and D Black.

Several songs from 1999 demonstrate clearly the speed and valence through
which hiplife gained local legitimacy. Obrafour's 1999 album *Pae Mu Ka* [To con-
fess], produced by Ghanaian producer Hammer, opened up the potential of the
genre to incorporate Akan traditions of moral proverbial speaking. Whereas Rockstone used simplistic Twi language constructions familiar to the polyglot urban
contexts of youthful Accra, Obrafour deploys complex Twi language forms, storytelling structures, indirection, and proverbial speech. His songs are noted for providing political and moral lessons. Reflecting the difference between Rockstone
and Obrafour, one aspiring rapper explained to me:

> Reggie was the first one to really make the music acceptable or popular rather. He
> showed us what we could do. That we could do what they were doing up there [in
> America]. Reggie was doing it, but there was this Western style [in his music]. Many
> [of us] were not too good in that Western style. . . . Obrafour . . . showed us that we too
> could enter this game; that the typical youth could make it. . . . He raps in pure, typical
> Twi filled with . . . proverbs. He brings in the authentic Ghanaian culture.

Hammer, a prolific producer, beatmaker, and music business entrepreneur, came
to prominence by making the beats for Obrafour's first album. His style emphasizes heavy electronic textures and synthetic drum loops. It does not focus on danceable rhythms, but rather uses layered rhythm tracks to highlight the rap flow. Their
music, as BiBi Menson of Radio Gold said, addresses "the problems faced by the
nation . . . giving people some incredible, deep lyrics." Perhaps the best-known
track from *Pae Mu Ka* was "Kwame Nkrumah," which presents a moral tale and
nostalgic lament about the history of Ghanaian politics and calls for national unity
and an end to corruption.

> You are our roots that is why we call on you
> Your intelligence redeemed Ghana
> When the skies got calm the white men shivered
> Because they saw your undefeated braveness
> Dr. Kwame Nkrumah, your intelligence dominates like the stars in the sky[19]

Obrafour's image reflects the multiple influences of the second generation of
hiplifers. He has dreadlocks and dresses in modest hip hop styles. His manners
and style of speaking are seen as highly respectful and in line with that of a good
Ashanti youth. It is often noted that he eschews fame and is not perceived as enjoy-
ing the trappings of success, as many artists do.[20] Obrafour's lyrics call for public
critiques of political corruption, sexual violence, moral degradation, and the violence of truck travel— the mundane and spectacular dangers and frustrations that
plague the daily lives of Ghanaians. His elegant use of storytelling and indirect pro-

verbial speech is highly respected by youth and older people alike and for many people it places him in the tradition of Akan poetry. He does not attract the critiques of foreignness and moral corruption that Rockstone and other more outwardly hip hop–oriented artists do.

Many consider the 1999 hit "Masan Aba" [I will come back again] on Akyeame's second album, *Nkonson Konson* [To link/weave], to be the first originally produced hiplife hit song that follows the formula that Rockstone prescribed—although he often did not follow it himself—of combining elements of highlife with Twi language rap, local humor, storytelling, and hip hop swagger. The cover of the cassette and CD shows the album's subtitle, *New York Meets Accra,* repeated across the bottom of a picture of the two artists wearing shirts emblazoned with "Versace" towering over the Manhattan skyline and the World Trade Center towers. A dollar sign ($), the symbol for the local cedi currency, and a new car are placed in the cityscape as well. This symbolism reflects their musical synthesis as well as broader generational hopes of travel and economic success.

"Masan Aba" begins with a rhythm highlife guitar over a simple three-stroke highlife percussion pattern, then bass guitar and synthesizer drums enter, backing the melodic highlife chorus and female harmonies. The chorus alternates with long raps by Okyeame Quophi and Okyeame Quoami.[21] The guitar, the harmonic style, and the slow patient rhythm in particular define this within a danceable highlife idiom familiar to older Ghanaian listeners. The cover of the CD reprints various critics' comments on the music. Adowa Serwaa Bonsu of the newspaper *Graphic Showbiz* flatly states, "My mother loves you guys. I don't know why, but it seems you're the only rap group she listens to." The contemplative, philosophical tone of the lyrics draw the listener, as one older fan told me, "to reflect on the conditions of life while also being compelled to dance." The rappers lilt lyrically through their rhymes—confessional and personal in tone—through highlife influenced voicings, and they use clear intonation rather than the more hardcore gravely style of Rockstone. In the same vein as Rockstone and Obrafour, here we see the self-conscious invocation of the power of words and public speaking. The name of the group and the reference to the Okyeame in the song lyrics reinforce the transformative power of words and the youths' right to speak in public. Typically, an Okyeame's ability is measured in his skillful use of proverbial oratory and rich referential language to fill out the message of the chief. This mediation acts as surrogate speech to "save face" in communicative situations that are potentially disruptive or dangerous while invoking important political and social issues (Obeng 1999).

In the same year, Ex-Doe had a hit song, "Comfort" from his album *Maba* [I'm here], in which he collaborated with older highlife star Dr. Paa Bobo adding vocals by Maggie. Ex-Doe's fast and forceful style of rap clearly reflects the influence of Rockstone's gritty hardcore voice; his style has a sense of apocalyptic menace that appealed to youth. This track opens with highlife acoustic guitar picking following a basic three chord progression before a heavy electronic bassline comes in as the rhythm track is repeated throughout. Dr. Paa Bobo and Maggie sing and harmonize in the lamentation of love lost while Ex-Doe intersperses his raps. The music video for the song also shows the growing importance of television to the genre's image. The camera pans across an older woman seated in a typical living room singing the chorus looking wistfully away from the camera, as Ex-Doe, dressed spectacularly in baggy white trousers, open shirt, and chains, presents himself in collaboration with the older generation but also with the swagger and force of a dominant youthful voice.

Many of these albums in the late 1990s seemed to be experimenting with what would appeal to audiences. They would have some tracks in English and some in Twi, some with more American-sounding beats and some with more highlife-oriented sounds reflecting attempts to find a musical formula that would be commercially successful.

In light of hiplife's sudden public presence on the radio and the rise in cassette sales, successful young highlife musicians also began to experiment with mixing hip hop and highlife, doing collaborations with rappers. This gave rappers commercial viability and cultural legitimacy among older and mainstream audiences and, conversely, gave highlife more youth appeal. For example, highlife singer Daasebre Gyamenah's hit "Kokooko", was celebrated for how it contrasted Gyamenah's highlife sung melodies and storyline with rap verses by Lord Kenya in a competitive dialogue.[22] Built around an electronic highlife beat, the song portrays an unstylish young man, Gyamenah, who cannot get the attention of a woman. He keeps knocking—seeking a woman's attention—and he is ignored. Lord Kenya's lyrics and style portray him as tough, confident, and successful with women. The joking juxtaposition of these two figures represents the way that many youth understand the relationship between highlife and hip hop and its implications for the political, social, and economic positions they occupy. Hiplife appears to many to provide an aspiring, self-fashioning masculine persona. The swagger and confidence of African American artists, picked up particularly by Rockstone, became a style for youth to use in facing daily frustration, lack of economic opportunity, and anxieties about social and sexual possibility.

As Panji, Hammer, Bakari, and other producers have noted, most of the initial creative energy was focused on lyrics, whereas there were only a few DJs and studio engineers who worked on making beats and mixing. This was partly due to the lack of foreign-made musical instruments. Many with musical interests had readily focused on the potential of rap and its ties to storytelling and lyrical traditions. At the same time, cheap, secondhand PC computers and software, such as Fruity Loops for sampling, beat making, and recording multitrack songs, became widely available, cutting down studio expenses. With available cheap technology, new informal studios sprang up, especially around Accra, Tema, and Kumasi. A few beat makers, such as Hammer and J-Que, and producers, such as Zap Mallet, who had worked on Rockstone's early recordings, came to dominate the hiplife industry in its first few years, and their musical sensibility shaped its initial orientation. Mallet influenced some artists by employing live instruments and sampling, although for most artists electronic beatmaking dominated production.[23]

Artists including Buk Bak and Tinny focus on rapping over electronic highlife, kpanlogo, and Ga jamma beats engineered by beatmaker J-Que. Buk Bak and Tinny from the Accra area, which is the indigenous home of the Ga people, rap in a combination of Ga and Twi. Buk Bak's album *Gold Coast* features hits like "Helepu" and "Gonja Barracks" with melodic kpanlogo and highlife harmonies and storytelling. "Gonja Barracks" tells the story of a man who would rather go to the infamous Gonja Barracks prison than not be with his woman. "Helepu" has a haunting pidgin chorus, "Make you no leave me for this place ooo. I go die." It again invokes the melancholy of highlife laments of lost love. Indeed, while Buk Bak dress in hip hop styles, their music is extremely close to 1970s highlife with little explicit rap in it.

Lord Kenya, Obour, Kwao Kesse, and Okomfo Kwade are associated with this school of hiplife, reclaiming the traditional role of elegant language use, morality tales, and proverbial speech. These artists use the Twi language with an elegance and precision that draws respect from young and old Ghanaians and provides a new direction for hip hop. Obour, who got his degree at the University of Ghana, explained to me that he was raised in a chief's palace. Reflecting the comments of many rappers, he said that in order to write his lyrics, he sits and listens to elders and tries to draw on their traditional proverbial wisdom. For him, even after becoming one of the most popular artists in the country, his clearest sign of success came when, after hearing one of his songs on the radio, an elder in his home village came to him and asked for an explanation of one of the proverbs in his lyrics. Obour also attempts to bring other Ghanaian musical traditions into his music, including adowa, agbaja, and adaha. Abrewa Nana [Wise woman], who is the first popular female rap artist, calls her music raglife and is the main proponent of the use of ragga and Jamaican patois flows.

Most hiplife has a national sensibility and is centered in Accra and Kumasi. The music industry has been dominated by Akan dialects (Asanti Twi, Fante, and Akuapem Twi), although Ga and some Ewe and Hausa are used in some songs. Some nationally known artists who work in Accra come from other minority groups in the country. Many of these rappers who rhyme and sing in Akan are not Akan. Some use their primary languages in secondary roles while further highlighting the domination of the public sphere of Ghana by Akan languages. For example, as another musician explained to me, "Okomfo Kwade is one of the hiplifers who uses the most proverbial, indigenous Twi. His lyrics are full of proverbs. But he is not even an Akan. He knows their language better than many people from Kumasi." More regional musical schools have developed as well with distinctive sounds.

Tamale, the capital of the Northern Region, has developed a local rap scene in Dag-bane. Musically, artists such as Tuba Clan and Big Adams use electronic reggae beats with Islamic musical inflections and sometimes sample versions of the dondo, the talking drum from that region.

VIP has been one of the most successful and enigmatic groups to work with the highly danceable jamma beats of J-Que to create a sound that relies on electronic highlife. Their high energy, aggressive stage presence, and powerful rap vocal styles project the tough ethos of the hip hop gangster. Coming from Nima, one of the poorest areas of Accra, where there is a high concentration of Ghanaians from the northern territories of the country, the group have translated their street toughness and lack of educational or economic opportunities into the symbolic language of gangster hip hop. They also rely on the authenticity of geographic iden-tification with this neighborhood to show their street credentials. Lazzy, Promzy, and Prodigal are known for their hip hop styles, American-style football jerseys, baseball caps, and heavy chains. In contrast, their most popular tracks rely on local dance beats and harmonic choruses. Lyrically, they demonstrate one of the shifts from relatively respectful gender relations within highlife storytelling by often fo-cusing on invocations of male power and celebrating the moral ambivalence of women, sexuality, and economic accumulation in contemporary urban society, all performed with the brash confidence of the hip hop star rather than the melan-cholic lament of the highlife. In some lyrics they address the devastation of AIDS in Africa and advocate the use of condoms. In others they are more materially ori-ented. The chorus of their track "Adoley" on their *Ahomka Womu* album repeats:

> *Me ye Mobile phone*   I have a mobile phone
> *Oba ring ring Ope bling bling*   The woman calls she wants money/wealth [bling]

Tic Tac's 2000 hit "Philomena," featuring Obrafour and Nana Quame and pro-duced by Slim Buster, also focuses on materialism and gender relations, although it takes on the characteristic humor and moral critique of more traditional forms of proverbial speech. As Collins states in this volume, the song describes a woman named Philomena and critically pokes fun at her for having too much hair under her arms and between her legs and adopting foreign habits that are deemed dis-gusting and indicate moral degradation.

> *Philomena petinge, Ewi waha ewi waha ewi waha, oooh!*
> Philomena, there is some [hair] here and here and here, oooh!

Linguistically speaking, this song is significant for several reasons. The song's chorus became a common phrase repeated all over town in reference to many and sun-dry things relating to sexuality, impropriety, poor hygiene, and the transgression of boundaries. The absurdity and embarrassing nature of this public commentary meant that, as Levi-Strauss says, it became good to think with. It became a coded way for young men to critically address anxieties about female sexual agency, uncleanness and moral impropriety, and women's adoption of foreign habits. For more conservative elements in society, this song was indicative of the moral absurdity of hiplife. The coded nature of the chorus—indexically and humorously indicating rather than directly naming the hair or the part of the body being discussed—reflects the indirectness of metaphoric and proverbial social commentary. While the meaning of the song was widely understood in this vein, its humorous ambiguity muted the dangerous force of these public verbal communications. It also draws on a tradition of public verbal shaming, particularly of women. This song—in the mobility of its crucial lines, its indirection, examination of female sexual impropriety and foreign styles, and its focus on the grotesque—shows the public effect of many other hiplife songs in content and form. As Collins describes in this volume, songs such as this are interesting in that, from the perspective of religious and government critics, they are often seen as being proof of the profanity, moral degradation, and foreign pollution of hiplife and the younger generation. However, from the perspective of many youth, these songs are critiques of moral behavior, pointing out the problems they face and providing forums for thinking through these issues.[24]

This chapter describes the development of hiplife, not as a singular musical style but as an eclectic blend of rap, electronic beatmaking, highlife dance-rhythms, and local language lyrical flow. Whereas highlife in the 1950s and 1960s focused on the massive transitions from rural to urban life that reshaped African society at the time (Cole 1997; Collins 1994), hiplife often addresses transatlantic travel and the frustrations and successes of Ghanaians in a cosmopolitan world. It offers youth an attitude of individual bravado in facing the predicaments of daily life. The music retains a sonic resemblance to highlife, appealing to audiences as distinctively Ghanaian, while acting as a vehicle for new forms of individual agency through hip hop lyrical dexterity and production techniques.

Karin Barber (1987: 38–41) argues that popular arts in Africa are syncretic forms that draw on multiple indigenous and foreign sets of symbols in order to create new conventions of expression. These polysemous genres dialogically produce new types of popular audiences in the context of urbanization and social change. Hiplife is not simply a reflection of existing collective and individual sensibilities; it also transforms them. It links African diasporic connections as well as poetic structures of proverbial speech and notions of Ghanaian-based wisdom and morality. Hiplife combined and rearranged highlife, afrobeat, American R&B and soul, and African drum patterns within the broad stylistic parameters of hip hop. Hiplife in Ghana shows that popular culture in Africa must be understood in the context of the historical dialogue of global black cultural forms. This music becomes a site for voicing young Ghanaians' changing relationship to what constitutes African culture. In effect, it provides a set of terms through which youth symbolically position themselves within local and global hierarchies of power. By reshaping hip hop in local aesthetic terms, hiplife embodies the multiple, intertwined cultural legacies of Ghanaian youth.

NOTES

1. *Daily Graphic,* March 3, 1971.

2. Interview with Mary Yirenkyi.

3. See May Joseph (1998) on pan-African popular culture, cold war politics, and African American soul culture in Tanzania.

4. K. K. Kabobo was also credited with linking proto-rap with highlife, and in the 1970s the Afro-rock group Osibisa was heavily influenced by funk and poetic ruminations.

5. According to several people in the music business, people associated with Dzato Krom traveled frequently to the United States, bringing new music and styles for urban street culture and nightlife back to Ghana.

6. DJ Azigiza Jr.'s album *Woye bia* (1998) features heavy synthesizers and simple electronic beats. Tracks in Twi include "Onukpa Photo," "Woyebia," "Love Azigiza," and "Shamo," which features a gospel beat and harmony and a chorus in English.

7. While Hesmondhalgh and Melville (2001: 106) focus on the importance of Caribbean peoples in the development of hip hop in Great Britain, they do not give much space to Africans residing there, such as Ghanaian or Nigerian artists who perform primarily for West African audiences.

8. Around 1994 Mahoney P returned to Ghana after releasing a cassette in Amsterdam on which he rapped in Twi over hip hop style beats.

9. This album was based on an EP with five tracks released in 1996 on Ossei Mix Records: "Tsoo Boi;" "Nightlife in Accra" featuring Cy Lover, Chocolate, and Sammy B; "Agoo, My Sweetie, Sweetie" featuring Root I; and "My Turn to Burn" featuring Freddie Funkstone. Rab Bakari was the executive producer and made the beats, Michael Smith-Horthman produced the tracks, and Zap Mallet did the mixing.

10. "Eye Mo De Anaa?" appears on the *Rough Guide to African Rap* (2004) compilation CD.

11. See the play *The Blinkards* by Kobina Sekyi, an early twentieth-century Gold Coast intellectual, which humorously highlighted the complex paradoxes of West African use of English as a way to appear elite and refined. See also Cole's (2001) analysis of this play and of concert party theater.

12. Information and quotations in this paragraph are from my interview with Korkor Amartefio, artistic director of the National Theatre of Ghana.

13. The inclusion of hiplife in the National Festival of Arts and Culture (NAFAC) in 1999 held in Ho, the regional capital of the Volta Region, points to the further intersection of state and other notions of cultural nationhood. NAFAC 1999 had a large segment of programming devoted to hiplife artists who performed alongside a durbar of chiefs and queen mothers accompanied by executioners (Obrafour), linguists/spokespeople (Akyeame), and drummers. Regarding the 1994 PANAFEST, Rab Bakari (interview) recounts, "The festival focused on 'back to Africa,' and they assumed African Americans did not want to see this kind of thing [rap]. It did not fit with their ideas of what was African. Traditional drumming and dancing are cool, but there is a technological side to Ghana.

We have state-of-the-art musical and computer equipment. We want to show them that we have this equipment and can make this music here." By the 1997 PANAFEST, however, ideas of what was African culture had shifted. Rockstone performed in Cape Coast for the festival and was one of the most popular acts among Ghanaians, although Africans from the diaspora who had come to Ghana tended to favor what they saw as more traditional performance styles.

14. Many older Ghanaians react negatively to hip hop and African American images of violence, moral corruption, and ill-gotten gain that they see in hip hop videos shown on local television and on satellite-accessible Channel O, the music television station based in South Africa. Ghanaians are less openly critical of the plethora of images of white American corruption, violence, and sexuality displayed in U.S. films on television, ironically reflecting histories of racial inequality that conscious hip hop has attempted to critique. This points to the often contradictory ways in which Ghanaians engage with global discourses of African diasporic identity (Pierre 2002). Black images seem often to resonate in a profoundly personal way. The symbolic excesses of hip hop and negative stereotypes about African Americans, for some Ghanaians, produce a (simultaneous) desire for material gains and fear of loss of local history that American culture seems to invoke in Ghana— and throughout the world. However, sometimes African American and white European and American images, which continue to saturate television and movie programming, are all considered foreign in contrast to local Ghanaian or African cultural programming. Hip hop music and styles became central to anxieties about how American culture was eroding what were considered indigenous African traditions. This can be compared to black middle-class responses to hip hop in 1980s in the United States, as well as to Ghanaian elite reactions to highlife in Ghana before it became "traditional."

15. It is widely recognized that it was only after Fela Kuti went to the United States that he developed a radical racial politics, transforming a musical form that reflected African musical sensibilities (Veal 2000; Collins 1994). In a similar way, hiplifers were radicalized with regard to the African content of hip hop by traveling and returning; musicians who have not lived abroad often make music that sounds more "Western."

16. Obour [Stone] described hiplife to me as being divided into two stylistic camps, reflecting how many understand the genre: artists who focus on local dance rhythms, and those who focus on lyrical dexterity providing morality tales that are "national treasures to the Ghanaian public."

17. Sidney is Rockstone's cousin, and a protégé of Eddy Blay of NFL and later a member of Nananom. He had been a part of the early Combined House of Music sessions.

18. See John Jackson (2005) for naming in hip hop.

19. Translated by Kwesi Brown.

20. *Graphic Showbiz* April 2000.

21. For an analysis of the lyrics, see Shipley (forthcoming).

22. Lord Kenya's album *Sika Baa* [Money woman], produced by Zap Mallet, was another important hiplife landmark in 1999, noted for its lyrical Twi rap over electronic hip hop style beats.

23. Many of the artists, including Zap Mallet, who were more interested in older Ghanaian musical forms and marking specific ethnic or cultural musical traditions, started through the National Theatre programs reflecting state notions of cultural representation. Mallet worked with Terry Bonchaka, who released *The Bonchaka Project 2004: Zoozey* just

before his death in a car accident, and Kontihene, whose first album was entitled *Nyankonton*. Both of these artists have focused on bringing live instrumentation and more traditional drumming rhythms and melodies into their music.

24. In 2004, VIP was invited to perform their hit dance number "Ahomka Wo Mu" [There's pleasure in it] at the Kora Music Awards in South Africa as Rockstone received his award for Best African Music Video. Their performance amid the elite of popular African music was a huge hit. But even though Rockstone's music has been played on television in South Africa for several years and he has toured with Positive Black Soul of Senegal and other African rap artists, not many Ghanaians have been able to attract non-Ghanaian audiences.

PERSONAL INTERVIEWS

Akoto, organizer of rap/hiplife programming at the National Theatre, December 1999
Korkor Amartefio, Artistic Director, National Theatre of Ghana, September and December 1999
Panji Anoff, Accra, December 2004
Kelvin Asare Williams, November 2002
Rab Bakari, October and November 2004
Paa Kwesi Holdbrook-Smith, January 4, 2003
John Mahama, Minister of Communications, 2000
M.anifest, Bronx, NY, March 6, 2008
Nii Moffat, December 2003
Obour, February 15, 2006
Reggie Ossei Rockstone, June and December 2004
Reggie Rockstone and Rab Bakari, October 1999
Adjetey Sowah, Director of Dance Factory, National Theatre, December 1998
Mary Yirenkyi, November 1999
Identity withheld, December 2004

A Genre Coming of Age

Transformation, Difference, and Authenticity in the Rap Music and Hip Hop Culture of South Africa

LEE WATKINS

As dominant elements in rap music are often attributed to Africa (e.g., Keyes 1996), I see South African rap music and hip hop as a diasporic genre at home—in Africa—but also as a genre having many homes.[1] Within these many homes claims to authenticity are expressively mobilized and contested. African Americans claim the genre as an authentic expression of their roots and routes, and as such it reflects their place within the racialized economic and political system of the United States. Adherents in other parts of the globe explain that their marginal statuses are reasons enough for identification with and participation in hip hop. The cross border associations facilitated through hip hop and rap music speak to a global consciousness, which is articulated substantially within a local discourse. This form of global consciousness is not only both real and imagined but also increasingly virtual, thereby rendering the notion of diaspora through hip hop performance even less secure in its moorings. If anything, this genre reveals that the notion of roots in the modern world is negotiable, changing, and subject to the tenuous nature of contemporary life.

Aspects of hip hop have been visible on the streets of South Africa since the mid-1980s. At the time, hip hoppers were motivated by what they learned in American hip hop films. They fervently embraced the music and dance and often performed at discos. Although they had an interest in unfolding political events, this was not their primary focus. As the political situation became more serious, however, hip hoppers were increasingly called upon to dance for high school and other community protest rallies. In the end, while hip hoppers were not political activists, they nonetheless formed an association with the political campaign against apartheid. Students and other youths also gathered on the streets of townships where they battled as rappers and break dancers. The sheer pleasure of performing on streets and designated performance venues such as the Base and T-zers disco in Cape Town, along with their presence in mass protest gatherings, strengthened the appeal of hip hop. Its visual impact was further authenticated by the vibrating effects of spraypaintings on the walls of buildings in the townships of Cape Town. Many of these spraypaintings were personal tags, love messages, and, at the height of apartheid repression in the late 1980s, demands for a South Africa free of military rule and white racial hegemony.

I initiated my research on South African hip hop in the late 1990s. The issues I recognized at the time, such as racism, marginalization, and musical creativity embedded in local and global frames of reference, remain much the same, but in this chapter I augment my findings of that time with the immediacy of the contemporary hip hop scene in South Africa. Like its counterpart in the United States, the movement has in recent years experienced transformation. Changes may be discerned in the racial constituents of the movement, the dissipation of its regional dominance, the growing presence of women rappers, and the influence of this genre on the emergence of kwaito, a form of urban popular music. Whereas before I had gained my information from hip hoppers only, this chapter juxtaposes their voices, many of which are now limited to the past, with rap music fans and adherents in the present. The first part of this chapter is a description of the numerous hip hop scenes in much of South Africa, including Cape Town, Johannesburg, Durban, and the seriously neglected—in music studies—cities of the Eastern Cape, such as Grahamstown and Port Elizabeth. The second part examines the issues emerging in these various locations. The third part contextualizes hip hop in South Africa more critically within a global performance culture. The fourth part is an analysis of hip hop's future potential.

A Survey of Rap Music and Hip Hop Membership in South Africa

South African rap music has come of age in its longevity, social reality, and representation of diverse interests in many national, racial, and class groups and as a creative influence in the emergence of kwaito. Kwaito has similarities with the compositional aspect of rap music, as considerable layering and extensive hailing of other artists' music are present in both forms. The relationship between kwaito and rap is amplified in their determined reliance on technological excess. Kwaito was spawned in the black townships of South Africa before 1990 and dominated the popular music scene after the apartheid government surrendered its authority. This music is produced mostly for entertainment, but a few artists convey social messages in their music.

In a previous publication I described the hip hop movement in Cape Town, from its inception in the mid-1980s to the early 2000s (Watkins 2004). Participation in the movement by women and young people across racial barriers was peripheral at the time of my initial research there in the late 1990s. Many studies or articles and programs on rap music and hip hop in the South African media are inevitably skewed toward Cape Town, since this is where rap first emerged and where the pioneering crews Prophets of Da City (POC) and Black Noise had shaped a considerable presence for themselves.

It is therefore exciting to see that hip hop has made a noticeable inroad in major cities such as Johannesburg and Durban and in the smaller towns of the Eastern Cape province. For the hip hop enthusiast, *Where You're At: Notes from the Frontline of a Hip Hop Planet,* Patrick Neate's 2003 book on hip hop in various parts of the world, including chapters on Johannesburg and Cape Town, is a rich contribution to an understanding of hip hop in South Africa. Although I discuss rap music in these locations, the intention of this chapter is to provide an impression of the general state of hip hop in South Africa and, through hip hop, an understanding of how South Africa is faring.

A misconception I harbored until recently was that when hip hop crews disappear from the scene, they disintegrate. This may be the case for many, but I have learned that the name of an inactive crew, POC, is still in circulation. The two members I met with many years ago remain active in hip hop. Shaheen has recently completed a master's degree in social anthropology in Canada and was involved in community work on the Cape Flats, a part of Cape Town that mushroomed as it became a destination for the many nonwhite people evicted from their homes in choice suburbs and the city center because of the Group Areas Act. This act was one of the pillars of apartheid. The majority of the nonwhite underclass of Cape Town resides here. Ready D was a mentor for Brasse Vannie Kaap (Brothers of the Cape, BVK) and is a DJ with international prestige. Shaheen, along with many other rappers of his time, are pursuing individual careers because age and family responsibilities mean they can no longer volunteer all their time for community development. When the opportunity arises, these members of POC regroup and recruit new members. The understanding is that the name POC and its core members are a permanent fixture while the rest of the crew is constituted by the here and now. New recruits refine their hip hop skills and then move on to pursue other interests. One such recruit is former POC rapper Ishmael Morobe. He is a leading kwaito artist and regards this music as liberating. His first album, released in 2002, called *Roba Letheka* [Break a Hip, a Sotho term for dancing], did remarkably well in sales and draws on a variety of styles such as house, gospel, and R&B. POC has performed with the Fugees, Public Enemy, and Afrika Bambaataa.

POC was a member of a community feeding scheme, called the Rhyme Unit Feed the Needy Organisation (RUFTNO). Shaheen was involved in radio education. In 2000 he coordinated an HIV/AIDS awareness program called "HIV HOP" on Bush Radio. Children were educated on issues relating to governance, labor, crime, colonialism, and apartheid. Another feature on Bush Radio was a Friday night hip hop show called Headwarmers. It featured a call-in open mic session. In 2007, Ready D and hip hoppers from other parts of the country completed a national tour sponsored by Red Bull. This brand sponsors an international Red Bull Streetstyle break dancing competition and hip hop programs. The Red Bull slogan is "Be original, be yourself." The purpose of the tour was to introduce the movement to young people and to create an awareness of drug abuse, gangsterism, and the immense problem with the AIDS epidemic.

Emile and his crew Black Noise are going strong and celebrated their twentieth anniversary in 2010. Emile has abandoned his surname, Jansen, because of its association with slavery and prefers being called Emile YX. The new appellation adorns the numerous Black Noise websites and Emile's publications. Black Noise has little interest in withdrawing from their commitment to social development. Since their inception they have been involved in community activism, through the resources of local government, private sponsorship by a company such as Adidas, and their own pockets. They have gone to great lengths to share the message of hip hop. The message they advocate is one of having pride in oneself; to understand who one is, and to uphold the positive messages in hip hop. They are tirelessly involved in sharing the skills of hip hop, such as the dancing and turntabling, particularly in communities where the levels of poverty and social rot are exceedingly high. Emile has started a hip hop school, based on the principles of the "Heal the 'hood" campaign (Haupt 1999). In 2003 he collaborated with Jamayka Poston from Angola on an album called *Conquering Lions*. Emile has written, published, and distributed several articles and self-help booklets on hip hop, and in March 2008 he served on a panel on hip hop in South Africa at Harvard University. Black Noise has several dedicated websites, including www.emileyx.co.za and www.music .org.za.

With the assistance of various government and corporate sponsorships, Black Noise has continued recruiting and mobilizing youths, conducting "Heal the 'hood" campaigns on a regular basis. Sponsors believe that the prosperity of the country depends on a new generation who may learn through hip hop to resist a range of social ills. Black Noise members regard themselves as performers who use hip hop as a tool for education and empowerment. Over the years, Black Noise has developed and maintained strong links with community organizations. This relationship is developed while sharing the messages and performance aspects of hip hop throughout South Africa. Emile has been organizing African Hip Hop Indabas, a platform for rappers, DJs, b-boys (break dancers), and spraypainting artists, since 1999, when it was known as the African Battle Cry. The Indaba emerged from a holiday program for schoolchildren from the Cape Flats, and it has discussion forums where the prospects and challenges of the movement are debated. The program includes the Battle of the Year National Break Dancing Championships. Each year the winners represent South Africa overseas in world championships.[2]

The crew named Brasse Vannie Kaap, consisting of Hamma, DJE 20 Envor (named after a Toyota model), and a group of break dancers, has steadily developed its profile and presence. One of its first and more charismatic members, Phat (Ashley Titus), died at 35 after a long illness on 28 November 2007. With the mentorship of Ready D, the appearance of BVK on the music scene in 1996 indicated a dramatic entry into what was then acknowledged as a post-apartheid music scene. They received accolades for their portrayal of the darker side and the positive aspects of life on the Cape Flats. The language they sing in is a spectacular and street-wise vernacular of the Afrikaans language. This version of Afrikaans is commonly spoken among the underclass in Cape Town and is a pastiche of prison language, street language, slang, and code-switching that only insiders may understand. The language shares these characteristics with ebonics in the United States. BVK is widely acclaimed in the mainstream media, at South African Afrikaans music festivals, and in Benelux countries where Afrikaans is understood with not too much difficulty.

The feature of hip hop appealing to marginalized people in various parts of the world has a particular impact on women in South Africa, who continue to inhabit the lower rungs of social empowerment in spite of the many rights they are supposedly guaranteed by the constitution. Marginality is experienced both in the larger society and in hip hop. In my first round of fieldwork I was informed by male hip hoppers that women were reluctant to participate in the movement because hip hop was associated with rebellion and street life. The men were adamant, though, that women were free to participate. In this context, a new development in Cape Town is the eminence of Godessa, an all-women crew that represents a challenge to the male-dominated hip hop movement. Godessa was formed by three women in 2000, and their music is produced by Grenville Williams, former member of the rock groups Nine and Firing Squad. The music video for their single "Social Ills" reached number four on the charts of Castle Loud, a television program sponsored by a brewery. Members of Godessa have new names. Vocalist and co-producer Eloise Jones from Mitchell's Plain, a sprawling township on the far end of the Cape Flats, has become EJ von Lyrik. She has performed with top crews such as the Neophytes, Darker Shadez of Funk, Brasse Vannie Kaap, and POC. Vocalist Bernadette Amansure from Lavender Hill, another township closer to the southern suburbs of Cape Town, calls herself Burni. She has worked with spraypainting artist Marco Polo and a producer called Silver Fox. The third member is Shameema Williams, who calls herself Shame. She started rapping in the mid-1990s.

Von Lyrik says their rap music is topical and recalls the past because people are inclined not to remember. She considers hip hop a two-faced beast. It has a social conscience but often communicates in the language of the commercial mainstream. Godessa has performed overseas in places like Amsterdam in November

2002, at a concert organized by the Netherlands Institute for Southern Africa, and Bush Radio, a community radio station in Cape Town. They performed at the USA Black August Festival with Dead Prez. The Black August event organizer, a member of the New Jersey Performing Arts Council, arranged for the crew to perform in New Jersey at the Planet Hip Hop Festival. In 2004, they performed at the Cuban Wemilere African Roots Festival at the invitation of the Department of Arts and Culture in South Africa.

In Johannesburg there are numerous crews, such as Skeem and Muthaload, who have come and gone. Skwatta Kamp, though, formed in 1994, has an ongoing presence. They signed up with Gallo Records in 2003 and have a large following, but their music and public image are derided by other hip hop heads (hip hoppers who adhere to the fundamental principles of hip hop) who feel that Skwatta Kamp has compromised the authenticity of the movement. Skwatta Kamp spokesperson Flabba says it does not matter what the hip hop heads believe because they have not moved with the times (Neophytou 2005). The Rhyme and Reason crew in Johannesburg are members of a larger crew, Cashless Society, who believe they represent the poorest of the poor and want to promote hope and progress. The crew was formed in 1998 and has seven members. They describe their music as streethop rather than hip hop. Their single "Blaze Tha Breaks" was released on vinyl by Fondle 'Em Records in 2000. They formed Unreleased Records in 1999 as a way to control the production and marketing of their music. Draztik of Cashless Society has been collaborating with Nations Uprising, a Johannesburg crew with international experience, innovative music, and increasing popularity.

In the early 2000s, a club called Rippingtons in the city of Johannesburg was the only performance venue for hip hoppers. On Saturday afternoons there were open mic sessions and DJs displayed their skill on the turntables. Elsewhere in Johannesburg, the first Sunday of every month in 2006 saw a growing number of hip hoppers assemble on the corner of Mji and Motlana Streets in Orlando West, a section of Soweto. This gathering where rappers and DJs shared their skills was called the Splash Jam.

Recently, the hip hop scene moved to the Slaghuis (Butchery) in Diepkloof, Johannesburg, providing a platform for crews such as Pitch Black Afro and Pro-Kid. In 2008, the hip hop scene in Soweto seemed to have broadened considerably. Rap music performances or emcee competitions were held on consecutive Sundays in the suburbs of Pimville, Meadowlands, Dube, and Dobsonville. In Pimville the performances took place on the second Sunday of the month in a large tent in an open field. The performances in Meadowlands were held on the third Sunday in a house operating as a *shebeen* [tavern]. Shebeens have long been the place where numerous music styles presented themselves in urban black culture. The performances in Dube take place in a derelict house on the first Sunday of the month. The key performers at the Dube event are Federation. They have released two mix tapes on the internet and claim that there have already been 300,000 downloads of their songs (as of early 2008). The performances at Dobsonville take place on the second Sunday of the month, at a site next to a graveyard. The rappers usually rap on everything from social issues to their love lives. There are turntablists and graffiti artists at events, but the focus is on emceeing. Msimango (2008) observes that the only problem with the performances in Soweto is that the emceeing usually transpires against a background of alcohol abuse and the excessive smoking of *dagga* (cannabis).[3]

The practice of Cape Town rappers drawing on the pool of musical sounds and various linguistic turns unique to that city is emulated by Zulu Boy, a prominent hip hopper from Durban who relocated to Johannesburg and whose language and musical influences affirm his roots and routes. His album, *Masihambisane* [Let's Go Together], released in September 2006 by the independent label Native Rhythms, is the first isiZulu language rap album released in South Africa. The music is influenced by the traditional music of Zulu performers who meet at the Jabulani Hostel in Soweto on a weekly basis. Some songs incorporate elements of the South African genres of maskanda, mbaqanga, and traditional choral music. These styles of popular music have their origin among migrants in Johannesburg, who migrated from Kwazulu Natal, where isiZulu is the dominant African language. In "Hail to the Kings," a sample of the praise singer of King Goodwill Zwelithini (present monarch of Zululand) describes the Zulu people's legacy of warrior kings. It is hoped the album may have a global impact because it is produced and marketed by Native Rhythms, established in 2005 by former Gallo deputy CEO Sipho Sithole, and distributed by EMI. Zulu Boy's streetwise attitude acquired in the city and his traditional cultural values, layered over hip hop beats, are believed to reflect an authentic Durban township experience. The music is influenced moreover by *bruin* [brown people's] funk, a form of township rap practiced by "colored" hip hoppers in Durban (Sosibo 2006).

In the port city of Durban there are Blazing Fridays, a forum where emcees and break dancers compete. One of the major Durban groups is a seven-member crew called Big Idea, formed in 2004. Members are MCs Q (Quincy Fynn) and Jet (Lee Wynn), vocalist/sampler King Babar (Nathan Redpath), drummer Gareth "2Gs" Gale, keyboardist Burton "Buttons" Naidoo, DJ LV (Leighsley van Wyk), and founding member Duane Nichols. Several of the members are from the south of Durban, which is heavily polluted by the effluent coming from oil refineries and oil-based industries; hence the name of their record company, Ruffinary Records. Their debut album, *Hot Box*, was released in 2006. Babar says rap music in Durban is more authentic and South African than the music from Johannesburg and Cape Town and its unique quality may be attributable to jazz and trip-hop. Their humorous and incisive lyrics incorporate the vernacular language widely used in the predominantly "colored" township of Wentworth. Their songs have a local orientation in language and in social awareness. While many of the songs are political, they are equally keen on creating music for dancing, believing that people may resent songs where the political messages are too strong. Journalist Niren Tolsi (*Mail and Guardian,* August 4, 2006) observes that the music is disappointing because it lacks effect and innovation.

Further down the east coast in Grahamstown, a small university town in the province of the Eastern Cape, Xolile Madinda (X) of DEFBOYZ estimates that there are around 50 crews. When thinking of marginality, the situation there is perhaps more striking because this part of South Africa is identified as one of the poorest and least developed provinces. Young people who are recruited by Xolile to join the Fingo Revolutionary Movement (FRM) are trained as rappers and are also educated in the creative and ideological aspects of hip hop. X Nasty, a crew that raps in isiXhosa, the dominant African language in the Eastern Cape, has a considerable following. Another crew called Bantustan released an album called *Banturap.* The word *Bantu* is a generic term used by colonial settlers to describe all sub-Saharan black Africans. The word *Bantustan* was adopted by the resistance in apartheid South Africa to refer to the ethnic or tribal homelands created by the social engineers of the apartheid regime. This name is evocative and strengthened by the social messages in their music. Their rapping is accompanied by smooth flowing R&B rather than the phat beats and sampling unique to rap music.

The hip hop scene in Port Elizabeth emerged after exposure to break dancing films such as *Breakin'* (1984) and *Breakin' 2: Electric Boogaloo* (1984). Dumza, Tobela, and Sebenzile were among the first hip hoppers, and they propagated hip hop in the townships of Motherwell and Zwide. They have used the Nkqubela community radio station as a vital tool for disseminating local rap music as well as educating young people and their parents about the positive attributes of the movement. The primary crews in Port Elizabeth are Shades of Blackness and Abantu. Their music is influenced mainly by South African jazz, anti-apartheid anthems, and religious music. Hip hop in Port Elizabeth also has a strong relationship with Rastafarianism. Port Elizabeth has an all-women crew called Alpha Phonetics (AP), whose marginality is exacerbated by not having access to the music industry the way Godessa has. They rap about black women in society and the challenges they have to endure, such as rape and drug and alcohol abuse. The aim of such lyrics is to have women recognize their power to change their behavior and thereby have a positive influence on their communities. AP performs in public spaces and parking lots in Port Elizabeth. They have a DJ and a sound system with turntables and speakers, and they rap in isiXhosa. As far as the music is concerned, the aim is to use U.S. hip hop bass lines and to combine them with raw black emceeing, like the French rappers do, observes Thulisa. This entails singing in isiXhosa and in the vernacular, identified as slang isiXhosa. The problem in the Eastern Cape is that rappers in small towns may be weak because they do not have much contact with the rest of the world. It is believed more competition will improve the standards of emceeing.

According to Shamiel X, the hip hop scene in South Africa is exploding. There has accordingly been a dramatic growth in turntabling, and there are now numerous schools in the country. Shamiel X says turntablists are required to train for at least three years and must practice a few hours a day because the technology is advanced and the scene is competitive. Break dancing has also become more competitive, as dancers need to blend innovation with styles from the old school. The difference with the past is that many new emcees do not have the political consciousness of the 1990s because the dynamics in South African politics have changed. The dominant message communicated in contemporary hip hop is influenced substantially by gangsta rap. With its emphasis on an excess of pleasure and women's sensuality, elements of gangsta rap are equally on display in kwaito music performances such as Arthur Mafokate's.

Negotiated and Contested Authenticities

Hip hop is a cultural movement expressively performed in spraypainting, break dancing, rapping or emceeing, and turntabling, and the human ethic of reciprocity is equally important. Most of the crews emphasize the reciprocal sharing of goods. These goods take the form of education and the learning of hip hop skills. Youth empowerment and authenticity, or "keeping it real," are emphasized.

Hip hoppers share their skills and the ideology of hip hop with underprivileged children, who acquire skills in performance and are given an opportunity to improve their social environment. Establishing a sense of communalism through hip hop is regarded as a means to combat the intense alienation most young people experience in the townships of South Africa. This sense of communalism depends on developing critical awareness and black consciousness among adherents and new recruits. The ideology of black consciousness in South Africa is a response to white supremacy and is not the opposite of white racism. It is instead aimed at restoring black pride after centuries of oppression and humiliation. Black consciousness as advanced by Steve Biko, who was assassinated by the apartheid government in 1977, is eagerly embraced by hip hoppers, and the ones in Grahamstown have formed an alliance with the Fingo Revolutionary Movement.

Hip hoppers do not subsume their individual status under the homogenizing impetus of a "rainbow nation," the racially inspired metaphor meant to show the world that South Africans can live in harmony despite their perceived cultural and racial differences. Instead, by authenticating their numerous identifications through language choice and an emphasis on their ethnic background, hip hoppers reveal the stirrings of a neo-apartheid consciousness in which rainbow nation politics are no longer valued with the same fervor as with its inception. The discursive regime of the new South Africa allows for the articulation of difference and the mobilization of the old with the new. Old forms of mainly ethnic identifications thrive while the state is at pains to promote visions of an advanced and nonracialized democracy. This reality in the new South Africa is problematized by the disillusion experienced in many communities after the euphoria of the first democratic elections in 1994. Durban-based emcee Iain says,

> Hip hop's story is almost like the democracy story. As democracy hit in '94, the excitement of it and everything was just so great and things started pushing that rainbow dream. We were living it and people were holding hands and were singing songs at the rugby. They were very excited, and then it started to get more real and started to whittle itself down. The politics started to become real, and we're getting to the stage where we're at right now where it's very, very serious. Now we've had to admit to ourselves that we were living the dream for a couple of years, and now the real work has to start to make that dream more sustainable.[4]

The fear of losing what is deemed authentic has dogged the hip hop scene since the mid-1990s. Hip hop has grown, but the challenge of resisting co-optation by the industry is difficult. Suddenly, after many years of the development of hip hop in cities other than Cape Town, Iain observes there is a reality check as many newcomers like Skwatta Kamp are regarded as not representing the social interests of the earlier movement.

Language use is one of the means by which rappers lay claim to their authenticity. The varied languages and dialects of South Africa can ambivalently reinforce the illusion of a rainbow nation, while hip hop challenges rainbow nation politics. The choice of language in rap music seems to have become a key indicator of differing authenticities. Language imbues the music with a sense of multiplicity and of ownership in diverse contexts; hip hoppers use language to reflect their roots, their social standing, and their multiplicity. They are assisted by the tone of their language and their irreverence for conventional syntax. Language, moreover, has an influence on perceptions of good or bad rap. According to Iain, good rap represents the individual's personal expressions, and it must be in the home language.

Performing in the vernacular is a challenge, for in relation to the hip hop movement in South Africa as a whole, hip hoppers in the Eastern Cape feel marginalized because they sing in isiXhosa, a language not widely spoken in South Africa. Much of their music is in the vernacular, and as a result their market is limited. They are not prepared to rap in English, as they believe there is too much English rap in South Africa. Their commitment to the language is reflected in their use of isiXhosa names rather than the Western ones that children often have to adopt when they enter school. In many Westernizing or aspiring South African societies, an indigenous name is considered inferior to a Western name. Nonetheless, many hip hoppers I spoke to argue that people like music in their own languages and that it is only a matter of time before they will be able to expand their market.

In the public domain of South African society, emphasis is placed on developing the dignity and rights of women. On a social level, many women are more confident than before, but in hip hop, breaking into a male-dominated movement is a challenge of a different kind. Performance or emceeing is the area in which the battlefield between male and female rappers is negotiated and produced. Women articulate their authenticity as women and specifically as African women. In *Counting Headz*, a film about women in South African hip hop (Magubane and Offer 2006), Godessa makes it clear they have no desire to be marketed as sex objects; neither do they consider themselves on par with the men in the movement, as the two genders have different experiences in society. Godessa member Shame says,

> There's a general perception that women should be organizers and that they can't be emcees. I stopped battling because it's just become public abuse. In America, emcee battling is less sexist and racist, but we are making history as the first female rappers in the country to release a single.

Thulisa, a journalism student and ardent emcee in Grahamstown, says women rappers find the hip hop scene intimidating, but the opportunity to perform is important, as their participation represents a challenge to male rappers. The style of rap she and her friends enjoy is called rap-poetry. She says they dig deep into the soul of the woman. She raps not about herself but rather about the situation most women find themselves in. In performance, women have yet to build their confidence because on occasion they cower if the male rappers are crude and overpower them with the flow of their rap. The best opportunity for testing their rapping ability is in the cipher, formed by rappers standing in a circle. The rapping moves from one rapper to another, or there is an exchange between two rappers standing in the middle of the circle and "killing each other off."

The challenge in keeping rap music real or authentic is motivated by the perceived dilution of the original meanings in rap music and the diversifying logics of the movement. This is more likely one of the contradictions that may be associated with the transformation in South African hip hop, that is, producing sounds that offer a radical critique of everyday life, and on the other hand, using hip hop performance styles to elicit sensuous pleasure and profit. Adding to the latter observation, Iain says the corporate world of South Africa has realized the popularity of the movement. Corporate leaders are enthusiastic about using rap music elements in selling their products. The music and the movement have become expendable. Iain says,

> My big problem is that now you have people who aren't in hip hop. You'll see a Yogi Sip advert[isement], and there's some guy rapping, and the way this guy got there is through an audition process. Crowds come in, and the corporation says, "We'll filter you down. You seem to have a good flow, so you go ahead and you're the Yogi Sip

guy." But this guy has nothing at all to do with hip hop. The same thing happens with our public broadcaster. The South African Broadcast Corporation has head-hunters, people who'll go out there and find the most hip hop looking person on the street.

The internationalization of rap music is one of the more important developments in contemporary popular culture. Its transformation in the United States from entertainment and an expression of marginality to a culture of bling is the presage to local forms such as kwaito which gaze wantonly to models in the United States. In South African rap and hip hop, the diasporic glance was at first motivated by black consciousness and its associated goals, such as the struggle against white racism. These days, hip hoppers in Cape Town especially have adapted their political consciousness to match the ideological unconsciousness of the state. While hip hoppers of the old school continue to influence novices with the positive aspects of hip hop, such as self-respect and reciprocity, their political ideals are at odds with the aspirations of the new elite. These old-schoolers refuse to sell out, as POC rapper Shaheen informed me years ago, unlike younger rappers whose primary interest is emulating the material excesses of their American counterparts and who show a cursory regard for politics. Many new rappers instead cross over into styles of music that offer much greater financial gain. One such style is kwaito, which provides access to a national market and a style of music heavily subsidized by the music industry.

Rap musicians of the old school and new recruits who envision a truly free South Africa remain on the fringe of the popular music scene. These hip hoppers are identified as members of an "underground," resisting commercialization and following their muse. The underground movement is flourishing in the Eastern Cape. The underground is a critical space for reflection and mobilization and is a space that the United Nations has recognized as a resource. In October 2005, the UN-HABITAT sponsored the first African Hip Hop Summit in Johannesburg, a follow-up on the Global Hip Hop Summit in Barcelona in 2004 and in preparation for the global summit in Vancouver in 2006. The UN called it the "Messengers of Truth" project, and the theme for this summit was "Youths under siege." The summit was a forum for collaboration between hip hop artists, youth organizations, NGOs, governments, the media, and the private sector. Its purpose was to raise awareness of the UN's Millennium Development Goals among the 300 million youths living in slums.

Underground hip hoppers are in conflict with hip hoppers who they believe have sold out, and they contest the legitimacy of a music industry that has always been associated with repression and exclusion. The problem with the music industry is historical, and there are few signs of transformation. Shaheen's observation of the music industry is an indictment on progress in other sectors of society: "The South African music industry is not established yet. All it has is the hype. It's full of people who know nothing about music, and most of them are holding top positions" (Neophytou 2005).

This is a perspective of the music industry at large, but owing to the increasing accessibility of production hardware and software, hip hoppers are now able to create their own music and to distribute it as they desire. Many new independent recording studios have emerged. Hip hoppers from Mitchell's Plain, such as the Drie Manskappe [Three Musketeers], to Soweto are transforming their bedrooms into studios. Bedroom studios have become a flourishing industry on the fringe. These hip hoppers produce a few hundred compact discs, sell them, and produce more when required. They do not have to depend on large production and distribution companies. They are on the periphery of the global and virtual flow of mass-produced music products and not subject to the influential power of companies in the global music industry.

Shamiel X observes that the music industry in South Africa has to orientate itself according to the requirements of global competitors and partners. These companies are not prepared to support politically motivated and unknown groups. The democratizing potential of technology in hip hop notwithstanding, the matter of the music industry continues to represent an ongoing problem for performers in South Africa. Iain says the situation has compounded the schism in the movement. In Johannesburg, record companies use scouts to find and recruit hip hoppers to invest in. Once they have been recruited, hip hoppers are informed that they will make their fortunes by following company orders. Examples are crews such as Pro-Kid and Skwatta Kamp. The latter was accused of following the style of gangsta rappers in the United States, with their lyrics consisting of overt sexual messages aimed at women and, paradoxically, also a concern for children's rights. Corporate money dictates how the scene evolves. Hip hoppers are also played off against one another, with record companies or other corporations negotiating for the lowest fees. According to Iain, the recording industry is saving money by fomenting division among hip hoppers because there is no corporate hip hop industry as such.

Another aspect of rap music in South Africa is its dalliance with censorship. The apartheid government exercised its authority by banning people who opposed it and by banning music and literature that they perceived as seditious or morally corrupt. Any gesture or utterance deemed a threat to the state was dealt with swiftly and often violently. POC was not a stranger to these efforts.

Xolile warns that "we will get to a place where black people are silenced by their own." The music of POC has often been banned from the airwaves and television, even in the new South Africa. POC won numerous overseas awards, including the Best Music Video/Clip ("Understand Where I'm Coming From," from *Age of Truth,* 1993) in the non-Francophone Africa category at the prestigious annual Cannes Midem festival. In 1994 a local television program, *Ezimtoti,* declared it the Best Video of the Year. The management of the sole television broadcaster, the South African Broadcast Corporation, found the song offensive and in conflict with the message of the Reconstruction and Development Programme, a government initiative aimed at developing infrastructure in underdeveloped areas and providing basic services to all. Fifteen of the twenty-one tracks on the album were banned from airplay, but "Understand Where I'm Coming From" was allowed (*Mail and Guardian* 1997). For those hip hoppers dedicated to social activism, this is one of the spaces where the magic in rap music resides. Music with an international following has the potential of threatening a nationalizing discourse. The sovereignty of the nation is subject to the mobilizing ethic of an international beat. Such is the power vested in rap. Deon (aka Ready D) attributed the poor sales of POC's records to the frequent banning of their music.

Rap in South Africa is no longer only a vehicle of expression but also a means of earning a significant income. This dual legacy of the genre has given rise to highly contested claims to its authenticity.

Globalizing Simulation

In an initial stage of rap music scholarship, one of the criticisms leveled was the flouting of copyright regulations and the wholesale copying and manipulation of preexisting music (Schumaker 1995). American jazz artist Wynton Marsalis, among others, condemned the lack of perceived originality and authenticity in rap music. But this argument was contested by numerous scholars (e.g., Krims 2000; Rose 1994) and rappers, who claimed that the incorporation of these sounds into their work was a form of homage and that older musicians should be grateful that their music is not allowed to perish. American rappers more often used and personalized samples of music from older black musicians who predated hip hop. This practice was adopted by rappers in South Africa as well. They drew on local and global repertoires, including sounds generally attributed to African American music styles. South African hip hoppers identified with the struggle of African Americans, claiming that hip hop is African and that these elements entitled them to the use of their sounds. The issue at stake here is the simulation and use of samples of music that may be deemed exclusive to a particular racial group. But while musical sound may have offered the possibility of solidarity across the Atlantic Ocean, the reality reveals that distance plays games with the musically inscribed racial imaginary. The simulation of musical sounds in terms of an imagined African origin increasingly comes across as a global language of differences rather than racial solidarity.

More to the point, musical sound may have the potential for building solidarity where racial divisions are evident, but individual practices emanating from the United States undermine the possibility of such solidarity. Neate (2003), for instance, describes the lack of faith South African hip hoppers have with their counterparts in the United States. Many hip hoppers I met in the 1990s similarly expressed their apprehension because even after having tailored some kind of agreement, the leading U.S. rappers failed to visit. In contrast, hip hoppers in South Africa have long enjoyed relations with European hip hoppers of all colors. Nonetheless, rappers in Cape Town draw on a sound pool, shaped in part by their American counterparts, to creatively develop their authenticity on their own terms. This practice is strategic, as it suggests solidarity through performance practice, and it is dissimilar in the sense that hip hop allows for the articulation of difference in a movement where the simulation of artistic forms is a standard practice. The question I have is what makes these conditions in hip hop diasporic and what makes them global?

The term *diaspora* is invoked when referring to the space that nonindigenous groups inhabit on arrival in foreign places or pass through on their way somewhere else, while *globalization* refers to these places as well as the cultural and economic influences of which everyone becomes the agents and subjects in the course of everyday life. Rap music in South Africa offers an understanding of globalization and the diaspora in which the two concepts are intimately connected. On the surface, at least, hip hop in South Africa signifies the black diaspora, but its various authenticities reveal that it has more or less established itself as a global or glocal (Neate 2003: 112) genre in which solidarity in color is no longer critical.

The globalization of hip hop has created conditions in which hip hop communities increasingly translate the experience of diverse musical influences and social realities into their music and performances. Thus, by familiarizing us with greater diversity in musical expressions and through simulated performance practices in a world of difference, rap music inverts the aesthetic of formalism in music creativity. Rap music is composed as such with a sense of double consciousness, where the utterances of musicians reflect roots and routes. But these days, roots must be understood as increasingly shifting, transient, and postracial. The freedom with which rappers appropriate grooves and samples from unseen others reflects a continuum with other musicians, such as those in the world music bin, who reinvent these musical elements and, in a manner true to much of our world, snap them up for sensuous pleasure. In this way, simulation in much of the globalized world is a dialogue with artifice, spectacle, and playful sensuousness.

In studying the global appropriation of rap and hip hop, the place Africa has weakened as a point of reference, since relationships among hip hop communities around the globe are increasingly keyed by the discourses of leisure, poverty, and marginalization. This relationship is further enhanced by the dissolution of geographical space and the development of virtual space. Looking at the way in which the local is contested and continually shifting, then, the term *diaspora* is a signifier not entirely of transnationality and racial imaginaries but also of political struggles to define the local, as a distinctive community, in historical contexts of displacement (Clifford 1994: 308). These conditions render the fixation with race and rap music shortsighted, as racial solidarity has been subsumed by the appeal of the sound and the sheer pleasure of participating in the numerous performance aspects of the movement.

Complicating an understanding of the mimetic and the diaspora in the South African context is Shaheen's observation that people in Cape Town took to the movement because the Cape and parts of the United States experienced the same kinds of colonization. Emile observes that Shaheen is referring to a common experience represented in a sense of displacement which "so-called colored people feel and the way that African Americans do not feel connected to the United States nor to Africa." Another point raised by Shaheen is that rap music is emblematic of blackness in relation to white oppression. Similarly, Deon's response to the popularity of rap music in other countries emphasizes the relationship between racial color and music:

> The whole movement basically enlightens people. There's a lot of people in western countries and especially white people that are coming to terms with themselves because we're living in the age of truth where a lot of things are being exposed. White kids see how their parents and forefathers have fucked them over mentally. White people should come to terms with the evil that they and their foreparents have done. If they truly want to come to some sort of racial harmony, it's much more than a simple verbal apology.

This relationship is not that easy to understand. The lack of material resources, and in this case a putative attribute such as being denied musical instruments in the public schools of the South Bronx, which aided in the development of rap music, articulates the interrelationship between music, racial color, sound, and an economy that is inaccessible to most. Colonization may have been the precursor to the development of this relationship, but the implication of a mutually obtained social experience being equal to shared musical experience does not carry much weight.

In the sonic world, the dependence on a limited pool of sound renders boundaries porous and racially expedient. Sounds from every corner of the world are accessible to the point that it poses a challenge to authenticity and keeping things real. Iain says one may recognize an authentic South African sound like maskanda as part of a production and think, "Well, that must be real." But, he continues, these days it could be any artist or a producer in New York who is using maskanda. Language is perhaps the only indication as to how real a song is, as once the language is removed, the beats and the music will erase any notion of authenticity or origin. One would not be able to tell where the music is from. As far as musical propriety is concerned, Iain, a young white South African, argues for the notion of place, rather than race, as a crucial determinant for the engagement between musical appropriation and authenticity.

The Beat Lives On and On

There is money to be made in this. People in Johannesburg pay a
fortune to have their kids taught. (mother of a break dancer in Port
Elizabeth, in Gillham 2008)

Hip hop has developed into a form of politics ideally suited to the neo-apartheid
era. Hip hoppers who are subscribing to the ethics of the early 1990s are in opposition to those who have embraced the possibility of instant wealth. The illusion
of wealth, especially in a city like Johannesburg, is juxtaposed with grinding poverty in the city's informal settlements and in the rural areas of South Africa. Performance enables hip hoppers to negotiate a sense of authenticity on their own terms
by articulating their awareness of their social conditions and the responses of
those in authority to social challenges. They resist, question, and construct meanings in a landscape that requires vigilance and innovation. Lipsitz's astute observation in 1994 continues to have purchase in the hip hop scene of South Africa.
He wrote that hip hop "brings a community into being through performance, and
it maps out real and imagined relations between people that speak to the realities
of displacement, disillusion, and despair created by the austerity economy of post-
industrial capitalism" (Lipsitz 1994: 36).

There is great disparity in the social and economic sectors in South Africa.
Based on appearances, the presence of hip hop suggests a potentially new kind of
internationalism that is the reinvention as well as the intensification of underclass
solidarity. The 'hood is global, but its romance is marred by the inevitable movement toward capital. Hip hop in South Africa displays an evolving, not a static,
identity. Hip hop in much of South Africa portrays and promotes visions of an
ideal world, and as a cultural movement rooted in sensuous pleasure and ideological praxis, it symbolizes change, transformation, and growth.

Culture is open-ended, mobile, relational, and virtual. In this regard hip hop
shares with culture the ability to reconfigure itself to the degree that many features of the movement may not have been anticipated by the original hip hop artists. South African hip hoppers of the old school resisted control by the recording
industry, whom they regarded as an enemy rather than as a business partner. They
mocked the apartheid state and are at a loss to understand the present government's failure to provide adequate services for the black underclass. Contemporary hip hop is affirmed in local practices and authenticated by the powerful need
for dramatic changes in the immediate social world. The struggle here is local, personal, political, economic, and artistic. In South Africa, much of contemporary rap
music represents an essentialized local morality in which there is little room left for
black internationalism and the diasporic intimacy of the first years of hip hop. The
rest of the rap music market in South Africa is fixated on emulating the crass materialism of what has become the mainstream in American hip hop and rap music.
This development is a problem of considerable weight for Emile:

South Africans are addicted to and obsessed with foreign actors, artists, personalities, and movies. Do we realize the amount of money that is lost to royalty payments to foreign artists? Do we know how many jobs are being destroyed by the constant preference given to U.S. and European artists? Do we realize why we have so few role models in our country? Do we see how it affects us when we play against these stars on the sports field and why we cannot believe we can win? Do we realize why our local artists cannot survive on their artistic skills?[5]

The increasing attention South African hip hop receives in the mainstream media in addition to the sponsorship of large corporations such as Adidas and Red Bull has raised the concern that the hip hop movement may be heading for an irreversible split. The award of Best Hip Hop album to Skwatta Kamp by the South African Music Awards in 2007 sends a message that the profitability of hip hop is now officially recognized. Grahamstown rapper Gcobani says that after twenty years of hip hop in South Africa, the genre should be standing on its own, but there are too many conflicts. The meaning of rap provides the ground for contestability, as there is a belief that true hip hop artists should rap in their vernacular or home language. Bad rap is when there is imitation of style and in situations where the emcee is inappropriately represented. Iain and Gcobani agree that many presumed hip hoppers have lost the plot with their belief that their style of clothing and extravagance qualify them as true hip hoppers. They suggest that those hip hoppers not representing the movement are blinded by money.

In Johannesburg, moreover, where the music industry is concentrated and lucrative deals are not difficult to obtain, rappers are compelled to soften the messages in their music. According to rap fans I spoke to in Grahamstown, many of these rappers are not true hip hoppers. Rather, for the right price they are fans willing to comply with the prescriptive demands of record companies. Nonetheless, hip hoppers are optimistic about the movement. In South African hip hop, certainly, there is power in its ability to move with the times while maintaining many of the initial goals of the movement, including reciprocity and the simulation of acts and sounds, combined with linguistic awareness. The ongoing commitment that hip hoppers have toward a better world is translated into positive actions and alertness to their social world, which is often articulated in strong messages to the state. The genre is coming of age. This is a process that will be prevailing for some time yet as changes in circumstances and negotiated and contested meanings all add up to a complex and glocal understanding of authenticity and difference.

NOTES

1. Emile YX and Shamiel X observe that many writers, including myself, are inclined to misrepresent aspects of the initial stages of hip hop in South Africa. In the early stages, they aver, hip hop was not associated with the struggle against apartheid. I take this opportunity to thank Emile, Shamiel, and the other hip hoppers for their contribution.

2. The DVD accompanying *Afrolution, Vol. 1* (Birch, Tapfuma, and Henen 2005) contains scenes from one of these indabas.

3. See the websites http://sowetohiphop.blogspot.com, http://1808hiphop.blogspot .com, and 1808 Sessions @ Pimville on Facebook for more information on the scenes in Johannesburg.

4. Unless otherwise noted, all quotations are from personal interviews and correspondence carried out by the author.

5. Emile from http://www.emileyx.co.za. Accessed September 19, 2007.

PERSONAL INTERVIEWS OR CORRESPONDENCE

Shaheen Ariefdien, 14 October and 11 November 1997, Cape Town.
Deon (aka Ready D), 17 and 24 October 1997, Cape Town.
Emileyx. Email correspondence, 3 September 2007.
Thulisa Jack, 24 August 2007, Grahamstown.
Siphiwo Kogere, 24 August 2007, Grahamstown.
Xolile Madinda (X), 28 August 2007, Grahamstown.
Tebogo Thebe Mogale (Emcee KasualT), 28 May 2007, Grahamstown, Bloemfontein, and
    Johannesburg.
Gcobani Ndabeni, 28 May and 24 August 2007, Grahamstown.
Iain Gregory Robinson (aka EWOK), 28 May 2007, Grahamstown and Durban.
Shamiel X, conversation 27 May 2007, Grahamstown, interview 3 September 2007,
    Johannesburg.

PART 2.
GRIOTS AND MESSENGERS
(SENEGAL, CÔTE D'IVOIRE, AND MALAWI)

The Rapper as Modern Griot
Reclaiming Ancient Traditions

PATRICIA TANG

> Rap music was born in Africa, grown in America
> and it went around the world to come back to Africa
> like a boomerang.
> —FAADA FREDDY OF THE SENEGALESE
> RAP GROUP DAARA J

What happens when hip hop, with its indisputable African American roots, returns to Africa? The past decade has seen an explosion of hip hop culture throughout Africa. Scholars and journalists often invoke the idea of the rapper as a "modern griot," linking rap to the ancient traditions of West African verbal artists or "masters of the word." When rap emerged in the 1980s in Senegal and exploded onto the Senegalese music scene in the 1990s, it could be seen as having taken a grand tour from its ancestral homeland, to its birth in the New World, and then back to Africa. But has hip hop really come full circle?

This chapter takes a critical look at the relationship between rap and griot traditions in West Africa. By examining the hip hop scene in Dakar, Senegal, it explores some of the ways in which African musicians reinvent both African American and African culture for their own purposes. Focusing on a case study of Positive Black Soul (PBS), the first African rap group to gain international success, the chapter reveals how Senegalese rap artists have seized upon and exploited Africanisms (particularly griotism) through various symbolic, linguistic, textual, and musical means.

Griot Traditions

Griots have played a significant role in cultures throughout West Africa for more than seven centuries, serving as oral historians, praise-singers, musicians, genealogists, and storytellers. Best known as hereditary artisans of the spoken word, griots also specialize in a variety of musical instruments, from the kora and bala-fon of Mande griots (*jali*) to the sabar drum of Wolof griots (*géwël*) in Senegal.[1] Written descriptions of griots date back to 1352–53, when the North African trav-eler Ibn Battuta described his encounters with griots at the court of Mali. During this time, griots served the kings and nobility and were responsible for transmit-ting the genealogies and histories of their patrons through their music and verbal arts.

Due to their ability to praise or critique individuals with their oratory skills, gri-ots have traditionally held an ambiguous social status, both revered and feared. Be-cause of their right to ask for money and gifts from the people they praise, griots are sometimes seen by others as greedy and opportunistic.[2] Regardless, griots con-tinue to play an important role in many West African cultures, though their role has certainly adjusted to modern times.[3] Despite changes in social structure (i.e., the decline of the hereditary class system) and other modern factors that have altered the original griot/patron relationship, griots to this day are active verbal artists and musicians.[4] Some griots specializing in the spoken word have become today's poli-ticians and figures in the media (radio and television), whereas griot musicians have found success in the burgeoning music industry, with many performing on stages and recording in studios throughout Europe and North America.

In the case of Senegal, griot singers and drummers are responsible for most as-pects of musical life, from life-cycle ceremonies to the popular music scene. Mbalax, the genre of dance music highlighted by Senegalese rhythms and griot vocal styles, is dominated by griot singers and features griot drummers as well. In the late 1970s, mbalax was created by infusing Cuban dance music with Senegalese percussion and Wolof lyrics. By the 1980s, mbalax had become a distinct genre of its own and is now considered the premier Senegalese popular music genre. The term *mbalax* was coined by Youssou N'Dour, who remains the genre's most famous and beloved singer as well as its international ambassador. Although mbalax is not an exclusive griot genre, the majority of Senegalese mbalax singers come from griot lineages (including Youssou N'Dour, Thione Seck, Alioune Mbaye Nder, Fatou Guewel, Kiné Lam, and Coumba Gawlo).[5]

Although griot singers dominate the popular music scene, griot drummers are prevalent in most aspects of Senegalese daily life. Wolof griot percussionists per-form at weddings, baptisms, neighborhood dance parties, wrestling matches, and political meetings. Géwël play the sabar drum as their primary instrument, and the sabar tradition has been passed down from one generation to the next for cen-turies (Tang 2007). Although nowadays some of the more successful griot drum-mers can be found performing with mbalax bands, they continue to perform in family drum troupes at traditional ceremonies as mentioned above.

What Is a Modern Griot? Terminology Broadly Defined

In recent years, the term *modern griot* has been employed by many schol-ars, journalists, music critics, and musicians themselves. In using this phrase, writers and musicians often invoke a romanticized and historically static idea of the griot—the traditional verbal artist who, for over a millennium, has served as keeper of oral history, musician, singer, and instrumentalist. The griot is usually historically situated, seen as a thing of the past, from which the modern griot has evolved over time, after crossing the Atlantic to the New World.

Several decades ago, few Americans had heard the word *griot*, let alone knew what it meant. Alex Haley's 1976 book, *Roots,* changed all of this, and the 1977 television miniseries based on the book drew the largest audience in the history of U.S. television at that time (Hale 1998: 2). The success of this miniseries led to a 1979 sequel in which Haley returned to The Gambia to trace his genealogy and learn more about his ancestor, Kunte Kinte. In this television sequel, Haley was told to consult a griot who would know his family genealogy.[6] Alex Haley's *Roots* has thus had an enormous impact on the international popularization of the griot as well as on African American interest in tracing genealogies. Suddenly the griot became an important figure in the way African Americans and others imagined Africa.

The term *modern griot* has since become a catchphrase broadly used in reference to modern African and African American artists. The late Senegalese novelist and filmmaker Sembène Ousmane considered himself a modern griot (Stoller 1994: 358); Youssou N'Dour refers to himself as a modern griot (Cullman 1991: 23); and Timothy Taylor (1997: 130) suggests that before N'Dour's international career took off, he was "a premodern griot, singing for various traditional rituals, including circumcision ceremonies." Hip hop/R&B singer Akon, who is the son of Senegalese griot percussionist Mor Thiam, has been described as a "new school griot," and the original timbre of his voice has been attributed to the style of African griots (Africahit.com 2006; Chartsinfrance.net 2007).[7]

In his book *Hip Hop Matters,* S. Craig Watkins (2005: 239) writes about the "new wave of urban griots in hip-hop lit." Quincy Jones also makes mention of the shared "traditions of the African griot storyteller that are continued today by the rappers" (in Gilroy 1991: 133), and David Toop (1984: 32) states that "the hip-hop message and protest rappers had an ancestry in the savanna griots." Geneva Smitherman (1997: 4) calls the rapper a "postmodern African griot," a verbally gifted storyteller and cultural historian in traditional African society: "As African America's 'griot,' the rapper must be lyrically/linguistically fluent; he or she is expected to testify, to speak the truth, to com wit it in no uncertain terms." Ndiouga Adrien Benga (2002: 82) adds that rap is rooted in the same origins as those of preachers: "From the tale teller to the praise singer of modern times, a kinship can be found in that this is a kind of 'oral literature' which takes place in 'urban poetry.'"

Indeed, many rap artists themselves point to Africa as a reference for their performance practices. In a 2006 interview with *Playboy* magazine, rapper Kanye West suggested that he would be a griot in a modern-day Bible, because he "bring[s] up historical subjects in a way that makes kids want to learn about them. . . . I'm an inspirational speaker" (Tannenbaum 2006: 132). Rapper Afrika Bambaataa says, "Although it [rap] has been in the Bronx, it goes back to Africa because you had chanting style of rappin" (Keyes 2002: 17). Lumumba "Professor X" Carson adds: "Once upon a time ago, a long long time ago, every Friday of the month, it was the duty of the grandfather in a tribe to sit down and bring all of the immediate children around him to rap. One of the instruments that was played while grandfather rapped his father's existence was a guy playing the drum. I guess that's why we are so into rap today" (Keyes 2002: 17).

Although he does not specifically refer to griots by name, Lumumba Carson's words serve as a perfect example of the romanticized way in which griots (or in this case, the village elders) are so often viewed. His statement "Once upon a time ago, a long long time ago" situates the grandfather in a distant yet timeless past. Carson then evokes the image of the grandfather in a tribe, a village elder, who gathers members of the younger generation around him in order to share his knowledge with them. He notes that the grandfather "rapped his father's existence," thus recounting his own genealogy to the next generation. Musically, the grandfather is rapping and is accompanied by the sounds of a drum.

The above statements by Kanye West, Afrika Bambaataa, and Lumumba Carson are clear examples of rappers creating an imagined Africa that gives historical prestige and precedent to their art forms. However, their language also situates Africa in a remote past. As Hauke Dorsch (2004: 108) points out, although hip hop plays a crucial role in connecting the different groups of the African diaspora, it also sometimes constructs representations of the African motherland which can be criticized for being "highly idealistic, mythical, and ahistorical."

Despite the many references to the griot roots of rap, few have attempted a truly critical examination of the complex nature of this relationship between rap music and the verbal art of griots. An exception is Cheryl Keyes, who looks more closely than others at this link between rap and West African musical traditions, calling it the rap music–African nexus. During the transatlantic slave trade, when many Africans (including griots) were transplanted to the Western world, they necessarily modified, reshaped, and transformed African systems of thought into their new contexts. Keyes (2002: 21) calls this foregrounding (both consciously and unconsciously) of African-centered concepts "cultural reversioning," citing rap music performance practices as representative of this. The case of African rap can thus be seen as cultural reversioning twice over, with African artists themselves foregrounding African-centered concepts which were once the domain of African diasporic traditions. A good example of this "boomerang" phenomenon is the hip hop scene in Dakar, Senegal (e.g., Daara J's 2004 album *Boomerang*). By the 1990s, rap in Senegal had experienced an explosion in popularity. This could in part be attributed to the shared qualities between rappers and griots. According to Frank Tenaille, rap has several reasons to thrive on Senegalese soil:

> The oral tradition remains important there. Between the griot, master of speech, and the rap MC, master of ceremonies, there is only a difference in surround-

ings. The art of discussion, of social communication, is a constant in African life, and the rapper speaks to this collective need. Africa has always been fond of "commentators" who take up and speak what is socially unspoken, who on their own level are rappers. And then of course there's the protomusical character of rap, founded on rhythm and tone, which suits the sensitivity of African tastes precisely with those two elements (Tenaille 2002: 222–23).

Rap in Senegal

The hip hop movement began in Senegal in 1984 with the arrival of the break dance craze and recordings of rappers such as Grandmaster Flash and the Sugarhill Gang (Herson 2000: 18). By the late 1980s, some young Senegalese rap groups had formed, as rap had become a growing medium for youth to express their frustrations with the many social, economic, and political problems of the time (including high unemployment rates and school strikes). Up until this point, mbalax had been the quintessential and dominant popular music genre in Senegal, appealing to all ages and socioeconomic groups since the early 1970s. However, by the early 1990s, the Senegalese music market experienced a rap explosion due to the sudden proliferation of new groups, the establishment of older groups, and a heady sociopolitical climate.[8] Indeed, hip hop is widely recognized as mobilizing Senegalese youth and advocating political change, which culminated in the 2000 election of president Abdoulaye Wade.[9] Nearly a decade later, when some of the Senegalese population had become frustrated with Wade's presidency, rappers once again spoke out against the government.[10]

Senegal's oldest and most internationally renowned rap group is Positive Black Soul, formed in 1989 by Didier (DJ) Awadi and Amadou Barry, aka Doug-E-Tee. Awadi was originally the leader of a rap group called Syndicate, and Doug-E-Tee was part of the King MCs. The two groups were rivals until Awadi invited Doug-E-Tee to his birthday party celebration on August 11, 1989. Here they rapped together and found that they shared the same musical vision and pan-Africanist philosophy. They then joined forces to create Positive Black Soul (PBS), a group that would be dedicated to promoting a positive image of Africa. In their battle against Afro-pessimism, PBS has been inspired by major African thinkers such as Kocc Barma (a nineteenth-century Senegalese philosopher), as well as Hampate Ba, Kwame Nkrumah, and Cheikh Anta Diop. The group started gaining airplay in 1990, and in 1992 they opened for the famed French rapper MC Solaar at a concert at the Centre Culturel Français in Dakar, gaining national attention. In the following years, they toured internationally and released numerous recordings, including more than a dozen cassettes on the Senegalese market and two CDs on the international market. Their first CD, *Salaam* (1996), was the first African hip hop recording to be released in the United States on a major record label (Island).[11]

PBS rapper Awadi elaborates on some of the connections, as well as distinctions, between rappers and griots:

A lot of people say that rappers are modern griots. But first one must understand what we rappers take from griots. The griots in traditional Senegalese society would sing for the kings; they would sing about the history of Senegal. They were like history books, like a journalist. And the griot was also someone who sang for money. So he wore several different hats. What we rappers have continued to do, what we have taken from the griots, is from the journalistic side. A journalist engaged in his society. But all of the other aspects of the griot, we don't do. That is, we don't sing for the purpose of receiving money. Of course, we are paid musicians. That's obvious. But we do not sing about people so that they will give us money. There is a big difference. Also, with regard to history, that is not really the role of rap. Of course, some rappers could specialize in history, but that's not the purpose. But I think that today the role of the griot here is different from the role of the rapper. The rapper is like a sentinel for society, saying what works or what doesn't work. And the griot's purpose is different. In any case, to the present day, the griot is here to sing for money. Period.[12]

Although most griots would argue that they do not sing for money per se, but rather that money is given to them in appreciation for their services, it is true that griots who perform at weddings, baptisms, and political meetings are mostly singing praises to the nobles, politicians, wealthy, and other prominent figures. Griot singers in the mbalax scene likewise have many songs in their repertories praising important figures, especially religious figures such as Cheikh Amadou Bamba Mbacké, founder of the Mouride sect of Islam widely practiced in Senegal.

In addition to praise songs, griots also sing commentaries on social issues pertinent to contemporary Senegalese society. Such topics include polygamy, immigration, the importance of respecting elders, and saying no to drugs. However, although these songs sometimes have moral or didactic messages regarding social behavior, they rarely speak out against specific individuals or institutions. This is in stark contrast to Senegalese rappers, who openly critique politicians and the government. Senegalese rap songs commonly address issues such as the importance of fighting political corruption, dealing with high unemployment rates, and rallying Senegalese youth together to demand and effect change.

One of the reasons why there is such a marked distinction between the words of griots and rappers is that in Senegal, most rappers are not from griot families. Rather than practicing a tradition of singing or drumming that has been passed down within the family for centuries, rappers were generally exposed to rap through initial contact with mediated American hip hop culture. Thus Senegalese rappers do not inherit their musical trade—they make a conscious choice to practice their trade, much as is the case with musicians who play modern instruments (such as keyboard or guitar). This freedom to decide their profession is further expressed in their freedom of speech, as rappers are expected to critique society and even the government, whereas griots tend to give moral advice or sing praises for money, as they have done for centuries.

Indeed, in Africa the term *griot* can have the negative connotation of one who sings empty praises to the wealthy. Therefore, it is somewhat ironic that African

American rappers (and those who write about them) would take on this word. Instead, rappers have redefined *griot* to fit their own circumstances. Their griot is the keeper of history, the village elder, and the powerful master of spoken word. In Senegal, the griot is also a practitioner of *taasu*, a verbal art form said to be one of the predecessors of rap.

Traditional Senegalese Roots: Taasu

Taasu is a traditional Senegalese Wolof style of rhythmic poetry, involving the declamation of heightened rhythmic speech over accompanying percussion.[13] The Wolof verb *taas* means "to bless" or "to praise." A kind of poetry, taasu is almost always declaimed to the rhythmic accompaniment of drums or calabashes or tin bowls. According to Mariama Ndoye Mbengue, "Taasu are formulas created by women in a variety of circumstances, often to mock, sometimes to glorify themselves or a third person. They are two or three lines long, [but] in any case, are rarely long. . . . The composer declaims her refrain, then the drum and the dance follow. It is an entertaining genre that takes place during family ceremonies. . . . It serves as a social regulator" (Ndoye 1982: 28; translated in McNee 1996: 67).

Unlike straight forms of praise-singing or speech-giving practiced by griots, the verse structure of the taasu poem is driven by an internal rhythm (McNee 1996: 67). Most taasu are improvised, although some well-known taasu poems have become part of griots' repertories.

As described by Deborah Heath:

> Wolof dances are associated with poems, frequently bawdy, which are called taasu. These poems are often associated with a particular dance step, so that its performance evokes the companion taasu whether or not it is spoken by the dancer or one of the drummers before the dance begins.
>
> The taasu provides women with a vehicle for social control, as well as creative word play. A poem may be composed specifically to respond to a particular situation, or an existing taasu may be modified to provide personalized commentary on specific individuals and local events. (Heath 1988: 93–94)

In Senegal, taasu has likely been practiced for centuries, primarily by women. In the late twentieth century, however, with the advent of modern music, taasukats (practitioners of taasu) began to produce commercial cassettes. The first female taasukat to release a commercial cassette was Aby Ngana Diop (*Liital*, 1994). More recently, male griot percussionists (including Bada Seck, Thio Mbaye, Pape Ndiaye Guewel, Pape Thiopet, Mbaye Dieye Faye, and Lamine Touré) have released sabar (percussion) based recordings featuring taasu, as griot drummers are often also skilled as taasukats.

Taasu is performed in a variety of contexts, ranging from life-cycle ceremonies (naming ceremonies), to neighborhood dance parties (generically called *sabar*, after the drum) and women's association meetings (*tur*). Although women typically perform taasu in these contexts, it is also performed by men, especially by male griots. Taasu can be performed by anyone, but tends to be associated with female *géwël*.

The desire to link rap to taasu has been taken up by Senegalese musicians themselves, both rappers and griots. In the 1990s, when Senegalese rap was at its initial height of popularity, rappers and griots began to claim that taasu was the "true" predecessor to rap. Senegalese rap group Gokh-Bi System, now based in the United States, released a recording in 2007 called *Rap Tassu,* which they hope "will enlighten people about the origins of rap music" (Gokh-Bi System 2007). Faada Freddy of the Senegalese rap group Daara J stated in an interview with the BBC that "rappers of today are all modern griots" and that taasu is "the ancestor of rap" (Pollard 2004). However, when questioned further about whether or not there is a direct link between taasu and rap, neither rappers nor griots whom I interviewed were able to provide a convincing explanation, nor did they seem particularly interested in doing so. As rapper Awadi states:

> What I think personally, is that rap is American music. OK. Second, like all black music, it has its roots in Africa. . . . We have taken American rap and created our own rap—we made it African. Thus it's clear. On the other hand, there are similar forms that exist here—taasu . . . all of this has existed for centuries, and it's the same principle, speaking a text over a beat . . . only the beat is created by women playing calabashes or by drums . . . but this has existed for a long time.[14] That's why people make the connection so quickly; they say rap is basically just taasu over big beats, but it's actually a bit different, because even if you perform taasu over a beat, it's different from rapping over a beat. . . . Thus rap has its roots in taasu; the roots are African, but I think it ends there. We like to make the connection a lot, but to be honest . . . [laughing].[15]

Both Senegalese griots and rappers work to connect rap to taasu, but this connection seems to be an oversimplification. Both are rhythmic verbal forms, but it would be difficult to show historically how rap evolved from taasu per se, because too many other African peoples have strong rhythmic poetic traditions to privilege any one as the primary source.[16] Whether or not rap is directly descended from taasu, Senegalese rappers have found creative ways to make use of griot traditions in their music and their messages. An excellent example is Positive Black Soul's song entitled "Return of da djelly."

Positive Black Soul's "Return of da Djelly"

"Return of da djelly" was released in 1996 on PBS's first international album, *Salaam.* An analysis of this song on multiple levels will demonstrate how rappers use the idea of the *djelly* (Mande griot).[17] Although Doug-E-Tee and Didier Awadi are neither djelly nor géwël in real life, in this song the first-person narrative, that of the djelly himself, is sung by Doug-E-Tee, who for the purposes of the song takes on a djelly persona.

Notably, PBS chose to use the Mande djelly instead of the Wolof géwël. Although géwël is most commonly used in Senegal, djelly is more widely used outside of Senegal and is recognized throughout the Western world. Yet PBS purposely chose not to use the English/French term *griot*. As Awadi has expressed, griots sing praises for money, thus their status in society is not always so admirable. However, *djelly* does not have the same negative connotations as *griot*. By using a native term, but one that is most widespread, PBS carefully situates the djelly as the authentic African storyteller, teacher, preacher, and historian.

Aside from the word *djelly*, the rest of the song is in English. The English text of this song gears it toward an English-speaking audience, although out of eleven tracks on the album, it is one of only two tracks in English (four are in Wolof, and five are in French). PBS's multilingual rhymes enable to them to address their immediate constituency as well as audiences in the United States and the world at large (T. Mitchell 2001: 5).

The song begins with the sound of a traditional flute native to a Senegalese ethnic group known as Peul or Fula, followed by a short synthesized melodic figure evoking the sound of a kora (a 21-stringed harp played by Mande griots). Then the drum and bass enter, and the first verse begins, sung by Doug-E-Tee in a ragga style. Although the text is not rapped per se (in that Doug-E-Tee's text is sung and not spoken), the ragga style is commonly used in hip hop music, and the rhythmic complexity of the lyrics displays Doug-E-Tee's strong rapping skills.

"Return of Da Djelly"

Flashback, it's time to check out history
Lemme tell you his story, a bit of mystery,
The way I say it is musical
As they used to bust it back in the African typical
Soul people, now you feel [that] I've got skills
My shit is real,
And my style kills
Just like the rainbow
I spread seven colors on your head
I'm the symbol of knowledge, call me djelly
One who transmits history, I'm like Koli [Senegalese hero],
More knowledgeable than a Bible
The knowledge involved like the Bible
My wisdom is my weapon
Reminisce the recital of the musical poetry,
Lyrical wizardry,
Mystic darkness meets majestic blackness
Africky, colly, that's the holy djelly
I nourish your mind but not your belly
Hangin' on my roots, I'll be a bliggey de bliggey

> Oh well, it's the return of the djelly
> Yes, it's the return of the djelly

In this first verse, the djelly speaks directly to the listener, explaining who he is and why he is so important. He says it is "time to check out history," then goes on to boast about his verbal and musical skills as well as his wealth of knowledge. He compares his knowledge to the Bible and talks about his wisdom being his weapon; the djelly is not only skilled but also a powerful and even holy figure. A symbol of knowledge, one who transmits history, he has now returned with a message for you, the listener.

> Yes, it's the return of the djelly,
> Yes, it's the turn of ola niggy Nubian,
> That's how they call me
> I expect respect, check the djelly
> Mention the man
> He's one in a million
> I will take you to places you've never been
> A ride back to the roots you've never seen
> Cos' I'm the storyteller, the teacher, the preacher,
> I wanna meet you
> Hey girl, hey boy
> I will teach you how to build
> And how to destroy
> How to live in harmony with the forces of nature
> Then nothing will never separate you
> From the motherland, *alkebu-lan* land
> With peace around the corner . . . Nubian
> Now that you've got an invitation
> Return of the djelly
> Come with the djelly in the land of meditation

In this second verse, the djelly continues to explain his significance to society. As a storyteller, teacher, and preacher, he will take you to your roots; by doing this, you will unite with the motherland, Africa. The djelly has invited you to come with him on a journey to the "land of meditation," where you will learn to live in peace and harmony.

> Haters always try to false my identity
> Showin' an African continent ain't no destiny
> Don't want black people to live in community
> And teachin' white is right, black is wrong and all that
> See, some people still faking the funk
> Saying that they love Africa
> But it's a funk on a dunk

If you should a know by now
The djelly—I will tell you now
Shout it out, people, shout it out loud
Lord have mercy, this the djelly
Listen, I have to tell you about your history
No matter where you come from
This is Don Doug-e-tee, the djelly, me have
To tell you some, black man
You have to know about your ancestry
No matter who you are, just come fe ball out fe we
Positive Black Soul, Awadi and Doug-e-tee
Lord have mercy
It's the return of the djelly
Come with the djelly to the land of meditation
It's the djelly

In this final verse, the djelly lashes out full force against Afro-pessimism. He speaks out against those who don't want blacks to live in the community, as well as those "fakes" who say they love Africa but really don't. The djelly seeks to rectify these problems by telling you, the black man, about your history and your ancestry. The djelly is returning so that he can educate today's black man by telling him about his roots. This last verse is also the first time that "you" is defined as the black man. Up until the very end of the final verse, the djelly is speaking to the unspecified listener, so his relevance and his message are more widespread.

Overall, the narrator talks about the djelly as one who transmits history and as someone with musical skills. In the rest of the song, he says he will teach the African about his motherland and to think about his history and ancestry, strongly advocating a positive Africanist philosophy. While the true, modern-day djelly are still constrained by certain traditional rules that dictate their place in society, rappers have the luxury of being djelly in a more metaphorical or symbolic sense; therefore, they are able to reach a broader audience and serve to critique, not just to praise. Whereas true djelly generally provide direct praise to patrons (e.g., by telling a person's genealogy and then listing all of his or her accomplishments), rappers communicate broader social and political messages, applicable to both Africa and the West. In a traditional context, a djelly would be praising someone, explaining that person's ancestry and the importance of his family lineage; the role of the listener would be relatively inactive, with perhaps the only action being the showering of monetary bills to show appreciation for the djelly's words. In contrast, this djelly, performed by a rapper, provides agency to the listener in a way that is much more socially proactive. The djelly may be advising the black man, the African, or even you, the listener. But it is up to you, the listener, to do something. In this case, the listener is not expected to give money but to listen to the djelly and get in touch with his/her African roots. Although he may be seen as a thing of the past, the djelly has returned to educate today's listener and to inspire positive action.

This case study of PBS and the song "Return of da djelly" is an example of how rappers use the idea of djelly for their own purposes, drawing upon Western ideas of the djelly as a romanticized and historicized African phenomenon. African rappers may indeed be modern griots, but in a global sense; at the same time, they share and negotiate their space in Senegalese culture with those who are true griots by birth, who themselves carry forward their own vibrant traditions, perform a vital role in society, and adapt to changing social and cultural realities. By invoking griotness, Senegalese hip hop artists construct a complex, new Africanized identity that draws upon American rap but then gains greater legitimacy through its roots in a historic African tradition. They then reclaim this tradition as their own, having the best of both worlds.

NOTES

The epigraph is from Terrell (2007).

1. The term *griot* is an umbrella term. Those ethnic groups that have griots each have their own native term for the word, including *jali* (Mande) and *géwël* (Wolof).

2. See Hale (1998) and Hoffman (2000) for further reading on the art of griot oratory and the power of griot words.

3. See Leymarie-Ortiz (1979), Knight (1991), Panzacchi (1994), Hale (1998), Charry (2000), Ebron (2002), and Tang (2006, 2007).

4. See Tamari (1991) and Diop (1981) for further discussion of caste in West African and Senegalese societies, respectively.

5. See Panzacchi (1996), Durán (1989), Cathcart (1989), Benga (2002), Tang (2005), Mangin (2004, forthcoming), and Stapleton and May (1987: 116–28) for further reading on mbalax and Youssou N'Dour.

6. Scholars have since shown that Kebba Kanji Fofana, Haley's supposed griot source, was in fact not a griot at all but a village trickster who fabricated Haley's genealogy according to what he thought Haley wanted to hear. See Wright (1981) and Mills and Mills (1981, 1984) for further reading.

7. Akon (born Aliaune Thiam) is the son of Mor Thiam, a well-known griot, djembe drummer, and jazzman who worked with the Katherine Dunham company. Akon is an unusual example of an American hip hop/R&B artist with Senegalese roots who actually comes from a griot family. However, Akon does not appear to use his griot roots in marketing himself or his identity; to my knowledge, he has not made any reference to his griot lineage in any interviews and does not seem to consider it an important part of his identity.

8. Various sources state that, at its height in the late 1990s, Senegal had as many as 3,000 rap groups, ranging from small neighborhood posses to internationally known groups such as Positive Black Soul (Mbaye 1999). However, I have been unable to substantiate these claims from their original sources, and I feel there is a possibility that this number has been exaggerated.

9. For more on Senegalese rap, see Herson (2000).

10. See *Democracy in Dakar* (Herson, McIlvaine, and Moore 2007) a film from Nomadic Wax and Sol Productions, about youth, hip hop, and politics in Africa.

11. See RFI Musique (1999). In 2003, Didier Awadi and Doug-E-Tee began pursuing solo careers.

12. Interview, 15 December 2006, Dakar. This is my translation from French.

13. Lisa McNee (1996, 2000) defines *taasu* as a panegyric performance genre.

14. For a discussion of women's calabash drumming associations in Bamako, see Modic (1996).

15. Interview, 15 December 2006, Dakar. My translation from French.

16. Portia Maultsby and Guthrie Ramsey have assisted in creating a timeline of black music that links the following: griots–verbal arts (boasting/toasting/signifying the dozens)–preaching–scatting–spoken-word poetry–rap (McBride 2007: 108–10). A close analysis of Senegalese poetic speech and African American poetic speech is beyond the scope of this study, but it is an important topic for further detailed investigation.

17. *Djelly* is a French variant spelling of the more widely used *jeli* or *jali*.

Promises of the Chameleon

Reggae Artist Tiken Jah Fakoly's Intertextual Contestation of Power in Côte d'Ivoire

DANIEL B. REED

In this chapter I explore the intertextual artistry of Ivorian reggae musician Tiken Jah Fakoly's 2000 song "Promesses de Caméléon" [Promises of the Chameleon]. I analyze elements of this song that reveal Fakoly's strategic choices, choices that contribute to the song's effectiveness in contesting political power. These choices, which I analyze as intertextual references, include: (1) the genre of reggae as his medium of communication; (2) singing a key phrase in the song's chorus in the Jula language; (3) inclusion of an explicitly militaristic musical motif in the song's introduction; and (4) his most potent of all—the daring inclusion of a recording of a speech by General Robert Gueï, the leader of the military junta then governing Côte d'Ivoire. I argue that it is the special ideological and identity-related implications of each of these choices—that is, the other texts and contexts that "Promesses de Caméléon" indexes—that renders the song such a loaded, powerful expression of protest. The song was so effective and popular that Fakoly began receiving death threats from Côte d'Ivoire military rulers and was forced to flee the country to live in exile, first in Burkina Faso, and later in Mali, where I interviewed him in 2003.[1] Fakoly's wide-ranging references lend themselves particularly well to an intertextual analysis, which can perhaps most effectively uncover a major aspect of his approach.

Intertextuality

Richard Bauman (2004: 1) notes that "the relationship of texts to other texts has been an abiding concern to literary theorists since classical antiquity," and that intertextuality has been central to the study of oral poetics since the late seventeenth century. In more recent history, however, the concept of intertextuality became popularized in linguistics and literary criticism to describe the transposition of one or more systems of signs into another. Alessandro Duranti (1994), Bauman and Charles Briggs (1992), and others have applied this concept to studies of oral texts in performances, adding that intertextuality involves not only the transposition of text but also the interlinkage of context. Duranti (1994: 5) explains, "Even the apparently most homogeneous or self-contained text exhibits, on close analysis, elements that link it to texts, with different contexts, different norms, and different voices." I find Bauman's (2004: 4) recent definition of the term—"the relational orientation of a text to other texts"—an apt entry into analyzing how "Promesses de Caméléon" works; part of its power as a song derives from its strategic references to other texts and contexts.[2]

The four elements of Fakoly's song that I am analyzing in this chapter function as three different types of intertextuality. The militaristic-sounding musical opening sonically signifies another text and context, almost like a jazz musician who, while soloing in one song, quotes a theme from another. The incorporation of the recording of Gueï's speech is similar to sampling in hip hop, in that it directly borrows something of another origin and recontextualizes it in the new song. The other two elements that I am labeling intertextual—the reggae genre and the languages—are more formal in nature, in that they are elements of the overall compositional structure of the song as opposed to passages within that structure. However, these choices do clearly orient "Promesses de Caméléon" to other texts and contexts, and in that sense, are every bit as intertextual as are the military music reference and recorded speech.[3]

Context for Contestation

On December 24, 1999, the first coup d'état in the history of Côte d'Ivoire overthrew the government of President Henri Konan Bédié and instated General Robert Gueï as leader of a military junta. Bédié had been in power since shortly after the death of President Félix Houphouët Boigny, who had been a colonial leader and then president from the time of Ivorian independence in 1960 until his death in 1993.

Until the period of political instability that began with the 1999 coup and continues to the time of this writing in 2010, Côte d'Ivoire had been an economic powerhouse of the West African region. Houphouët Boigny led a markedly pro-Western, pro-capitalist, mildly dictatorial state for over three decades. "The Ivorian Miracle," as the country's economic boom period from the 1960s through the early 1980s was called, was based largely on the export of cash crops such as coffee and cacao, grown on plantations in the verdant southern half of the country. Critical to this economic success was Houphouët's deliberate openness both to foreign investment and to immigrant workers from poorer neighboring countries like Burkina Faso, Mali, and Guinea, who labored on plantations for little pay. This flood of immigration, which continued well into the 1990s, was so great that, by 1998, more than 25 percent of the inhabitants of Côte d'Ivoire were foreign immigrants, mostly from poorer countries to the north (F. Akindès 2004:10).

Declining prices for agricultural raw materials, the increase in the dollar exchange rate and the price of oil, the rise in international interest rates, and skyrocketing national debt combined to undercut Côte d'Ivoire's economic health in the late 1980s and early 1990s (F. Akindès 2004: 17). As the economic downturn worsened, the huge population of northern immigrants became scapegoats for the failing economy. Under Bédié, an ethno-nationalist political rhetoric developed, called Ivoirité [Ivori-ness], which was based on both economic and political justifications. Government reports critically evaluated "the impact of immigration on the country's natural demographic equilibrium, its political life, its economic life in terms of the rise in unemployment of 'native-born' Ivorians, and on security and social cohesion" (27). This scapegoating was not limited to foreign immigrants, however, but lumped those immigrants together with people of northern Côte d'Ivoire, commonly called "Julas" (see below) whose belonging in the "Ivorian nation" was also increasingly questioned. Northern Côte d'Ivoire is historically majority Muslim, and Muslims furthermore account for 86 percent of immigrants to the country. Further fanning the flames of national tension, Ivoirité also valorized Christianity—more common in the south—as the "historically adopted culture" of the nation (28–29). The net result was a gradually increasing politicization of regional, ethnic, and religious difference, and northerners and immigrants came to understand Ivoirité as state-sponsored xenophobic discrimination. This ethno-nationalism was further realized in the Ivorian constitution by the addition of restrictive eligibility clauses for the position of president. In sum, these restrictions, which narrowly defined nationality according to numerous criteria, including whether a citizen's parents were born in the country, were read by many as a bald attempt by Bédié to exclude his main political rival, former prime minister Alassane Dramane Ouattara, from political eligibility. That Ouattara is a northerner led to the interpretation that his exclusion was state-sponsored discrimination at the highest levels.

The military junta that seized power in December 1999 accused the Bédié government of using identity definitions for political purposes to perpetuate a "legitimacy of exclusion." Gueï, a former army chief of staff with a reputation as an ethical person, was widely hailed as a savior who would surely right the Ivorian political ship that had gone so wrong under Bédié's rule. In the first months after his seizure of power, Gueï was highly critical of the ideology of Ivoirité—calling it a threat to national unity—and of government corruption (F. Akindès 2004: 21). He furthermore vowed to move quickly toward open elections so that Ivorians could choose a civilian government. To the astonishment of many, however, within a few short months Gueï began completely reversing course. He became what Ivorian scholar Francis Akindès calls "Gueï Version 2," characterized by "increasing and sustained doubts as to his will to cede power to civilians, remarks close to xenophobia, a hardened tone toward Allasane Dramane Ouattara, the re-appropriation of the rhetoric of 'Ivoirité' (although without explicitly using the term), the abandoning of the 'clean sweep operation' (an anti-corruption campaign), selective arrests of a political nature, and the recruitment of former PDCI-RDA (the political party that had been in power since independence, that he had overthrown) office-holders into his cabinet as advisers and to other posts" (21). It was in this context that Tiken Jah Fakoly hurriedly wrote, recorded, and released his album *Le Caméléon,* an album full of hard-hitting songs like "Le Pays Va Mal" [The country is ill] and the intertextual masterpiece "Promesses de Caméléon."

Since 2000, when "Promesses de Caméléon" was released, Côte d'Ivoire has experienced continued instability. In September 2002, following two controversial elections that excluded Ouattara, an armed rebellion led by a coalition of northern rebel groups seized control of the northern half of the country. Côte d'Ivoire remained divided for eight years. The southern half of the country was led by the government of Laurent Gbagbo, who was elected president in a highly contentious election in late 2000, while the north was held by rebels who became known as the "New Forces." Although there was little active fighting after 2004, the two sides remained separated by UN peacekeeping and French forces throughout the rest of the decade. In October 2010, a long-delayed election was held, in which Outtara—finally deemed eligible—defeated Gbagbo. The incumbent refused to concede, and a stand-off, which ultimately turned violent and claimed 4,000 lives, ended in April 2011 when Outtara's forces stormed the presidential palace and captured Gbagbo.[4] Throughout the period of conflict, Fakoly remained in Bamako, where he continued writing and releasing albums full of politically charged reggae, much of it concerning the fate of his divided home nation.

Choice of Reggae as a Genre

Since it is the frame within which all of Fakoly's other intertextual choices function, I begin by discussing the most fundamental intertextual decision that he made: his selection of the genre of reggae as his medium of communication. Some might take issue with my assertion that genre choice in and of itself is an intertextual move. However, in selecting reggae, Fakoly purposely positions his songs in relation to others in the genre; that is, to employ Bauman's concept of the term, he orients his text to other texts in the reggae idiom. Reggae as a form, as a genre, itself intertextually indexes, through its association with Bob Marley and a host of other post-Marley African diaspora reggae protest singers, a sense of pan-African identity and resistance to injustice. As Lisa McNee (2002: 232) writes, the identification of West African youth with reggae represents a kind of "double movement"— the first connecting to what is often referred to in reggae lyrics (again, intertextually) as "Babylon"—that is, the international reggae discourse against oppressive power, postcolonial power, and imperialist injustices levied against peoples of African descent—and a second connecting the youth to protest of local issues.

Fakoly clearly had these thoughts in mind when he chose to begin writing songs in the reggae genre. As he told me, "Reggae is a militant music. It's the music of those without means. It's the music of opinions. . . . it is a music that is the soul of the poor."[5]

> [Jamaican reggae artists] spoke of justice, of the issue of equality in Jamaican society. They spoke about slavery and colonization. So I said to myself, "These themes of injustice that they have found, there are cases of injustice like that all around me." We had those same problems in Africa, even in my village. And so that's why I began to write songs. . . . There are [reggae] songs about colonization, about slavery, about the exploitation of Africa by the West, etc. But there is injustice here at home and so before you say to others—"things are messy, you have to clean up," you have to clean up your own house first. So it was that I wrote my first song about the griot.

Fakoly's first song, written when he was still a teenager, concerned what he saw as the unjust treatment of griots (singular, *jeli*) in his own culture, who are highly valued for their many contributions to society (including praise-singing, maintaining oral history, and various ritual functions), yet are also, in Fakoly's words, oppressed and discriminated against, to the extent that, for example, they are not permitted to marry outside of their own families. Fakoly thus consciously chose reggae, because of its association with protest against injustice, to offer a musical critique of injustice in his own backyard. Choice of this genre itself was a strategic choice—an intertextual reference—that placed his protest songs within an international context of protest against injustice, imbuing each of his songs about problems in Côte d'Ivoire with a sonic signifier of the general fight against "Babylon." Again, intertextual references link not just to other texts but to other contexts as well, and Fakoly's choice to write reggae songs clearly functioned in that manner.

Following his initial critique of his society's treatment of griots, Fakoly has gone on to exploit the reggae medium to offer critiques of many aspects of Ivorian political and social life. Most notably, Fakoly rose to national and international prominence in 1997 with his album *Mangercratie,* which included songs protesting the policy of Ivoirité ("Le Descendant") and governmental corruption and ineffectiveness (the title song) (see also S. Akindes 2002: 94–95).[6]

Fakoly was but one of several reggae musicians, including his Ivorian reggae forebearers Alpha Blondy[7] and Serges Kassy, who defined reggae in the Ivorian context as *the* primary music of rebellion and political protest in the 1990s. For example, immediately upon seizing power in the 1999 coup, which (ironically) instated General Robert Gueï, mutinying soldiers "seized the state radio station and put back on the air the recording of Ivorian [reggae] musicians whose banned music had inspired them" (Vick 2000). Reggae singers "are the people who tell the truth," declared Sergeant Oliver Zadi, one of the soldiers involved in the coup. "They say exactly what happens. It's because of them that we became conscious of what's going on and said, 'Enough is enough'" (Vick 2000). Reggae was a means of expressing discontent in Côte d'Ivoire, and when Fakoly sang in this genre, that association preceded him, and he perpetuated it. Furthermore, with the exception of Kassy, the best known Ivorian reggae artists (including Fakoly and Blondy) were from the north, leading to associations of reggae with northerners, both culturally and politically (S. Akindes 2002: 97).

Choice to Add a Jula Phrase to the Song's French Lyrics

The lyrics of "Promesses du Caméléon" are in French with the exception of one very important phrase, which is in the Jula language. The Jula phrase "Militairi cè"[8] [military man] comes at the beginning of the song's chorus, which, in its first two instances, immediately follows lengthy recorded excerpts of General Robert Gueï's post-coup speech. What makes this particular passage so important is that it occurs at the moment in the song when Fakoly's lyrics (sung by a female chorus) formally and directly address Gueï. How one addresses a figure of authority in Africa is a matter of great importance and is not taken lightly. That Fakoly chose to do so in Jula, in the context of a song otherwise sung in French, is significant and bears analysis from the perspective of intertextuality.

In his introduction to *Global Pop, Local Language,* Harris M. Berger asserts that language choice in popular music is informed by language ideologies. That is, language is never neutral—it is never without substantial ideological meaning. Language choice in popular music thus connects popular music to larger social contexts (Berger 2003: xiv), which, I suggest, is yet another example of intertextuality—the relation of a popular song to the texts and contexts of language politics in any given setting. Language choice is not merely a reflection of those contexts, as musicians use language choice to "actively think about, debate, or resist the ideologies at play in the social world around them" (xv). This is especially true in substantially multilingual contexts, in which an artist has more than one language at hand that might seem natural to select as the communicative code for any given song. In such circumstances, an artist might ask, as does Berger, "Which language or dialects will best express my ideas? Which will get me a record contract or a bigger audience? What does it mean to sing or listen to music in a colonial language? A foreign language? A 'native' language?" (x).

Language politics in Côte d'Ivoire are similar to, but nonetheless distinct from, the language politics of other former French colonies in Africa. As in most of these other ex-colonies, French is the official language in Côte d'Ivoire and as such is used in all political contexts, in formal commercial contexts, and in nearly all mass media. What distinguishes Côte d'Ivoire from many of its neighbors is the extent to which dialects of French are used to communicate across ethnic lines and, for that matter, even between members of the same ethnic group, in informal and daily interactions. To be sure, the sixty languages indigenous to the country continue to be regularly spoken, but the percentage of Ivorians who can speak some French, and who regularly choose to do so, is quite high relative to other former French colonies in the West African region. In that sense, French truly is the lingua franca of Côte d'Ivoire. However, it is not the only language that warrants that label. An African language, Jula, serves as a kind of secondary lingua franca of the country.[9] Most Ivorians know at least a few words or phrases in Jula, and many can carry on conversations in the language, especially in markets and urban neighborhoods, where Jula is widely spoken. A great many people living in Côte d'Ivoire are also fluent in Jula, especially those people who are identified by Ivorians as "Jula"— those who either live in northern Côte d'Ivoire or originate from other northern regions such as parts of southern Burkina Faso, southwest Mali, and northern Guinea.

Fakoly sings in both French and Jula, sometimes in the same song, as is the case in "Promesses de Caméléon." Fakoly told me he chooses which language to sing in "depending on the context" of the message he is attempting to relay. Both French and Jula index larger and very different ideological, social, and historical contexts. What does speaking, or singing, in French or Jula mean in Côte d'Ivoire? While there can be no single answer, it is not difficult to outline some of the larger contexts that Fakoly's linguistic choices implicitly or explicitly reference. Clearly, the strategy of singing in French enables Fakoly to reach his largest possible audience: that of most Ivorians, the rest of Francophone Africa, and the Francophone world generally, including, of course, the lucrative market in France. But a certain amount of ideological and historical baggage is inherent in any use of a colonial language in a postcolonial setting. The widespread fluency and use of French in Côte d'Ivoire can be directly linked to the pro-Western, pro-French economic and ideological program of Houphouët Boigny. At the very least, as in most postcolonial contexts, the colonial language in Côte d'Ivoire is the language of political and economic power (see Perullo and Fenn 2003). And yet French in Côte d'Ivoire has become *so* common that its use and meaning are not as loaded as in other former French colonies. While there are unquestionably ideological and identity-related reasons that Ivorians prefer local languages and choose *not* to speak French in certain contexts, French is taken for granted to the point of minimizing its associations with the colonizer and Houphouët's pro-Western policies. Those associations, in popular music contexts, are far outweighed by the language's ability to maximize the potential market for a popular musician like Fakoly. French is the language of economic and political power, and so to sing in French accords Fakoly the maximum of each, in that it maximizes his potential audience and market and the impact of his attempt to spread his political messages.[10] In Côte d'Ivoire, Fakoly can sing in French without being labeled a colonialist for having done so.

Jula, on the other hand, is undeniably associated with the peoples of the north, and at the time of the release of "Promesses de Caméléon," not to mention in today's divided Côte d'Ivoire, the Jula language has an even more loaded association than in prior times. The word itself, *Jula*, has rather complex meanings and connotations. "Jula" means "trader" in northern Mande languages like Jula, Bamanankan (Bambara), and Maninkakan (Malinké). Again, all immigrants from the savanna and sahel who have settled in central and southern Côte d'Ivoire, and all residents of the north of the country, are identified by other Ivorians as Jula. A small percentage of them actually come from the Jula ethnic region in north central Côte d'Ivoire and southern Burkina Faso, but many belong to other ethnic groups, including non-Mande groups (such as the Gur-speaking Senufo and Mossi). Yet, in part due to their dress (often bubus associated with Islam), northerners are automatically associated with Islam and called "Jula." To further complicate the matter, even converts to Islam who are from the forest region sometimes identify themselves, and are identified by others, as Jula. Simply put, when discussing the hundreds of thousands of various northern peoples of myriad nationalities and ethnicities living in Côte d'Ivoire, northerner=Jula=Muslim.[11]

Therefore, in the context of the present conflict, the language Jula, though widely spoken by many Ivorians, indexes the northern region, meaning the New Forces, and the struggles over Ivoirité and what many northerners see as discriminatory policies of the state. That Fakoly sings a key phrase in Jula, and is himself from the northern town of Odienné, leads many to associate his music with the northern rebels and their concerns. Indeed, Fakoly did sing explicitly in response to Ivoirité in such songs as "Le Descendant." However, he does not see himself as being on either side in the Ivorian conflict. Rather, Fakoly told me that before the war his role was to inform people "that the country was ill, that there was too much injustice, that we must pay attention. They didn't listen to us, so the war broke out." Once the country was at war, Fakoly saw himself as being on the side of peace and reconciliation. Whether the Ivorian audience, and in particular the Ivorian government, saw Fakoly that way is another matter.[12]

Deeper than any current associations of the Jula language with the military and political conflict in the country are the language's roots as a widespread trade language that links its speakers to the Mande world, which has its origins in the ancient Mali Empire. Singing even just one phrase in Jula situates Fakoly as a truly African reggae artist, anchoring him in a local identity, which, ironically, is a key to success in the global world music marketplace (see McLaughlin and McLoone 2000). Furthermore, singing in Jula, Fakoly taps into the large Mande-speaking audience that populates portions of many West African countries, from Senegal in the west to Burkina Faso in the east. Fakoly's Mande language can be simultaneously a language of resistance—it was, after all, the language of Samori Touré, the famous leader of the military resistance to French colonization—and a language that taps into a large market. In other words, Fakoly need not sacrifice his audience in order to resist governmental power and express his regional identity by singing in Jula.

Yet I would suggest that in many cases Fakoly speaks to and reaches different audiences with his lyrics in Jula than he does with his lyrics in French (see Perullo and Fenn 2003: 22). Songs that are primarily or exclusively in Jula are really for the Mande-speaking world, while those in French reach out to all Ivorians and the rest of the Francophone world. A song like "Promesses de Caméléon," however, which is nearly all in French but has a refrain mixing French and Jula, speaks simultaneously to both audiences, a strategic move that maximizes Fakoly's audience but also intertextually references his Mande identity and the ideology of resistance to the discriminatory policies of the Ivorian government.

Choice to Open the Song with an Explicitly Militaristic Motif

A rapid, insistent trumpet line—not unlike a bugle reveille—accompanied by a drum roll crescendo opens "Promesses de Caméléon," musically setting the stage for the protest message to come (see music example below). This reference to military music suggests several meanings simultaneously. Firstly, it functions like a reveille, indexing the long-standing tradition of waking up military troops with a bugle call. It is as if Fakoly were saying to his audience, "Wake up! This is urgent. There is a battle at hand." In conversation with me, Fakoly distanced himself from the military dimension of the Ivorian conflict, and clearly preferred reconciliation and a diplomatic, rather than military, solution to the problem. The troops Fakoly was attempting to rouse were the Ivorian people, and the battle he implored them to fight was of an ideological rather than a military nature. Just as Fakoly chose not to take up arms but rather to employ reggae songs to fight injustice, he asked his audience to become activists for a peaceful solution. And by opening the song with a reveille, Fakoly positioned himself as a general of peace, embracing the identity he had become known for—that of a leader of the conscience of the Ivorian people. The wake-up call might also have been directed toward Gueï himself, whom Fakoly clearly believed needed to be awakened to the tragedy that his misdirected leadership was sure to bring on.

Second, opening the song with a military motif served to characterize Gueï, whose speech begins just seconds later, as a military rather than a political figure. Support for this interpretation can be found in the lyrics of the song itself, which repeatedly ask Gueï not to follow in the footsteps of other African military leaders but to exit the stage quickly, as he had promised to do, and allow a civilian government to take power. Again, in the song's chorus, Gueï is portrayed as a military man; of course, Gueï was a general, and his professional identity prior to the 1999 coup was nothing but that of a military man. Fakoly's military opening suggested the central issue his song would address: the problem of the military, as opposed to elected civilians, running the government. As Fakoly told me, "The music that we make is based on the message" that he endeavors to communicate in any given song. Opening "Promesses de Caméléon" with a military musical motif is a clear example of a musical choice that was informed by the message—the primary focus of Fakoly's songs.

Inclusion of a Recording of a Speech by Junta Leader Robert Gueï

Ethnomusicologist John Collins (1992b: 192), in an article about the anti-hegemonic aspects of African popular music, observes that "usually in African music, political protest against those in power is not direct but oblique." In both traditional and popular musical forms, there is much evidence to support Collins's claim. Indirectness and metaphorical lyrics are common means of expressing discontent and protest in music of Africa. On this point, Tiken Jah Fakoly's music, and in particular "Promesses de Caméléon," stand in stark contrast to the general pattern.[13]

While Fakoly praised his Ivorian reggae predecessors Alpha Blondy and Serges Kassy for having used their music to speak out against injustice, he noted to me that

> they usually sang in parables. What changed when I arrived was that I started to sing "Allez dire aux hommes politiques" [Go tell the politicians, the opening line of his hit "Mangercratie"];[14] that's to say that I directly addressed the politicians. And it's as if I added an ingredient to the sauce, some salt maybe, or no, perhaps there was already salt but there was a little hot pepper missing. So when I came, I added that voice, and it was a great success.

Fakoly was convinced that it was precisely his directness lyrically that had brought him success and fame. He explained,

> That's our role and that's what made us successful. When people see us they say, "Ah! I am happy because you said what I have wanted to say." You see? So that's our role in society. And so we take risks, because in Africa the people have no confidence in politicians, because they say things but never follow through on them. As a result the people want to express their discontentment. But there is no channel through which they can do so.

Fakoly could have left out the recording of Gueï's speech in "Promesses de Caméléon" and his own lyrics would still have been powerfully direct criticism. But the inclusion of Gueï's speech, coupled with the direct and immediate critical sung response to the speech within the same song, is about as far from oblique as one could be. The song takes Gueï to task for precisely what Fakoly mentioned in the quote above—having made promises that he had not followed through on—thus the title, "Promises of the Chameleon." And it is in moments like this that an inter-textual analysis can be so effective in analyzing some of the song's power.

The speech that Fakoly inserted into this song was delivered by Gueï the morning after the coup of December 24, 1999. In this speech, Gueï promised "to sweep out the house," meaning to clean up the political corruption that had plagued the Bédié regime. Many Ivorians took this to mean that, among other things, the mis-guided policy of Ivoirité would finally be laid to rest and that among the results would be a free and fair election, one that would not exclude former prime min-ister Ouattara. Comparing himself with military leaders of other African nations who had seized power and remained at the helm, sometimes for decades, Gueï declared, "We have come to sweep out the house. Once we have put it in order, believe me—I am not a man of power ambitions. Otherwise, I [would] have the same qualities as my brothers in arms in certain other countries." As described above, early in his tenure, Gueï seemed intent simply on overseeing the transi-tion to true democracy, but within just a few short months he was backtracking on those promises. Ten months following the coup and Gueï's speech, the Ivorian people had ample evidence to suggest that Gueï had every intention of manipu-lating the system to remain in power, and Fakoly felt this needed to be expressed publicly. In the song, Fakoly's direct response to the speech first manifests in the haunting refrain, sung by a female chorus: "Military man / remember / you prom-ised us / the people are watching you." Finally, near the end of the song, Fakoly's own voice enters, singing, "Be part of history / By putting civilians in power / Keep your honor / Sweep out the house / Return to your neighborhood / Like you had promised, ohh!" (See transcription and translation below.)

Fakoly explained to me his motivation for recording the song and the reaction he received from the military government:

> In fact when I put out the album *Promesses de Caméléon* [author's note—the al-bum is actually titled *Le Caméléon*], it was under the military regime during a mo-ment when the military was in power and the army was in the streets and all that. . . . The album came out because people didn't want military leaders to be candidates in an election. . . . I had one sole means of expressing myself and that was through my music. I wanted to tell the president not to present himself as a candidate, because [he] had already told the people that he wouldn't do that. . . . I didn't know how to reach the president, so I entered the studio and I put out the album in a rather hasty manner. Then I was threatened over the phone—there were military officers who said that if they saw me, they were going to kill me. There were some who came by my house, but they didn't find me at home, etc. That's when I left Côte d'Ivoire for refuge in Burkina Faso.

Judging by the military regime's reaction, Fakoly's strategy of incorporating the recording of Gueï's speech into his song was an extremely effective means of protesting Gueï's plan to run for office. What made the song so effective was that

Fakoly did not just speak out against the president's words reassuring the public that all was well, but he appropriated those very words and recontextualized them, imbuing them with new meaning—the very opposite meaning—that in fact the country was not well but increasingly unstable. As Fakoly explained, "[In my song] I said the country was ill while on the television every day they made us believe that everything was fine." Herein lies the brilliance of Fakoly's intertextual move: he used the government's own propagandistic text to counter their very message.[15] By reperforming Gueï's speech, Fakoly was boldly assuming his license to do so, which clearly was read as a transgression by the military regime.[16] The result is bone chilling, and it is no wonder that Fakoly began receiving death threats and was forced to flee the country.

An Intertextual Contestation of Power

In Côte d'Ivoire where many people are illiterate or marginally literate, popular music, which transcends the bounds of literacy, emerges as an especially effective means of asserting and contesting political ideologies (Kwaramba 1997: 6). In "Le Descendant," Fakoly resists Ivoirité—the Bédié government's attempt to define Ivorian identity. In "Mangercratie," he contests the same government's portrayal of itself as an administration acting in the best interest of the nation. And in "Promesses de Caméléon," he refuses Gueï's attempt to define himself as a trustworthy leader and a worthy presidential candidate; in this same song, Fakoly defines himself as worthy of leading the Ivorian people's conscience and their ideological battles. By contesting the government's power to define the truth, Fakoly's music stands out as a model case of popular music issuing "serious challenges to hegemonic power" (Garofalo 1992: 2).[17] One of Fakoly's most effective methods in this effort is his deft manipulation of the power of intertextual references.

In "Promesses de Caméléon," Fakoly strategically and forcefully communicated through recontextualization and reference. Fakoly's choice of reggae positioned his message in relation to the larger international movement for economic and political justice and equal rights; his choice of French and Jula indexed some of the issues associated with language politics in Côte d'Ivoire, including the north/south conflict; his choice to open the song with a military musical motif positioned him as a leader calling troops to action and indexed Gueï's military identity; and his incorporation of Gueï's speech appropriated and subverted Gueï's message that all was well under his rule. As is always the case with such intertextual moves, the larger social realities were indexed, and yet the artist's strategic recontextualizing imbued the borrowed texts with new meaning. Just as Dan mask performers in 1990s Côte d'Ivoire borrowed musical, dance, and spiritual elements and recontextualized them for strategic purposes (Reed 2001, 2003), Fakoly's use of intertextual references positioned and strengthened his communicative efforts. His intertextual references strategically drew upon the power of identity-related and ideological associations that rendered his musical contestations of power all the more effective.

"Promesses de Caméléon " [Promises of the Chameleon] by Tiken Jah Fakoly, 2000
Transcribed and translated by Daniel B. Reed

(Tiken Jah, speaking):
Quand un général s'engage
[When a general commits himself]

(Prerecorded voice of Robert Gueï):
Aidez-nous à aider les Ivoiriens et les Ivoiriennes
[Help us to help the Ivorian men and women]

Voilà, mesdammes et messieurs les journalistes,
[There it is—ladies and gentlemen the journalists,]

Ce que je tenais à vous dire,
[That which I am anxious to say to you,]

Pour que les choses soient claires dans les esprits
[So that things may become clear in our minds]

Et que des quiprocos ne puissent pas nous diviser
[And that misunderstandings may not divide us]

Nous sommes venus pour balayer la maison
[We have come to sweep out the house]

Une fois qu'on aura mis de l'ordre, et croyez -moi,
[Once we have put it in order, believe me]

Je ne suis pas un ambitieux du pouvoir
[I am not a man of power ambitions]

Sinon, j'ai les mêmes aptitudes que mes frères d'armes
[Otherwise, I have the same qualities as my brothers in arms]

De certains pays
[In certain other countries]

(Female chorus)
Militairi cè
[Military man]

Rappelle-toi, rappelle-toi, rappelle-toi
[Remember, remember, remember]

Tu nous avais promis
[You promised us]

Rappelle-toi, rappelle-toi, rappelle-toi
[Remember, remember, remember]

Militairi cè
[Military man]

Rappelle-toi, rappelle-toi, rappelle-toi
[Remember, remember, remember]

Le peuple te regarde
[The people are watching you]

(Prerecorded voice of Robert Gueï again):

Que le peuple soit rassuré
[May the people be reassured]

Que les diplomates soient rassurés
[May the diplomats be reassured]

Que nos ambassadeurs, auxquels j'ai expliqué
[May our ambassadors, to whom I explained]

Les détails de ce qui s'est passé,
[The details of what has happened]

Je croix qu'ils comprendront
[I believe they will understand]

Que ce qui est dit actuellement
[That what is said now]

Dans les polices, ne sont que des rumeurs
[Among the police are only rumors]

Nous sommes venus pour faire au mieux
[We have come to do our best]

Pour ques les Ivoiriens puissent effectivement orchestrer
[So that Ivorians may be able to essentially orchestrate]

La bonne politique qui puisse être dans l'intérêt supérieur
[Good politics, in the best interest]

Du pays, pour le bonheur du peuple
[Of the country, for the good fortune of the people]

et pour le salut de la République
[and for the preservation of the Republic (of Côte d'Ivoire)]

(Female chorus)

(Tiken Jah singing):
Rentre dans l'histoire
[Be part of history]

Avec civils au pouvoir
[By putting civilians in power]

Garde ton honneur
[Keep your honor]

Balaye la maison
[Sweep out the house]

Retourne au quartier
[Return to your neighborhood]

Commes tu l'avais promis, ohh!
[Like you had promised, ohh!]

Retourne au village, balaye la maison
[Return to your village, sweep out the house]

Garde ton honneur, le peuple te regarde
[Keep your honor, the people are watching you]

Rentre dans l'histoire, avec civils au pouvoir
[Be part of history by putting civilians in power]

Le peuple te regarde
[The people are watching you]

Comme tu l'avais promis, ohh!
[Like you had promised them]

(Female chorus)

Promesses de Caméléon

Tiken Jah Fakoly

Opening Trumpet Line (notated at pitch)

NOTES

1. I would like to thank Boubacar Diakité for transcribing the text of my interview with Tiken Jah Fakoly; Bakary Sidibé, Boubacar Diakité and Drissa Konè for helping me work through ambiguous aspects of the song's lyrics and translation; and Bakary Sidibé and Fadjinè Konè for helping set up the interview. Translations into English were made by the author.

2. The word *text* is of course central to the concept of intertextuality. Scholars in many disciplines have used this word not just to refer to passages of written or oral language but also to identify the communicative properties of any number of other expressive forms, from fine art to architecture. Popular music scholar Simon Frith (2004: 1) asserts that what is meant by text in popular music varies according to genre, and might include a song, a

record, a performance, or a star. Elsewhere, I have employed the term intertextuality to describe the referencing of sources of disparate origins in the full range of expressive modes in operation in Dan mask performances, including spoken and sung text, other musical sounds, movement, and visual art (Reed 2001, 2003). Similarly, my use of the term *text* in this article will encompass sound and words, and *intertextuality* will indicate the referencing of other sounds, words, and their associated contexts and meanings that Fakoly drew upon in creating "Promesses de Caméléon."

3. The concept of intertextuality has been criticized on the basis that "text" commonly implies a fixed object and that use of this word reduces performance to a one-dimensional fixed thing that can be "read" like a book. While this borrowed term might seem to negate precisely the kind of richness that music has and literature does not, I embrace it here because it so effectively emphasizes the *process* of composition, the strategic choices that make up this process, and by extension, the agency of the artist. Intertextuality emphasizes the notion of music as a communicative medium that, like all communication, is anchored in historical precedents, which are creatively manipulated to express new ideas in the present. Finally, as rich a song as "Promesses de Caméléon" is, the version of the song that I analyze is fixed like a text, in the medium of a commercial recording which, while multidimensional in its combination of words and music, is as static as a book. An intertextual analysis works well to highlight the effectiveness of such an art form.

4. USA State Department, Bureau of African Affairs, "Background Note: Cote d'Ivoire." http://www.state.gov/r/pa/ei/bgn/2846.htm.

5. All Tiken Jah Fakoly quotes come from an interview with the author, Bamako, Mali, 2003. Fakoly was initially drawn to reggae music of artists like Bob Marley and U-Roy during his teen years because of its sound and its danceable beat. Not understanding English, Fakoly was unaware of the meaning of the words of these songs. He explained to me, however, that over time he began asking any English-speaking person he could find to translate reggae songs for him. As he explained to me, "Each time I ran into someone who said 'Hello' in English, I wouldn't let them go until they explained to me what the Jamaicans were saying. So that's how I began to understand what the Jamaican songs are about."

6. From *manger* [to eat] and *cratie* [form of government]. The ambiguous meaning could be taken literally, as a government that puts food on the table, taking care of people's needs or metaphorically (to steal or use inappropriately) as corrupt government.

7. Alpha Blondy's reputation as a proponent of resistance to injustice was to some extent undercut by his relationship with Houphouët (McNee 2002: 239), which led many to label him "Houphouët's griot." Still, Blondy has released many songs critical of various aspects of Ivorian life, including political policies.

8. Technically, the word *militairi* is a Jula-ized French term. This is a common practice in Jula, in which altered French words gradually work their way into Jula vocabulary. Thus the French *militaire* [military] becomes *militairi* in Jula, just as the French *table* [table] becomes *tabali* in Jula.

9. Jula, also spelled Dyula or Dioula, is a language in the northern Mande family, which also includes Bamanankan (Bambara or Bamana) and Maninkakan (Malinké or Maninka) and is essentially mutually intelligible with those languages.

10. A dialect of French that is particularly loaded with ideology and meaning is that which is variously called Nouchi, Street French, Ivorian French, or, pejoratively, Moussa's French. Simon Akindes (2002: 92–93) writes that this French dialect "developed as a me-

108 GRIOTS AND MESSENGERS

dium of communication among illiterate labourers, house servants, shop attendants, and other low-rank workers with little or no formal education, and people originating from Burkina Faso. Currently, it has grown into an urban language nationwide that does not abide by the rules of French grammar, and it incorporates words, sentence structures, images, and forms of expression from local languages. More and more popular songs, plays and comedies, written by literate and illiterate artists alike, use Nouchi for its spontaneity and to reach larger audiences. . . . Nouchi has been pejoratively called *Francais de Moussa* [Moussa's French]. 'Moussa' was used to designate the uneducated Burkinabe laborer because it is a common name among Muslim Northerners in general." Fakoly does not use this dialect in "Promesses de Caméléon."

11. For excellent discussions of the complexities of Jula identity in Côte d'Ivoire, see Launay (1982, 1992).

12. Following Abu-Lughod, I have argued elsewhere (Reed 2005) that in engaging in acts of resistance against hegemonies, agents sometimes unwittingly back up into other hegemonies and are caught in a web of power interrelationships. Fakoly, in speaking out against corruption in the Ivorian government and Ivoirité, by logical extension becomes associated with the New Forces who, as their own dominating force, have controlled the northern half of the country for nearly eight years as of the completion of this writing in summer 2010. Fakoly might have a clear vision of himself as neutral and an advocate for reconciliation, but he cannot control how his audience receives his message.

13. Fakoly, however, is far from the only exception to this rule. Another well-known exception was Nigerian popular musician Fela Anikulapo Kuti, whose lyrics, especially late in his career, were extremely direct, which led to numerous confrontations with the Nigerian government (Olaniyan 2004).

14. "Mangercratie," better known as "On a tout compris," was Fakoly's first smash hit in 1997. It opened with the lines "Allez dire aux hommes politiques / Qu'ils enlèvent nos noms dans leur business / On a tout compris" [Go tell the politicians / That they remove our names in their business / We've understood it all].

15. During the writing of this chapter in May 2006, Neil Young released a song entitled "Let's Impeach the President" (on the album *Living with War,* 2006, Reprise Records), which makes use of the same method as does "Promesses de Caméléon." Young's song opens with a trumpet playing military taps and incorporates bits of speeches by President George W. Bush into his song, in which he directly criticizes Bush for lying about the justification for the war in Iraq, violating the constitution, and failing in leadership.

16. Duranti (1994: 6) asserts that the right to perform certain genres is an indication of power relations in any given context. In other words, not everyone has the license to perform just any genre, and transgressing these social norms can be interpreted as an act of strategic appropriation.

17. Garofalo (1992: 2) asserts that mass expressive culture, such as popular music, can operate as "contested terrain" in which "ideological struggle—the struggle over the power to define—takes place."

Style, Message, and Meaning in Malawian Youth Rap and Ragga Performances

JOHN FENN

Rap music from the United States and ragga from Jamaica feature prominently on the youth cultural landscape of Malawi.[1] As imported urban dance-oriented music with strong global connections to youth demographics, these two genres hold cosmopolitan appeal for Malawian youth. This appeal manifests locally in two important components of rap and ragga culture in Malawi, both of which feed processes of youth identity: style and message. Style comprises both physical and ideological elements. Malawian youth draw on several styles attached to imported rap and ragga while simultaneously reconfiguring them in terms of local contexts (Collins 1992b; Hannerz 1987). Message infuses Malawian youth discourse on rap and ragga, often to the degree that the mere presence of messages overshadows their content. Young Malawians talk about messages they find in imported rap or ragga, and they talk about the messages they put into their original compositions. In both cases, the concept of message is more important than the literal meanings of the words carrying a message. To Malawian rap and ragga performers, messages certainly relate to linguistic meanings of words and phrases, but, more importantly, messages signify various kinds of identities and social practices. In this chapter I investigate the interplay between style and message as found in rap and ragga musical performances from the urban environment of Blantyre, focusing on the messages young singers put in their original lyrics and in the styles they create or embrace. This interplay between style and message undergirds what I call "musical sociality" among youth in the city, ways for building peer networks and identities via participation in popular music cultures. As such, styles and messages are mechanisms of everyday practice and musical performance through which youth negotiate social, economic, and political structures in daily life in Blantyre.[2]

The Rap and Ragga Scene in Blantyre

According to scholars such as Sara Cohen and Will Straw, scenes are social and material entities, as well as "meaningful concepts" within which people engage music (Cohen 1999: 241). Scenes also represent localized manifestations of widespread cultural phenomena, anchoring globalized musical forms such as rap and ragga in particularities of place and group dynamics (Straw 1991; T. Mitchell 2001). The rap and ragga scene in Blantyre in the late 1990s consisted mostly of young males and divided along class lines in ways that differentiated it from other scenes across Malawi. Clothing, language use, and value systems were important elements of the scene, comprising both imported and local streams of influence that merged the visual and the conceptual with the musical. Almost all of the rap and ragga music heard on radio or sold on cassette in Blantyre was of foreign origin (primarily U.S. and Jamaican), while the performed music was local in that youths composed their own lyrics and occasionally their own music.[3]

Blantyre is the largest city in Malawi, and though not the seat of government, it is home to many government offices and ministries. It is the commercial capital, with manufacturing and goods distribution based either in Blantyre itself or in the conjoined city of Limbe; together these two places form an urban cosmopolitan entity. As home to the national radio stations, practically all of the private radio stations, and, most recently, the national television station, Blantyre is a key site for media in Malawi. Many of the recording studios in the country can be found there, and the cassette duplication industry is based there as well. Several of the country's popular musicians live in the area and often have standing gigs at hotels and bars in the city. Blantyre is also the distribution center for a large number of recordings and other music-related products, such as posters or videos. Consequently, items often unavailable elsewhere in Malawi can be had in the markets, shops, and street stalls of Blantyre or Limbe. By virtue of the city's position in the cultural and commercial matrix of Malawi, youths living there have potentially had more ready access to the cultural material—sonic, visual, and biographical—of rap and ragga music than their peers spread throughout the country.[4] Blantyre, therefore, has been central to the growth in popularity for rap and ragga in both its imported and local manifestations.

The rap and ragga scene in Blantyre consists of several facets that extend beyond primary activities of listening to and performing music, such as fashion, language, and worldviews (or value systems). These facets interlock, forming a musical culture extensive throughout Malawi, yet differentiated in specific places by a range of factors connected to locale (urban vs. rural), class (elite vs. poor), and gender (see Fenn 2004). Rap and ragga denote "youth," with a large portion of fans and performers being of school age; there are many college-age participants, because Blantyre is the site of one campus in the University of Malawi system.[5] Following a general pattern in Malawi, the scene in Blantyre in the 1990s was overwhelmingly male, especially when it came to public performance. Such male dominance reflected broader patterns in popular music production as well as the near-exclusive appearance of male performers in the corpus of imported rap and ragga available in Malawi (see Gilman and Fenn 2006).

Sounds, Styles, and Identity

Youth in Blantyre rarely listened to locally produced rap and ragga recordings, in part because these were not readily available on the market, but also because imported music held greater cosmopolitan appeal and carried higher status. The bulk of available listening material, then, consisted of rap from the United States and ragga from Jamaica (or the UK).[6] Private and state-run radio stations stocked their playlists with recent songs by foreign rap and ragga artists, and cassette vendors on the street and in markets displayed pirated tapes by U.S. and Jamaican stars. In addition to providing a soundtrack of sorts, radio broadcasts and commercial cassettes also proved to be the source of instrumental backing tracks used in rap and ragga competitions. A significant portion of the rap heard in Malawi stemmed from the genre of gangsta rap, as the diverse styles and subgenres of hip hop culture in the United States were not necessarily known in Malawi. While rap has been present in Malawi since the late 1980s, it only gained widespread public acceptability and accessibility following the shift to multiparty democracy the country underwent in 1994. A general liberalizing of society, as well as a policy of economic liberalization, enabled a flood of imported music into the cassette market. As gangsta rap was one of the most popular subgenres in the United States during the early and mid-1990s, it was poised for worldwide distribution through legal and illegal channels. Pirated copies of second-generation gangsta rappers such as Tupac Shakur, Notorious B.I.G., and Snoop Doggy Dogg were widely available at cassette stalls throughout Malawi in the years immediately following the democratic transition, and the popularity of this handful of artists cemented gangsta rap in Malawian youth consciousness as the aesthetic model for fans and performers throughout the country. Other non-gangsta artists, such as Will Smith or Busta Rhymes, provided some diversity to rap music heard in Malawi, largely due to airplay on radio stations or, in Smith's case, exposure garnered through film projects. Given the overwhelming prominence of gangsta rap in Malawi and the lack of access to many resources for information on the history of the genre, many youths in Blantyre know little of rap produced before Tupac Shakur started his solo career in the early 1990s.

Beyond the sonic, though, these imports contributed important visual and conceptual components to a range of youth identities connected to rap and ragga. Imported music provided material for gangsta or rude boy identities via "style," for example. Body language and postures copied from magazines, music videos, and posters became ways of moving for young males in Blantyre that signaled to their peers they were part of and knew about rap or ragga. A related realm of visual communication tied in to imported rap and ragga musical culture was clothing. Contemporary urban fashions such as baggy trousers, heavy sneakers or work boots, and oversized T-shirts constituted the uniform of choice for fans and performers alike in Malawi. The manner in which an individual's particular set of clothes came together—used clothing vendors, upscale boutique shops, hand-me-downs—depended on social and economic class, and so a range of brands, quality, and styles were acknowledged as appropriate clothing for sartorial expression of rap and ragga participation.

Urban imagery associated with rap and ragga extended to language use, with youths often adopting American accents associated with black speech patterns in the United States or vernacular speech stemming from Jamaican English. As one of two official languages of Malawi, English is taught in primary school and is the language of instruction at the secondary level, so most youth have some proficiency with English.[7] Class and gender add dynamics to the issue of English proficiency that reflect broad patterns of social stratification in Blantyre (and Malawi in general). Males are more likely to complete secondary school and work or socialize in situations that encourage English language skills. Youth of either gender who come from upper classes in Blantyre (political and economic elite, middle class) are likely to have extensive (and sometimes private) education as well as a wider range of access to models for English language usage, such as music videos, travel, and overseas living.

Interwoven with fashion and language were value systems that youths throughout Malawi constructed from the cultural material of imported rap and ragga. These value systems reflected elements such as overt consumerism associated with hip hop in the United States (e.g., emphasis on material possessions and money), but were far from simple internalizations of attitudes or worldviews gleaned from foreign recordings, magazines, and videos. The value systems I encountered were more hybrid, combining and recombining bits of localized experience and cultural framework with imported (and reinterpreted) manifestations of modernity, globalized youth culture, or status. These emergent value systems anchored in musical culture and practice became bases for lifestyles or musical "pathways" available to Malawian youth (Fenn 2004).[8]

Performing Local Music: The Rap and Ragga Competition

The most prevalent public performance opportunity for rap and ragga artists in Blantyre during my fieldwork (1999, 2000) was the rap and ragga competition, and at these events the various components of the rap and ragga scene were onstage. Though recognized as distinct genres by fans and performers alike throughout Malawi, an important set of relationships held between rap and ragga due in large part to competitions. Many youths found musical parallels between the genres, often articulated with reference to "heavy" beats, the strong presence of bass frequencies, and the spoken quality of the vocals. Second, competitions were always billed as "rap and ragga" competitions and could be found in Malawi's larger urban centers as well as some smaller towns. The high frequency with which they occurred in Blantyre was related to at least two important factors: the city's musically dense environment, and the large number of sponsoring organizations for competitions. For the most part competitions were sponsored by nongovernmental organizations (NGOs), often locally based but funded with international donor money. These organizations generally focused on particular issues (e.g., HIV/AIDS) or constituencies (e.g., youth) and targeted their projects accordingly. Rap and ragga competitions were useful as a means of attracting attendees to NGO events, sitting at the overlap of promotional devices and participatory events. That is, youths would often go to an event because of a competition and were thereby exposed to the sponsoring NGO's program. As such, there was an important connection between NGO sponsorship of competitions and the messages in Malawian rap and ragga.

An ideal structure for a typical rap and ragga competition existed, especially in discourse about the events. In practice there were many variations on the ideal, and perspectives on these variations themselves varied depending on a given individual's or group's final ranking; people who won were more likely to be satisfied that a given competition met expected standards than those who failed to make it to the prize round. One significant source of disagreement among youth about the ideal or normal structure for competitions arose from the relationships between the two genres, rap and ragga, within the competition. Participants held strong convictions about whether or not rap artists and ragga artists should compete separately or against each other, but many fans and performers in Malawi connected the two genres. A group such as C.O.B. Connection elided the problem of genre by successfully folding both styles into their performances.

Conflicting evaluations by youth participants aside, a rap and ragga competition in Blantyre involved several core elements. An appropriate venue was a necessity, often a nightclub or other public space that housed or could accommodate a sound system and had adequate space for performance and dancing. The element of time was also important: all competitions took place during the afternoon hours on a weekend. The afternoon timeframe was especially significant in the cases where the venue was a nightclub. Nightclubs and bars are not youth-oriented spaces, and holding competitions at them after nightfall would directly contradict the goals of youth-oriented NGOs. Daytime eradicates (or at least mediates) the negative associations with nightspots. Weekends allow for those attending school to participate (Gilman and Fenn 2006).

Another important element was the structure of the event as a competition. This structure consisted of a period for contestants to register, often while music played in the background and attendees danced or socialized; an initial round of single-elimination performance; and a final round from which judges selected the top performing acts (often three) to receive prizes—cash as well as hats, T-shirts, and posters promoting the NGO or cause associated with the competition.

A significant element of rap and ragga competitions was the broad cast of participants. Competitors were primary figures, but the audience was often just as important. Consisting of close friends of competitors, other artists registered to compete, and the more general peer group of youth in the rap and ragga scene, the audience was the intended recipient of messages in the lyrics. Other participants included the judges and the deejay responsible for playing each group's instrumental backing track.[9] Often individuals somehow associated with the organization sponsoring a competition, judges served as targets for disgruntled artists' complaints and were therefore a common source of tension in the discourse of competitions among Blantyre youth.

Beyond these competitions there were essentially no other performance opportunities for youth in Blantyre, indeed, for the entire Malawian rap and ragga scene. Therefore, these events are central to youth culture, providing artists with opportunities to disseminate messages in a heightened context ripe with processes of identity construction and expressive practice. Thus, even though individual competitions could fall short of participants' expectations, the general category of competition as a cultural performance provided a vital interpretive frame for youth with regard to creating identities and strategies for navigating their surroundings.[10] Blantyre, as a cosmopolitan urban center rich with media and music, provided an environment dense with the current political, economic, and social dynamics radiating throughout the whole country. And it was within this environment that competitions operated as performance events, peer gatherings, political soapboxes, and identity forges. I now turn to the interplay of message and meaning as filtered through the style and performances of a particular group: the C.O.B. Connection.

Education, Entertainment, and Message: The C.O.B. Connection

Formed in the 1990s, the C.O.B. Connection was a loose collective of small performing groups from the neighborhood of Chilobwe, a high-density area in the hills south of downtown Blantyre. Busy and relatively poor, though by no means destitute, Chilobwe claims a market, a raucous minibus depot, and hundreds of homes dotting the hillside. Office workers, school teachers, and market vendors lived alongside partially employed and unemployed residents, as Chilobwe simultaneously reflected the social economic diversity of Blantyre and the growing divide between the rich and the working poor.

All members of the C.O.B. Connection called the neighborhood home, often referring to it as their "ghetto" in line with the popularity of the term in North American hip hop vernacular. The name they chose for their group underscored their identification with the area: "C.O.B" was a common abbreviation for Chilobwe, and "Connection" highlighted the rhizomorphic structure of the group as well as the shared residential links. Membership in the group hovered near twelve individuals (all male) in the late 1990s, but this was a flexible number. There was a core membership—present at all the interviews and meetings we held, as well as all the performances I observed—that consisted of three individuals: Meckai B, Red Gun, and Mad Ghost.

This group moved through a scene in Blantyre characterized by several perspectives on and interpretations of rap and ragga.[11] Members of the group specialized in either rap or ragga singing, but in performances they merged the two genres to create an idiosyncratic sound that often set them apart from other artists. They eschewed extremely popular imagery such as "gangsta" or "thug" embraced by their peers in the Blantyre scene, often distancing themselves from such styles of urban toughness by emphasizing their collective interest in educating through musical performance.

The C.O.B. Connection made the most of limited performance opportunities to pursue a twofold mission. One component of the group's mission was to promote Chilobwe as a home for rap and ragga talent. A core member of the group, Meckai B, told me that prior to the formation of the C.O.B. Connection, people— emcees from other neighborhoods, competition organizers, peers in general— did not think of Chilobwe in terms of rap and ragga singing. But now, he explained, "people know Chilobwe is a place where our rhythms can flow. People know C.O.B.," indicating that the group's public performances at competitions had brought notoriety to the neighborhood. Members of the group embraced their name as a unifying element, a way to indicate that they were all part of the Chilobwe scene and, consequently, were a "family." In various reports by members about the group's history and goals, the theme that most often emerged was one of peer solidarity based in place. The C.O.B. hung together for each other, to promote their musical abilities in rap and ragga and to celebrate their "ghetto" as an important place in the Blantyre scene. They did this by enveloping the place in the name of their group and in their performances—they always sang as inhabitants of Chilobwe, as voices from up "on the hill." As Red Gun expressed in an interview, "Everybody does represent [Chilobwe]. I and him, when we play music, we register 'C.O.B.' Him and him: 'C.O.B.'" explaining that when any combination of group members performed at a competition they signed up under the C.O.B. Connection moniker.

The second component of the C.O.B. mission related more directly to the concept of messages. They defined themselves as rap and ragga singers in terms of both entertainment and education, with peers as their target audience. Red Gun stated in an interview, "In all the songs I have composed, there is no song just for fun. I'm trying to educate somebody. Myself, I'm an educator. I'm a musician, but I'm an educator, right? Educate the youth, because 'education is the key, that's why we pay the fee.'" The concluding phrase quotes Red Gun's own lyrics and illustrates the kinds of messages C.O.B. members put into their lyrics, messages intersecting with the nascent youth identity politics tied to social issues and power dynamics impacting Malawian youth.

Discourse and Messages: The Politics
of Identity and Performance

The thematic spread of the messages C.O.B. embedded in their discourse through lyrics or embodied verbal performance covered concerns of Malawian youth or concerns the group felt their peers should have: HIV/AIDS, poverty and truancy, and political woes such as corruption and the economic gap between high government officials and citizens. The C.O.B. Connection hoped that by spreading such messages through musical performance they would foster unity and knowledge within their peer group. The use of rap and ragga was central to this goal for two reasons. First, members of the C.O.B., along with many others that I spoke to, identified rap and ragga as youth-oriented; these were heard all over the country, and young people were the primary consumers and producers of the musical culture. Second, the members of the C.O.B. were solid fans and practitioners of both rap and ragga. They believed in the music as a tool for communicating messages because they were heavily invested in the music. Following the stars, songs, and stories of rap and ragga from the United States and Jamaica as closely as they were able—and trying to stay as true as possible to what they interpreted as core authentic elements for each genre—constituted central processes of identity creation. It is at this nexus of social practice and musical performance that a youth identity politics emerges, with members of the C.O.B. Connection employing rap and ragga performance as a way to generate awareness, if not effect change, among Malawian youth. Paying attention to their immediate surroundings in Chilobwe, as well as the broader contexts of Blantyre and Malawi, the C.O.B. crew set out to engage the power structures around them through their music. Folded into their attempts to educate and entertain was a nascent political consciousness hinged on a dialectic of identity—as youth, rap and ragga performers, fans, students, friends, and Malawians—and practice.

The C.O.B Connection's youth identity politics did not explicitly refer to an agenda they adhered to, nor did they present themselves as active in ways normally thought of as political in Malawi.[12] However, there were several aspects of the group's shared attitudes and actions that led me to interpret their collective perspective as youth identity politics, especially in relation to broader power relations and structures in Malawian society. A portion of this youth politics had to do with the discourse of cohesion embraced by the C.O.B. From the name of the group to the rhetoric of family often used by members in discussing the C.O.B. Connection to the manner in which they approached competition performances as a unit, the group espoused cohesion as a political dynamic and praxis. Members of the group explicitly disagreed with divisive discourse attached to gangsta perspectives on rap in Malawi, routinely manifested in "eastside/westside" allegiances that youth in Blantyre professed in accordance with the prevalence of such divisions in media discussions of rappers from the United States. Instead, the C.O.B.

Connection articulated a group position anchored in the idea that youth in Blantyre, and Malawi more generally, needed to stand together to acknowledge and propose solutions for social concerns. The messages in their lyrics were public-service announcements to this effect, encouraging their peers to take responsibility for their own lives as part of a group: Malawian youth.

Another factor behind the concern with youth issues that defined C.O.B. identity politics, in addition to influencing the messages in the group's lyrics and their performance opportunities, was the handful of NGOs dedicated to Malawian youth. These organizations functioned largely as education agents, focusing on health-oriented and behavioral concerns such as HIV/AIDS, drinking, and drugs. Youth NGOs also dealt with civic education, dispensing information on voting rights or the responsibilities of citizens. An NGO such as Blantyre-based Youth Arm Organization was a local entity, based in Malawi and staffed by Malawians. Funding by international NGOs, such as Save the Children or foreign donor organizations such as USAID, was in the form of soft money, meaning that budgets were always tight and NGOs often disappeared after short periods of operation. Many survived, though, due to the determination of staffers and agents in the international funding institutions. Partnering with the Malawi government, which mainly meant seeking economic assistance, usually involved navigating a bureaucratic quagmire and was rarely fruitful for local NGOs of any sort.

The overwhelming emphasis of youth NGOs was HIV/AIDS education and prevention. The organizations distributed posters and pamphlets, coordinated support groups or clubs in schools, helped put on dramas about HIV/AIDS, and sponsored rap and ragga competitions. In Blantyre, these competitions occurred much more frequently than in other locations in Malawi, and the members of groups such as the C.O.B. Connection participated as often as possible. There was a strong connection between NGO-sponsored competitions and youth-conscious rap and ragga lyrics such as those embraced by the C.O.B. Connection. A common requirement for participating in competitions was that lyrics addressed the theme around which the event was organized, usually HIV/AIDS awareness. In the years since the advent of multiparty democracy in Malawi (1994), NGOs and public discourse about HIV/AIDS proliferated, and a feedback loop developed that encompassed youth desire to perform at competitions as well as practical constraints on their lyrical themes. That is, if youths wanted to compete, then they had to sing about HIV/AIDS, even if it was not something with which they were personally concerned. The result of this feedback loop was that some youths ended up singing about HIV/AIDS just so they could participate; others took the issue to heart. This analysis may overly polarize the situation, as my research did not focus on HIV/AIDS among youth. My ideas here stem from what individuals told me and what they rapped in their verses—domains of discourse that may have varied significantly from actual behavior or social practice. Since I was not explicitly investigating how, if at all, behavior related to lyrics or messages, it is difficult to posit anything beyond the possibility of a link between lyrics and identity politics embraced by performers.

Self-awareness was another root of the youth identity politics that enveloped C.O.B. Connection lyrics and performance. This self-awareness arose from individual life experiences as well as peer group interactions. Members of the group held strong and nuanced notions of who they were—as individuals and as a collective—and how they fit into the world around them. They often positioned themselves as educators for their peers, taking on a type of substantive social-moral role not common in the Blantyre rap and ragga scene. Of the many styles that emerged from rap and ragga coming into Malawi from outside—gangstas, monied thugs, playas, rude-boys—members of the C.O.B. Connection embraced one that was not very prominent: educators. Socially conscious figures in both rap and ragga have been a presence on the U.S., UK, and Jamaican scenes, but their music has had low public and commercial profiles. And commercial success in the United States or UK has been a key determinant of which styles flow into countries such as Malawi (legally or otherwise). C.O.B. Connection members, then, were not familiar with the more conscious/education-oriented rap produced in the United States over the past decade or two by artists such as Poor Righteous Teachers, Roots, or Lyrics Born. Therefore, while members of the C.O.B. Connection did not have specific role models in developing their "conscious" style, other youth in Blantyre invested in the "gangsta" style turned to artists such as Tupac Shakur or Notorious B.I.G. as cultural blueprints of sorts. Members of the C.O.B. Connection, such as Red Gun or Mad Ghost, were familiar with one or two popular ragga artists from Jamaica known for singing conscious lyrics, and they would connect themselves to these stars by calling attention to a shared predilection for delivering "messages" in songs. The concept of messages served as a cohesive agent in the formation of identity, in this case providing a skeleton for style that intersected with conscious rap and ragga at a global level. This style constituted an interpretive frame for the surrounding social environment of Blantyre. The peer educator style reinforced relationships between message and identity in musical performance. Unwrapping this idea requires a brief discussion of the concept of style I am developing.

Borrowing from Dell Hymes's 1974 work on ways of speaking, I take style to be a way of doing something. Admittedly broad, this description of style focuses analysis on the goals of expressive practice rather than its aesthetic details, which are often associated with discussion of style, instead asking what should be done. This refocus of analysis strikes a balance between what should be considered two facets of style—the "how" and the "why" of doing something—and highlights what I believe is an important dynamic at play: style is both product and process. In approaching style, then, it is important to think about the motivations behind an action as well as the way that action can be evaluated aesthetically. In addition to Hymes, I draw on Dick Hebdige and Raymond Williams in formulating this notion of style. From Hebdige I absorb the important distinction between style as surface-level appearance (aesthetics, again) and style as a tool people use to make meaning and identity visible through symbolic display—material and/or kinetic (Hebdige 1979). It is in the tension between these two levels of style that practice becomes coded as significant, and people rely on style to identify and differentiate themselves in relation to others. And from Williams I derive the connection between style as a general set of observable characteristics and style as the experience of social life, what he refers to as "structures of feeling" (R. Williams 1977: 128–32). Here the "observable characteristics" are similar to Hebdige's "surface-level appearance" or what I refer to as aesthetics above, while Williams's notion of "experience of social life" bridges Hebdige's notion of a "conceptual tool" and Hymes's idea that style is a "way of doing something," or what I called practice. Style for Williams, then, is a way of doing something but also a way of interpreting the experience of doing it in a world populated by others.

As I use the term, style is a constellation of aesthetic and performative elements that comprises a way of doing something. In the case of the C.O.B. Connection, that "something" was ultimately navigation of the dynamic nested in the social environs of Chilobwe, Blantyre, and Malawi. They used style—collectively and individually—to map the world around them as they made their way through it. Style operated as a catalyst for interpretation of social life at the same time that it emerged from experience, as the youth involved with C.O.B. crafted idiosyncratic styles that converged in a group style. The C.O.B. group style, anchored in the education-entertainment dynamic they often articulated to me, emerged from members' individual pathways through life in Blantyre as school-age males living under the shadow of HIV/AIDS, economic insecurity, and corrupt power structures. Their collective and individual perspectives fueled their efforts to interpret and comment on their surroundings with the goal of informing their peers about problems and ways to avoid them. The expressive form the C.O.B. chose for articulating their messages—the pairing of rap and ragga—was an entertaining and popular musical phenomenon that they also saw as a tool for education. The C.O.B. was not alone in investing rap and ragga with moral weight, but their ability to articulate the twin goals of entertaining *and* educating their peers stood out in my fieldwork. Their style, then, was a way of moving through the world around them, making sense of it for themselves and their peers, "doing something" that they believed in, and, despite little chance of economic reward, pursuing it as if it were a career.

From perspectives on rap and ragga as imported musical forms, members of the C.O.B. Connection traded on each other's understanding, knowledge, and experience in order to figure out where they stood and how they could stand together. The stage at a rap and ragga competition served as one site where they could do this publicly, enacting group cohesion and generating meanings through style. Here "meaning" is more than the literal level of messages served to peers, as it also encompasses identity as the symbolic presence of individuals and group in the world. Thus style as a component of identity connected onstage performance with offstage life. Messages and the way youths talked about them contributed to identity and musical sociality in public space, constituting practice while simultaneously representing the world through lyrics and performance (cf. Berger and Del Negro 2004: 3–20).

Of Meanings, Mediations, and Messages

In considering relationships between identity, meaning, and message as delineated through performance at competitions, I am concerned with overlapping bands of signification rather than absolute meaning. There is a semantic layer for messages, but there is also a social layer that emerges through the particularities of performance. This layer is multifaceted, with identity being one important element carried through style and performance. Other important facets of meaning—some of which intersect processes of identity creation and maintenance—imbricate notions of cultural capital (Bourdieu 1984), status, and position in the everyday environment, moving us beyond the immediate scope of this chapter but indicating trajectories for further thought on the subject.

For youth in the Blantyre rap and ragga scene, the intersection of messages and musical performance involves significant expressive practice. Competitions represent the most common site for this intersection, and members of the C.O.B. Connection actively disseminated their messages at competitions.[13] Peers, such as fellow artists and other youth in the audience, were the intended recipients for the group's messages, and the themes that the C.O.B. explored were almost always issues of concern to young Malawians, like HIV/AIDS, poverty, corruption, or lack of employment. One level of meaning in the messages had to do with these themes. Whether the message in a song was a warning about HIV/AIDS or a critique of corruption, audience members could engage the first-order denotation of the message through semantic understanding. That is, they would hear the sung words, interpret them, and generate some sort of response: disagreement, confirmation, dismissal, internalization. When youth in Blantyre discussed messages—whether in their own songs or imported rap and ragga—it was this order of meaning that situated the concept as central to the importance of the music.

The peer-generated significance of the message concept, while certainly intertwined with the semantic import of messages, offered a distinct analytical window onto context and what I refer to above as musical sociality. The concept of messages, as opposed to their semantic content, served as a vehicle for musical sociality, that is, for group cohesion based in musical practice that provided youths with interpretive frameworks for the world around them. Rap and ragga artists, represented here by the C.O.B. Connection, rallied around the notion of messages by discursively constructing the concept as meaningful, often without explicitly elaborating on the particular content of a given message. Thus there was consensus throughout the Blantyre scene (and in Malawi as a whole) that "messages" were central to rap and ragga. The broader recognition of messages as important often led to more narrow groupings, as young performers and fans allied themselves to particular kinds of messages: celebration of one's neighborhood or peer group, valuing of family or traditional culture, or expressing concern about widespread problems being a few examples. Narrower group cohesion emerged as youth forged politically motivated styles and identities around themes they felt morally compelled to educate their peers on via performance: political corruption and economic insecurity, the plight of orphans, and explicit warnings about behavior linked to HIV/AIDS (sex, drug and alcohol use).

To say that young rap and ragga performers or fans at competitions were often more concerned with the presence of messages than the messages themselves by no means implies that Malawian youth did not grasp or articulate lyrical messages. In the context of competitions, it was more important that performers had messages in their songs than that those messages were explicitly articulated in evaluating performance. Knowing about frameworks represented a kind of knowledge that carried cultural capital in rap and ragga scenes throughout Malawi, particularly so in Blantyre where the density of the media environment surrounding those genres heightened or intensified perspectives on them. These perspectives, in turn, helped youth construct identity, make sense of their social environments, and connect to immediate peers as well as imagined communities. Messages, then, were part of a cascade of symbolic communication stemming from rap and ragga musical practices in Blantyre.

Within the context of competitions, intersections of message and meaning are thrown into relief by tension between impact and intent. On the side of impact, questions can be posed about whether or not youth-oriented messages in rap and ragga songs actually do anything to educate, warn, or otherwise affect individuals who hear the songs. Behavioral impact is difficult to measure directly, and it falls beyond the reach of my research, but it is important to note that this is a kind of meaning aligned with the semantic layer discussed above. A message might have meaning for a youth if he or she hears it at a competition and goes on to recognize a connection between the message and his or her lifestyle, as in the case of HIV/ AIDS. This kind of meaning stays close to the individual and, in many ways, defies sharing. Impact of messages is not, however, the only trajectory for meaning in rap and ragga performances in Blantyre.

Just as impact of messages in rap and ragga songs is difficult to measure, so is intent of the performers. As I noted above, participants at competitions in Blantyre often sang about certain topics so as to meet entrance qualifications posted by the sponsoring organizations. However, intent was a key element in the way members of the C.O.B. positioned themselves in relation to their peers. They based their styles and identities on the dynamic of education and entertainment that infused their music. And for the group, intent undergirded performance, especially public performance on the competition stage. Comments by Meckai B and Red Gun concerning the reasons young singers might enter a competition recurred in our interviews. Some youths simply wanted to hear their own voices, some wanted to "boost" themselves or brag, and some wanted to embrace a style such as gangsta that was not "real," according to members of the C.O.B. Connection, because it had little connection to the world in which they lived.

The C.O.B. Connection worked with several well-articulated intentions: to educate, entertain, and bring attention to talent in the Chilobwe area. By no means did they think themselves the only youth in Blantyre who had such intentions, for they often spoke of other groups and individuals they respected as emcees that combined talent and messages. After a particularly controversial competition, Meckai B told me that there were many artists there who knew "how to flip" (sing rap or ragga), but who also had good messages; he respected their technique as well as their intentions. In a group discussion we had after another competition, Meckai B critiqued a peer's performance that consisted largely of rapping about his prowess as a rapper. Meckai B summed up the performance by saying, "His style may be good, but his message was not." He did not isolate a particular message—such as the rapper boasting—but instead based his critique in a good/bad polarity, with the implication being that there was in fact a message in the song but not one with any redeeming qualities. Intent served as an evaluative measure spanning meaning of the words and significance of the performance.

The tension between impact and intent is not resolved by arguing that groups such as the C.O.B. Connection wanted to educate their peers with messages in their songs and should therefore be lauded for taking a strong stand on youth-oriented issues. Questions of impact touch on a range of issues: the limited scope of the audience, as competitions generally attract fifty to seventy-five attendees and the performers are rarely heard outside the competition context; effectiveness of NGO programs on issues such as HIV/AIDS (infection rates in Malawi continue to be quite high on a global scale); or shifting power structures, as the ongoing experiment with multiparty democracy in Malawi continues to yield economic disparity and social change to be faced in the near future by younger generations.

Conclusion

My interest in the tension between impact and intent within the context of rap and ragga competitions has less to do with behavior that responds to the literal messages and more to do with the layers of meaning and message found in practices that I have outlined above. In that the C.O.B. Connection intended to educate and entertain with their performances, their performances entailed another sort of intention, more tacit and abstract. In focusing on messages, C.O.B. members inscribed identity through participation in rap and ragga musical culture; their messages were at once dialogue with peers and statements about who the group members believed themselves to be. This process of identity creation and maintenance served to give C.O.B. members firm ground to stand on together while everything shifted around them. The group cohesion around the concept of messages became one significant element of the styles embraced by the C.O.B. Connection as well as many of their peers. Style ultimately helped these youth navigate the economic, political, social, and cultural structures of daily life in Blantyre.

Focusing on the performative practices of a particular group of individuals foregrounds the ways that the concept of messages underscored a sociality rooted in styles encompassing youth identity politics as mediated through musical performance. Ongoing change in Malawi accelerated by a shift to multiparty democracy in 1994 refracts through institutions, issues, and experiential frameworks with high profile such as HIV/AIDS, the economy, the government, and foreign donor aid. These forces impact the daily lives of Malawian youth in various ways, and young performers draw on these forces as themes for lyrics. Rarely political in the explicit sense that they call for formal action or actively promote platforms, these lyrics engage broad power dynamics in that they are efforts on the part of the performers to make sense of the surrounding social, political, economic, and cultural environment. The C.O.B. Connection, for example, explicitly emphasized themes such as HIV/AIDS, corruption, or poverty as central to the messages they disseminated to their peers via musical performance. By doing so, they engaged in an ongoing cycle of identity creation and maintenance that provides stable ground from which to interpret or make sense of the shifting structures around them.

In 2004, when I returned to Blantyre for some follow-up fieldwork, the scene had changed. Many of the youths I worked with during my earlier visits were no longer involved with rap and ragga, often despite the many "promises" they had made never to turn away from the music they loved. Some had been "born again" and therefore viewed rap and ragga in a negative light; some had moved on to other musical forms, seeking financial return that would not come with local rap and ragga; and others had taken on more adult responsibilities, such as jobs and families. While I was not able to locate all the youths I worked with, even all the members of the C.O.B., those that I did talk to echoed each other in describing a scene that featured far fewer competitions. Studio work was still popular, though as before young artists recording rap and ragga were doing it primarily for their own consumption. So while I would not emphatically state that the scene has died, rap and ragga had lower public profiles in 2004 than they did at the turn of the millennium. Circumstances had changed, for individuals and Malawian society on the whole, catalyzing shifts in musical style and performance embraced by youths in the ongoing construction of meanings and identities.[14]

NOTES

1. An urban dance music connected to dancehall culture in Jamaica, ragga is essentially reggae made with digital instruments (Barrow and Dalton 1997: 273). Also see Stolzoff (2000) for a discussion of ragga, dancehall, and "gun talk" or hardcore lyrics. Youth in

Malawi are most familiar with hardcore ragga stars such as Shabba Ranks and Buju Banton, who have characteristic vocal styles that hover somewhere between singing and rapping.

2. Two important texts in my thinking on this central point have been Margaret Drewal's 1991 article, "State of Performance in Africa," and the recent collection of essays by Harris Berger and Giovanna Del Negro (2004). Drewal makes a strong case for studying performance as an integral part of social life in African contexts, urging researchers to investigate the many ways that individuals forge experience and meaning through performance. Berger and Del Negro's book provides a wide-ranging set of reflections on the intersection of identity, practice, and what they cogently articulate as the interpretive domain of the "everyday." Specifically, see 19–20 and 125–57 in the collection for passages I draw on.

3. There is a prominent local music industry in Blantyre based on cassette sales and live performance by artists playing reggae, gospel, and what is often called "Malawi sounds" or local pop. Local rap and ragga have little market appeal and are therefore not commercially viable, for a variety of reasons ranging from the aesthetic to the economic.

4. Lilongwe, the political capital of Malawi and the second largest city, presents a slight exception to Blantyre's dominance of the cultural material aspects of rap and ragga. As of June 2004, young performers in Blantyre reported to me that Lilongwe had become an important center for rap and ragga, but radio stations and recording studios are still found largely in Blantyre.

5. The Polytechnical College of the University of Malawi is in Blantyre, while the main campus of the system is in Zomba, some 40 km away.

6. With rare exceptions, youths record original rap and ragga at local studios almost exclusively for their private consumption. One of the few commercially successful ragga artists of the past decade in Malawi was San B, a young producer and singer who released an album in 2002 that brought local ragga high visibility for several months. This artist quickly shifted styles after this record, releasing a gospel album next. This combination of recording for private consumption and genre-switching by pop musicians in Malawi deserves further examination yet moves beyond the scope of this chapter.

7. Chichewa is the other official language of Malawi. See Perullo and Fenn (2003) for a comparative discussion of language choice and usage in Tanzanian and Malawian hip hop.

8. Ruth Finnegan develops the notion of "musical pathways" in her 1989 book, *The Hidden Musicians.* I borrow and adapt it, as her robust idea proves to be useful in explaining the many ways that musical practice intersects social life.

9. The "instrumental," as it was called by all rap and ragga performers I worked with, was usually an instrumental backing track found on many commercially available cassettes by U.S. rap stars or Jamaican ragga singers. There was not a large diversity of instrumentals available, and not every performer owned one, so the same tracks were often heard several times at a given competition. Some artists had custom-made backing tracks that they obtained from recording studios in Blantyre; these were much more expensive and therefore quite rare.

10. I use the term *cultural performance* in accordance with the definition put forward by Milton Singer (1972).

11. As developed by Ulf Hannerz (1987) in his work on creolization, a perspective comprises a position from which an individual interprets and reconfigures cultural influences.

This position is itself influenced by the social and cultural environment within which the individual lives. I draw on Hannerz's formulation in order to emphasize that youth in Blantyre are always interpreting imported rap and ragga from the frame of their own life experiences.

12. The term *political* in Malawi immediately conjures up the realm of formal state politics for most people and is not a type of activity that many people would tie themselves to given the ways power differentials have manifested themselves in the context of the past two elections. Instead, I invoke a broader definition of *political* as awareness of and engagement with general power dynamics. For an instructive discussion of this definition in relation to popular music, see Balliger (1999).

13. While competitions are the primary performance context, and therefore the most common way for artists to disseminate messages, some youth do produce recordings of their songs. There are two significant obstacles to such recordings as vehicles for messages: most youth cannot afford studio work, and few people actually hear the recordings. It is common for them to be heard once or twice on the radio, but most rap and ragga artists produce recordings that only they and their friends will hear.

14. In the summer of 2010, I returned to Malawi for a brief stay and found that "urban music" (hip hop, ragga, and R&B) had swelled in popularity. While I was not conducting research in 2010, several informal conversations with colleagues and friends, as well as observations on the kinds of music heard on Malawian radio, indicate that locally produced hip hop has achieved a foothold in the sonic market.

PART 3.
IDENTITY AND HYBRIDITY
(MALI AND NIGERIA)

Mapping Cosmopolitan Identities
Rap Music and Male Youth Culture in Mali

DOROTHEA E. SCHULZ

Over the past fifteen years, street life in urban Mali has come to pulsate to the word-rhythms of rap. Even though various musical styles enjoy great popularity among young urbanites, it is rap that has achieved a privileged status among many male adolescents, particularly in the capital Bamako.[1] Rap's triumphant national career has been facilitated by the diversification of the media landscape in the wake of the introduction of multiparty democracy and concomitant civil liberties in 1991. Yet in spite of the diversification of marketing structures and the plurality of views and styles broadcast on private radio stations, Malian national television remains the primary channel through which new trends in rap are popularized because it regularly features talent shows such as the Saturday afternoon program *Jouvance.* Accordingly, many young men in town make sure that they spend Saturday afternoon in front of the television screen to acquaint themselves with the most recent fads and fashions in the Malian rap scene.

At a most immediate level, rap indicates a musical style. Yet whenever used synonymously with hip hop, the polysemous practices of Malian rap stand for the dreams, self-understandings, and projects of self-making of an entire generation. As fans in Mali commonly emphasize, rap not only perpetuates traditional forms of social criticism but also allows young people to combine a critical attitude toward society and established authority with a modern, cosmopolitan orientation, which they expressly associate with an authentic African identity.

To be sure, only to some groups of young media consumers does a rapper identity appear as desirable and hip. In many small towns of southern Mali and their surrounding rural areas, for instance, the majority of male adolescents express a clear preference for musical styles that are coined as typically local, such as balafon music and the hunters' (sing., *donson*)[2] music and poetry, all of them genres many consider emblematic of Mali's rural traditions and therefore more authentic. The aesthetic preferences for a genuinely Malian music of these consumers who live in semi-urban or rural areas are echoed by many adults in town. Most of them are mothers and fathers whose perception of youth culture is shaped by their daily struggle to manage large households. They find the protest stance of rap threatening and argue that this music, along with its posture of social critique, lends a fashionable outlook to intergenerational conflicts that are currently unsettling most urban households as an outgrowth of economic liberalization measures imposed on Malian society since the mid-1980s (Brand 2001; Schulz 2004: 97–158; 2005). Similar to many young music consumers from the countryside, these adult opponents to rap culture commonly posit a contrast between rap as culturally foreign and other musical styles, which they identify as authentically local. They point to the attitude transported in rap as a sign of youngsters' propensity to mimic Western consumerism, and scathingly denounce the moral and social degradation under foreign cultural influence that rap music facilitates. They thereby wholeheartedly dismiss rappers' self-portrayal as those who educate society, as well as their assertion that rap helps them live a modern, cosmopolitan, and authentically African identity. The portrayal of rap by these critics thus hinges on a conceptual dichotomy. Certain musical styles are presented as being rooted in rural society, traditional, and morally superior, and they are contrasted to the stylistically foreign and thereby impure music and immoral lifestyle of the city.[3]

How should we understand these contradictory accounts of the nature of rap and its social import? And why are issues of morality and educational value highlighted when it comes to evaluating a musical genre that in other areas of the globe is commonly associated with youth protest?

The second question had been nagging me for years, since I began my research on the political biography of Mali's praise singers (*jeliw*)[4] and on some of their most prominent female representatives, pop stars such as Ami Koita and Kandia Kouyate (Schulz 2001a). In the mid-1990s, I was mainly interested in understanding the reasons for their breathtaking popularity among women and girls, and therefore focused, to borrow Raymond Williams's evocative phrase, on the appreciative "structure of feeling" of female listeners. But I also wondered what the male counterpart was to the culture of sociality and debate that emerged around women's and girls' consumption of jeli pop music (Schulz 2001b, 2002a). It was already evident that to those young men and adolescents who understood themselves to be hip, "kuul," and oriented toward things modern, rap was the music and lifestyle of the future.

Whereas most women and girls expressed a strong preference for national musical styles (among them the songs performed by jeli singers), and enthusiastically followed the trials and triumphs of their favorite pop stars, the young men I used to hang out with took a very different view. For them, jeli performers, their music, and lyrics belonged to the world of yesterday, of "traditional" culture, and of antiquated norms of conduct and ways of dressing, speaking, and moving around in the world. Over the years, the longer I followed these friends' engagements with an emergent Malian hip hop scene, the more I became intrigued with the stark contrast between their views of rap (and its significance in a Malian context) and the ways rap is often portrayed in scholarly literature. That is to say, whereas fans and musicians in Mali highlight the educational value of rap, many scholars, particularly those who work on Francophone hip hop, tend to foreground its political and critical potential and its role in articulating a global culture of youth protest (Krims 2000; Kimminich 2001, 2004b; Auzanneau 2002; Silverstein 2002; Osumare 2005; Lipsitz 1994; Potter 1995). Most of these authors emphasize that hip hop, as a globally circulating idiom, is translated and appropriated into locally specific material and aesthetic forms and practices of signification (see Androutsopoulos 2003). At the same time, the assumption seems to persist that hip hop around the globe articulates a culture of youth protest. Often implied in this portrayal is that young people throughout the black diaspora face the same dilemmas and experiences of racial discrimination and come to articulate their "connective marginalities" (Osumare 2005) in the shared idiom of hip hop. As insightful as this focus on protest and marginality is, it cannot explain why rappers in Mali evaluate rap lyrics primarily according to their edifying and moral value, and self-consciously portray themselves as those who bring "moral lessons" (*ladili*) to a society divided by egotism and material greed.

Clearly, to grasp the social significance and repercussions of rap in Mali, we need to pay closer attention to the specific aesthetic conventions, moral standards, and social institutions within which hip hop emerged and, since the 1990s, has enjoyed such spectacular success among male youth. I begin by sketching out basic characteristics of hip hop as it emerged in the United States, in an attempt to identify important differences between the U.S. model and its adapted and reappropriated forms in Mali. This will allow me, in a second step, to elucidate the particular situation of marginality that young men and adolescents in Mali face, and to discuss why and how hip hop seems to offer them a way to come to terms not only with their personal dilemmas but also with their desire to imagine themselves as modern, cosmopolitan, and kuul citizens of the world.

Rap/Hip Hop as a Musical Style and Globally Circulating Idiom

Starting in the early 1980s, various subcategories of rap emerged in the urban ghettos of American metropoles, especially in New York and Los Angeles, often in competition with, and contradistinction from, each other. The social environment in which rap materialized as a new musical style offered adolescents very little opportunities for upward mobility, economic success, or turning their cultural creativity into a professional career. Because of the specific racial composition of the ghetto population, these restraints had more severe consequences for nonwhite segments of the urban lower classes. In this environment, rap articulates the logic of street life characterized by honor, freedom, competition, and self-assertion. From this follows a pervasive tendency in rap lyrics and performance toward raw autobiography and self-aggrandizement.

The social and sometimes political critique formulated by rappers tends to bear a strong racial undertone (Anderson 1995; also see Keyes 1996).[5] That is, many of the lyrics composed by U.S. rappers are characterized by what Paul Gilroy (1993: 101–102) ironically refers to as "powerful magic of alterity." Gilroy thereby castigates what he considers an unacceptable inclination to define one's social identity through the category of race. According to Gilroy, this category of race is based on a reified and essentialized notion of African American culture and its unmitigated rootedness in the African homeland.[6]

Gilroy's insistence on the need to recognize class as a marker of difference rightly captures the fact that many of those involved in the rap production process continue to struggle in a stigmatized social environment, at least as long as they have not yet been discovered by a broader public. At the same time, rap has been discovered and marketed as both a musical style and a lifestyle, and has therefore turned into an object of consumption by a racially diverse, broader range of (mostly youth) consumers.

The lyrics of U.S. rap reflect a broad spectrum of ideological orientations that range from political and social criticism (including symbolic references to the 1960s Black Panthers and Nation of Islam) to more apolitical forms, among them those heavily geared toward commercial mainstream music as it is presently marketed on MTV and other popular music channels. Whereas the tendency by numerous rap groups to articulate misogynist, anti-Semitic, and homophobic views has been decried by many critics, apologists argue that these contents simply reflect on the genuinely subversive nature of rap and its breaking with conventional forms and understandings of music making on one side and with established ideas of musical, acoustic, visual, and poetic aesthetics on the other (Potter 1995; Darby and Shelby 2005). Whether or not one agrees with this rationale, it is certainly true that rap music moves beyond conventional categories used in the assessment of musical harmony and beauty, and of performance skills, by replacing them with criteria such as technical virtuosity on nontraditional musical instruments, such as a DJ's turntable, and the mastery of a different repertoire of symbolic and verbal skills. In this process, the slang of rapping and improvisation becomes, to borrow once more from Gilroy (2004: 92), the "dissonant soundtrack of racial dissidence."[7] Rap generates and resonates with a "moral panic" (Baker 1993: 5, 13, 20). It shatters conventional musical and verbal aesthetic standards of harmony, beauty, and taste and challenges prevailing, often gender- and age-specific, measures of morality and propriety.

Hip Hop in Mali: The Social Locations of a Youth "Protest" Culture

Earlier in this chapter, I cautioned against a tendency to study hip hop in African societies without due consideration of established standards of performance and taste that allowed this seemingly global idiom of youth protest or idiom of a "global diaspora aesthetic" (Manthia Diawara 2005: 252–53) to be appropriated and integrated into music making across the African continent. The immense success of hip hop in Mali as well as the fierce reactions it generates on the part of its mostly adult critics can be only understood if we relate it to established forms of youth sociality and critique, to its embodied modes of performance, as well as to key metaphors through which social critique is commonly articulated across different genres of Malian music and oral culture.

I start with the forms of sociality in which hip hop in Mali, as an expressive culture of forging individual and group identities, is embedded and from which it draws its dynamics. Perhaps the most striking continuity between hip hop and earlier music youth cultures is that they all emerge around the same institution of male sociality. Most rappers with whom I talked recounted that their musical activities started in a so-called *grin* (an informal structure of male socializing).[8] Grins exist in each neighborhood and can be seen as the backbone of male social life—not just of adolescents (Brenner ms; Schulz 2002a; also see Manthia Diawara 1998: 99–104; 2005; Kiefer 2006). What brings men together in a grin is not so much a shared educational and socioeconomic background (in fact, the absence of the latter is a striking characteristic of many grins), but experiences and concerns that derive from a similar standing in the Malian age and status hierarchy.[9] Male friends, some of them from different neighborhoods, convene on a daily basis (mostly in the afternoon) to drink tea, play cards or board games, and talk. As I argued elsewhere, perhaps the most important social significance of the grin is that it offers men of all ages a space where they can address their concerns in a sphere outside of the household among friends. Married men discuss worries, such as concerns about financial hardship or marital conflicts, which their role as head of the household prevents them from doing otherwise. To young and unmarried men, grins are the place where they can articulate feelings and views that norms of filial respect would prevent them from doing within earshot of their parents (Schulz 2002a; also see Sessay 2001).[10]

As Manthia Diawara (2005: 252) recounts in his recollections of his youth in Bamako in the 1960s, grins brought together young people (mostly but not exclusively men, and mostly from the middle classes) thrilled by the music, lifestyle, and self-assertiveness of musicians such as James Brown and "other diaspora aestheticians from North America." Diawara observes that his and his friends' enthusiasm for the "diasporic aesthetic" articulated by African American musicians translated into embodied performances of an African modern identity through dress, dance, and musical activity. It also resulted in the organization of musical happenings modeled on Woodstock and other sites of the performance of global youth culture. The fact that contemporary Malian hip hop, too, is deeply rooted in grins points to the persistent relevance of this form of male sociality for the generation and reconfiguration of male consumerism, musical creativity, and possibly protest culture.

If the structures of socializing and conviviality within which hip hop is lived are similar to earlier forms of urban youth culture, what are the particularities of hip hop and in what ways do they reflect on the specific situation and dilemmas of today's youth?

The majority of producers and consumers of rap are males between fourteen and twenty-five years old, yet their most important common denominator is not age per se but a shared experience closely related to the worsening of economic conditions for the urban middle and lower middle classes. Large-scale unemployment and a rampant lack of opportunities for adolescents to make a living (regardless of the kind of diploma they may have received) limits opportunities for many young men to marry and to establish an independent homestead. Many young men are obliged to rely on their parents' income and to put up with the equivocal constraints and expectations such a dependency generates. In more privileged families, this lack of financial autonomy often goes hand in hand with a dependency on the political connections that older family members can provide. Most adolescents are highly ambivalent about their ongoing dependence on parental resources. Even though they might benefit from it, they simultaneously resent and deplore their lack of self-sufficiency (Schulz 2004: 159–202).

It is important to distinguish between musical producers and consumers in Malian rap. The consumers include those who establish a rapper identity not only through music consumption but also through dress style, bodily comportment, and speech. So far, most young men (and the few women) who have set new musical and stylistic impulses and initiated new trends in fashion, appearance, and body movements come from a privileged family background.[11] Although influences of Senerap from neighboring Senegal are palpable in Mali, inspiration for local trends in dress, lyrics, and modes of expression is mostly drawn from French hip hop and introduced by young men who have spent some time in a European metropolis (mostly Paris or Brussels). Here, for the first time, they had the experience of being discriminated against because of their skin color and cultural origins. This experience made them highly susceptible to the protest stance of French rap, much of it made by immigrants from North and West Africa. As illustrated by many personal biographies of male rappers that I collected, the (entirely novel) experience of discrimination prompted them to conceive of their identity in terms of race and being black.[12]

Once returned to Mali, they translated their experience into musical productions and into personal narratives of an adventurous marginality recounted to friends and peers at their grin. I suggest that in this process of translating experiences of racial and social discrimination, the very meanings of race, blackness, and a youth protest culture are remediated and significantly transformed. Malian rappers do so because they speak and appeal to local audiences and their concerns, thereby appropriating and simultaneously redirecting the idiom of a common transnational black experience of marginalization.

Most of the rappers are autodidacts. Lacking the necessary technical equipment and training, they initially rapped to the accompaniment of a boom box and to improvise with various versions of rap and other local musical styles. The inspiration from an international Francophone hip hop culture is undeniable, yet most rappers self-consciously describe themselves as "self-made men" (pronounced in English) and trace their ideas about being "black" (which most of them pronounce in what is locally considered U.S. ghetto slang) and black culture back to the adventure accounts, movies, photographs, and video recordings of friends who managed to "embark on the adventure" (*partir à l'aventure*) across the Atlantic Ocean and who, once returned to Mali, are often celebrated as heroes, very similar to earlier generations of young males who migrated to neighboring countries in search of new opportunities and fortune.[13]

Most rap crews make their first productions in private recording studios, either in their homes or in a facility provided by a sponsor, who is often a relative. Some groups gain wider renown through participation in events organized at the neighborhood level and that bear similarities with talent shows organized and sponsored by Malian national radio. A group may then gain wider popularity and renown by making recordings at commercial recording studios. Yet, although private recording studios have multiplied over the past ten years, national television and radio remain the privileged channel through which rap musicians seek to circulate their musical productions. Rap music and lifestyle thus enter the national market of mass-mediated entertainment culture through the same venue as various other music styles, which over the last two decades have achieved wide prominence and public recognition. And as it is the case with the latter category of musicians, having personal connections to employees of the national broadcast station is often the first step in one's national career, a step only the privileged ones may realize.

Among these privileged rapper crews are those which, at least in the initial stages of their career, are funded by their parents or relatives. Fathers who are willing to provide their sons (much less their daughters) with the technical equipment necessary for their musical activities usually do not have any particular liking for the music their children perform. Rather, their financial support springs from their hope that, in the absence of other job opportunities, their children will be able to embark on a successful musical career. Very few rap groups, even those who have already gained some renown, manage to attract the attention and support of their internationally successful compatriots, who can offer financial, institutional, and personal assistance.[14] The more professional support these star musicians provide often affords these fortunate rap groups an entry into the international music scene. But even for those rappers whose success remains limited to the national arena, the assistance they received from their sponsor translates into a higher level of professionalism which, once reflected in their recordings, significantly increases their income. For all these institutional and financial reasons, those in Mali who become nationally or even internationally renowned rappers do not represent the socioeconomic background or the marginality that many of their U.S. models claim.

Given the specific institutions and socioeconomic locations of hip hop in Mali, this raises the question of how rap, as a local appropriation of a global "diasporic aesthetic" in Mali, differs from its historical predecessors from the 1960s described by Manthia Diawara (1998, 2005). A major difference resides in the radically altered political situation within which hip hop culture today can unfold its social critical and political potential. Malian youth culture in the mid-1960s was realized in a politically repressive atmosphere. The state, represented through vigilantes, sought to exert almost totalizing control over its citizens' comportment, consumption, and taste, yet also promised its youth new opportunities for upward mobility and achievement in the new state apparatus. The contemporary status quo appears almost as the opposite. Following a worldwide surge of a neoliberal ideology of self-reliance and self-realization, political liberalization since the early 1990s has brought unprecedented liberties for self-organization, yet fails to provide the urban youth with opportunities for employment and regular income. It is against the backdrop of these seriously forestalled opportunities of self-realization that one needs to explore the particularities of contemporary youth culture in Mali and the kind of protest it articulates. As a first step, it is useful to look more closely at the formal characteristics of rap as it is performed and appreciated in Mali in order to understand how it continues with, and possibly departs from, conventional forms of oral narrative and social critique.

Word Music: The Pulse of Social Critique

Characteristic features of rap music in Mali, and elsewhere in Africa, are the playful jockeying of words and sounds and the combination of rhetorical ingenuity and inventiveness with a rhythmic patterning borrowed from established genres of popular music. In many of their songs, the group Les Escrocs [The Crooks], for instance, ingeniously relies on the kora to introduce additional layers of complexity into their instrumental and speech performance. Other rap crews commonly mobilize a partly novel linguistic repertory by combining different national languages with a French, English, or Arabic lexicon, thereby infusing their lyrics and music with cosmopolitan prestige, greater credibility, or an authentically local outlook.[15]

Rhythm plays a pivotal role in rap, in Mali and elsewhere. To a greater extent than the text, which significantly appeals to one's intellect, rhythm integrates and congeals rappers and listeners into a shared experience of community or "communitas" (see Turner 1969). The privileging of rhythmic speech over melody leads Malian critics of rap, among them many adult men and women, to question whether rap constitutes music at all and to assert that it lacks not only morality but also pleasing appeal. Their denouncement of rap deserves closer attention because it implies an evaluative framework that highlights melody and musical harmony as evidence of a rap song's quality and moral value. Yet this assessment is at variance with the pivotal position of rhythmic speech in local aesthetic performance conventions. The spoken word is said to mobilize emotions inaccessible to listeners' conscious efforts and to move them to extraordinary action. In other words, fast, well-measured, and articulate speech is commonly perceived as essential to the moving effects of a successful oral performance (Zahan 1963; also see Charry 2000: 94–96, 322–27). And it is precisely this verbal and rhythmic virtuosity that consumers of rap highlight whenever they rave about a particular song or performer. To deplore the absence of musical form in rap thus seems to be a way to express one's uneasiness with the critical posture implied in both the form (edgy, speedy speech) and contents of rap.

Clearly, the appreciation of rhetorical virtuosity in Malian rap cannot be interpreted (as critics of rap sometimes do) as an indication of their mindless imitation of U.S. rap performance conventions and its logic of competitive self-display. Rather, the popularity of rap among Malian male youth is in line with established notions of the aesthetically and ethically moving powers of rhythmically patterned speech. Moreover, similar to areas of East and Southern Africa, the appreciation by fans of a rapper's verbal and rhetorical virtuosity perpetuates the conventional high valuation of verbal rivalry, often combined with subtle derision or satire directed at those in power. In Mali, the most significant of these traditional genres of youth critique is the *baara,* a Bamana musical form performed by female and male youth, combining song with evocative body movements and other embodied forms of criticism directed mostly at the parental generation and local authority. These musical, nonverbal forms of criticism used to be particularly well suited to subverting existing standards of conduct that prohibited any form of critique on the part of juniors. Rappers and their fans frequently refer to baara and other conventional forms of youth criticism to claim that they continue an "older" social function "just with new means." Rappers, in other words, employ a distinct repertoire of lexical forms, symbolic gestures, and body movements that allow them to perform a modern kuul identity and to subvert standards of bodily deportment that require a downplaying of any allusion to sexuality. But they understand themselves as being in continuity with long-standing local traditions of social critique, mockery, and speech contest. To emerge from this contest as the winner, the "master of the word" (*ngaara,* in Bamana), one needs the ability to keep the longer breath and eclipse one's rivals through compelling speech.

Lyrics: The Subtle Assertion of an African Particularity

Many rap songs in Mali borrow substantially from the symbolic repertory of U.S. hip hop culture. That is to say, Malian rappers assume the critical posture of their "brothers" in the U.S. diaspora and thereby imply that hip hop culture refers not only to a shared performance aesthetics and lifestyle but also to a common experience of racial discrimination.[16] Yet closer scrutiny reveals that their espousal of a rhetoric of racial confrontation characteristic of some strands of U.S. rap is ambivalent. One reason for this ambivalence is that the critical stance that Malian rappers assume draws on central terms and metaphors of U.S. rap, yet ultimately refers to a significantly different context of social and political inequality. The specific context within which Malian rappers operate and voice their critique marks their distinctiveness from the situation in the United States and France and also within the African continent. A closer look at the specific dilemmas that the youth in Mali faces and decries warrants new insights into the actual meanings of the "connective marginalities" (Osumare 2005) of youth around the globe, but also into their locally specific conditions of marginality.

Compared with southern Africa (taken by Osumare as a representative example of Africa's youth protest culture), where the legacy of apartheid continues to haunt and fragment the political imaginary, in Mali and other areas of sahelian West Africa, settler colonialism and its attendant forms of racial discrimination have never been significant. In this latter situation, the category of race easily acquires the status of a free-floating signifier. Rappers refer to it in shifting and contingent ways to denounce various aspects of the colonial past and of postcolonial forms of political and economic dependency. In this process, and similar to hip hop cultures in other African countries, such as Senegal (Biaya 2000; Havard 2001; Wittmann 2004), the exact contents of racial discrimination are redefined, partly as a result of the specific colonial heritage that bears on contemporary state politics as much as on the internal restructuring of family dynamics. Accordingly, much of the criticism made by Malian rappers is directed toward what they perceive as the most serious social evils of Malian society, among them rampant unemployment, AIDS, the ongoing attempts of family elders to maintain control within the family, the arbitrary treatment of women by their husbands, and the deeply eroding effects of money on society and love relationships. More important, the sliding meanings of blackness allow Malian rappers to draw on a symbolic register of sameness to American hip hop, yet also to mark their own authenticity as African rappers. Involved in their conflation of an African with a black identity is therefore a double movement of authentication that yields an ambiguous outcome.

Malian rappers borrow heavily from the U.S. expressive repertoire by inserting key terms of the black political struggle into their songs and self-portrayals. For instance, *Cikan* [Message], the title of a recently released CD of the rap group Tata Pound, translates and brings a concept from the broader hip hop linguistic culture to a Malian context. Similarly, *fangafin*, the literal translation of Black Power, has been chosen as the name for one of the most successful Malian rap groups. As a neologism in Bamana, this term only makes sense in reference to a global black protest culture. At the same time, employing key notions of U.S. hip hop culture also allows some Malian rappers to subtly assert an identity as "veritable" (*yèrè* in Bamanakan) Africans, as opposed to their American brothers whose preoccupation with race they do not share. For example, similar to their U.S. superstars of rap, some Malian rappers emphasize their pride in their African cultural and historical roots through the adoption of names of legendary historical heroes (such as Shaka Zulu) who confronted white hegemony. Yet, underneath this claim to sameness, a subtle assertion takes place of a genuinely African, not just black, identity. Although not everyone in the Malian hip hop community lays claim to a more authentic African identity, the claim pinpoints the somewhat ambivalent positioning of Malian rappers within a diasporic aesthetics.

There are yet other significant elements of Malian rap lyrics that mark their specificity within a global black culture. Contrary to the subversion of conventional moral standards in many U.S. rap songs, many Malian rappers subscribe to a highly moralizing discourse that is conservative, if not reactionary, in nature. And they are self-conscious about their moral mission: they frequently point to their role in improving society and morals, and assert that, compared with the "self-centered" and "culturally alien" nature of U.S. rap lyrics, their own educational vocation proved that they were deeply rooted in African cultural norms and thus more "genuinely African" than their U.S. counterparts.[17] Several rap crews, among them Fanga Fing and Tata Pound, understand themselves as articulators of a "message" of political criticism and as mouthpieces of a youth disaffected about the promises of democracy that were not borne out. Yet the majority of rappers consider edification and exhortation to be their primary objectives and feel that this practice is more significant and of higher value than the striving for self-aggrandizement and antagonism many of these rappers associate with U.S. hip hop.[18] Accordingly, their songs denounce the moral degradation of society and the fact that feelings of love and empathy have been emptied out by a greed for money instilled under the influence of Western imperialism and corrupt political elites.

Also pervasive in many lyrics is the tendency to present women as both agents and beneficiaries of the erosion of friendship and love. The conservative tenor of rap lyrics, in Mali and other countries, has been largely overlooked by scholars whose preoccupation was with the subversive politics (Lipsitz 1994; Krims

2000) and protest culture of a global youth. Wittmann (2004), one of the few authors who addresses this phenomenon, views it as a conundrum and rightly concludes that "protest" or resistance does not necessarily entail a progressive politics (also see Abu-Lughod 1990). What both interpretations miss is that the moralist-conservative tenor of many rap lyrics echoes established aesthetic conventions for oral performances. That is to say, there is a common perception (not only among fans of rap) that the true value of a song shows in its moralizing and edifying effects and that it teaches "moral lessons" (*ladili*). Also, the image of the "greedy," "immoral" woman and its corrupting effects on men and the social order at large is a recurrent figure of speech in local accounts of social change and degeneration (Schulz 2001a: 235–80; 2001b). This means that rap lyrics are successful, not in spite of their conservative outlook but because they frame their social critique as a moral concern and thereby draw on, and respond to, commonsensical understandings of Malian society, its ills, and ways to remedy them.

But there is more to the marked emphasis of many Malian rappers on the social usefulness of their performances.[19] And this brings back the question of the particular conditions of marginality with which Malian youth grapple. I noted above that those who perform, consume, and enjoy rap in Mali share problems that arise from a situation of postponed autonomy from parental control and that foreclose any possibility of being accepted into the world of adults. Given their marginal position in economic and social life, rappers' insistence on their educational mission should be seen as an attempt to claim a place and a function as morally responsible members of society (Schulz 2002a, 2004: 97–158, 203–61; H. White 2001; Weiss 2002). To assume the function of a moral watchdog in a situation of relative exclusion allows them to reclaim some elements of an adult identity which otherwise remains unattainable. This search for recognition by, and integration into, the adult world comes out clearly in the ways in which many of the rappers with whom I interacted on a regular basis envision their futures. They dream of the reputation or "name" (*tògò*) that their musical career will afford them and that will materialize in visible signs of success such as lavish outfits, a mansion, and a sports convertible (see Hacke and Roch's 2004 documentary *Bongo Flava*). Most significantly, they daydream about future, unlimited possibilities to "put their parents in better conditions," possibilities that would enable them to live up to the expectation that an obliging and dutiful child should pay respect and "show gratitude."

Whereas social and moral critique is central to the self-understanding of rappers in Mali, this critique sometimes stands in tension with the privileges many of them enjoy because of their family and economic background, as well as with the actual dilemmas that arise from their socioeconomic positioning. As noted above, a theme that figures centrally in numerous rap songs is the denouncement of the attempts by parents, particularly by fathers, to maintain or extend control through economic dependency. Although rappers thereby adequately portray the conflicts waging in many urban households, it is also a fact that many of them depend on the financial and social support of a father who either occupies an influential position in politics or administration or engages in highly successful business ventures. Parents' continued hold over their juniors is thus often the precondition for rappers' poetically and musically mediated criticism of parental control and of other sources of intergenerational conflict.

A final notable difference between Malian rap and its U.S. counterpart consists in their respective social vocations and their repercussions. Whereas rapping in U.S. cities takes place in, and reflects on, a highly competitive setting, rap in Mali as a musical and performance style often serves to confirm and expand social relations. Many rap songs contain lengthy passages in which the performer greets people in a neighborhood or at a particular grin. This form of public greeting is highly popular among urban and rural audiences, especially among those individuals, families, or grins whose reputation a singer boosts by addressing them in person. Simultaneously, greeting people also helps the rapper to establish himself as someone who is popular and to whom one should feel indebted because of the public kindnesses he showed to friends and acquaintances in public. By inserting personal address forms into their performances, rappers continue with the social function that other conventional forms of cultivating social bonds through oral public performance assume, such as those practiced by jeli singers and radio speakers (Schulz 1999). The group Tata Pound, for instance, combines in the song "Badala" allusions to specific places, events, and instances of performance with the greeting of specific individuals. This and other songs thus allow the group to expand existing forms of sociality through the medium of music, partly by evoking an insider knowledge that binds listeners and performers into a common realm of shared experience and extends it to new public arenas. Here again, rap illustrates how a global genre acquires specifically local properties and significance through the process of its appropriation and translation into local social and aesthetic conventions.

Sartorial Practices and Other Forms of Embodiment

To many rappers in Mali, clothing and other embodied expressions are as important in conveying "the message" (always pronounced in English) as do the critical-yet-edifying lyrics. The central importance of their visual and embodied performance of a kuul, cosmopolitan identity, is evidenced in the spontaneous, often nonverbal reactions of their fans and of hip hop consumers in general.[20] Bodily posture and movement of rappers form, together with a complex gestural apparatus, a symbolic repertoire of mimetic acts that is modeled on the example of prominent U.S. rappers that helps them articulate a political-ideological orientation, a critique of the establishment ("the elders," "the system"), and a youth identity that is commonly described as kuul, associated with a cosmopolitan orientation. Significantly, this notion does not simply borrow from U.S. notions of coolness but is informed and shaped by conventional local understandings of dignified conduct: whoever wants to be considered an adult needs to display a capacity for self-restraint, illustrated, among other things, in speaking in a "cool" way (*suman*, literally cool, as in temperature), that is, in a low-volume and measured way, and contrasted to the "heat" of someone whose immaturity shows in his impatience, quickness (*teliya*), and thoughtless speech (Schulz 2001a: 235–280).

As a reference to a shared black identity, numerous rappers in Mali, as well as their fans and other consumers of hip hop culture, favor corporeal expressions and forms of ornamentation such as dreadlocks, skullcaps and colors associated with the Rastafari movement.[21] They also seek to obtain consumer objects, such as posters, stickers, and dress accessories that many Malians associate with a global black culture.[22]

Yet not everyone supportive of this type of Malian youth culture, and of the project of self-making associated with it, has the actual institutional and financial capacities to partake in it, either as a producer or as a consumer. Moreover, in Mali, outside articles, signs, and gestures become operative as elements (emblems) of a global black culture only if they make sense in local and personal frameworks of meaning and signification practices. In this process of insertion and appropriation, some articles gain new meanings, such as the association with a cosmopolitan identity, as in the case of "I love New York" T-shirts. And so can the definition of an authentically African identity gain new meaning, as in the case of certain gestures and body movements that reflect on local concepts of dignified behavior.

Thus, similar to hip hop culture in settings outside the Euro-American West, the project of constructing one's identity in which rappers and rap consumers engage is effected through powerful, globally circulating representational forms that tend to be associated with a black global culture and are shaped by the forces and exclusionist tendencies of an entertainment market (see Wade 1999: 457). Their attempts to carve out a space for self-expression and for recognition by the adult world are located within this market-mediated arena of material and symbolic practice. Although many symbolic and expressive elements of a rapper identity circulate at a global scale, their meanings are restricted by way of their insertion into local contexts of signification practices.

Conclusion

Similar to other popular music styles in Mali, rap has emerged as an area of cultural creativity at the interface of several social, technological, and economic developments. One is the spread of new technologies that allows for new ways of producing music, such as sampling and cut and paste. Another process consists in the appropriation and selective revising of aesthetic conventions, standards of musical appreciation, and markers of social distinction. New dynamics also emerge at the interface of globally circulating objects and emblems of a modern, cosmopolitan orientation and of a black youth protest culture and of the practices of signification they generate in various local and regional arenas. In the case of Malian youth culture, rappers draw on consumption objects and images that circulate along transnational commercial structures and have a decidedly global outlook. By inserting themselves into this global consumer culture, rappers contribute substantially to the objectification of their protest culture. Simultaneously, however, they attribute distinctive and sometimes particularistic meanings to these objects, in an attempt to map the self, to envision an African adult identity for themselves that is in line with local norms and expectations (see Wade 1999: 457). Seen in this light, Malian rap culture continues with, and is representative of, conventions of appropriation that, for a long time, have enabled the adoption and partial transmutation of transnational musical and verbal repertoires, in accordance with local aesthetic sensibilities and preferences.

A word of caution is in place, however. The transnational symbolic and aesthetic repertoire of hip hop culture offers rappers in Mali opportunities to imaginatively define themselves as modern Malians. Yet it is important that their possibilities for mapping a kuul, hip, and cosmopolitan image of themselves are circumscribed by the limited conditions under which most African urbanites may engage in consumption. Rather than heralding the contemporary moment as an era in which consumption constitutes a site of seemingly unlimited opportunities for identity construction (see Miller 1995; Remes 1999), we should recognize that this is a site with restricted access (Schulz 2002b, 2004: 203–261; see Ferguson 2002). As we have seen, most of the urban youth supportive of rap in Mali lack the financial means and social networks that would enable them to partake in the making of a rap culture that is local in outlook and orientation. For them, mapping a future self remains an affair of embodied imagination and "mimicry" (Ferguson 2002) of a transnational idiom of black protest.

This leads me back to my earlier concern with the common emphasis on protest and a politics of subversion in writings on the global circulation of hip hop. Not only do we need to recognize substantial diversity within the category of Francophone rap. But studies of hip hop in African societies and beyond need to pay closer attention to the specific socioeconomic locations of those who perform rap, as well as to the specific dilemmas that they, as well as hip hop consumers, face. True, young people across the African continent share certain experiences of exclusion or marginality (e.g., Honwana and de Boeck 2005). Yet the dilemmas that emerge from this situation, the answers that adolescents of different economic background envisage, and the forms of sociality that accompany their (makeshift) solutions differ widely, along with the regionally specific social and aesthetic conventions from which they draw inspiration. Viewed in this light, a nuanced understanding of African hip hop and its complex social repercussions will allow us to refine the analytical categories we bring to bear on hip hop as a polysemous and shifting idiom of a highly diverse diasporic aesthetic.

NOTES

This chapter is based on research conducted in Bamako and San between 2001 and 2006 (altogether fourteen months). Earlier versions were presented during a roundtable discussion on popular music in Africa during the 2003 African Studies Association meetings in Boston, and as the habilitation lecture to the Faculty of Social and Political Sciences, Free University Berlin, February 2005. I thank Jochen Seebode for helpful comments on earlier versions of this article, and Lamine Doumbia, Tonton Kulibali, and Teyan and Boa Keita for teaching me the first important lessons about hip hop and male youth culture in Mali.

1. See Polak (2004, and this volume) for the popularity of djembe drumming in Bamako. Some authors distinguish between rap as a musical activity and hip hop as a way of life that, in addition to musical practice, comprises a particular orientation and attitude, which manifests itself in specific patterns of consumption. However, the dividing lines between the two notions remain fuzzy. In this chapter, I employ the term *rap* to refer to a musical culture in a broader sense, to describe a specific, even though highly heterogeneous, musical genre and the process of oral performance and technical production. *Rap* also refers to the various symbolic and social acts which are associated with the consumption of this music and follow particular conventions of self-representation. I am interested in rap as a practice of signification whose social relevance stretches beyond the immediate production process. In other words, the meanings of rap are constituted both in the immediate production process and in the course of consumers' engagements with it, which taken together constitute a field of socially situated acts of signification.

2. Unless noted otherwise, all foreign expressions are rendered in Bamanakan, the lingua franca of southern Mali.

3. They understand the impurity of urban musical styles to derive from their mixing of various foreign influences, among them the use of new or electrified instruments, rhythmic patterns, and lyrics.

4. The *jeliw* [French: griots] belong to a professional group (*nyamakalaw*) that forms one of three status categories of Bamana society in southern Mali. The conventional tasks of jeliw are to serve as genealogists, praise singers, and mediators on behalf of their patrons.

5. Herein consists an important difference to British rap and the less exclusionist and racially defined project of self-identification that many British rappers formulate.

6. Gilroy (1993, ch. 3) criticizes the idea and claim by numerous rappers of rap as an authentic and uniquely African American cultural form. Instead, he proposes to see rap and hip hop as illustrations of the hybrid nature of all black cultural forms as they exist and travel throughout the African diaspora. He emphasizes that rap has its origins as much in the booming electronic culture of Jamaica as in the preference for orality and oral mastery that continues to shape aesthetic performance conventions on the African continent (also see Lipsitz 1994; Klein and Friedrich 2003).

7. Yet as Houston Baker Jr. (1993, ch. 3) cautions us, this soundtrack also bears its risks, especially if it is employed by writers such as Henry Louis Gates, who as "experts" of rap translate and simplify its contents and agenda for racially mixed audiences (also see Anderson 1995: 17).

8. The literal meaning of the Bamana word *grin* is "reunion."

9. In a certain sense, grins are the equivalent of age groups in rural societies. These groups, very often formed on the occasion of life status transition rituals such as circumcision, allow men of approximately the same age to move together through the different phases of life.

10. Brenner (ms.) argues that grins, particularly those of unmarried and unemployed men, acquired a central political significance as centers of popular protest and opposition to the government of former president Moussa Traoré in 1991.

11. Malians distinguish between three kinds of social categories that historically could be roughly correlated with different socioeconomic backgrounds. People of free-born (*horon,* from Arabic *hurr,* free) or noble descent were usually the most powerful and wealthy in an area. Dependent on them were different groups of clients of *nyamakala* (artisan) background, among them the jeliw, whose expertise was to perform music and various oral genres on behalf of their free-born patrons. And finally there were the people of serf background (sing., *jon*). Although these status distinctions hold sway in everyday life, it is important to note that today, particularly in urban areas where rap is mostly performed and consumed, social background cannot be correlated to socioeconomic position or class. In other words, the economically privileged background of many rappers does not indicate that they are of horon birth.

12. Rappers usually use the term *black* in the untranslated English version.

13. The practice of *partir à l'aventure* has been a long-standing rite of passage for male adolescents. Various oral genres recite the trials and triumphs of heroes who established their claim to military and/or spiritual leadership by surviving various travels to foreign lands.

14. The most prominent example of this kind of sponsorship is provided by Salif Keita. Toumani Diabaté, who lent money to musicians in the mid-1990s, has since stopped his support.

15. Cases include well-known passages from particular *suras* (Koranic verses) or loanwords from U.S. slang or French argot. See Auzanneau (2002), Auzanneau and Fayol (2004), and Kimminich (2004b) for interesting parallels to the mixing of linguistic repertoires in Senerap.

16. I suggest below that their choice of names (e.g., Les Escrocs, Black Panthers) allows rappers to claim commonality with the gangsta identity of their U.S. role models and that blacks around the globe share the same concerns emerging from uniform modes of discrimination.

17. Expressions in quotation marks (translated from French or Bamanakan) without citations here and throughout this chapter are taken from conversations with my informants.

18. This perception is in line with a conventional evaluatory framework that places the highest value on moral education, empathy, trust, and mutual reliance.

19. Many consumers of rap in Mali denounce the competitiveness and boosting of U.S. rappers as an indication of their selfishness and lack of social responsibility. Rappers in Mali, as well as their fans, often contrast ego-centered and insulting U.S. rap lyrics with Malian rap lyrics and argue that the latter have a superior value because they do not aim at personal aggrandizing but at the improvement of society.

20. These reactions are gestures, facial expressions, and body and dance movements.

21. Yet in Mali as well as in numerous other African countries, these rastafari colors coincide with the colors of the national flag. Accordingly, consumers propose contingent and sometimes contradictory interpretations of the meaning of these colors.

22. Pop icons of Malian rap consumers (who see themselves as supporters of this black culture) include Bob Marley, Lucky Dube, the basketball star Michael Jordan, and U.S. American rappers such as Public Enemy. This suggests that rap consumers fashion an identity for themselves that is conceived as an unbroken continuity of black resistance in North America, the Caribbean, and in Africa (see Wade 1999: 457).

Nigerian Hip Hop
Exploring a Black World Hybrid

STEPHANIE SHONEKAN

Throughout the twentieth century, there was a dynamic two-way crossing of cultural influences between Africa and her diasporic people. Economist Roger Wallis and musicologist Krister Malm (1987: 118), in their study of popular music, conclude that many small countries that have become marginal markets for international products are also sources of new raw material. The spread of hip hop has generated exciting tentacles of hybridity that have encroached on, but not always subverted, existing traditions, art forms, and cultural mores. The case of Nigerian hip hop presents one of the many dynamic cases of cultural hybridity to emerge at the end of the twentieth century and continues to evolve in the new millennium. Indeed, the people of Nigeria have embraced and imbibed African American popular music for decades and in the process have created new cultural and artistic products.

By the early 1990s, the most popular music produced by young Nigerian artists was reggae and ragga. Local artists like Ras Kimono, Blackky, and Daniel Wilson became popular among the youth. Their music enjoyed radio and television airtime, and both Kimono and Blackky appeared on television shows and at public events. By 1995, African American rap had made its way to Nigeria, and Nigerian rappers tested their skills with this new genre. Junior and Pretty first emerged on the Lagos scene with their trademark humorous lyrics embedded in pidgin English, which ensured mass consumption. Baba Fryo also surfaced with funny and socially conscious lyrics. After a reasonably enthusiastic reception, mostly in the urban centers, other artists began to venture into the arena of rap. Artists like Daddy Showkey, probably recognizing the enduring power of reggae, mixed reggae with rap. As African American rap music spawned more commercial and formulaic styles that were broadcast on MTV and BET via satellite and cable, emerging rappers in Nigeria tried, not always successfully, to adopt the formula. An exception was the Trybesmen, whose hit "Shake Body" was popular around 1998 because it mixed local and imported references. In the new millennium, a fresh generation of rappers represents a spectrum of styles and focus. This includes the award-winning 2Face and Blackface (formerly of the group Plantashun Boiz), the popular Eedris Abdul-Kareem, the London-based Unsung Heroes, and one of the only women on the Nigerian rap scene, Weird MC.

From its inception, styles of Nigerian hip hop music ranged in scale from the more Americanized sounds of the Trybesmen to the more localized music of Junior and Pretty. However, the character of Nigerian hip hop always presents itself as an offspring of two distinct musical and cultural influences—African American hip hop and Nigerian afrobeat. The concept of hybridity, which has a relationship to reproductive biology (Young 1995), provides a useful metaphor for examining the relationships and interactions between the parents and the offspring or new raw material that is Nigerian hip hop.

Nigerians have little access to what is considered underground socially conscious hip hop from the United States. Underground artists based in the United States, like Immortal Technique and Dead Prez, are not promoted internationally. This subgenre, by its politically confrontational and therefore noncommercial nature, is unpopular among the gatekeepers of pop culture. The underground hip hop world in the United States refuses to remain within the misogynistic and apolitical boundaries set by popular media and the popular music industry. As such, this music, heavy with political and social justice messages, has no chance of joining the comparatively placid music that gets imported. So, while the images and overall form of Nigerian hip hop are appropriated from African American hip hop, the social and political tones, as well as the devices used to convey these ideas, must come from the familiar and powerful legacy of Nigerian popular music—afrobeat and, to a lesser degree, highlife.

This chapter examines the way in which these musical antecedents have influenced the evolution of Nigerian hip hop in the last decade of the twentieth century and made it a viable, distinct cultural product that amplifies both local and foreign stylistic elements. It is based on research and analysis of Nigerian rap music utilizing radio shows and questionnaires and interviews of artists, listeners, and disc jockeys.[1] Interviewees and respondents to my questionnaire, ranging in age from 16 to 40, revealed that they listen to more African American R&B and hip hop than anything else. However, they also appreciate Nigerian hip hop, which features a wide range of subgenres or flavors—from fun and light, to social and thoughtful, to political and heavy. Yet there is agreement among the artists and listeners that Nigerian rap is a unique form of music, distinct from African American rap and unlike other forms of Nigerian popular music. This chapter will explore the elements that make this musical genre relevant and appropriate within the local Nigerian setting. I will reflect on how young Nigerians have reinterpreted this African American musical form to produce a unique hybrid rap style that fits the Nigerian youth identity.

Hybridity and Nigerian Hip Hop

Nigerian hip hop provides a vibrant example of a creative expressive form that follows the principle of hybridity inherent and exemplified in pidgin English. The colonial experience that led to the creation of pidgin English as the vernacular of Anglophone West Africans reflected a duality of the internal and external, of the colonizer and colonized, of the oppressor and the oppressed. The concept of hybridity, as it relates to language, connotes the historical merging of two or more forms that nevertheless retain sufficient resemblance to the original sources (Bakhtin 1990: 37).

Broadly speaking, theories of cultural hybridity tend to fall into two categories: kinship or genealogy, and diasporic or "rhyzomic," where different influences merge in a sometimes chaotic fashion, creating an exciting new national cultural form (Wade 1998: 4). The hybridity inherent in Nigerian hip hop culture lends itself to an in-depth interrogation of both the kinship (roots) and diasporic (routes) tropes that characterize the development of new cultures.

Analysis of Nigerian hip hop in the kinship mode follows a trend of black music research that has been carried out by ethnomusicologists like Richard Waterman (1963), Kwabena Nketia (1973), and Portia Maultsby (1990). The hybrid character of each succeeding black musical genre has revealed an evolved form that retains elements from preceding genres even as it possesses its own distinct qualities. The escalating influence of the mass media in the second half of the twentieth century enabled a vibrant loop so that African American music traditions stretched and looped back to the continent of Africa from where it had originated, transforming a continuum from Africa into a dynamic cycle. Manifestations of this cycle have been seen in Nigeria for at least the past 50 years. It stands to reason that Nigerian hip hop should be considered a part of the cycle of continuity of black music within the African diaspora.

Nigerian hip hop music and culture cannot be seen only in one-dimensional terms. Black identity and experience are unique in every part of the globe. As Paul Gilroy notes, "Compton is as foreign to some blacks in New York as Kingston, London, Havana, Lagos, Aswan, or Cape Town." He therefore urges a careful examination of "the complex dynamics of black cultural production and use" (Gilroy 1993: 199). Thus the rhyzomic or diasporic model of hybridity lends itself well to this cultural product that is Nigerian hip hop. Gilroy's ideas of the crossroads that intersect in the diaspora are also useful here, even though his focus is primarily on the black British. He sees the notion of the crossroads as "a special location where unforeseen, magical things can happen, [where there is a] tension between cultural roots and cultural routes, between space constituted through and between places and the space marked out by flows" (193). In the case of Nigerian hip hop, the influences that explode at this crossroads include those that come from within the country in terms of the merging and mixing of different ethnicities and the tradition and modernity that exists in an evolving postcolonial environment, together with the impact from the British colonial past and the media's perception of what African American identity and culture are supposed to be.

Oludare Art-Alade, a disc jockey at the Lagos Cool-FM radio station, revealed in an interview that Nigerian FM has been affected by MTV, BET, and *Soul Train*. "Nigerian rappers get a lot of their style from copying American artists. But we are lucky because our artists fall back on our culture, our language, in producing their work." Thus they produce their own hybrid style. Following the trend of preceding Nigerian popular music genres, Nigerian rap reflects the transformation of an African American musical genre into a localized medium that is readily identifiable as Nigerian. This generation has listened to contemporary African American music on television, cassette tapes, and radio, but local conditions have influenced the lyrics and stylistic elements of Nigerian rap to create a vernacular tradition.

Context: Nigerian Youth Identity

The influence of African American music and culture on Nigerians affects not only the music but also the identity of an entire generation of Nigerians, many of whom have never traveled overseas. Perhaps a useful way to see this is in the clear terms that W. E. B. Du Bois presented in his 1903 exposition of double consciousness where he described two streams of heritage running through the veins of African Americans at the turn of the twentieth century. His thesis finds special resonance in the present-day Nigerian sociopolitical fabric, which has been the birthplace of Nigerian rap because the postcolonial entity called Nigeria is still a space for external influences (British, African American, Jamaican) and local allegiances (national and ethnic traditions). These influences mingle, creating an awareness that constantly negotiates between the external and the internal, leading to either a schism or a fusion between the imported and indigenous. A dichotomy continues between the socially conscious and the economically expedient. These intersections of identity continue to reverberate in the creative expressions of young Nigerians.

Through the ever-present media conduits like cable television, magazines, and the internet, Nigerian youth are able to reinterpret and appropriate African American style and music so that they form a legitimate arm of black world culture. These influences are injected into the local culture, which is colored by the experience and challenge of life and progress. The development of popular music in Nigeria is linked to historical, social, and political circumstances before and after World War II. Although Nigerian rap appropriates an African American musical genre, many agree that it is undeniably Nigerian and reflects the Nigerian experience. Eldee of the Trybesmen insists: "We're not representing where we're from if we're kicking some New York style. It's better for us to have our own identity; that's why we put in our own thing" (interview July 1998).

Their "own thing"—the larger part of their identity—is built on a strong local culture that has nurtured them and an unfortunate political and economic legacy that has impaired them. A Yoruba proverb states that when two elephants fight, it is the grass that suffers. In Nigeria, it is the majority of people who suffer from the power struggles, the recurring cases of blatant economic mismanagement and political upheavals that have plagued the country since independence. This suffering undergirds the evolution of rap music in Lagos, the commercial capital of Nigeria. In many ways, parts of Lagos are similar to the inner cities of the United States where rap and hip hop originated. Lagos is divided into several inner-city sections, such as Ajegunle, Oshodi, and Isale-Eko, which contrast sharply with the more affluent suburbs in terms of economic development and infrastructural facilities. According to sociologist Oladipo Okege (1992), a number of factors have led to the poor conditions in such inner-city areas, including poor political leadership, corruption and embezzlement, general lack of discipline, and unequal educational and employment opportunities. Most of my questionnaire respondents agreed that there are very few opportunities for the Nigerian youth. A twenty-five-year-old respondent opined bitterly that "there is little or no hope for young people in Nigeria," and Ayo Osun, a Nigerian journalist respondent, confirmed that most rappers are from the ghetto and are uneducated.

Many of the youth in these inner-city areas have dropped out of high school, but many more have simply not been privileged enough to gain admission to a tertiary institution of learning (even though they may be in every way academically qualified), due to the political nature of the process. Nigerian educator Cordelia Nwagwu explains the problem of education in Nigeria:

> Unfortunately, the educational environment has not fostered positive attitudes toward the acquisition of essential knowledge, values, and skills as a condition for deserving an educational certificate. With educational institutions very poorly funded and with great shortages of qualified teachers, instructional facilities, and materials, very little effective teaching and hence learning takes place in the schools. Confronted by employers and a society that are so certificate-conscious and competitive entrance examinations into higher education institutions, the environment for admissions racketeering, examinations malpractices, and membership of secret cults is properly set.[2]

A quick glance at the economic and social place of these young people suggests that mountains were moved in the 1960s but that ground was not necessarily gained. In 2009, a study from the United Nations Development Programme (UNDP) revealed Nigeria's deplorable record of human deprivation—one of the worst in the developing world—and it was ranked among the poorest 10 percent of countries. World Bank and UNICEF statistics for 2008 reveal that life expectancy in Nigeria is 48 (below average for sub-Saharan African countries), and 70 percent of the population lives below the poverty line.[3] From these circumstances, Nigerian youth create a fantasy-driven culture for themselves derived from African American culture that has been presented to them through the usual pop culture media outlets. This may be their way of escaping the realistic hardships of a life that shows no sign of reversal.

African American Roots: Image and Persona

Among the Lagos inner-city youth in the 1990s, the processed wavy Americanized hair and haircuts and baggy hip-hanging jeans conspicuously overshadowed the dreadlocks and red, gold, and green clothes characteristic of Jamaican rastafarian culture that was so popular there since in the 1980s. Some radio announcers of the Nigerian FM stations and television personalities like Prince 2000 and Joe Black derive their names and pattern their speech after African American media stars to attract attention to themselves and add flavor to their image. Likewise, artists who live in the inner city have reached out to embrace styles that are culled from African Americans and Jamaicans observed on television and radio.

Within the difficult yet colorful inner-city environment, Nigerian rap artists like Junior and Pretty, Baba Fryo, and Daddy Showkey emerge, seeking to express themselves creatively, advance a message, and earn a living. The popularity of hip hop music and culture in Nigeria reflects the ongoing influence that African American music has had on Africa throughout the twentieth century. From the 1970s to the 1990s, aided by the widespread availability of televisions, stereos, and VCRs due to a short oil boom, other African American musical genres such as funk and soul were well received in Nigeria. For many young Nigerians, Nigerian music is a supplement to other forms of imported American music. Since independence, Nigerian FM stations have played both Nigerian and American music throughout the day. After music is released in the United States, original products and illegal reproductions swiftly find their way to Nigeria via people who visit the United States.

The newly introduced African American musical genres of the 1970s and 1980s were received and reinterpreted by young musicians in light of the ongoing Nigerian social, political, and economic problems. This heavily influenced the direction of Nigerian popular music. I grew up in the 1970s and 1980s listening to the vibrant sounds of James Brown and the Ohio Players emerging loudly and defiantly from my eldest brother's bedroom. *Shaft in Africa* and *Superfly* were shown in cinemas along with the popular East Indian movies, and Nigerian youth began to wear bellbottoms, platform shoes, and Afro hairstyles.

I interviewed Nigerians who were in their twenties during the 1970s, and they spoke of the passion with which they embraced African American music. They heard it all over the radio, purchased LPs, and reveled in the performances on *Soul*

Train. These impressionable young Nigerians listed their favorite artists as follows: Teddy Pendergrass, Bobby Womack, Parliament, Funkadelic, Aretha Franklin, Ray Parker Jr., James Brown, Stevie Wonder, and Barry White. At parties, they would dance to the funky sounds of George Clinton and the Ohio Players, among others. They felt comfortable with this music.

Like the audiences, many Nigerian musicians wholly adopt images based on what they see on television of American artists. They use these "props" as a means of arresting the attention of the audience. For instance, John Collins's (1992a: 107–109) review of Afro-rock in Nigeria in the 1980s contains photos of rock star Chris Okotie with sunglasses and jheri curled hair and Nigerian female soul singer Patti Boulaye sporting makeup similar to that of Diana Ross. The dance routines of Igbo highlife performers Bright Chimezie and Oliver de Coque are reminiscent of James Brown's gyrations.

Television programs like *Sunday Rendezvous* were modeled after *Soul Train,* which was being aired on Nigerian television in the 1970s and 1980s. Nigerian media hosts like Prince 2000, DJ Joe Black, and Patrick Oke tried to imitate the professionalism of Don Cornelius and the suaveness of Donnie Simpson of BET when presenting their own local musical shows on television and radio.

Although most Nigerians who are part of the hip hop generation have never left the country, they have been deluged by cultural influences from the diaspora mostly through print and electronic media. Eldee, one of the Trybesmen, says that he grew up with a Western influence from cable television. Likewise, all my questionnaire respondents revealed that most of their ideas for fashion come from film, television, video, and magazines like *Essence, Ebony,* and *Jet.* Rappers' images reflect this, even on their CD and DVD covers. Tony Tetuila's unusual blond hair and Soji's FUBU T-shirt are examples. Baba Fryo proudly displays his Bootsie Collins style glasses. The CD cover of the popular Nigerian R&B/hip hop group StylePlus shows the group in a familiar pose that is similar to one used by African American male groups like Boyz II Men, 112, and Jagged Edge. One of the most popular Nigerian rappers, 2Face, seems to emulate Tupac Shakur in name and also on his CD cover, which is reminiscent of Tupac's pose on his album *Me against the World.*

This American influence may stem from the oil boom of the 1970s, when wealth enabled elites to travel and return with new styles and also made American television and magazines readily available. The UK gave Nigeria its educational and legal systems. But for style, many Nigerians turned to the United States.

Apart from image, young Nigerians are affected by the style of articulation of African American rappers. Nigerian rappers and their listeners have listened closely to and absorbed the style and structure of verbal delivery unique to African American artists. When asked who their favorite African American artists are, younger Nigerians are quick to put forth names like Black Rob, Notorious B.I.G., Tupac, Dr. Dre, Ja Rule, 50 Cent, NWA, Diddy, Busta Rhymes, Joe, Nas, R. Kelly, Mystical, Nelly, and Wu Tang Clan. Nigerian rapper Freestyle, also a self-professed music critic, is hard on Nigerian rappers who do not measure up to the likes of Nas: "We're trying to be as good as or better than the people we got the rap from."

There is therefore some pressure to emulate African American artists. In "Dangerous Mix," the Black Reverendz adopt the Busta Rhymes' "Dangerous" track. The Remedies, in "Desire," adopt a sample used by Puff Daddy and Faith Evans in "Love Like This Before" and include a section almost identical to LL Cool J's tune created for his sitcom *In the House*. The song "Me and My Girlfriend" by Nigerian rapper Stonecold is almost identical to Tupac's "Girlfriend" and Jay-Z and Beyoncé's "Bonnie and Clyde" tracks. Nigerian rappers also rejuvenate earlier forms of African American popular music to flavor their own creations. In "Sade," the Remedies sample the Michael Jackson track "Liberian Girl," and Zaki Adzee's track "My Darling" uses Michael Jackson's "Don't Stop Till You Get Enough" (which itself was borrowed from Cameroonian Manu Dibango).

Apart from the utilization of various expressions and samples of African American music, there is more evidence of a strong influence of African American rap particularly in the speech patterns. In "Jealousy," the Remedies are influenced by Wyclef Jean when they chant, "one time . . . two time" after different phrases. Zaki Adzee's smoky deep tones, cadence, and delivery on "OK Now" are reminiscent of the unmistakable Tupac sound as on, for example, "Young Niggaz."

One cannot help noticing the many African American–sounding oral exclamations like "uh," "uh-huh," "yeah," and "come on" that permeate Nigerian hip hop music. Tony Tetuila sends shout-outs to his "homies" and "niggaz in the house" using language that is completely borrowed: "I know you got my back. . . . Hey, you feel that?" The same is true of Eedris Abdul-Kareem, who introduces his DVD with an attempted imitation of an American accent and constant peppering of the phrase "you know wha'am sayin?"

This emulation in image and articulation of the popular African American rappers appears clearly in some of the performance stylings of Eedris Abdul-Kareem. On footage of his live show in Lagos, Eedris stomps from one side of the stage to another, wearing a "wife-beater" stretched across his chest and a do-rag on his head. His towel is over his shoulder, his pants are sagging. His "posse" zips back and forth with microphones, chiming in when necessary. Halfway through the performance, a naked girl, who is obviously mortified, comes on the stage and begins to dance. This prop takes the image of the African American video girl to a whole new level.

With this scene in mind, one may tend to agree with the severe note of disapproval in a recent statement made by Nigerian poet laureate Niyi Osundare. He condemned "the hip hop hysteria" pervading Nigeria. "It urges one to take leave of one's very self and assume the borrowed clichéd mask of the other," he laments (*Guardian*, September 18, 2005, 70). However, the next section, in dealing with the indigenous roots of Nigerian hip hop, will reveal that, contrary to Osundare's statement, Nigerian youth are actually able to appropriate and customize African American hip hop to produce a distinct amalgamation of indigenous afrobeat influences and African American hip hop.

Indigenous Roots: Content and Structure

Nigerian rappers selectively utilize elements of style and thematic content inherent in a long line of Nigerian popular music genres, including highlife and, more markedly, afrobeat. From the latter, it draws themes of social and political criticism, and from the former, it draws themes of relationships and humor. Highlife, the popular West African dance music that is influenced by African jazz, juju, and other West African indigenous music, was popular in the 1950s and 1960s, and thematic concerns were lighter than those carried by Fela Anikulapo Kuti's afrobeat. Just after independence, Nigerians were filled with hope and excitement about the prospect of wealth and self-governance. The need for social and political criticism was not as pronounced as in the 1970s. The popular theme of love and relationships between men and women is an element that Nigerian rap has borrowed from highlife. However, in both Nigerian highlife and Nigerian rap, this theme is always portrayed in a humorous and entertaining manner, rather than the more serious disposition seen in African American rhythm & blues and soul music. The use of humor by Nigerian rappers seems reminiscent of the early African American minstrel performers who "laughed just to keep from crying."[4] In fact, Nigerians are known to find humor in many difficult situations, and this seems to be a way of dealing with pain and suffering. This humor has helped to tide the people over as they have been plunged through numerous waves of economic hardship and political upheaval.

Building on this innate cultural mechanism to deal with unpleasant situations, this lighthearted approach of Nigerian rappers was enthusiastically received. Junior and Pretty began to popularize this theme in their 1994 single "Monica." In this song, they quip about a lover, Monica, who has an affair with the neighbor while her man is away on business. When Monica is asked why she does this, she explains she is following the Bible teaching to "love your neighbor as yourself." Similarly, in "Fatimah," Junior teases Pretty about his future in-laws, and Pretty swears that in spite of their wickedness, he will still marry his love, Fatimah:

> Fat fat fat Fatimah ba-be
> Fatimah please don't make me go crazy
> Fat fat fat Fatimah

Humorous lyrics in Nigerian rap are common and illustrate encounters with and among friends and lovers. They are rarely used in reference to parents and elders, as is the case with Jazzy Jeff and the Fresh Prince in "Parents Just Don't

Understand." Clearly, this is a function of the culture of Nigerians. Nigerian societal values consider it disrespectful and in bad taste to openly discuss parents in such a humorous manner. Also, romantic relationships are considered private, discussed only within the boundaries of family and close friends. Therefore, these songs by Nigerian rappers do not reveal the heartfelt depth that is palpable in romantic ballads and rap songs by African American artists like LL Cool J ("I Need Love") and Jay-Z ("Song Cry").

Another theme that dominated highlife and found its way into Nigerian rap was a focus on women. Although much of this focus on women was set in a humorous light, it is rarely perceived as offensive to Nigerian women. Flagrant disrespect and disdainful behavior by men toward women in Nigeria is typically not well received or tolerated because respect for women is tightly interwoven and ingrained in the culture such that any defiance of this unwritten code is seen as more an aberration than the norm. Another highlife song, "Sweet Mother" by Prince Nico Mbaga, reveals the esteem with which mothers are regarded. "Sweet Mother" is often played at Nigerian weddings as a way of paying tribute to the mother of the bride.

This tone of respect for women has carried through into Nigerian hip hop. Junior and Pretty do this in their song "Fatimah":

> Fat-fat-fat Fatimah
> I swear I go go home tell my mama
> say I don reach time to get my woman
> because Pretty don become a man

Like Mbaga's "Sweet Mother," the rapper shows his mother respect as he seeks her approval and blessing before getting married.

While highlife was popular among Nigerians, its influence was concentrated mostly in southern Nigeria and embraced mostly by the generation who were young adults in the 1950s and 1960s. Afrobeat, on the other hand, reached further across geographic and generational boundaries, and therefore, remains a more powerful influence on contemporary Nigerian hip hop. Afrobeat is a combination of funk, soul, and distinct African beats created by Fela Anikulapo Kuti. The emergence of this genre in the late 1960s marks a milestone in Nigerian music history. More than ever before, the enduring Egba tradition of resistance and militancy burst forth and was reshaped in the spirit of truth and boldness. As a citizen of the proud Egba (Yoruba) ethnic group, and as a son of revolutionary parents, Fela created a musical genre that had critical appeal to the common man.[5] As Dele Morakinyo (1990: 18) states, "Fela believes music is a weapon against societal ills and he shoots with it." From the 1960s to 1980s, Fela Anikulapo Kuti used his afrobeat to criticize the perpetuation of colonialism in the vicious but stealthy cloak of neocolonialism. Having studied at a prestigious musical institute in London and spent time in Los Angeles, Fela intertwined the militant nationalistic philosophies of Malcolm X and the activist tendencies of his heritage with both African and African American musical bases and began to mold a vibrant new musical genre (C. Waterman 1998: 3; Veal 2000; Olaniyan 2004).[6]

Nigerian rapper Freestyle appropriately referred to Fela as "the late great" (interview, July 1998). He emphasized the role that afrobeat played in the evolution of Nigerian hip hop. This influence is evident in much of the hip hop music that is created by young Nigerians. An obvious example of this is in the beginning of the Black Reverendz' track, "Check Yourself." It drips of Fela's afrobeat with elements like the repetitive bass line, the percussiveness of the shekere, the call and response, and the vocal quality. It is almost as if Fela were there performing with them. A definite influence of Fela and afrobeat is also found in the thematic content of much of the hip hop tracks that Nigerians create. According to rapper Eldee, "Hip hop is a way of life that needs to be expressed in a certain manner so we use our music to express the feelings of the people" (interview, July 1998). With a strong and fearless precedent set by Fela, some Nigerian rap focuses on social and political criticism. The unpleasant prevailing socioeconomic circumstances have encouraged a reflective and bold discussion of the government's inadequacies and the reality of the environment as revealed in Junior and Pretty's "Gallows," Eedris Abdul-Kareem's "Nigeria Jaga-Jaga" (which was banned for a while), the Remedies' "Peace Nigeria," and the Trybesmen's "What Kind Life Be Dis."

Apart from the musical quality of afrobeat, Fela's thematic trademark was a fearless critique of the political and social circumstances of the 1970s and 1980s. The ordinary Nigerian, whose cause is boldly advanced in Fela's music, has, according to Emeka Ojukwu (1989: 34), "become the obscene donkey on whose blood, sweat, and toil the entire edifice of a monstrous omnivorous and grotesque state is given life support." Fela reveals how the prevailing Nigerian environment necessarily shapes thematic concerns for the Nigerian musician:

> Yes, if you're in England, you sing of enjoyment. You sing of love, or who you're going to be with next! But my society is underdeveloped because of an alien system imposed on my people. So there's no music for enjoyment, for love, when there's such a struggle for people's existence. (Fela quoted in Grass 1986: 142)

This theme of social and political criticism pervades the music of Fela and then younger artists like Lagbaja and Nigerian rappers. Examples of Fela's stringent social critique include "International Thief Thief (ITT)," "Big Bad Country (BBC)," and "Zombie." In "International Thief Thief" from 1979, Fela goes as far as calling the names of leaders and other popular and corrupt politicians who are "international thieves, rogues." In "Zombie" from 1976, he directly confronts the military government.

In the same manner, some Nigerian rappers venture into this area of social criticism. By the 1990s, conditions for the masses had not improved. Instead, they had continued in a steep downhill dive, and artists found a need to continue the tradition of social and political commentary. In "Gallows," rappers Junior and Pretty lament the deplorable conditions in the inner-city areas where most of the Lagos youth live. In this song, Junior and Pretty reflect on the hopelessness of the situation for the masses:

> This generation is lost for lust
> No one cares but the love of us
> it used to be days when we lived in peace
> but now brothers crumble
> Nowadays, children don't play in the street
> blood flowing back and forth like a stream
> no pain no gain life is but a dream
> I pray you temper justice with mercy
> for this your hunger I no longer fancy
> my friends how many times shall I cry
> see how hard it is for me to stay alive
> Every meal I eat becomes my last supper
> Eat your last and die like a pauper
> this situation in the nation, no occupation
> enough is enough in this your situation
> my brothers my strength is spent
> I want to see this nation excel
> not live in the penury just like hell

Daddy Showkey's "What's Gonna Be Is Gonna Be" reflects this same theme:

> Many brothers they die and they go
> Many youth they die and they go
> Remember if you live in the ghetto
> I always try and feel it in my mind oh
> . . . .
> kekekeke the sound of the gun
> people don't live long by the shot of the gun
> kekekeke the sound of the gun
> people don't live long under oppression

Here Showkey discusses the bleakness of life for the youth. Educational opportunities are few for the underprivileged, for those who "live in the ghetto." Thus dreams for a better life are quickly snuffed by the prevailing conditions. Showkey also points an accusing finger at the military dictatorship that governed Nigeria in the 1980s and 1990s (with a brief respite of inept and ineffective democracy from 1979 through 1983).

It is pertinent to point out, however, that these earlier Nigerian rappers were not as outspoken as Fela. A conceivable reason for the subdued boldness of Nigeria's pioneer rappers is a situation engendered by the government's vicious hostility to free speech in the early 1990s. The Nigerian artist continued to operate within an atmosphere of a very hostile military dictatorship, which often proved its brutality to those who showed any form of opposition to it. Throughout his career, Fela and his family experienced this ruthlessness. Artists like Junior and Pretty and Daddy Showkey understandably decided to tread softly in order to stay safe and out of prison.

More recently, as Nigeria has remained in a reasonably stable democracy, rappers and artists have grown bolder. The perception of freedom of speech seems to be lauded and embraced. A good example of this is shown in the bold lyrics of rapper Blackface's "Hard Life":

> It's a hard life wey we dey live for Nija [Nigeria]
> Na so them do, dey done chop our money go
> Them say me and you no go know
> Na lie oh; See them as they pass and go
> With their siren from Opebi [Lagos neighborhood] to Otukpo [city in Benue
>   state] . . .
> See as our lives just dey bitter, eh,
> 'Cos our roads are bad
> How can we be glad
> When our children are suffering everyday . . .
> Which kind life we dey today
> When we work and then get no pay, I say
> This government is bad, oh

Here Blackface bemoans tough living conditions. He indicts the leaders who flaunt their power (sirens) in a way that suggests they do not think or care that the common people will notice the corruption.

Related to this theme of social and political criticism is the theme of anti-Europeanization or antimodernization. Again, Fela laid a strong precedent for this theme. Often he accused the elite of throwing away their traditional values to embrace an alien and inappropriate way of life, which is evidenced in the neocolonialist actions of the postcolonial leadership. In "Lady," Fela berates African women who try to be less African and more European. Nigerian rappers embrace this theme with their usual humor. Junior and Pretty's "Body Fila" is a good example. They speak out against Nigerian women who use too much makeup in an attempt to gain what they perceive as more "sophistication" and therefore become less African:

> That pancake wey you dey rub for face
> the lipstick you rub for lips
> the mascara you rub for eyes
> oh . . .

> she no get rival for town
> na shock absorber [i.e. juicy and cushiony body]
> ready to attack and still under cover
> when the girl call am the bobo [boyfriend] still dey pose
> with her funny look and her hair like cover girl
> Bobo jump on top of girl start to dey kiss
> e no no say this kiss na six feet [is six feet deep]
> dey no do well well he come collapse for ground
> they rush am go hospital for inside town
> doctor examination be say na operation
> the sickness na cosmetic indigestion
> too much pancake de bobo don swallow
> now dey de tear belly to remove eye shadow [operation to remove the
>   consumed makeup]

Here Junior and Pretty exaggerate the effects of the application of Westernized forms of makeup, describing an impossible situation where the boyfriend of the "sophisticated girl" is diagnosed with "cosmetic indigestion" because he has come into contact with so much of the makeup. In their song "Monica," Junior and Pretty continue to taunt women who fall into extreme categories of social interaction: the unrefined on the one hand and the overly sophisticated on the other hand. Here they ridicule a socially unexposed girl who is taken to a restaurant for a meal and naively orders a "satellite dish" for dinner.

Baba Fryo also criticizes Western behavior in "Hip Hop Pose," in which he chides the Nigerian who returns from the United States with new ways and attitudes, intending to make his old Nigerian friends look inferior. Many of these "returnees" believe that the acquisition of American mannerisms is somehow better than their "Nigerianness." Many actually return with affected bogus accents and queer fashion sense, which is neither American nor Nigerian. They therefore fall out of favor with friends and family and into ridicule. Baba Fryo laments:

> Once they go America
> na dat time they start to de speak like foreigner
> Den go dey pose
> Den go de waka kuru kere [walk in a crooked way] . . .
> Some of dem dey waka like say they too big
> Some of dem dey waka like say they no dey shit

Common Ground: Black World Devices

While the influences from African American hip hop and afrobeat (and to a lesser extent, highlife) help to create and localize Nigerian hip hop as a popular music genre, there are some features that reveal a sharing of a common ground for black music across the diaspora. Nigerian rap artists have adapted a foreign, but in many ways familiar, musical tradition and localized it to fit the environment and their circumstances just as other musicians had done with earlier African American genres. The musical connections between Africa and black America are not just a continuum but can also be viewed as a powerful and unrelenting cycle.

Perhaps at the center of this cycle are the long-standing traditions of West African orators, griots, praise singers, and town criers, vital sages and performers within their local societies. African communities found expression of their history, events, and issues through these important persons. Black musicians across the diaspora share this heritage. The tradition bequeathed by these oral traditions lays the foundation upon which both traditional and modern African—and in this case Nigerian—music grew. Musicians adapted their style and lyrics according to the times and the circumstances in which they found themselves. They also embraced and fused the sincerity of expression and oratorial creativity meticulously handed down with their own musical innovations.

This legacy touches both Nigerian and African American rappers. Cheryl Keyes (1996) concludes that some African American rappers have drawn elements from the "African crossroad" such as repetition, language use, timbre, and texture as well as other nonmusical elements such as dress and posture. It is the Nigerian rappers' customization of these elements that makes Nigerian hip hop uniquely "Nigerian."

The vital role of the audience is a clear instance of what happens at the African crossroad. Use of a special language for in-group communication is an example of how Africans and African Americans share a common approach to music making. Describing James Brown's songs, Maultsby (1983: 56) states that they "were in the dialect and musical style that Black people recognized." Like Fela and other Nigerian artists over the years, most Nigerian rappers keep their art uniquely localized by using pidgin English. This medium of communication is acceptable and well received by the community because of its special appeal to a large number of people across social, class, and ethnic lines.

Most Nigerian rappers use pidgin English because the people can relate to it. When rappers substitute this language with what they perceive to be a more refined American style and accent that they have not mastered, audiences do not understand their lyrics. When Baba Fryo's sidekick attempts his American accent in "Pose Hip Hop Version," it becomes very difficult to understand and not nearly as popular as Junior and Pretty, who call themselves "the Kings of Pidgin Rap" and consistently rap in the vernacular.

Other elements of African oral performance are shared by Nigerian and African American artists. According to Nigerian scholar Isidore Okpewho (1990: 14), African oral performance is characterized by repetition, parallelism, piling and association, tonality, ideophones, digression, imagery, allusion, and symbolism. Junior and Pretty consistently use symbolism and metaphors to flavor their pieces. In "Gallows" they rap:

> I want to see this nation excel
> not live in the penury just like hell
> the breast milk of wisdom is sour
> how many of us will see the next hour

Reference to breast milk in Nigerian speech is not uncommon, and the audience immediately understands that wisdom and truth are essential to the healthy growth of the nation just as breast milk is to the growing child.

Junior and Pretty's "Body Fila" is saturated with symbolism and metaphor:

> In the night you turn to sunlight
> in the morning you turn to midnight
> yellow baby don turn to charcoal
> with your chewing stick leg just like macaroni
> Young girl I swear you dey look funny

Here, they joke about a woman who bleaches her skin to a lighter color (turning it to sunlight) and compare her skinny legs to sticks and macaroni. In "Theresa" they use more symbolism:

> When she come to settle one of our fights
> na the chemist from our street wey dey de enjoy
> na so so money I dey pay for those she injure
> every sanitation Theresa must quarrel
> her mouth go dey fire like double-barrel

Junior and Pretty liken Theresa's mouth to a double-barrel gun because of her quarrelsome nature. In most of their lyrics, Junior and Pretty use familiar and humorous symbolism and metaphors that are readily received by the audience.

Other Nigerian hip hop groups, such as London-based Unsung Heroes (Ty and Breis), show more depth in their use of symbolism and metaphor. The sophistication with which they craft their message is complex and impressive, reminiscent of some of the well-established African American hip hop artists such as Mos Def, Jay-Z, and Lupe Fiasco. In "Right Here in Front of You," Ty rhymes:

> Watch the drummer sing, Rum-pa-pa-pum-pum
> Love where I come from, Rise above the hum drum
> Mainstream, can I piss in the puddle
> Then represent a frog like a kiss and a cuddle . . .
> With more support than a big girl's girdle
> I've got the sunshine cap while you leap frog hurdles . . .
> And drop a cold rhyme to let your blessing curdle . . .
> I think you'll find that this style is critical
> Ten naked girls in my room, still miserable . . .

Anger, the only thing in us you can provoke
Too many headlights caught up in my antelope
Street marching and I don't have to tip toe
Carbon dioxide up against my window
I'm only rapping my fingers on your windowsill
Watching the World Cup, we're forced to win it like Brazil
Not many heroes are unsung
Try and test the group
End up in the soup like won-ton
That's like trying to fight an army with one gun

Ty uses interesting imagery to convey his message of self-pride and activism. In this track, he separates himself from the mainstream by "pissing in their puddle" and explains why his lyrics are different, more "critical," and provocative. References to Brazil and the World Cup and the ten naked girls further exemplify his clever play with language and stylistic devices.

Stories and tall tales also function as important stylistic devices used in the lyrics of rap at the crossroads. This follows a very old West African oral tradition of storytelling. Pioneer MC, British-born American rapper Slick Rick, and more contemporary Columbian-born Immortal Technique use the medium of hip hop to tell stories. Nigerian rappers draw on this same tradition. In "Fatimah," Junior and Pretty tell a vivid story in pidgin English of how Pretty goes hunting armed with a cutlass and a gun. When Pretty suddenly encounters a lion, he drops his arms and runs for dear life:

Another day den say Pretty go kill animal
na the kind of animal you go tink say na man
Me I no agree, then I start to quarrel
Pretty carry gun with cutlass
enter inside forest
for inside bush he see lion wey de wait for breakfast
na in he tear race, forget the gun and cutlass
now Pretty dey run—na in dey fall for ground
when de lion catch am Pretty still dey roll around

Another vital stylistic element is the use of boasting and competition in somewhat the same way it operates in the lyrics of African American rappers like Lil' Wayne, Ludacris, and Kanye West. In "Fatimah," Junior and Pretty compete. Junior starts by teasing Pretty about his affair with Fatimah and how Pretty could not easily win her hand in marriage:

Another day they say make we do traditional wrestling
The man wey dey do Pretty
Na one Summo wrestler

> Ma people you know say Pretty be like pikin [child]
> When de man deal with am finish
> e be like fried chicken

Junior, using pidgin English, explains to the audience how Pretty's strength was tested. A fight with a sumo wrestler leaves Pretty like "a pikin" (a child) and turns him into "fried chicken." Pretty immediately responds and counters what Junior has said.

Another track that exemplifies the art of boasting is the Trybesmen's "Shake Bodi":

> No need to rush the mic, Eldee is the doc
> Cos now yo Mama and Papa
> they be singin my song
> Intelligent rhymes and lyrics
> you all be singing for long
> No need to talk much
> Go buy the album
> It's the bomb
> Now I'm keeping it real and being like I was
> The only thing that changed is to see me now you have to buzz
> Cos now I'm a business man no time to waste
> like Microsoft now "Billy" is coming through my "Gates"
> I've got my own label
> make dough because I'm able
> We don't rush, we spread ideas upon the table
> to see how we can keep you dancing, waving your hands
> so follow the Trybesmen we'll take you to the promised land
> Come on—stop trying to sound like us fool

The metaphors and images in Nigerian rap lyrics draw on both foreign and local scenes. Again, this reflects the duality of this musical tradition. Junior and Pretty constantly make familiar Nigerian references like "Taribi West," "The National Cake," "Ayinlara Street," "Akin Adesola," and "Mammy Water." These are all localized registers that only Nigerians or foreigners well acquainted with Nigerian sociocultural conditions will understand.[7] Yet, in the lyrics of groups like the Trybesmen, there have been references to "Rambo," "Schwarzenegger," "Hasta la vista," "Holyfield," "I believe I can fly," and "Clinton and Lewinsky," which reflect the influence of American popular culture.

The Future of Nigerian Hip Hop

Anthropologist Andrew Causey (1999: 430–31) urges caution in applying the concept of hybridity to material culture because of its assumptions that the offspring is supposedly "stronger, healthier, or more 'effective.'" It is this same concern that confirms the utility of this concept for analyzing Nigerian hip hop. This essay has explored the strength of this hybridity in Nigerian rap music by interrogating the internal/local and the external/international influences, while also examining the contribution of the common foundation of African oral traditions.

Hip hop has taken root, especially in the large, bustling cities. Nigerian artists have cleverly merged several stylistic elements from African American music to create a vibrant new style. However, rappers do not partake of the prosperity that their counterparts in the United States enjoy. Piracy of original tapes and compact discs has stripped the music industry of any profits comparable on a relative scale to those achieved by artists in Europe and America. The rappers are forced to record in very small, unsophisticated studios where basic facilities like air-conditioning are lacking. This results in crude output in terms of the technical quality of the recordings. However, the artists' creativity remains incontestable.

According to Graham (1992:18), "Most modern Nigerian musicians have come to rely on live shows for income, not through gate fees but through the custom of spraying whereby a rich individual is mentioned in song and in return 'sprays' the forehead of the musician with as much money as status demands." Nigerian rappers are not particularly popular among the more elite or wealthy members of society, nor do they praise rich people, so they do not gain much from the spraying. The culture, scope, and mission of Nigerian rap music are antithetical to sycophancy as manifested in other genres of Nigerian popular music such as juju.

While Nigerian society enjoys rap music, it looks down on the people who perform it, possibly because they perceive that there is limited economic potential in rap music or other forms of popular music. It is not unusual for parents to be upset when their children choose that line of work. The reception to popular music artists is lukewarm at best. When rapper Lanre D. of the group Trybesmen, the son of upper-middle-class parents, found himself being drawn into the art of rapping, he knew that his family would not support him. He knew that only a handful of artists had successfully broken through societal biases. Artists like Fela Anikulapo Kuti, Onyeka Onwenu, Evi Edna Ogoli, and Sunny Ade had made that leap and earned respect from Nigerian society as a whole. Lanre hid his art from his family until the day that he was with his father in the back of a chauffeur-driven car. As they approached the gates of a business, the security man recognized Lanre as the artist whose music his children were crazy about. The security man greeted Lanre enthusiastically and ushered the car in through the gates. Lanre then had to explain to his bewildered father that he was indeed better known to young Lagosians as a member of the Trybesmen (interview, September 1998).

The hard life of a Nigerian artist can also be attributed to the ongoing economic slump that continues to beset Nigerians. The depressed economy does not encourage the purchase of nonessential luxury items. Food, shelter, clothing, education, and health are areas much more valued and essential. Music and other forms of entertainment fall out of favor with the pocket. This leads to the society's selfish use of the music—to be enjoyed but not to be supported or remunerated—a situation that is unfortunate but understandable. DVDs and CDs are bootlegged, reproduced, and sold on the streets, prompting the Nigerian Music Association to include harsh warnings on music videos against piracy.

Although the economic situation is bleak, this new Nigerian hip hop follows in a long line of evolving Nigerian popular music genres and continues to thrive. In 2010, rap music is still the number one music of the youth, followed by R&B. Since the late 1990s, A-list African American artists have performed for enthusiastic crowds in Lagos and Abuja, including Jay-Z, Beyoncé, Akon, Chris Brown, and 50 Cent.

Ronnie Graham (1992: 18) explains that Nigerian popular music forms such as "juju, fuji, apala, waka, highlife, afrobeat, and Ibo blues remain vibrant, living idioms with clear and identifiable roots in traditional styles. . . . Hip hop, rap, and ragamuffin have thousands of adherents, while many older styles are slowly but steadily dying." In contrast to this contention of the strength of these contemporary pop music genres, Stapleton and May (1987: 5) contend that "everywhere there is mixture, collision, and collusion. Africa impacts on the West; the West on Africa. Pessimists predict that African music will lose its identity as a result of this global give and take." The elements in the hybrid of Nigerian hip hop remind us that there is indeed mixture, but because of the very strong local cultural and musical foundation and sense of nationality on which Nigerian rappers build their art, there is no likelihood that this form will ever lose its identity. As long as afrobeat and African American hip hop survive, Nigerian hip hop will remain a strong offspring, and one can argue that even in the unlikely event that these "parents" begin to wane, Nigerian hip hop, nourished by the legacy of its roots, will continue to flourish for generations to come.

NOTES

1. After much collaborative planning, I provided my research assistant Godwin Oragbon with the resources to carry out the interviews on my behalf. He provided me with the original tapes when the interviews were done. Unless otherwise cited, Godwin carried out all personal interviews quoted in this chapter in Lagos between July and September 1998, the same year that my questionnaire was distributed.

2. Cordelia Nwagwu, "The Environment of Crises in the Nigerian Education System," *Comparative Education* 33 no. 1 (March 1997): 92.

3. UNDP: Human Development Report, Nigeria 2008–2009, http://hdrstats.undp.org /en/countries/country_fact_sheets/cty_fs_NGA.html; World Bank Report, Nigeria at a Glance (December 9, 2009), http://data.worldbank.org/data-catalog/at-a-glance-table, http://devdata.worldbank.org/AAG/nga_aag.pdf.

4. In his autobiography, *Big Sea,* Langston Hughes quotes a blues song that reflects this sentiment: "You don't know / You don't know my mind— / When you see me laughin' / I'm laughin' to keep from cryin'" (1993: 53).

5. From the end of the eighteenth century and into the nineteenth century, the Egba fiercely resisted threats and incursions from the Oyo Empire and from slave traders. In

spite of large numbers of fatalities and captures, they survived as a group and settled in Abeokuta. Fela's parents were both active in their fight for women's rights and educational equality (Johnson-Odim and Mba 1997).

6. Afrobeat remains a strong musical force among the people of Nigeria, carried on after Fela's death in 1997 by Lagbaja and Femi Kuti, among others.

7. Taribi West was a Nigerian national soccer player, the "National Cake" referred to a share of the nation's riches, Ayinlara Street is a ghetto in Lagos, Akin Adesola is a street in the highbrow area of Lagos Island, and Mammy Water is a water spirit.

PART 4.
EAST COAST
(KENYA AND TANZANIA)

The Local and Global in Kenyan Rap and Hip Hop Culture

JEAN NGOYA KIDULA

In 1996, I was invited by a bossa nova musician to participate on his album by rapping in Kiswahili alongside a Brazilian rapper invoking Angola using a genre known as maracatu. The idea in part was to demonstrate the reciprocal interconnections that have marked developments of popular music between the African continent and its diaspora. Africans on the continent have appropriated genres born in the diaspora, such as reggae or rhythm and blues, to globalize themselves, while people of African descent outside the continent constantly draw on African continental forms, textures, structures, and performance practices to invoke cultural and artistic heritage. I was therefore invited to represent the African roots of rap and to reinvent them in an African lingua franca.

With my street Swahili and an ambivalence to the niceties of the language as it was taught to me in high school, I enlisted the help of a Kiswahili Ph.D. student to suggest, correct, and guide my poetry. His suggestions were in such difficult and correct idioms that I dismissed them and rewrote the text in a semiliterate form, first to suit the poetic style I had selected and also to fit in the musical framework constructed by the producer and main DJ—a Brazilian jazz pianist. In the process, I realized that my "composition" was informed not just by the general structural characteristics of rap but also by Kiswahili poetic structure and delivery, and concerns I felt were important to a musician from Kenya. The Brazilian rapper, in Portuguese, invoked maracatu, a genre associated with ceremonies of African diasporic groups in northeast Brazil. The rhythms and instruments used in maracatu evoked its African musical roots and cited the continent for lyrical inspiration. Both of us summoned local Afrogenic musical underpinnings to propel our product into the global space whose most potent genre at the time was rap.[1]

This chapter examines the local and the global in Kenyan rap music and the accompanying hip hop culture. After outlining the place of rap in the Kenyan music industry, I will analyze some of the characteristics that distinguish Kenyan rap as a musical genre derived from global representations. I will trace part of the history of the establishment of rap in Kenya and the main players in its production and dissemination. Further, I will examine antecedents to rap stylings emanating from indigenous ethnic and popular musics, describe the veneration and nostalgic role of rap for Kenyans residing in the United States, and locate Kenyan rap alongside hip hop culture as understood from a global perspective and as localized in the country.

Rap and the Kenyan Popular Music Industry

Since the beginning of the twenty-first century, the Kenyan popular music scene has been dominated by rap and gospel music. Both genres are popular in that they are readily available and accessible. They are vitalized by their propensity to absorb other musical styles as subgenres. Each genre relies on performers' manipulation of its characteristics as well as the critique of its consumers. Gospel music is characterized by Bible-based lyrics, social and moral messages, and opinions purported to be Christian religious. Rap, while most differentiated by semi-spoken declamations against a rhythmic backdrop, may contain religious lyrics, in which case it is called gospel rap. Gospel has a variety of performance ensembles, from soloists, to family and small chamber groups, to choirs of 12 to 100 members. Rap artists work in much smaller numbers, from solo acts to a very popular combination of two rappers, or a crew (more than two people) or a leader with backup vocalists. Ubiquitously present is the DJ, who might also MC an event. Most gospel artists use regular names like Esther Wahome or Reuben Kigame. Rap artists always have stage names, such as Necessary Noize, Redsan, or Deux Vultures.

While both genres are widely disseminated, gospel generally outsells rap for a number of reasons: rap appeals to young people with little cash; it is associated with youthfulness and rebellion; as an urban phenomenon, rap sells little in small towns and rarely in rural areas; and many rap artists produce single hits rather than albums. Radio is rap's largest disseminator, with home dubbing as the primary method of circulation. Gospel, on the other hand, became popular in the late 1980s (Kidula 2000) and has an expanding market due to an explosive growth of Christian denominations in Kenya. Both genres as entertainment arts incorporate dance, acrobatics, and other types of gimmicks. Often there is little difference in their presentational styles. Because gospel has a longer history as a mediated popular genre, its elements of continuity can more easily be traced (Rycroft 1977). Rap, on the other hand, is presently the most accessible avenue for youth to express themselves musically in the urban space where communal music making occurs in schools, churches, dance halls, or watering holes (bars or pubs).

Both rap and gospel are locations for legitimizing popular language slogans, promoting novel ideas, and discussing contentious issues. In both genres, consumers often edit performers' styles and lyrics during concerts, on radio call-in programs, or on websites and chat rooms. Artists, congregations, and consumers further edit gospel and rap lyrics to accommodate performance contexts and audiences. These edits are incorporated into later recordings by original or cover artists, creating a blended composition. While gospel lyrics may be global, given their biblical associations, rappers often draw on local contexts, places, people, and immediate events. Rap has become the space for political and social lobbying whereas gospel is for moralizing, although its artists also provide social critique. Rap commentary can be brutal, honest, and earthy, just as it is elsewhere.

Making Rap Kenyan

Rap initially emerged with African Americans in the late 1970s. "It is characterized by semi-spoken rhymes declaimed over a rhythmic musical backing, drawn from the sampling of pre-existing recordings and the use of DJ mixing techniques" (Toop 2005) and initially based on funk and soul music. Rap was part of the hip hop complex involving disc jockeys, emcees, break dancers, graffiti writers, and "an attitude rendered in the form of stylized dress, language, and gestures associated with urban street culture" (Keyes 2002: 1). It was this composite that was introduced to the Kenyan public through films, video, radio airplay, and television. Jimmy Gathu inaugurated a program in 1993 on the Kenyan TV station KTN to popularize the genre (Rebensdorf 1996). He aired North American artists and a few Kenyans, but no definitive local voices emerged. By 1996 various Kenyan rap wanabees had engaged the genre for self-expression, particularly since rap invites personal opinion in a public forum.

The success of gospel and reggae in Kenya as commercial products attested to the fact that for any global genre to speak Kenyan, it must address local and national issues and draw on distinctively Kenyan traits. Gospel had established the commercial and popular viability of drawing on ethnic resources for difference (Agawu 2003) when marketing to Kenyan and other African audiences. While artists, including Gathu, appropriated rappers' penchant for social commentary and critique, they did not initially earn public sanction as the people's representatives.

Musicians who had failed to earn a reasonable living playing Congolese-style rumba began to draw on features that Kenyan rap embraced to regroup, in particular, the use of Sheng—a fusion of Swahili, English, and Kenyan languages (Nyairo and Ogude 2003). In addition, Kenyan musicians became increasingly aware of what the country brought to the global table, as demonstrated by the success of such artists as Ayub Ogada (1993) using indigenous Kenyan instruments, languages, and tunes on the world music circuit. Kenyans without knowledge of, or access to, copyright patents had their ideas looted and even reworked by poachers. Musicians thought that the best way to avoid this plagiarism was to make audio recordings. For example, in the 1990s, gospel musician Shari Martin was shocked to hear his song credited to his cousin during a TV broadcast. He called the station to protest. Ownership was only properly ascribed after the producers ascertained through live audition that the singer on the recording to which the cousin was lip-synching in the earlier airing was indeed Martin.[2]

Exposure on radio and TV, in performance venues, and on newly created award shows was a primary means of establishing ownership. Further, a lack of proper jurisdiction in copyright matters forced rap artists and their producers to perform live in order to claim possession of their work and to earn income from shows. In Kenya, Ted Josiah inaugurated the Kisima Music Awards in 1995 to acknowledge local talent, some of whom received pan-African exposure at the Kora Awards where musicians in different popular genres interacted with their continental counterparts.[3] Rap musicians profited from this network that landed them new gigs and wider audiences abroad, particularly since Ted Josiah, as a producer, seemed to understand the international market. Rap slowly gained widespread exposure at local urban joints and on the national and pan-African stage. The process of its legitimization began first with localizing rap and its broader associations in Kenya, then globalizing the resultant Kenyan expression. How indeed did or does rap become Kenyan?

The production of rap at the musical level involves procedures such as sampling, mixing, spinning, scratching, reciting poetry, chanting, and singing. Some of these practices grew out of reggae, possibly the most appropriated diasporic form in Africa. Rap acquired distinctive Kenyan features from at least four dimensions: the artists who composed and produced it originated in Kenya, whether or not they lived in the country; the lyrics, language, and issues voiced concerns that were politically or culturally rooted in happenings in Kenya; the musical forms, types, and styles appropriated had cultural roots or underpinnings in Kenya; and the music sampled was from Kenyan cultures or had been composed by Kenyan popular icons. These four aspects are merely fluid indicators of what initially endeared rap to Kenyans.

Nationalizing Kenyan Rap

Kenyan rap became a national phenomenon through the release of a single in 1999 called "Tafsiri Hii" [Swahili: Interpret this, Read this, or Get behind the sense of this] by the group Kalamashaka.[4] But hip hop gained Kenyan national iconicity in 2002 when "Unbwogable" by the duo GidiGidi MajiMaji was adopted as a theme song by the primary political opposition coalition that eventually won the elections.[5]

Various rappers—alone, in duos, or in crews—had already localized the genre by invoking their social, street, and ethnic musical and linguistic identities for difference and market value. However, Kalamashaka's "Tafsiri hii" was the most important watershed for the appropriation of rap as a Kenyan expression. The word *tafsiri* entails such an expansion of the concept of interpretation or translation that one needs a dictionary to begin to understand the different dimensions of what is being rapped about. The text addressed the various levels of poverty and injustice prevalent in Dandora, a semi-slum section of Nairobi that was originally middle class but had deteriorated as economic conditions worsened.[6] Kalamashaka had previously rapped in English, imitating North American gangster and ghetto rappers. The group identified with the situations described by the tough street gangster lyrics of their Dandora 'hood. But in English, the language alienated the singers from the conditions they claimed to represent.

"Tafsiri hii" was a major departure in that it was not just in Swahili, the language of the urban middle and low class. It was in the street Swahili associated with a particular section of Nairobi, full of metaphors, hyperboles, and tongue twisters. It was spoken in a dialect called Sheng, whose underlying meaning and idiom was evident to insiders. Sheng is based on Swahili and English, but it incorporates Kenyan languages. In Kenya, the language of the people living in the vicinity where Sheng is spoken further distinguishes its specific dialects. Thus Kikuyu words preponderate in Sheng in an area populated by Kikuyu speakers. It is therefore possible for two Sheng speakers not to understand each other at all if they come from different neighborhoods or there are generational differences that delineate slang currency. Additionally, English words can be Swahili-ized (e.g., *mathé*, a Swahili-ized accentuation of the word *mother*), and Swahili or other languages can be anglicized (e.g., the Luo word *bwogo* [scare] can take on an English prefix and suffix to form un-*bwog*-able). By using street talk, Kalamashaka brought rap home to its own neighborhood.

"Unbwogable" (2002), on the other hand, demonstrated that rap was Kenyanized by more than just street language. The anglicized word *unbwogable* [unshakeable, fearless] is rooted not in Kiswahili but in the Luo language, engraving a more profound indigenization than Kiswahili inscribes as a nationalizing language. As the song gained notoriety, Nyairo and Ogude (2005) note, audiences and producers hijacked and edited the text beyond the intentions of the singers to create several versions of the piece. The lyrics of "Unbwogable" are rebellious from both a youth/social standpoint and a political position. The main refrain based on these two lines became a political slogan.

> Who can *bwogo* me
> I am *unbwogable*

Youth and social rebellion are contained in the language and in the way that language is employed. In these lines, the singers posit themselves as immovable. Several lines from the text demonstrate youthful dare, confidence, and rebellion.

> *Nyakwar Ajengo jokobodo ng'ama tugo koda*
> [Ajengo of Obodo, who dares play with me?]
> Listen nobody can bwogo me, neither nobody can bwogo this
> Gidigidi big name am saleable, *kama* [like] *pilipili* [pepper] yes am terrible . . .

Majimaji *nyakwa*r Ondijo [son of Ondijo] am a Luo but who are you?
What are you? Who the hell do you think you are?

By anglicizing the text, the singers' lyrics targeted a broader audience. Instead of marginalizing the song to an ethnic market, the consumers were now urban youth whose identity is ethnic (Luo), yet international (English), grounded in tradition yet embracing change, speaking a local language (anglicized Luo) yet appealing to a national crowd (Kenyanized English). The style (rap) in which the lyrics were coated presented an elitist social position, at once local, regional, international, and in the moment, attracting a national audience, an urban demography with some distance from rural residence, yet still bearing ethnic identity markers set in their names.

The linguistic construction also points to the languages the singers are most comfortable with, a Kenyan construction rooted in urban residential neighborhoods (Kioko and Muthwii 2004). Some of the lyrics are appropriated from "Lookin' at Me" by North American rapper Mase (aka Mason Durell Betha), reflecting the international fraternity of the situation and age group.[7] The political stance in this song is at once local and national. Using Luo indigenous lyrical and epic style, the vocalists introduce themselves, declare that this is their viewpoint, take a social position (that they are young), and acknowledge their ethnic heritage; here they localize themselves. They then position themselves as representing Luo culture with its political martyrs and detainees from various regimes that have ruled Kenya. It is this allusion to political detainees that was taken up by members of the then national political opposition coalition, some of whom were the children of those who had been assassinated, detained, or displaced by political powers and pundits.

> *Agwambo gini tek manadeni, yawa gini pek manadeni*
> *Jobondo gini tek manadeni, you are unbwogable*
> *Orengo gini tek manadeni, yawa gini pek manadeni*
> *Jougenya gini tek manadeni, you are unbwogable.*

Translation

> Agwambo this thing is really difficult, heavy, weighty, hard
> People of Bondo, this thing is difficult, you are unshakeable
> Orengo, this thing is really difficulty, heavy, weighty, hard
> People of Ugenya, this thing is difficult, you are unmovable.

Agwambo is a pseudonym for Raila Odinga (then a member of parliament but an opposition leader), the son of Oginga Odinga (Kenya's first vice president), who was himself detained, as was Orengo. Bondo and Ugenya are names of the places these two originated from.[8]

The Luo word *bwogo* became national common parlance, and its anglicized structure legitimized this way of creating Kenyan English words derived from indigenous languages. This was not the first time that language was transformed in this way. It was usual to adopt English words and "ethnicize" them or to anglicize ethnic words to convey a depth of metaphor or association lost in a literal translation. In the case of "Unbwogable," the factors that propelled the song to political and popular fame lent a type of credence to this method of creating new words that has been debated by Kenyan linguists since Sheng gained prominence.[9] Musically, "Unbwogable" used a technique that is recognized as indigenous to epic and ballad singers from the Luo ethnic group, establishing a groove that enables verbal extemporization, but which can be used as a counterpoint by the singing chorus. Both of these ideas are used in commercial rap that has sung and rapped sections against a rhythmic backdrop.

Rap in Kenya, though extremely popular among urban youth, is less lucrative economically than it is trendy. It has become a significant form in which urban youth can hold court for themselves and with the population at large, as there are no other public forums where youth are actually heeded. Therefore, individuals, duos, or crews cut singles and seek radio airplay. Artists also get exposure on local TV stations, at local and international rap festivals and contests, in "godowns" (warehouses that have been converted for televised performances), in clubs, and in national and international events set up to raise funds for causes or to educate the public on issues such as health or human rights. Thus rap artists are featured at concerts set up by UN environmental and educational agencies to educate the public on human rights or about HIV-AIDS, although not at locally organized government events or national celebrations. Artists also tour internationally, performing for their fan base in the Kenyan diaspora in Europe (particularly in Great Britain and Sweden), and in the United States. Some Kenyan artists are based in these alien lands and provide additional critiques to the rap and hip hop culture. Websites and chat rooms have also become forums for discourse about rap and for rappers to market their wares.

However, it is only since 2003 that some Kenyan musicians have signed contracts with international companies. Prior to this development, artists were managed by Kenyan producers, the most significant being Ted Josiah, who was associated with a number of studios before he legitimized his Blu Zebra Records company.[10] In addition, some DJs like Pinye (Peter Chuani), Ogopa (Francis and Lucas Bikedo), and Clemo (Clement Rapudo) also became managers and producers. Otherwise, rappers marketed themselves by way of radio DJs, particularly on private FM stations (Wetaba 2009: 212–40).[11] This was the preferred method of controlling sales and output by originating artists (Nyairo and Ogude 2005). Radio stations polled listeners to determine the most popular rap in a given week or month. Additionally, musicians achieved national and international acclaim through music awards, such as Kisima (Kenyan/East African) and Kora (pan-African), and by invitations to be opening acts at large international festivals and award ceremonies in Europe and the United States.

As a genre that has traditionally drawn from and absorbed other forms, Kenyan rap represents various locations as well as social and economic layers, more so than it does ethnic and age groups, through the types of subgenres associated with these populations. There is ghetto rap that through the language used—dialects, slang, idioms, street talk—bespeaks groups that either live in, or were brought up in, slums or in abject poverty in cities. Some of these groups are further identified as performing genge (gangster rap), particularly those groups in sections in the city with male or female gangs. Certain locales are well known for producing rappers; for example, the Eastleigh and Dandora sections in Nairobi are well known for genge, to the extent that the groups sometimes rent social halls to hold emceeing and cutting contests. When a particular rap song performs excellently on the airwaves, it gains a certain status associated with the phrase "it has bombed," meaning it has done well, contrary to associations that *bombed* might have elsewhere. Then it is described with the word *bomba*.[12] Other subgenres include rap taarab (or taarap), when mixed with the popular genre taarab that fuses Arabic and Indic elements, or Afro-Indic, when it is mixed with Indian film music (filmgit) stylings. Additional variants include rap-rumba, when elements from Congolese rumba and Cameroonian music are incorporated, or ragga-rap when intoned in ragga and reggae styles. Upper-middle-class youth engage in a rap style known as kapuka, which incorporates elements of North American rap, ragga, and house. Kenyan youth identify with North American and other African rap artists who may have come from ghettos and used rap as a way out or who may have come from affluent neighborhoods and, because they already had the means, used rap for other purposes. Through these various subgenres, rap appeals to different social classes. Moreover, rap popularized the notion of using local street language. When Kenyan artists rapped in African American street English, they were ignored. It was not until they began to use Sheng—urban local street language in form, structure, content, and context—that they gained a following.

Apart from achieving airplay on radio, rappers have tapped into the video industry, especially since 2003 when MTV became widely accessible in Kenya. However, the video images and storylines are localized to portray issues, situations, and locations familiar to Kenyan and East African consumers. One of the most popular videos of 2004 was "Amka Ukatike" [Get up and dance] by C'zars (Abdulkarim Mohammed).[13] The video begins in an activity familiar to any Kenyan high school student: verse recitation at music and drama festivals. These spaces were invented for youth to exhibit their musical, dramatic, and artistic talents (Kidula 1996). The music festival is known to be as conservative as the drama festival is its opposite: creative, innovative, and contemporary. Music and poetry feature at both festivals with a greater variety of languages and musical combinations at the music festival.

C'zars' rap is a satire on public verse speaking. It begins with a recitation of a *shairi* (a Kiswahili poetic form with a specific type of delivery) before a group of three adjudicators. The audience is usually other competitors, who in this case are classmates and friends. A pair of Kenyan comedians from the group Redyku-lass plays two of the adjudicators.[14] The producers of the video portray teachers or professors (a usual crop of adjudicators) with a certain disdain, for while teachers know the forms, they do not perform these poems on a regular basis. It is students who compose and perform them. The performer in this case decides in the middle of the *shairi* that he cannot continue to pretend to deliver a poem in a style that is so far removed from the reality of performances that typical teenagers engage in. It is not in the classic poem posited by school authorities that expression resides, but rather in the structure born in and among the people, that speaks to the sensibili-ties of the people. He therefore shifts from regular Swahili to Sheng. C'zars' type of rap is called genge, and the student is from Genge Secondary School.

It is not only the portrayal of the teachers that is at stake; it is also the depic-tion of women in the video that speaks to stereotypical expectations of women's roles and actions. One portrayal is characteristic of how women are featured in popular music—mainly as dancers—and the other is an archetypal image of a fe-male teacher, usually an underpaid mother. The character playing the mother-type teacher, incidentally, is a male impersonating a woman, a parody for which Redykulass is famed in their political/social satire. The attire of the two female ad-judicators is a typical depiction of a motherly but vocally assertive high school teacher and a fashionably trendy recent graduate, closer to the students' age and therefore more sympathetic and in tune with teen life and the poet's rebellion. In fact, the young adjudicator enjoys the piece so much that she joins in the dance. The audience also participates. In the video, the dictatorial male adjudicator tries to restore order but is overruled by the audience, to his shame, and in the end, even the motherly teacher tries a few dance steps. Such an action suggests that maybe women are cognizant of their children's activities, even if they might not approve of them, or maybe she is not as "country" as she has been forced to ap-pear by her job, by her financial situation, and by society. I selected this video to demonstrate societal stereotypes of women and how students, who are socialized to image women, parents, and authority figures in this manner, enact these stereo-types. I also sought to demonstrate how rap highlights, legitimizes, or protests so-cial mores and understandings.

Association with the Hip Hop Postnation

Hip hop is mostly associated with urban youth regardless of social class and ethnic group. As a culture, hip hop in Kenya has incorporated global rap, which has then been appropriated and reconstructed using indigenous creative forms, popular national and pan-African languages and styles, and African diasporic figu-rative poetic language and genres like R&B, funk, reggae, ragga, taarab, and others. Hip hop also includes DJing at clubs, events, competitions, radio, and TV outlets, emceeing, and dancing. Graffiti art was initially portrayed on small public transport vans known as *matatus* (sing. *matatu:* minivans of different shapes and sizes, which are a ubiquitous public transport system in Kenya), popularizing a form of the art depicting images associated with youth, urbanity, rebellion, and experimentation. The vans were covered with graffiti and given names. Matatus were notorious for playing the latest and most popular rap songs and also for showing videos made by the artists.

Other global aspects of hip hop include the names that artists use, such as Hardstone, Nameless, Kleptomaniax, Ray C, and Gidigidi Majimaji. Artists rarely use a normal version of their names. For example, Gidigidi formulated his pseudonym from the last four letters of his last name, Ogidi, and repeated the construction. The resultant sonic impact is one of hypnosis or creating giddiness. Other artistic expressions associated with hip hop, including fashion (dress, costume) and the business of styles, are part of the Kenyan scene. Artists strive for the raw look, tough gang, and street appearance. Other global associations and practices feature the connection of rap with street life, drugs, fights, gangs, territorialism, occupation, loudness, resistance, and other social or political accoutrements.

The African roots and counterparts of emceeing and rapping in the diaspora made for a smoother appropriation of the practices in Kenya and for the genre to resonate with older generations and educational institutions. As such, rap, for all the criticism it receives as corrupting proper language and speech, has never been censored in Kenya, unlike reggae, rumba, and other African and diasporic genres that were banned at one point or another in Kenya's post colonial history (Wallis and Malm 1984: 257–59).

Rap lyrics can be both local and global in subject matter and approach. They address familial and social relationships, territory, disenfranchisement, representation, repression, social and political ills, and critique political, ethnic, and generational ideologies. The type of language employed includes street to slang to pidgin, to popular language, to metaphors and other linguistic devices that suggest multiple layers of meaning. The poetics of language are a major artistic and expressive feature with street, school, and national competitions co-opted to select the best lyrics and editing of texts in chat rooms on the web.

The relationship between the local and the global is evident in lyrics that address sexual and romantic relationships. "Atoti," a song performed by GidiGidi MajiMaji, addressed this topic in local terms, but also expanded it to portray Kenya's affinity to global hip hop culture. The song is about a girl called Atoti.[15] The theme is romance, sex, and emotion. The genre is localized by the name of the subject to whom the lyrics are addressed, the use of the Luo language rather than the national language Kiswahili (although Kiswahili is invoked), and by blatant sexual allusions, a practice that is acceptable in Luo public courtship expressions of song and dance. Localizing the genre also brought awareness of the huge role that Kisumu (the urban epicenter of the Luo ethnic group and a smaller town than Nairobi) occupies as a major rap and hip hop center. Luo aesthetics are so accepting of rap that the Kondele club scene (in a suburb of Kisumu) holds music contests, pitting youth using indigenous instruments for a backdrop against those who generate grooves from studio equipment and other sounds, and also younger against older singers who invoke some of the stylistic elements present in contemporary rap.

Wicky Moshi and MajiMaji wrote the lyrics of "Atoti." The dual authorship caused some problems because of the notion that a rapper's fame is due to the ability to craft one's own lyrics, rather than looking for a professional verbal art scripter. That Wicky Moshi was included created some interesting dynamics in the country, particularly when Moshi was killed in 2003 by a matatu in the Nairobi suburb of Githurai. That the accident occurred in the early morning when Moshi was returning from an all-night celebration after winning an award for "Atoti" creates further associations with global rap greats whose lives were snapped off at crucial points in their careers. That he was killed by a matatu, the very vehicles that were perceived as physical carriers of rap art in sonic and visual form, was indeed an irony.[16] Until the government banned music in matatus, these vehicles were the prime places to sample the most current music. Some matatus had such quality audio equipment that one experienced not just the sound but also the vibrations of the drum and the bass lines. Moshi's demise in a matatu accident symbolized the contradictions associated with the business of music and the function of rap—that it builds and it demolishes, it creates and it destroys, it toasts and it criticizes.

Rap composers and consumers in Kenya have mostly been under 30. This is a demographic for whom rap represents a changing of the guard, because they were part of an education system that embraced the U.S. structure from the 1980s rather than the earlier British-based system. This group also boasts of trailblazers who were motivated by social and political liberation rhetoric only to be disenfranchised or disillusioned by formal education. Their dream of having a job as university graduates was no longer guaranteed due to national economic problems and by imperialist global control. This populace embraces local, national, and global perspectives and represents itself as such. It further invokes its indigenous identity so as not to be misrepresented by the very powerful Kenyan diaspora that competes for similar prospects with more opportunities.

Rap and Kenyan Diaspora

In a 2007 interview with Dickson Ngujiri Thirima of True Blaq entertainment, I asked him who he considered the hottest Kenyan music group in the United States. His response, Kleptomaniax, was not surprising, as Thirima's company markets and promotes them, and they were then on a U.S. tour organized and promoted in part by True Blaq. The three guys who make up the group (D. E. P. Collo aka Collins Majale, Munkiri aka Robert Manyasa, and Nyashinski aka Nyamari Ongegu) actually began to produce music and perform while still in high school.[17]

According to their blogs and other reviews, they "have a lot of firsts" on their proverbial plate, including being the first group to release a successful single, be nominated for an award, and win an award while still in high school. Not many artists have a similar claim in Kenya.

Achievements of the Kenyan Group Kleptomaniax (www.sambazainc.com/Klepto.html)

- First Kenyan group to release a successful single while still in high school
- First group to be nominated while still in high school: Favourite Male Group, *Chaguo la Teenies* 2002 (Choice of the teenagers)
- Won Favourite Male Group, *Chaguo la Teenies* 2002
- Nominated Favourite Male Group, 2nd year running, *Chaguo la Teenies* 2003
- Won Favourite Male Group, 2nd year running, *Chaguo la Teenies* 2003
- Nominated Best Group, Kisima Music Awards 2004
- Rated 2nd Most Popular Kenyan Music Video (Tuendelee) by the TV show *The BEAT*, year 2004 Roundup
- Nominated Favourite Male Group, 4th year running, *Chaguo la Teenies* 2005
- Nominated at the Kisima Music Awards 2005 in three categories: Best Group, Best Song, and Best Rap Song
- Won the Kisima Music Awards 2005 for "Best Group"
- FIRST and ONLY nominees ever in eastern Africa for "Best African Act" for the MTV Europe Music Awards 2005
- Nominated in the "Best Group from East Africa" category for the KORA Awards 2005
- Rated 2nd Most Popular Local Music Video (Swing) by no. 1 music TV show, The BEAT, year 2005 Round Up

One of their most popular songs, technically their fourth single, a 2004 release, "Tuendelee" [Should we continue/proceed?], is both a *shairi* (Swahili sung poem) and rap.

Kleptomaniax performed in Atlanta, Georgia, on March 10, 2007. Thirima had traveled with the group from California and New Jersey before coming to Georgia. Kleptomaniax are marketed as contemporary urban music. The general clientele in the United States who frequent their performances in clubs, parties, or celebrations tend to be Kenyans 15–32 years old, although Thirima informed me that the age bracket had expanded to 40-year-olds. Apart from Kenyans, the audience is drawn from the East and Central African complex, including Tanzania, Uganda, Rwanda, Burundi, Somalia, Malawi, Mozambique, Angola, and the Congos. Such a large clientele is attracted not just by the marketing and promotion of deejays on stations featuring African music or people who enjoy African music. Other lures include the language and musical styles of African urban pop confluences—the intersection of global, pan-African, national, and local indigenous musics. Kleptomaniax rap and sing in various dialects of Kiswahili, Sheng, and English. The language and contemporary urban factors, more than any others, have, in my opinion, opened the market to audiences beyond East Africa and its diaspora.

The arts are a vital connection in the cycle of life. They have historically served as an avenue and recourse for establishing, negotiating, and reiterating identity. Much has been written about how African slaves in diaspora invoked their musical memory to affirm their humanness to the extent that their distinctive musical characteristics are a result and function of the fusion of mimetic horizons. This is especially evident with Africans who orally reconstituted musical structures, forms, and instruments. The fusion of their memory, their new contexts or situations, and their encounter with other cultures led to the creation of new forms, styles, instruments, and new ways of playing European instruments. While Europeans could still freely draw upon their ancestral lands for language, instruments, and musical styles and import these into their new world, Africans without a similar freedom were forced to create new styles. Some of these musics were eventually remarketed to Africa, including jazz, blues, rumba, reggae, and rap that grew out of a diasporic African nostalgic or even romanticized past.

Kenyans in diaspora are patriotically nostalgic, hence the popularity of such groups as Kleptomaniax. The performances allow migrants to mediate and reconcile sentiments of nostalgia, memory, and belonging. They offer a bridge to a remembered past or a distant land. They also provide a window into current Kenyan issues, trends, and developments in entertainment and social affairs. These touring musical arts target Africans who grew up in urban rather than rural areas, who are cognizant of international mainstream music standards, and yet have a patriotic Kenyan memory. In fact, Thirima, other promoters, and DJs purposefully market to this crowd, which is accustomed to better equipment, better studios, and therefore better recordings. But there is also an older generation of recent immigrants with strong and original links to the country who nostalgically imagine life in contemporary Kenyan towns such as Kisumu and even appreciate rural sounds and places portrayed in rap lyrics and videos. A third target audience is contemporary urban youth, who may be recent immigrants or second, third, or fourth generation with occasional or no visits to Kenya, who may just know it as a place idealized by parents or friends. This utopia is represented not just in song but also by the singers. Musicians such as Ida, who grew up in the United States but invokes her parents' heritage for marketability, belong to this group seeking ideological, historical and social connectivity, explained by Tim Rice (1994: 206) as "symbolic of the rural past they and their families had abandoned."

In my cursory survey by questionnaire of Kenyans in Atlanta, Kansas City, Oklahoma City, and Dallas (December 2006–March 2007), the most listened to Kenyan musicians performed gospel and rap. In the survey, Kenyans said they learned about the latest Kenyan gospel and religious songs from visitors in churches or from CDs. Gospel is a lucrative business. It competes with a genre referred to by Thirima and others as Afro-pop, where according to Thirima, *pop* is a generic word for any urban type secular music. The two genres' substyles are diverse. The sacred product is not necessarily different from the secular one. Rap, on the other hand, was accessed on the web, in socials, and in clubs. Increased tours by musicians, savvy business practices, and access to better technology help promote these products. Thirima stated that the most successful artist has been rapper Nameless, whose real name is David Mathenge. Mathenge has a university education (with a bachelor's degree in architecture). I believe his education factors in the greater and more diverse appeal to urbanites in diaspora than do rural groups with ethnic roots such as Abana ba Nasery.

It is no easy task to bring live Kenyan acts to the United States. Musicians such as Kleptomaniax have to undergo quite an ordeal to obtain a visa. Thirima explained that in order to get a visa, musicians, after passing the Kenyan appeal test, must (a) have a CD, (b) have already traveled to other countries, (c) have awards or credibility in different markets, (d) have a manager for tours or recording, (e) have an agent, (f) have writing about them in newspapers in and out of Kenya, and (g) have been performing for at least two years, or been in the group for two years. Kleptomaniax had fulfilled these visa requirements. Respondents I surveyed felt that the musicians were successful, based on some of the following factors.

a. Language: "it is our language"—Swahili, Sheng—big Swahili base. Sheng incorporates Kenyan languages such as Luo or Kikuyu and so attracts the demographic with such roots;

b. Lyrics: the messages, the issues addressed are current concerns; for example, the relevant AIDS message on "Vuta Pumz" by Logombas made the musicians a hit;

c. The lyrics sometimes mention places people remember of the homeland, particularly those who have not been back to Kenya for a long time ("Brings home close to you"); and

d. Their style has aspects of R&B and hip hop from the different production houses and types of music (e.g. genge, kapuka, hardcore, westlands).

Few people understood the actual cost of bringing the memory of home to the United States. I was shocked from my survey because some people, while they went to clubs where original CDs were sold, still indicated that they mostly dubbed the CDs and VCDs. They also tried to enter clubs without paying the cover fee, and they rarely gave love offerings for the gospel musicians at the concerts or events they attended. At least the music is getting disseminated, I thought. I hope, however, that Kenyans in diaspora, in acknowledgment of the historical, cultural, and artistic embodiment of musical works and their creators, will financially support music and musicians of Kenyan origin and descent.

Afterword: Artistic Imagining of Africa in Rap and Rap in Africa

Much has been said about the presence of African performative and musical practices as bespeaking the Afro-centricity of rap. Maybe the elements most invoked are those of groove and improvisation, which are the musical postures and practices of praise and entertainment balladeers and oral historians. Much less invoked is the practice of a public critique of a work in progress through performances for peers and other publics (Nyakiti 2002), with latent ideas privately or publicly incorporated in different renditions (Barber 1997). While this practice is prevalent in chat rooms of rap lyricists and their fans, it does not seem to me to be present in North American rap.

Analysts also note a number of other African practices, such as using music as a peaceful means of protest or as an avenue of resistance in which sounds and movements can be used to categorically state one's position and allow another to respond without either party losing face. Another is exploiting the ambiguity that can be created by using two seemingly opposite media or emotions (e.g., mourning while dancing or accompanying a sad text with energetic movements), and the subsequent side effect of taking a different reading justified by metaphors inherent in both lyrical and musical speech. Also evident is the use of music as a way of publicizing private thoughts and emotions, as a platform for the oppressed to express disaffections and publicly moralize or castigate oppressors, where words usually spoken in private can be spoken publicly without fear of reprisals (Avorgbedor 2001), and as a space for the silenced youth to speak openly to their community—now of diverse cultures under one nation—and have their contributions acknowledged. These are some ways of understanding the invocation of utopic Africa in rap performance practice.

Perhaps the initial resistance to rap in Kenya was due to its association with and representation of youth. It may be this association with youth, the now and the present, that is responsible for some of the ways rap is perceived: as always in flux—like the youth it represents—faddish, incoherent, yet pervasive because of its loudness and seeking to destabilize tradition while invoking indigenous heritage for life and continuity. At the same time, these very elements can justify the legitimization of rap, that as a text—a style of music, a manner of performance, a creative synergy—once exposed encourages potential interpretations that the continuing dialogue between the elements that inform the genre and the readers and consumers of the product is vitalized by the ability to create endless possibilities.

Popular music has been a favored negotiating nexus for indigenous, national, continental, and global culture. Fluidity and contradictions determine and construct identity and affiliation in terms of rural versus urban, ethnic-national versus continental, Euro-American and Asian systems versus African ethnic and indigenous systems. Music has been a space to confer, discuss, bargain, and reiterate tradition, transition, potential, opportunity, and outlook. Rap music in Kenya has been one of these popular pieces on the table in the urban space.

NOTES

1. The resulting piece, issued as "Maracatudo" on Sergio Mendes's 1996 album *Oceano* produced by Polygram Records, is available from online retailers.

2. Shari Martin, interview with author, July 1995.

3. Although Kisima Music Awards were initially intended for Kenyan musicians, Josiah and other organizers expanded competition to Tanzania, then Uganda, and to other eastern African nations. They also expanded the categories beyond secular genres, to religious and "roots" musics. Essentially, Kenyan artists were exposed to the larger eastern African live, audio, and television viewing public, and musicians from these countries secured a fan base in Kenya and began to tour clubs and churches and perform in Kenyan festivals.

4. Kalamashaka was made up of Zacharia Mwaura, Robert Gakuyu, and Kamah Ngige.

5. Gidigidi is Joseph Ogidi Oyoo, and Majimaji is Julius Owino.

6. For full lyrics, see Wetaba (2009: 133–34).

7. See discussion in Shitandi (2002) and Njane (2001).

8. For an analysis of the whole piece, see Nyairo and Ogude (2003, 2005) and Hofmeyr, Nyairo, and Ogude (2003).

9. See Githinji (2003), Samper (2002), and Sure (2004).

10. See Brown (2003).

11. Wetaba's (2009) text provides insights into ways urban youth engaged rap as a unifying identity construct, a function of rap not only in Kenya but also in the neighboring countries of Tanzania and Uganda where rap artists regularly tour.

12. The term *bomba* acquired other meanings after my initial fieldwork was done in 2004, but its original meaning is still recognized in rap lexicon in Kenya.

13. An internet search for "Amka Ukatike" will bring up the video on various sites.

14. Redykulass, formed in 1998, is a popular comedic troupe made up of John Kiarie, Tony Njuguna, and Walter Mongare, whose satire commented on Kenyan politics and politicians and provided a comical reading of local and global social and political events.

15. An internet search for "Atoti" should identify sites with the full lyrics.

16. For details, see Amos Ngaira, "Tragedy as 'Atoti' Singer, Wicky Mosh Dies," *Daily Nation on the Web*, www.nationaudio.com/News/DailyNation/18042003/News /News1804200364.html, April 18, 2003. Ngaira covered the demise of other rap artists, such as "Popular Local Musician Buried," *Daily Nation on the Web*, March 18, 2003, and with Dan Tengo, "Kenya Rap Star K-rupt Shot Dead," News kilimanjaroentertainment.com /K-rupt%20Carjacked.htm, December 2, 2003.

17. Ngujiri D. Thirima, interview with the author, March 29, 2007.

Imitation and Innovation in the Music, Dress, and Camps of Tanzanian Youth

ALEX PERULLO

The imitation of foreign music has been central to the formation of several Tanzanian popular music genres. In the late 1800s, taarab, a genre that imitated Egyptian song, appeared as royal court music in Zanzibar. In the 1920s, *dansi,* a form of upbeat dance music that remains popular in Tanzania, originated as a form of ballroom dance music for expatriate Europeans living in Tanganyika. And kwaya, a mixture of European Christian choral music with local rhythms and melodies, started as a form of hymn singing at missionary facilities throughout the country. A general pattern for these genres was to imitate foreign styles, localize the sounds, words, and meanings into Tanzanian culture, and then innovate on the newly formed genres in distinctive ways. Over time, composers and performers of these genres purged some of the Western sounds and incorporated more local, national, and pan-African aesthetics into their music, a process which helped move these genres toward being regarded as distinctly Tanzanian or East African musical forms.

Bongo flava, a category of music that encompasses several genres, including rap, R&B, zouk, and ragga, is the most recent form to move from imitation to localization. Currently, bongo flava, a name that connotes the "wisdom" (*bongo*) that one needs to survive in Tanzania, is the most popular and financially lucrative musical form in the country. The genre emerged during the country's liberalization in the mid-1980s among middle- and upper-class youth who had access to foreign records, cassette tapes, and videotapes (Perullo 2007). Through imitating the music they heard on these albums, these artists learned the basic forms and structures of hip hop, but eventually began altering their use of language (from English to Swahili), rapping style, message, and many other elements to make the music more meaningful to other Tanzanian youth. Due to these musical and cultural shifts, bongo flava moved beyond the small circle of hip hop aficionados who initially supported the genre into a popular musical form that appealed to a broad array of Tanzanians.[1]

In this chapter, I examine three areas of bongo flava—music, dress, and camps—to comprehend the ways youth innovate on physical, aural, and ideological elements associated with rap music. In particular, I suggest that innovation occurs in the ways that youth modify their music, appearance, and lifestyle to connect with the many communities with which they want to be a part. Whether an artist composes a song meant for an international audience or for peers in Dar es Salaam, s/he shifts various elements to reach his or her audience. Albums frequently feature a broad array of songs aimed at different listening communities. A composition for an international audience may contain references (musically and lyrically) to American or European songs, and the meaning of the song may deal with general topics about youth rather than specific Tanzanian issues. Alternatively, songs composed for a local audience of peers may have slang terms and local ideas that only make sense to them. Vocal style may remain steady throughout an artist's compositions, yet an album can show the ways that artists understand and relate to many communities. It is in an artist's understanding of each of these communities that innovations are made.

Each of the areas of this chapter is critical to the identity of bongo flava as well as to the identities of the people involved with the genre. The first area, music, refers solely to the "beats" that support the lyrics. Elsewhere I discuss language use and meaning in bongo flava lyrics (Perullo and Fenn 2003; Perullo 2005). Here, however, I focus only on the ways producers, who compose, perform, record, and mix all of the beats for bongo flava, use foreign and local genres to create music meant to reach different communities. The second area, dress, analyzes the clothing styles that many urban youth use to create a bongo flava fashion aesthetic. Youth combine international concepts of beauty, American hip hop culture, and locally available clothes and materials to create distinctive styles that visually distinguish bongo flava youth from other members of Tanzanian society. Finally, camps refer to the organization of youth into groups based on similar interests, backgrounds, and ideological views. These camps exist as support networks for artists and fans of bongo flava and offer a critical means for urban youth to find direction in Tanzania.

In the 1950s, as dansi and taarab were becoming increasingly popular as urban forms of expression, scholars discussed theories of cultural imperialism, using the terms *Americanization* and *Westernization* to describe the impact of Western cultures on the music of the non-Western world (Tracey 1954; Bose 1959; Mensah 1959). In writing about the impact of "western and other foreign intrusions" on the Bantu peoples of Africa, Hugh Tracey (1954: 34) lamented that African music had changed for the worse and that local culture "was exposed and vulnerable to attack by determined proselytizers, both progressists and priests." Tracey's analysis put forth a center-periphery model where Western colonialists, whether administrative officials or priests, impacted or "damaged" local cultures to the point where the locals could not prevent the changes taking place in their music.

In more recent years, scholars have critiqued this position and offered alternative notions of local interaction with global flows of cultural ideas and practices. Many of these theories, such as creolization (Hannerz 1987), syncretism (Herskovits 1966), hybridity (Kapchan and Strong 1999; Gross, McMurray, and Swedenburg 2002), and glocalization (Robertson 1992), attempt to show the ways people interact with local and global cultural flows, presenting people as more engaged in the world around them rather than as passive observers. These theories often dismantle the center-periphery model and, instead, posit a movement of ideas, even if unbalanced, between the West and other parts of the world and also between "peripheries" (Inda and Rosaldo 2002; Adelt 2005).

While theories of creolization and hybridity are helpful in moving scholarship beyond notions of cultural imperialism and articulating the complexities of daily life, there is a tendency to reduce the various ways people interact and engage with the world around them to simplified notions of cultural assimilation or cross-fertilization. Synchronization theories can set up dichotomies between the merging of two different things (e.g., global/local, Western/African, traditional/ modern). While, theoretically, most scholars attempt to move beyond these dichotomies, a tendency remains for ethnographic analyses to return to the merging of two elements thought to be in opposition. (One only has to look for the abundance of articles that draw on the global and local dichotomy.)

One means to overcome these dichotomies is to consider the many ways that people use music in their daily lives. While bongo flava is certainly influenced by the movement of sounds from the United States to Tanzania, each artist, producer, and composer uses music in different ways. Innovation occurs as artists alter the sounds, uses, and interpretations of music. It is a means of subtly transforming words and sounds in ways that make them appear new within a specific context. The issue then is not how is bongo flava a synchronization of global and local sounds but how do artists apply their conceptions of music to different communities and in different contexts? How do they draw on various sources to achieve a desired result? The establishment of a musical sound or identity particular to a person's interests and community involvement is central to informing his or her choices in music, dress, and lifestyle. Thus a person does not merge or synchronize various elements in a repeatable manner but continually innovates on sounds, symbols, language, and ideologies to interact with others in different communities and social contexts.

In Tanzania, youth who participate in bongo flava place themselves within several communities that are intrinsically connected yet often socially separate. International hip hop, African youth, and urban Tanzanian youth communities, as well as communities associated with class, ethnicity, and family background, critically affect the approach that artists take in their music. Youth respond to sonic, linguistic, and physical elements from different parts of the world by creating music to participate in several communities. They merge or mimic foreign sounds, local aesthetics, and community ideals to various degrees depending on their desired audience.

Members of the group X Plastaz, for instance, wear traditional Maasai clothing during their performances abroad, a modified version of Maasai clothing in local performances, and similar styles of dress as other Tanzanian youth wear offstage. The Maasai look sets the group apart in local performances, but is particularly important in foreign shows where images of the Maasai—red outfits, sandals, beaded necklaces—has come to represent Tanzania and, to some extent, Africa as a whole. X Plastaz plays on this representation of Tanzania to promote their music abroad, but also to encourage engagement with their cultural background. For international audiences, the Maasai-ness of the group is a selling point even though only one member is actually a Maasai. Ntarangwi (2009: 40) notes that the use of the Maasai identity becomes a "tool for youth to access an international market for their music by reverting to essentialized 'African culture' that affirms the stereotypical images of Africa." It also may be a means to endorse certain cultural traditions historically admonished in Tanzania and stereotyped abroad. Internationally, using the Maasai identity can create moments of intense outside interest in something imagined to be proto-African, which can then be subverted in socially conscious lyrics being delivered in a technologically sophisticated rap song. In Tanzania, the use of Maasai dress becomes a means to highlight national pride and ethnic identity, thereby establishing originality within the local music scene.

Interest in being part of the American hip hop community is particularly strong. Most youth look to the United States as an important center of hip hop culture and to African Americans as progenitors of rap music. Ramadhani Mponjika, a Tanzanian rapper popularly known as Rhymson, explains the view of many Tanzanian youth during the early years of bongo flava:

> If you look at African Americans, they unconsciously look at Africa for cultural inspirations. But we [Tanzanians] do the reverse. On the radio or in the newspapers—we did not have TV—we see people who are like us, but they live in America. I remember when I was young, I saw a picture of Mohammed Ali. It really inspired me. Yes, that is the champion, and he looks like me. Like he was one of our people. Music was the same. When we heard the music of black people, it interested us. At that time [late 1980s], anything foreign was considered good.[2]

Professor Jay, another Tanzanian rapper, also found African American culture appealing, particular the messages in the music and the empowerment of black people:

> I started to rap in O level, when I was in the seventh grade. In 1989, there were many different styles of rap music being heard in Tanzania. During this time, I was listening to rap, such as Public Enemy, "Fight the Power." This music really drew me straightaway to become a rapper because I saw the way that a black man was able to search for his own thing [identity]. Public Enemy had the power to stand somewhere and speak with people. Those people listened to what the group had to say and followed their message. So it was this type of thing that drew me to rap. People such as Public Enemy, LL Cool J, KRS-One, and others like that.[3]

Many Tanzanian youth borrow symbols and styles from the United States, even if those elements mean something different. A Yankees cap, which many Tanzanians wear, for instance, does not symbolize baseball, a powerful team, or even an American city, as it often does in the United States, but rather notions of blackness, Americanness, and power. This mimetic process provides youth with the means to identify and associate with an international and imagined community of hip hop culture.

Aside from African American culture, Tanzanian youth are also keenly aware of their roles and connections to local communities. They identify with local trends and believe that their success as members of the hip hop scene depends on how well they connect with local audiences. To do this, they have to compose music, assemble a fashion sense, and follow a lifestyle that makes sense to their understanding and interpretation of the local music scene.

For some youth, the promotion of more Tanzanian aspects of bongo flava has led them to envision traditional African music as a precursor to hip hop, thereby grounding their connection to hip hop in real historical terms and overcoming the notion that hip hop is a product of Western cultural hegemony. In an online chat room, for instance, one writer commented, "I used to buy a lot of hip hop on vinyl since the mid 80s (e.g., Run DMC) and will take them home to tz [Tanzania] with me. I'll be playing them and my grandmother would tell me I am playing the *ngoma zakwetu* [native ngoma]. *Na nikibisha* [And, if I argued with her] she used to remind me when we go *vijinini* [rural areas] and listen to the drummers play, the beats were the same."[4] In the Tanzanian hip hop video *Hali Halisi* [The Real Situation], Mr. Mashili from the National Arts Council (BASATA) comments, "When I was young, there was a particular rap that was performed by the drum players. I still remember those raps they used to sing. So when I heard the modern raps, I compared them with those from the past. Then I realized that rap has been with us since the past." Neither of these commentators link the actual sound of hip hop to traditional Tanzanian culture. The electronically produced beats are a distinctly foreign phenomenon. Instead, they hear the rapping and rhythmic makeup of songs as something reminiscent of traditional ngoma. The argument that African American music as well as many forms of Western popular music are indebted to African cultures is not new (Saakana 1995). But in the case of bongo flava, it helps empower youth and others to see hip hop as more than just an American or Western musical form.

Producers Imitate to Innovate

Upon first listening to bongo flava, most Western audiences comment on the American sound of the music. The pulsating snare, deep throbbing bass, and synthesized harmonies are common sounds in the production of hip hop, both in the United States and Tanzania. For many Tanzanian listeners, the reliance on foreign sounds is a sign of a lack of originality and an unhealthy fascination with the West. Fredrick Sumaye, the former prime minister of Tanzania, gave a speech at the Bagamoyo College of Art at which he said: "They [hip hop artists] copy foreign music and then they just change the words and put them into Kiswahili" (Mlekani 2002). Sumaye told his audience that Tanzanian musicians should stop being "lazy" by copying other people's music and turn to traditional music for creative inspiration. Many other government officials, non–hip hop–based musicians, and music fans echoed Sumaye's comments, lamenting the Western quality of Tanzania's latest and most successful musical form.[5]

These criticisms are difficult to refute. The majority of producers in Tanzania borrow heavily from foreign studio techniques, musical arrangements, and timbral sonorities. For instance, numerous producers layer the bass part of songs over several octaves, including those not easily heard by the human ear at the low frequency range, which creates the thumping sound that listeners of rap feel more than hear. Many producers digitally manipulate vocal tracks, such as the use of Auto-Tune, which was first popularized by Cher in the song "Believe." And the majority of bongo flava songs center around a steady rhythm created from electronically produced sounds; real drum kits are rarely used by bongo flava producers. The result of these and other practices is a sound that many people, both inside and outside Tanzania, dismiss as imitative of foreign music and uninspired for the country's popular music scene.

It is critical to realize, however, that producers purposely mimic American hip hop songs to educate themselves about production techniques, and the results of this imitation are innovations localized in urban Tanzania aesthetics. The first point is partially a result of the history of Tanzanian musical production. Before 1994, no one in Tanzania knew how to produce music for bongo flava. A handful of recording engineers worked at the government-owned radio station, Radio Tanzania Dar es Salaam (RTD), which recorded dansi, taarab, and ngoma music, but no one had tried to create complex and multilayered digital sounds such as those heard on Notorious B.I.G.'s "Things Done Changed" and Nas's "The World Is Yours," both released in the mid-1990s when Tanzanians first attempted to create their own beats. When youth started producing music, most were at a loss for equipment and methods to create hip hop sounds. Attempting to imitate foreign artists became central to establishing credibility as a producer and learning the basic skills necessary to create hip hop beats.

Some of the earliest producers, such as Boni Luv, Master J, P Funk, and Malone, learned techniques from foreign producers who either showed them how to use equipment, play instruments, or organize recording projects (P Funk also studied engineering in Holland). Master J, who studied business in England and learned some recording techniques from a college friend, Owen Paris, recalls one of his earlier recording projects upon returning to Tanzania:

> I returned from England with a synchronizer and then started recording the song "Moja kwa Moja" [Straight ahead, a song by II Proud, who is now called Mr. II or Sugu]. When we started recording the song, II Proud dropped the vocals with just a click, a metronome [vocalizes metronome sound—tick-da-da-da—and laughs]. And II Proud was looking at me like, "This guy's insane, there's no beat." But he recorded the verses and choruses anyway, and then left. So after he left, then I started making the music. I would do a beat according to the vocals, and add chords, bass, rhythm, etc. After three days, I told him, "Look, the track is ready." "Yeah, okay, let me hear it." And he came to hear the music for the first time. He was shocked—they [artists] used to go wild. And I used to do tracks for free, just for the fun of it.[6]

The three days spent in the recording studio were a key period for Master J to experiment in composing, recording, and mixing beats. Working with his newly purchased recording equipment, learning how to manipulate the computer and sequencer, and composing a backing track using a keyboard, drum machine, and bass, Master J assembled a multilayered hip hop beat behind II Proud's vocal track (see figure 9.1).

In listening to "Moja kwa Moja," obvious links to American hip hop sounds can be heard. The basic beat of the song is made by a drum machine simulating a drum kit with a sharp strike on the snare for the downbeat. A sample of a trumpet solo also signals the chorus of the song, similar to "Rebirth of Slick (Cool Like Dat)" by the American group Digable Planets. The use of sampling and a drum kit are common in American hip hop, and Master J admits that some of his inspiration comes from studying the music of foreign artists.

> Since I never studied sound engineering, I learn the most from reading books and listening to a lot of foreign music. At home, I put on headphones and just listen for a half hour or hour a day. I want to listen to how they [the foreign producers] use the stereo spectrum; what do they do to the chorus, the vocals; what effect do they use and how do they use it; you know, these are things that I listen to a lot. Because, I don't know, I didn't study [to be a] recording engineer. So I learn a lot of things through listening to foreign music and reading books.[7]

Using CDs and cassettes of foreign artists, which are widely available in Tanzania, Master J learns techniques for composing and recording bongo flava songs. The

Figure 9.1. Master J (center) in the studio with members of Gangwe Mobb, Inspekta Haroun (left), and Luteni Kalama, July 2001. Photo by Alex Perullo.

sounds he hears in his headphones certainly appear in his compositions. Thus, as the music changes in the United States, Europe, and elsewhere, so too do productions of bongo flava.

Nevertheless, a great deal of innovation and localization exists in Master J's backing tracks. "Moja kwa Moja" is a bit more laidback than most of the foreign hip hop that Master J was listening to in the late 1990s. It opens with a four beat, three chord keyboard sequence—Dmin, Emin, Fmaj7—followed by four beats of sustaining the Fmaj7 chord. The effect, which is repeated throughout the song, adds a sound reminiscent of dansi (the seventh chord is commonly used in dansi music). Master J also layers the song with an arpeggiated guitar part, again hinting at the dansi tradition in the country where rhythm guitarists make strong use of this technique. Since Master J's father was a dance band musician, the influence of the dansi sound on his composition is not surprising. It does, however, provide aesthetic qualities of Tanzanian culture within the American hip hop framework, an innovation central to much of the studio production of bongo flava. Further, the basic layering of parts—bass, drums, keyboard, guitars, and samples—in Master

J's initial composition has continued to follow him in his later work. Listeners can, therefore, frequently identify a song composed and produced by Master J simply by listening to the backing track of a song.

In the decade since the emergence of independent recording studios in Tanzania in the early 1990s, the local production of music has grown dramatically.[8] Around 50 commercial and hundreds of home studios now exist in Dar es Salaam to record bongo flava artists (Perullo 2011: 244-45). Many young producers also apprentice with the more experienced producers, thereby avoiding the need to purchase their own equipment. (Before temporarily closing his studio in 2004, Master J had two bongo flava producers working for him and one producer who worked with other genres of popular music.) Although it is difficult to provide an exact number, some producers estimate that more than 100 producers work in Dar es Salaam composing and recording beats for bongo flava compared with only 4 a decade earlier in 1996. The dramatic rise in the number of studios and producers and the cost of recording highlights both the popularity of the genre and its market potential.

During this period of dramatic increase, the sound of bongo flava production also evolved to reflect a broad array of styles and production skills. While producers remain the engineers and composers of bongo flava songs, artists are more central in creating ideas for a track. Frequently artists arrive at the studio with lyrics and an idea of the sound of the backing track. Some arrive with an American track that they want to emulate. Mr. Blue, for instance, based his recording "Holla Back" on the American artist Fabolous's song "Young'n." Often the producers discuss ideas with artists until an agreement is made about the best way to produce new material and establish an audience, since producers rely on hit songs to bring quality customers to their studios.

When not based on American or other foreign sounds, artists frequently refer to the rich array of genres contained within bongo flava to guide producers to the sound that they are seeking. Frequently artists appropriate foreign and local genre names to mean something specific to bongo flava. Zouk, for instance, refers to slow, romantic R&B ballads rather than the upbeat West Indian genre; bomba, which emerged in Kenya as boomba, is a more aggressive sound with upfront vocals and thick layering of an urban, east African keyboard sound; taarap, mainly created by the artist Cool Para, is a combination of taarab melodies and rhythms with rap vocals; ragga is vocally similar to the Jamaican style of guttural rapping but, in Tanzania, often has less aggressive rhythms than its Jamaican counterpart.

Several styles are associated with only one producer or artist. Mr. Nice created *takeu* (which stands for Tanzania, Kenya, and Uganda) to advance both his vision of an East African sound and his style, a dancehall rhythm with regionally inspired African harmonies and a heavy use of Auto-Tune. The artist Zozo's style is bongo culture, and it borrows from traditional ngoma music. Saidi Comorieni, who runs

Metro Studio, produces beats that he calls African American or Africa–U.S.A., a reference to the mixture of African and American sounds in his productions. Some producers never label their style, but create consistent hits in a way that artists want to emulate.

Due to the vast array of styles, bongo flava producers need to be able to compose a broad spectrum of backing tracks, from those that imitate American hip hop to those that sound similar to other forms of African or Tanzanian popular music. Bizman, for instance, learned to produce from P Funk in 2001, and he also plays in a hotel band called InAfrika Band. His production for the artist TID on the song "Zeze" is similar to the work of Master J in that it merges sounds from both American popular music, particularly R&B, with Tanzanian aesthetics in a standard Dar es Salaam rap production. Yet Bizman's solo album, *Ningekuwa Kwetu*, relies more on the sounds of dansi and ngoma than on American hip hop. The title song features traditional drumming from the Mwanyamwezi ethnic group. Bizman explains the diverse recording practices as a combination of artists and producers attempting to achieve a certain sound and find access to different music markets: "The bongo flava artists, from what I can see, are just keeping up with what is happening in the world. If we compose really good beats, it can be heard throughout the world. The beats are a means of capturing the interest of many people."[9]

In many ways, the producers of bongo flava are repeating the practices of early dansi composers, who incorporated elements from foreign styles into their music. Some bands, such as the Sparks and the Comets, attempted to write music that more directly emulated the sound of their foreign counterparts. Other bands, such as Tabora Jazz Band, Dar es Salaam Jazz, and Western Jazz, appropriated foreign rhythms and melodies to create music that reflected an urban cosmopolitan view but still sounded distinctly Tanzanian. Due to the political movement toward socialism in the late 1960s, foreign music faded as a dominant force in the country, and Tanzanian artists established a dansi sound based more on local and national aesthetics of that period.

A similar process of mixing foreign and local sounds of various consistencies—depending on worldview and aesthetic interest—is occurring with bongo flava. Unlike dansi, however, bongo flava producers are able to innovate within a liberalized economy, which provides them with more latitude to decide the future direction of their music. Producers do not need to refocus their compositions to accommodate dominant political views of national identity. They can consider their place within a global economy, borrow ideas from foreign music, localize their music using Tanzanian sounds and ideas, and ultimately cater to the interests of artists who hire the producers to give them a backing beat for their music. This results in various production styles, such as transnational, African, Tanzanian, or Dar es Salaam hip hop.

Wearing Clothes, Defining Style

On the March 2005 cover of the Tanzanian lifestyle magazine *Bang!* appear three "bongo flava Divas": K-Lyinn (Jacqueline Kanyana Ntuyabaliwe), Ray C (Rehema Chalamila), and Renee (Irene Lwelamira). Each wears a sheer white top with either torn blue jeans or form-fitting stretch pants. They all wear makeup, have eyebrows trimmed to a perfectly thin arch, and have well coifed hair. The glossy full color cover could easily be mistaken for an American or European fashion magazine, as there are few symbols that can identify the women as being Tanzanian or African: removed are the bright colors, the complex patterns, traditional hairstyles, and conservative dresses that typify Tanzanian daily fashion.

Over the past decade, clothing in Tanzania has become a symbol of the bongo flava generation. Most fans and artists modify Western clothing to establish identities that connect them to various communities. *Bang!* represents one part of the Tanzanian fashion style associated with youth. It is a glossy spread where the publishers create a sense of belonging to an international community, mainly for upper-class urban youth who want to emulate foreign fashions.[10] Other youth in Tanzania innovate on the symbols of Western clothing to create styles that take on new meanings in local contexts. They also create their own items of clothing, such as jewelry and locally made T-shirts. For instance, the popularity of "I Love Dar" T-shirts highlights the connection that many bongo flava artists have with Dar es Salaam and the respect they have for it as an urban environment unlike other parts of the country. Selecting clothing, both to buy and wear, becomes an art form that helps youth find connections to other like-minded people within the city while also asserting their own identities. In other words, youth assemble styles out of the "material culture available to them in the effort to construct identities which will confer on them 'relative autonomy' within a social order fractured by class, generational differences, work, etc." (During 1999: 441).

Western clothing has always been a part of the Tanzanian popular music scene. Starting in the 1920s, artists who performed ballroom dance for expatriates at clubs, such as the Dar es Salaam Club, wore tuxedos during concerts. Decades later, tuxedoes were shed for suits, particularly as performances moved out of exclusive clubs and into other local establishments. After the country's independence in 1961, many musicians continued to wear suits, while others adopted the styles of American soul and Motown artists. Magazines, such as *Nyota Afrika*, promoted images of James Brown, Aretha Franklin, and others, which encouraged young people to wear afros, bellbottoms, and miniskirts. Due to the strong nationalist movement, however, many youth worked together to ban the overt Western fashions that were seen as indecent.

During the country's liberalization (after 1984), many performers and dancers modeled their own clothing on the fashions seen in Western movies and music videos, which were flooding the local market. Since it was difficult to purchase foreign clothing locally, many artists modified available materials. Fresh X, one of the first Tanzanian rappers (he started rapping in 1984), often appropriated the fashion style of American artists and, for one event, cut his jeans, painted graffiti on his boots, and cut his hair in the style of Cameo, the American funk group.[11] Although this practice was unusual for everyday dress in the 1980s, it was prominent in clubs with dancers imitating Western stars.

Once independent television and radio stations emerged, clothing became an increasingly important symbol for youth to show that they were cosmopolitan and knowledgeable about foreign trends. The government station, Radio Tanzania Dar es Salaam (RTD), had limited the airing of foreign music on its local services since the late 1970s, and no television stations existed in the country until the formation of ITV in 1994 (Perullo 2003; Sturmer 1998). RTD had controlled the local music market since the country's inception, which left little locally produced material available to the newly independent stations. Independent stations, therefore, spent a great deal of energy and money traveling abroad, purchasing foreign records, and airing them in Tanzania. Listeners, the majority of whom had little means to hear foreign music under the government ban, clamored to hear the "new" sounds coming out of Europe and the United States. Additionally, music videos provided strong visual cues for youth to learn about foreign styles. A short time after foreign videos began broadcasting to the Tanzanian public, youth more directly emulated what they saw on television.

Beauty pageants and fashion shows have also influenced local concepts of dress in Tanzania. With the exception of the Vazi la Taifa (national fashion shows), the majority of beauty competitions, such as Miss Dar City Centre, Miss Sinza, and Miss Ubungo, all of which take place in Dar es Salaam, draw heavily on international standards and styles of modeling shows. At these competitions, women typically wear Western style evening gowns with long slits up the legs and low-cut necklines and extremely revealing "beach wear." Hair is often straightened and occasionally bleached blonde, and nails are extravagantly manicured. Women imitate runway models in walking, turning, and posing, and most have the international modeling body shape—tall and thin—rather than the more stereotypical full-figured women promoted in other areas of popular culture. (Take, for instance, the songs "Jimama" [Big Mama] by Babloom Modern Taarab and "Nyambizi" [Large Woman] by Dully Sykes, which praise women with large, shapely figures.)

Even with historical connections to Western forms of dress and the popularity of television images and beauty pageants, the most important reason for the use of Western clothing in Tanzanian daily dress is the importation of *mitumba* (second-hand clothing). During the late 1980s, wholesalers imported large bales of used clothes from the United States and Europe. Because the Tanzanian textile market was already in a state of decline, partly due to its reliance on government subsidies (de Valk 1996), the market for mitumba grew dramatically.[12] By the late 1990s, it was difficult to visit a part of Tanzania where mitumba clothes did not feature prominently, and only the kanga—a thin, colorful cloth typically worn by women around the waist, shoulders, and head—remained as prominent a fashion as used clothes. Due to the intense infiltration of inexpensive secondhand clothing in Tanzania, bongo flava artists and fans in the country's major cities, such as Dar es Salaam, Arusha, Mwanza, and Morogoro, rely on the importation of used clothing to furnish their bongo flava style, especially since they cost far less than the other options available to them.[13]

Despite the many uses of Western clothing, Tanzanian youth are not "powerless recipient(s) of an imposed" system of foreign styles (Ivaska 2002: 587). They use clothing to participate in international and local concepts of hip hop culture and to establish specific identities for themselves within their various communities (home, school, work, or with other hip hop enthusiasts). The presentation of self is thereby dependent on an individual's position and interest in a given context. For instance, in live performance, many youth use the stage to display the identity of communities with which they want to be associated. These communities are known as camps in Tanzania and refer to the gathering of youth in specific locations throughout the city who share common ideological perspectives. Displaying the proper forms of attire onstage is important in communicating to local audiences and building a fan base of like-minded youth. Off the stage, youth vary their clothing considerably, from those who maintain their stage presence to those who blend into everyday life in Dar es Salaam. This fluctuation of dress allows youth to identify themselves as being part of specific communities. A marijuana plant symbol, a Yankees hat, FUBU shirt, an American sports jersey, locally beaded jewelry, baggy pants, Timberland boots—all carry local meaning.

Figures 9.2 and 9.3 represent examples of dress among youth interested in bongo flava. King Crazy GK wears a shirt with the name of the camp he belongs to (East Coast Team, although it is written as East Coast Army), a white winter Yankees cap, and an armband with the Jamaican Rastafarian colors and a peace symbol. The clothing is reminiscent of American hip hop trends, particularly the Yankees cap, yet the style connects a specific representation of GK and his target audience. The Yankees cap, for instance, is an obvious reference to New York City, a place that gave rise to hip hop. The cap is also meant to position GK as being affiliated with the "east coast" of Dar es Salaam, just as New York is on the east coast of the United States. GK lives in Upanga, which is centrally located and more or less in the eastern part of the city. This location not only symbolizes privilege—it is one of the wealthier communities in the city—but also references the belief that the artists here gave rise to bongo flava. The shirt strengthens the notion of location and identity, specifically mentioning the camp that GK helped found in Upanga with other local artists. Since the shirt is locally made, as are many of the T-shirts worn by youth in live performances, GK adds to his credibility as a locally conscious performer. Finally, the armband borrows on the images of peacefulness in Jamaican

Figure 9.2. GK performing in Dar es Salaam, Tanzania, July 2005. Photo by Alex Perullo.

Figure 9.3. Members of the rap group Mambo Poa in Dar es Salaam, Tanzania, December 2000. From left to right: Steve 2K, John Mjema, Spider, and Vincent Magige. Photo by Alex Perullo.

Rastafarian culture. It can be read as a symbol of marijuana use, or it can highlight GK's view on the importance of peace.

Outside of live performance, the use of camp symbols and names often becomes less important, and many artists return to typical forms of Dar es Salaam dress. Figure 9.3 shows the rap group Mambo Poa hanging out in front of a small store in downtown Dar es Salaam. Vincent Magige wears business attire: slacks with a short-sleeved shirt. Spider and Steve 2K wear a style frequently worn by youth, a relaxed collarless shirt with pants. And John Mjema dons his purple suit, which connects him more to other forms of popular Tanzanian music, such as dansi, than to bongo flava, where suits are almost never worn. In their dress, none of the members of Mambo Poa have obvious markers of American hip hop culture, and each easily blends into other forms of dress commonly found in Dar es Salaam. At concerts, these artists may put on attire more easily recognizable as part of a broader hip hop culture, yet in their daily interactions, nothing they wear marks them as being artists or fans of bongo flava. Style, therefore, fluctuates according to context and community interaction.

Style in Tanzanian dress can also be thought of as what local youth do not emulate. For instance, most males refrain from wearing flashy jewelry, tattoos, or pants worn low enough to show their underwear, all of which has become important in the images they see of American rap artists. Men also tend not to braid their hair, a custom heavily criticized by elder community members in Tanzania, since it is a feminine style. Exceptions obviously occur, such as Steve 2K, who has his hair partially braided in rows. Women tend not to wear revealing clothes outside of a performance situation (the assumption being that revealing clothes signals being a prostitute), and if jewelry is worn, it often borrows from Tanzanian aesthetics and design.[14]

Style therefore becomes a mixture of trends that are modified for a particular situation. Innovation occurs in the ways that meaning is attributed to symbols and items of clothing regardless of their place of origin. Being constantly aware of the meaning of these clothes and dressing in ways that properly display one's connection to various communities is central to any person's participation in bongo flava. The American rapper Chuck D said in an advertisement, "SO YOU WANNA BE IN THE MUSIC BUSINESS . . . WHATCHA' GONNA WEAR?" (cited in Negus 2004: 537). The quote, aimed at the burgeoning hip hop movement in the United States, is just as applicable to bongo flava: clothing is a visual symbol of youth commitment to international hip hop, East African urban culture, and the local bongo flava movement, all communities that youth relate to in as many ways as possible. How artists put the clothing together has less to do with their reliance on foreign items of clothing than in their choice of styles and materials, all of which create appropriate identities for themselves in the shifting dynamics of urban African communities.

Camps and Urban Communities

When not working in the recording studio, filming a video, or performing onstage, most artists and many fans pass their days sitting with each other in "camps." Camps exist mainly in Dar es Salaam as a home base for artists or a gathering place of an artist's most ardent fans. Camps can be any physical location: a bar, street corner, a lean to, wall, tree, or neighborhood street. While these camps could simply be considered hangouts, they serve as centers for youth to support and educate one another about current events in bongo flava communities. They allow artists to test new lyrics and discuss ideas about stage performance or video production. They provide places for youth to make contacts, network, and in some cases attain financial support for a musical endeavor. Most important, camps are critical for establishing a community of youth who share similar backgrounds and ideological viewpoints.

One of the better known camps in Dar es Salaam is Wanaume Unity Family, typically referred to as Wanaume (Men).[15] KR, a rapper and founding member of Wanaume, explains its importance:

Our camp is a way of showing unity, sharing ideas on everything, and discussing life and the music business in a calm place, without any violence or noise. Practicing is also important because you cannot practice on your own; you learn from practicing in front of others. If you sit in front of others, it is easy for them to tell you "this is good" or "this is bad." This has brought unity to the group and strengthened our music.[16]

Almost every day, some of the fifty members of Wanaume gather near a bus stop in Temeke, Dar es Salaam, to ruminate about current events, jobs, and music. They also create TMK T-shirts and armbands (TMK stands for Temeke) and coin new words and phrases, such as *cheua-beiua* [cough up the money]. The group uses the axe as its symbol, and members make a hand gesture—essentially two fists together with the index fingers crossed into an "X"—to represent the axe and their camp. Modeling themselves after the military, they shout "Eh" in unison when one of the group members bellows "Wanaume."

Of course, Wanaume also records and performs onstage. Often a single artist, such as Juma Nature, will perform and the other members of the camp will go onstage to support his music. The live performances are popular throughout the country due to the highly choreographed routines, which merge military movements with a contemporary dance aesthetic and socially engaging lyrics. In creating the dancing and rapping, the group draws from the identity and image promoted by Wanaume camp. KR comments on the image that the camp portrays: "The members of Wanaume try to squeeze out a life for themselves. If you look at us, no one is proclaiming to be rich; we come from a poor environment. Tanzania is a country of poor people. So we try to speak for those who are poor."[17] Using an ideology of poverty and a military concept of unity and discipline, the camp members use their music and performances to inform people about the problems that many Tanzanians face. They do this, according to KR, to support the poor and to counter other camps in Dar es Salaam that compose songs about having fancy cars, clothes, or jewelry, material possessions anathema to Wanaume's purpose.

In Wanaume and most other artist-based camps, apprenticeship is important; artists are brought in if they are recognized as having "skills" that can be developed. They start out by learning from the more established members how to rap, dress, and conduct business. In these circumstances, the camps act as schools. As artists improve, senior members feature them in songs in order to give them exposure (featuring involves inviting another artist to perform a verse or a chorus in a song). Once the artist is capable of recording on his or her own, other camp members assist in paying for studio time, negotiating contracts, or finding places to perform.[18]

Most informal estimates by journalists and artists are that 1,000 camps exist throughout Dar es Salaam. Camps provide defining and salient forms of identity for members. They can be descriptive, characterized by shared values and backgrounds, and prescriptive, giving members direction in their lives and musical careers. Bongo flava camps are also evaluative, which means that members of camps are constantly motivated to adopt and maintain behaviors of a group (Hogg, Terry and White 1995: 260). For this reason, camps often adopt symbols, language, dress styles, and other defining characteristics that members constantly assess in order to maintain in-group status.

Being a member of a camp does have a cultural precedent in dansi and taarab bands. During the same time that bongo flava artists sit in their camps, dansi and taarab bands gather at their home base, often a local club, to practice new songs, discuss current events, and hone their skills on individual instruments. Young artists often sit in with the bands to learn performance techniques and improve their playing, singing, or dancing. The music business is often discussed, as are future plans for the band. Among many bands, money can also be borrowed to help pay for funerals, weddings, or other important events in a member's life. For these reasons, camps and bands offer similar support in dealing with the complexities of music, business, and urban life.

The most important distinction between the practice spaces of dansi bands and the camps of bongo flava is the way they function as centers of power. Dansi bands certainly wield power as culturally influential entities within urban centers. Most of the economic power of these bands, however, rests with organizations or individuals who own them. Bands members are paid salaries for their work, and few have any control over where they perform, who they record with, or what songs they should record. The more democratic groups allow members to vote, yet the ultimate verdict rests with the members or individuals who hold economic power. For bongo flava, the established artists enter the camps with economic stability. Many drive cars, possess extensive wardrobes, and enjoy disposable income. When they enter the camps, they do so with the knowledge that they do not have to rely on the other members for financial support, though they also can turn to the camp members if need be. Even artists who have not yet succeeded in the music business recognize that their financial success is determined by their ability to release a hit song and not by an overarching organization that pays them a regular salary.

The movement from organizational control to individual empowerment is a significant transformation in the local music scene and one that has greatly impacted the identity of musical organizations. Youth understand themselves to be connected within camps by similar interests, backgrounds, and skills, but they also recognize their independence. It is up to them to write music, record in the studio, perform onstage, attain airplay, and sell records, even though camps provide a critical support network. Certainly, the liberalization of the local economy and the trend toward individualization within the local music economy have placed more emphasis on the individual. Camps, however, act as a means for youth to ground global and local trends toward individualization with a stronger notion of community. They allow youth a chance to remain independent but still be a part of a strong social network that assists them in establishing a career and moving their message out to other communities.

In the past few years, dansi bands also opted to create camps for their fans. African Stars Band was the first group to form camps of die-hard fans that attend almost all of the band's concerts. Mfano Mchangani Camp, Wagumu Camp, Home Alone Camp, Wazee wa Njaa Camp, Wazee wa Bandari Camp, and Wazushi Camp are all located in the Mwananyamala section of Dar es Salaam, and the African Stars managers provide them with tickets for upcoming shows and clothes that help promote the band. By supporting these camps, African Stars can guarantee that they will have large, enthusiastic crowds at their shows, which further entices people to attend and typically provides good reviews in local newspapers and more airtime on local radio stations.

Bongo flava also has fan-based camps, although clothing and tickets tend not to be provided to its members. These camps support and praise individual artists, such the camps Choka Mbaya (for the rapper Professor Jay), Dar Skendo (DuduBaya), and Misifa Camp (Dully Sykes). At bongo flava concerts, some camps brandish homemade shirts or flags. When their artist appears onstage, members dance and sing, and a few join the artist onstage. They act as a critical support network in the increasingly competitive music market and provide a sense of purpose for fans who want to identify with a particular artist.

Although Tanzanian youth, as well as other Africans, have long been localizing foreign sounds, one significant difference exists between the previous generations and those currently innovating on the sounds of hip hop: the ability to easily communicate with various communities. The internet, texting, the rapid availability of magazines and CDs, and the frequent travel of artists within and outside of eastern Africa allow youth to maintain constant connections to people, practices, and sounds at a rate that would have been impossible in the past. An artist can e-mail a backing track to the United States, have the song remixed, and then record the vocals before the song is mixed down to be sold. Many artists tour Kenya, Uganda, Europe, and the United States. Youth watch broadcasts of local, regional, and international hip hop videos as soon as those videos are released in their home markets. International stars, such as Jay Z and Sean Paul, find Tanzania an important place to tour and present their music. And numerous individuals post websites with songs, photographs, and videos for listeners to view.

The transnational public sphere of hip hop culture, which moves beyond national borders or localized communities, informs youth about current trends (Gupta and Ferguson 1992: 9). Youth reify this knowledge of international hip hop and apply it to communities of which they wish to be a part. This provides them with a sense of power as they assign meaning to notions of cosmopolitanism and urbanness to other youth and other communities in East Africa. Partially through bongo flava, youth continually inform each other what it means to live in an African city, such as Dar es Salaam, as well as assert what it is to be young, urban, and Tanzanian.[19]

Often the interest in foreign music and styles is interpreted solely as the dominance of the West. In a recent *Kenyan Times* opinion piece, Dominic Omondi writes about the impact of globalization on Kenyan society. At the end of the article, he addresses local music:

> As a matter of fact, unlike Tanzanians, who have expertly and strategically fused their local music and Hip-hop, thus culminating into much acclaimed "Bongo Flava," Kenyans have given monkeys a contest by not only singing like 50 Cent, but also dressing like him; speaking his language, putting on his garbs; and with a most daring audacity, claiming to be proud to be Kenyan![20]

While initially criticized as being solely a form of imitation, bongo flava is increasingly being recognized as an innovative form of music that embodies the communities and identities associated with Tanzanian youth and music. Omondi dismisses similar innovations occurring in Kenya and instead points to the direct forms of imitation that exist in that country. Of course, these forms of imitation occur in Tanzania and other parts of Africa as well, where American stars, such as 50 Cent, take on powerful roles as cultural icons. Yet in Kenya, too, numerous groups appropriate the symbols, sounds, and ideas of foreign artists and incorporate them into local aesthetics and ideologies. The dualism of imitation and innovation is central to any form of popular music where artists seek to connect to the initial purveyors of the musical form and still compose for local audiences. The increased speed of communication and travel provides artists with the ability to appropriate local, national, and international trends, thus giving them resources to establish styles and identities most useful for the various communities with which they want to be a part.

NOTES

1. The abundance of academic writing on bongo flava emphasizes the social and cultural importance of this genre in Tanzanian popular culture. See Englert (2003); Haas and Gesthuizen (2000); Higgins (2009); Lemelle (2006); Mangesho (2003); Ntarangwi (2009); Perullo (2005, 2007); Remes (1998); Reuster-Jahn (2007); Saavedra (2006); Suriano (2006, 2007); and Thompson (2008).

2. Rhymson (Ramadhani Mponjika), interview with the author, Canada, May 23, 2004.

3. Professor Jay (Joseph Haule), interview with the author, Tanga, January 19, 2001.

4. This quote was posted October 14, 2004, on YoungAfrican.com on the Ya Tanzania Tupo (All Tanzanians) pages.

5. Many critiques of bongo flava can be found in online forums. In May 2005, the website darhotwire.com asked users about the imitation of foreign beats and lyrics in Tanzanian bongo flava. Of the nearly 500 people who voted in the survey, many of whom live outside Tanzania, 57 percent stated that copying beats or lyrics from foreign sources showed that local artists had "nothing original left"; 30 percent felt that copying was common, while the remaining 13 percent perceived the practice as a form of creativity.

6. Master J (Joachim Kimaryo), interview with the author, Dar es Salaam, November 29, 2000.

7. Ibid.

8. Before 1991, only two recording studios existed in Tanzania: Radio Tanzania Dar es Salaam's studio and the Tanzania Film Company's studio. A department of the Tanzanian government owned and operated both studios (see Perullo 2011: chapter 2).

9. Bizman Ntazyo, interview with the author, September 10, 2005.

10. The 50,000 who read *Bang!* are well-connected members of the popular music industry (radio presenters, deejays, business owners, etc.), and the models and clothing used in the magazine represent some of the fashion trends occurring among the wealthier youth in the local scene. The magazine also features photographs and discussions with Tanzanians living abroad, thus creating direct ties to fashion trends abroad and in Tanzania, Kenya, Uganda, and South Africa, where the magazine is also sold.

11. One of Cameo's band members had the sides and back of his head shaved close, with the top hair standing straight up. From his description, this is most likely the style that Fresh X imitated.

12. Recently, a debate has ensued in Tanzania concerning whether or not to ban mitumba in an attempt to support local clothing manufacturers. Although this debate has occurred before, it is now being discussed among members of the East African Community (EAC), which would be able to lobby appropriate officials to pass legislation banning the importation of mitumba ("Mitumba Days Are Numbered," *Arusha Times,* August 27, 2005).

13. Other options include new clothing stores, such as D-Jungle and New Look, both in Dar es Salaam, which feature brand-name clothes. Also, several local designers, such as Slim A. Slim and KP Clothing, make original lines aimed at bongo flava artists.

14. Since 2005, when this article was originally written, many of the trends listed in the previous paragraphs have significantly changed. Tattoos, for instance, are more common, even though few people are knowledgeable about creating tattoos and there has been a strong media attempt to curb the practice. For example, on December 20, 2006, the *Guardian* printed an article titled "Common Problems Associated with Tattoos." Four days later, *Nipashe* published an article by the helpful advisor Anti Flora Wingia that described a youth frightened of the dangers involved in tattooing (this story lacked a great deal of credibility and appears mostly fabricated).

15. The discussion of Wanaume in this article concerns their activities before the camp split into two competing camps in 2006.

16. Rashid Ziada (KR), interview with the author, Dar es Salaam, November 9, 2000, and September 10, 2005.

17. Ibid.

18. Camps are predominately a male enterprise, although there are female members. Many female artists perform in Tanzania, such as Zay B, Witness, and Nakaaya. Among these there is a conflicting opinion about gender dynamics in the music economy. Some argue that there is discrimination against female artists and less opportunity to perform or record. Others state that the discrimination is not in the music economy but in the home and society, where people are not as accepting of solo female artists. Several female artists explained to me that urban centers, such as Dar es Salaam, have changed significantly over the past decade to become far more accepting. As more prominent female artists have distributed and broadcast their music, discrimination has become less prevalent.

19. See Magaldi (1999: 313) for this notion in a Brazilian context.

20. Dominic Omondi, "Opinion," *Kenyan Times* (January 26, 2007).

PART 5.
POPULAR MUSIC PANORAMAS
(GHANA AND MALAWI)

Contemporary Ghanaian Popular Music since the 1980s

JOHN COLLINS

The development of Ghanaian transcultural popular dance music from its origins in the 1880s can be divided into three broad historical epochs. First, as a result of colonialism there was, in southern Ghana, the introduction of foreign regimental brass band music, the classical and ballroom music of Western orchestras, and the guitar and accordion music of foreign seamen. There was a gradual African-ization of these genres up until the Second World War, sometimes linked to the spread of popular music genres from the coastal urban centers to the provincial and rural hinterlands.[1] This resulted in transcultural music forms such as adaha and konkoma marching band music, the coastal osibisaaba and more inland and rustic odonson guitar styles, and street music by local elite ballroom dance orchestras that by the 1920s was being referred to as "highlife" (i.e., high-class life) music. By the 1940s, *highlife* became the generic term for all these new forms of Ghana-ian music, whether played by brass bands, guitar bands, or dance orchestras and bands.

The independence ethos of the 1950s ushered in a second epoch when there began a more self-conscious Africanization of the highlife dance bands and also of the guitar bands and their associated "concert party" popular theater groups.[2] Many of these supported Kwame Nkrumah's Convention People's Party (CPP) and, as a quid pro quo, when Ghana gained independence in 1957, Nkrumah supported the local popular music and entertainment sector. Then in the 1960s came im-ported soul music and its associated Afrocentric fashions that triggered an Afri-canization of imported Western pop music leading to Afro-beat and Afro-rock.[3] By the early 1970s these developments resulted in the country boasting more than seventy guitar bands (linked to concert parties), scores of private and state-run highlife dance bands, dozens of Afro-rock and Afro-beat bands, and hundreds of pop bands that emerged through school-student pop chains (competitions).

Catering for these bands were large numbers of nightclubs (sixty in Accra alone), four recording studios, and two pressing plants that produced hundreds of thousands of records a year.

This second epoch ended in the late 1970s with the general collapse of the Ghanaian economy due to the mismanagement and corruption (*kalabule*) of the Acheampong/Akuffo military regimes, which came to power in 1972. After a honeymoon period, the economy quickly began to decline and finally ground to a halt at the end of the 1970s, and Ghanaian artists left the country in droves.[4] This was followed by a period of political instability (two military coups by J. J. Rawlings in 1979 and 1981) and a curfew (1982–84) that affected the country's nightlife and entertainment sector. This break or interregnum in the commercial popular music industry between the late 1970s and 1984 was followed by the imposition of huge import duties (160 percent) on band equipment, and music education was demoted in the school curriculum. All these factors negatively affected the highlife and other popular bands, which were often of large size, depended on access to Western instruments and know-how, and needed audience gate revenues. Furthermore, highlife bands began competing with a new generation of smaller "techno-pop" bands whose dance music was mediated through "spinners" (mobile discos), video, and television.[5]

This brings us to the topic of this chapter: the third epoch in the development of Ghanaian popular music that began in the late 1980s, when the country's economy was liberalized and Ghana began to move back toward civilian rule. By then much of the old-time classic highlife guitar and dance band music had been wiped out, and new styles of popular dance music emerged linked to changing music technologies, local Ghanaian churches, and new imported music styles such as reggae, rap, and world music. Moreover, folkloric music found a niche with the many foreign visitors due to a boom in the tourist industry resulting from political stability. Nevertheless, some of the old-time highlife groups did manage to survive, and new highlife bands, artists, and genres surfaced during the 1980s and 1990s.

Classic Highlife Survives and Burger Highlife Arrives

Many of the old-time dance band and guitar band highlife musicians survived the problems of the 1970s/80s by going abroad. For instance, guitar bands (like those of Kofi Sammy, Alex Konadu, and T. O. Jazz) moved to oil-rich Nigeria, particularly eastern Nigeria, where its own version of highlife was already popular. Others moved to or partially operated in North America, Europe, and Australia, including Jerry Hansen (Ramblers), Eddie Quansah, Bob Pinodo, Gyedu Blay-Ambollay, Pat Thomas, A. B. Crentsil, Jewel Ackah, Eric Agyeman, C. K. Mann, and Amekye Dede.

Some simply stuck it out in Ghana. For instance, a handful of concert party highlife guitar bands that had large rural followings survived, such as the City

Boys, Kumapin Royals, African Heroes, African Brothers, Alhaji Frimpong's Cubana Fiesta, and Teacher Boateng's Afrikana, while the Osofo Dadzie and Obra groups found a niche in long-running television series. The only urban-oriented big highlife dance bands that survived the 1980s were those connected to state hotels or the armed forces.

However, by the early 1990s there was a revival of highlife big bands, partly linked to a public outcry against the lip-synched music videos on TV and a demand for live televised shows. A new generation of highlife big bands was formed that included Papa Yankson and the Western Diamonds, the Marriots, the Golden Nuggets, Ankobra, and Ghana Broadcasting Band, led by Stan Plange, leader of the famous 1960s/70s Uhuru and Black Star Line dance bands. These were followed by the Megastar and the Vision bands, the Gold Coasters, Desmond Ababio's Alpha Waves, and, more recently, a reformed Ramblers band and the university music department bands on the Legon and Winneba campuses, directed by Ebo Taylor and Bob Pinodo, respectively.

Many of the large number of Ghanaian musicians who moved abroad from the late 1970s settled in Germany, where immigration laws were relaxed. The port town of Hamburg was a favorite destination for these economic migrants, and it was there that "burger highlife" was born. This was a musical fusion of highlife music with the drum machine and synthesizers of disco dance music created there by guitarist George Darko, singer Lee Dodou, keyboardist Bob Fiscian, and bassist B. B. Dowuona, whose Bus Stop band released the very first such burger disco/highlife album in 1983, called *Friends* (which included "Akoo Te Brofo"), which was a smash hit with young Ghanaians. Other Ghanaians abroad followed the burger highlife trend, including the Lumba Brothers (Nana Acheampong, Charles Kojo Fusu, and Sarkodie), Rex Gyamfi, McGod, Albert Jones, and Charles Amoah in Germany, Sloopy Mike Gyamfi, Chikinchi, and Captain Moro in Holland, and John K. and Ben Brako in Britain. This music subsequently became even more popular in Ghana after the mid-1980s when the economy started to pick up, and many of these burger Ghanaian musicians began visiting or returning home.

This techno-pop style of burger highlife was favored by the Ghanaian youth of the times who began to see the older brands of highlife that used live percussion and horns as "colo" (colonial) or old-fashioned. Another reason this music became popular was that burger highlife bands had just a small number of personnel and so were more economical to operate than the older large highlife bands, an important consideration taking into account the large import duties at the time on musical instruments. Furthermore, burger highlife was produced mainly by recording bands that made music for discos, spinners, and television video clips. As a result, when performed onstage, this music was usually mimed or lip-synched. One of the most popular burger highlife artists is Charles Kojo Fusu (or "Daddy Lumba"), who had an enormous hit in 1998 with his song "Aben Wo Ha" [It is cooked], which was banned by some radio stations due to its lyrics thinly disguising the idea of a sexually aroused women. Other popular burger artists today are "Lover Boy" Nana Acheampong and Nana Aboagye Da Costa, who rose to fame in 2000 with his love song "Odo Menkoaa." Indeed, most of the lyrics of burger highlife are about romantic or erotic love. This is quite unlike old-time highlife in which love was a minor theme, with the majority of lyrics covering a range of topics that included witchcraft, sociopolitical commentary, broken homes, moral advice, money "palava" (quarrels), sickness, and death.[6]

NAKOREX was an important highlife group formed in the late 1990s that bridged the gap between old-time and burger highlife. Like burger highlife, NAKOREX used hi-tech instruments, but combined these with standard musical instrumentation and put an emphasis on live performance. It was the brainchild of three young musicians who wanted to create a world music brand of highlife, and it became the launching pad for the solo careers of its founding members, Nat "Amandzeba" Brew, Rex Omar, and Akosua Agyepong.

Ghanaian Reggae

Jamaican reggae music first became popular in Ghana in the mid-1970s through the records of Desmond Dekker, Jimmy Cliff (who visited Nigeria in 1974), and especially dreadlocked Bob Marley when he released his *Exodus* album in 1977. Indeed it was that year that the first reggae sound system was brought to Ghana by the Jamaican Raas Wolde Mikael.

From the late 1970s a number of Ghanaian reggae bands sprang up who imitated the Jamaican style. There were the Classic Handels and the six-piece Classic Vibes, which included Kwadwo Antwi, Obibio, and Ayi Soloman and which left Ghana for Denmark in 1983 and then Switzerland in 1985.[7] Another early Ghanaian reggae band, Roots Anabo, was set up in Germany in the late 1970s by Ekow Savage Alabi and Sammy Nukpere. This group toured Ghana in the early 1980s, and in 1984 it became the first African reggae band to play at the Jamaican Reggae Sunsplash Festival. Ghanaian reggae bands and artists singing in Jamaican patois and operating in Ghana in the early 1980s were SO2 Squad (later called Sons of Zion), Felix Bell, Kojo Ashakanor, Kindred, and Grassroots. In 1984 a reggae and ragga sound system called Hi Power was bought to Ghana by Jah Rhapsody, a West Indian from Britain who worked with the Ghanaian emcees or toasters Preacher Levi, General Marcus, and Wahesh Simeon.

Due to the economic problems in Ghana during the 1980s, there were few visits there by performing bands and artists from outside Africa.[8] Nevertheless, during these difficult years three West Indian reggae bands did manage to come: Misty and Roots, Musical Youth (from Birmingham, UK), and Yellow Man. However, it was Bob Marley, through his records and videos, who was most influential. As a result, many members of the early local Ghanaian reggae bands and sound system groups began to sport his matted rastafarian dreadlocks, typifying an emerging Ghanaian youth subculture.[9] This urban subculture was, like the West Indian model, marked not only by hairstyle and Jamaican patois but also by the rastafarian diet, its use of marijuana as a religious sacrament, the worship of Jah (Jehova), and its criticism of Western civilization or "Babylon."

Reggae bands multiplied in Ghana during the 1980s and early 1990s and included Root of David (leader Ras Kente), Black Empire, Nazarite Vow (Ras Korby and General Stano), Shadrach, Sons of Zion, and Shasha Marley. Student reggae bands included Kente (run by Fred Dred) and Sly Dennis and his Exodus group, formed in 1987 at the University of Science and Technology in Kumasi (they toured Germany and the UK in 1997). Another was Local Crisis, formed at the University in Accra in 1991 by Rocky Dawuni, who has become a major star and today regularly tours the United States and releases successful albums. The Nigerian lady reggae performer Evi Edna Ogoli (whose band included Ghanaians) toured Ghana in 1989, while records by other Nigerian reggae artists such as the Mandators, Majek Fashek, and Ras Kimono (who performed in Ghana in 2004) also became popular with Ghanaian reggae fans.

Whereas the initial Ghanaian reggae bands were based on Jamaican models, reggae rhythms were quickly absorbed by some of the local guitar band highlife artists who sang their lyrics in Akan rather than English. The earliest of these artists who began playing a reggae influenced highlife style as early as the mid-1970s were J. A. Ampofo (City Boys), Nana Ampadu (African Brothers), and Teacher Boateng (Afrikana Band), followed by Amekye Dede (Apollo High Kings), the Kumapim Royals, and K. K. Kabobo. A group that performed reggae in the Ga language of Accra was Salaam's Cultural Imani Band, set up in the early 1980s by Ellis "Salaam" Lamptey, who had originally been a guitarist for the Tempos, Barristers, and El Beats highlife dance bands.

Another factor encouraging Ghanaian reggae artists to use their own local languages were the late 1980s tours of reggae star Alpha Blondy of Côte d'Ivoire, who sang in his country's Mande and Baoule languages. Also important in the vernacularization of Ghanaian reggae lyrics is Kwadwo Antwi, who left the Classic Vibes and since 1986 has released a string of albums of Twi love songs that combine highlife with the sentimental "lovers rock" form of reggae pioneered by the Jamaican Gregory Isaacs.

The impact of reggae and the Ghanaian rasta subculture has been strengthened since the 1990s by an influx of West Indian and other foreign reggae and ragga artists. With the establishment of the biannual PANAFEST in 1992,[10] there have been visits by Gregory Isaacs, Zion's Children, the toaster-poet Mutabaruka, and Shaba Ranks from Jamaica, United Spirit from Germany, and Bob Marley's widow, Rita, and son Ziggy. Indeed, Rita Marley has settled in Ghana and established the Bob Marley Foundation school and recording studio at Aburi near Accra. Besides this foundation, other West Indians have set up organizations that cater to reggae music, such as the Twelve Tribes of Israel Foundation (established in 1997), the

Afro-Caribbean Center in Accra, and the Union of African States Foundation run by Ras Calab Appiah-Levi.

Besides PANAFEST, reggae bands play at special events, such as Bob Marley's birthday, Haile Selassie's birthday, and Caribbean Emancipation Day (celebrating the freeing of Caribbean slaves on July 31, 1838), which Ghana began celebrating in 1998 and which has involved reggae shows at the Children's Park in Accra. Other Accra venues that host or cater for reggae are the Jehrah Restaurant, Akoma Village, and on occasion the Alliance Française (French Cultural Centre). Furthermore, the annual Ghana Music Awards (the country's equivalent to the American Grammy), established around 2000 by the Charter House Company, gives out awards for best reggae artist; winners include Shasha Marley and Kwadwo Antwi in 2002, and Shariff Ghale and his Seven For Peace group in 2005. Other Ghanaian reggae musicians include Nana Fynn, Kwesi Selassie, Ekow Shailo, Black Prophet, Carlous Man, Alaine Courage Man, Sheriff Ghale, Ras Tonto, and Mokin.

Afro-Fusion Music and Local Jazz

Except for the London-based Osibisa, none of the early Ghanaian Afro-fusion bands (Afro-rock, Afro-funk, and Afro-beat bands) survived the 1970s/80s musical downturn: indeed, many musicians left the country (Okyerema Asante, Kwaku Morton, Nat Hammond, Stanley Todd, Kofi Ayivor, Herman Asafo-Adjei, Afro Moses, and Alfred Bannerman). However, from the late 1980s Afro-fusion music resurfaced with a new generation of musicians or through musicians returning from abroad.

In the mid-1980s, Lash Layrea and Jagga Botchwey of the 1970s Hedzolleh band formed Amartey Hedzolleh, while Jerry James Larteh, who had played with Basa Basa Sounds, founded the band Saka Saka.[11] In the 1990s, the Bawasaaba Afro-rock band was put together by the ex-Boombaya and Zonglo Biiz drummer Smart Urpah Pozo on returning from Britain, followed in the late 1990s by Dabatram, run by the university lecturer Kojo Gavua, who had studied in Canada, and Dzidudu, formed by Nana Kwesi Danquah after returning from Sweden. Also in the 1990s there was the Ninkribi band led by the Sierra Leonian percussionist Francis Fuster, which became partly based in Ghana. Like the earlier Osibisa, many of these new Afro-fusion groups featured some traditional instruments. For instance, Ninkribi teamed up with Captain Yaba of northern Ghana, who plays the traditional Frafra two-stringed koliko or kologo lute,[12] while Djidudu worked with the Group Afrika percussionists, and Dabatram used the local one-stringed Dagomba goje fiddle.

Another group that combines Western and African instruments is Takashi, formed by singer Kojo Essah and guitarist Cliff Asante, which uses guitar and horns with traditional percussion, including the giant gome frame-drum that provides a bass line. From northern Ghana come Atongo Zimba and King Ayisoba, who combine the koliko/kologo lute with Western instruments and play a range of styles from Frafra songs to Afro-beats. A final example is Mac Tonto, one of the founders of Osibisa, who returned to Ghana and set up the Osibisa Kete Warriors, in which his trumpet and flugelhorn are backed by a battery of local percussion.

Afro-rock and Afro-fusion music is not particularly liked by the current generation of urban youth of Ghana, who see it, like highlife, as being too old-fashioned. This music is, rather, appreciated by foreign visitors, musicians, and world music fans, as well as by older Ghanaians returning home after long stays abroad. It is precisely this class of Ghanaian who also patronizes local jazz.

From the late 1950s through the mid-1970s, the Ghanaian jazz scene was stimulated by a number of African American jazz musicians who visited the country, such as Louis Armstrong, Max Roach, Randy Weston, James Riley, Patti Bown, Eddie Harris, and Les McCann. Also important was the late Guy Warren (Kofi Ghanaba), who had been the drummer for the Tempos dance band before going to the United States in the mid-1950s and releasing *Africa Speaks, America Answers* and a string of other pioneering Afro-jazz albums.

As with other areas of popular entertainment during the military regimes of the late 1970s to mid-1980s, little happened on the local jazz scene; Kofi Ghanaba became almost a recluse. However, the improvement of the Ghanaian economy and tourist industry from the late 1980s stimulated things in two ways. First of all, foreign jazz musicians started coming to the country again. Randy Weston and Max Roach returned, and other Americans came: James "Plunky" Branch, Andrew Cyrille, Donald Byrd, George Cables, Nathan Davis, Idris Muhammad, Milton Mustapha, Clark Terry, Joe Williams, and Nick Roberts, as well as the Black British sax player Courtney Pine and the German free jazz percussionist Robyn Schulkowsky.

Even more important was that many who had left Ghana for economic reasons began to come back with the liberalization of the economy. Some of them had been exposed to jazz and were also relatively well-to-do. A number of exclusive jazz clubs, therefore, sprang up in Accra and elsewhere to cater to them. In the early 1990s there was Jimmy's Jazz Club run by reed player Jimmy Beckley; others followed, like Diane's Café, Village Inn, Baseline (later called the Jazz Optimism Club), Bywells, the Jazz Tone Club (established by African American jazz vocalist Toni Maneison), the Odo Jazz Club, and jazz clubs embedded in top hotels like the Golden Tulip and La Palm Beach. These jazz spots are patronized not only by middle-class Ghanaians but also by foreign visitors and residents. As a result, small jazz groups have multiplied in recent years, including Jimmy's Jazz Combo, Ebo Taylor and Ray Allen's Unconditional Love, the D Minor Band, the Karmah Jazz Band, Wellington's Magnificant Jazz Trio, and Cliff Eck and Soroko's Febeja, as well as trumpeters Osei Tutu and Long John, singer Rama Brew, and Cameroonian horn player Fru "Fats" Tanga.

During the 1980s the grand old man of Ghanaian Afro-jazz, Kofi Ghanaba, established his African Heritage Library and became an inspiration to a young generation of local jazz and Afro-jazz enthusiasts. He collaborated with a number of local artists and bands, including his own son, Glen Warren, and the Afrika Obonu drummers led by Nii Amah Okomfrah. More recently, Ghanaba worked with the sax player Nii Noi Nortey,[13] who ran Mau Mau Musiki, and later Musiki w' Afrika, which combines African and Western instruments and is particularly influenced by John Coltrane. This growing jazz interest resulted in the formation in 2004 of the Jazz Society of Ghana, which began organizing jazz festivals at venues such as the W. E. B. Du Bois Center in Accra.

Ghanaian Rap or Hiplife

Ghanaian vernacular rap or hiplife has its origins in American hip hop, and it became popular in the early 1990s when Ghanaian teenagers and schoolchildren danced to rap at Greater Accra clubs like the Matador, Red Onion, Balm Tavern, Ringway Hotel, Pizzazz, and Miracle Miraj, at the Orion and Globe cinemas, and at beach parties at La Beach. Their heroes and MCs who rapped in English over a beat-box included Burgey, Joe B, Bubee, Areka, Ded Buddy, Jellycone, Sammy B, Chief and the Tribe, Taboo Tribe, Swiftman, Little Shaba, Eddy Blay Junior, General Marcus, Best MC, KKD, and Cy Lover.

From rapping and toasting in English, some began using local Twi and Ga languages. One of the earliest to do this was Mahoney P, based in Holland in 1994, who released the album *In Gang Amsterdam* that contained the rap song "Ebe Ye Yie." More important was Reggie Rockstone, who released the single "Tsoo Boi" in 1995 and went on to popularize the name "hiplife," a fusion of the words *hip hop* and *highlife*. Rockstone, considered the godfather of Ghanaian rap, was born in England and so spent most of his childhood between London and Accra. He later traveled back and forth between London and New York, where he witnessed the emergence of the hip hop of Grandmaster Flash and Lil Rodney C. In London he worked with Sierra Leonean partner Freddie Funkstone in their PLZ group. Rockstone began to visit Ghana in the early 1990s and moved back there in 1996 when he formed Kassa Records with DJ Rab, a deejay from Queens, New York.

Other early hiplifers were Nananom, who released their first album, *Nana Kasa,* in 1997, Lord Kenya, Akatakyie, Lifeline Family, Buk Bak, the DC All Stars, and the Native Funk Lords, who sang in pidgin English. Then there was Nana King, who was raised in Los Angeles and performed with the late Tupac Shakur before returning home to Ghana and releasing his first hits, "Ama Serwah" and "Champion," which uses music loops from Fela Kuti's "Lady." Some of the hiplifers concentrated more on the West Indian dancehall ragga style of rap, like Mad Fish, Batman, Yoggy Doggy, Bandana, Sonni Borley, Aberewa Nana, Slim Busterr, and the late Terry Bonchaka. A striking feature of hiplife is its lack of women rappers. An early exception was Jyoti Chander (Joe T), who was a member with Omanhene Pozo and Sidney of Nananom, but she then married a pastor and moved into gospel music. Currently there are only a few female rap artists, such as Aberewa Nana, Triple M, and Mzbel. However, in 2005 the lady gospel singer Jeal Wiafe released a rap version of local gospel music ("hip-gospel") called "Me Yi W'aye" [I'll worship you].

Many of the older Ghanaian generation complain that hiplife lyrics are too *kasa hare* [Akan for hurried talk] to be deciphered, or that they are sexually explicit and misogynist, or are of the violent African American gangsta rap variety in which hiplifers denigrate each other in song. For instance, Batman Samini's insulting of other musicians (in "Igwe") and the musical duels between Ex Doe (in "Maba") and Chicago's rude reply (in "Wo Beko") have resulted in negative newspaper comments.[14]

Newspaper reports also condemn lyrics they think promote teenage promiscuity in songs, such as Batman Samini's "Linda," Kaakyire Appiah's "Nketewa Do" [Small love], Lord Kenya's "Bokoboko" [Slowly], Max Kofi's "Akaada Ketewa Bi" [Youngster], and Michael Dawamena and Cool Joe's "Te Bi Di" [Take and eat].[15] Examples of sexist lyrics are Sidney's "Abuskeleke," which makes fun of a recent female fashion of baring the midriff, Nana Nsiah Piese's rap about a woman being sexually attracted to a policeman's *aba* or baton,[16] and Tic Tac's "Philomena," which criticizes the imported female fashion of allowing genital and underarm hair to grow.

In 2002 the director of the International Federation of Women Lawyers (FIDA) stated that some hiplife lyrics "debase femininity and the bodies of women" and constitute "violence against women on the airwaves." As a result, FIDA threatened high court actions against some radio stations and disc jockeys.[17] Furthermore, both FIDA and the Musicians' Union of Ghana (MUSIGA) asked the Ministry of Information and the Ghana Media Commission to closely monitor the local FM stations for indecent lyrics.[18] At a seminar in Kumasi in April 2005, the Center for Moral Education suggested that the National Communication Authority of Ghana should ban hiplife and profane songs. But as the journalist William Asiedu commented in the *Mirror* on December 28, 2002, hiplife songs that are banned for immorality "become instant hits and chart busters." Not only does all this criticism by the older generation make hiplife more commercially popular, as Asiedu rightly says, but this criticism is precisely what the hiplife musicians and fans like, for the controversial local rap puts a distance between them and the older generation.

Hiplife, with its outspoken lyrics, electronic instrumentation, solo artists, and video clip format, became an identity symbol for the Ghanaian city youth who were moving away from the live bands and performance venues of the older generation. The very artificiality of the sound also helped distance this new music from popular dance music of the older generation, for the emphatic use of electronic drum beats, vocoders, and other hi-tech gadgets added a distinctly modern flavor. This artificiality is not a result of some sort of failed imitation of Western electronic techno-pop but, rather, the flavor of the month. In short, hiplife became an antiestablishment musical icon for the youth. As such it was partially de-contextualized from its American rap precursor, an aggressive street music gangsta rap linked to the violence, drugs, and oppression in American black city ghettoes. Although there was a generational factor in the development of American rap, in Ghana this generation gap was paramount.

A more serious objection to hiplife from the older generation than its lyrics and artificiality was that hiplife is not performed live. With a few exceptions (Sidney and VIP), early hiplife musicians usually mimed or lip-synched to prerecorded, computerized backing tracks, even when appearing onstage in front of audiences. However, it is not fair to blame the youth, for as already discussed, during the 1970s and 1980s Ghana's live popular music scene collapsed due to a succession of military regimes. Furthermore, in 1988 music was demoted in the school syllabus, and so hiplifers were not trained to play instruments. Indeed, without the easy-to-produce-and-perform electronic music of hiplife, Ghanaian youth of the 1990s would not even have had their own musical idiom, for where were all the live high-life bands, concert parties, and student pop-chain competitions of yesteryear? And without them, who was going to teach the youth how to play musical instruments and acquire live stagecraft techniques? In the 1990s the youth, therefore, had no musical instruments and no one to teach them to play. But every generation has to find a musical medium, and so the youth did the only logical thing. They borrowed and adapted musical backing tracks from American hip hop, and with the assistance of local studio technicians they overlaid these with a rap session. So hiplife provided a voice for the youth even if the older generation did not like it.

Despite what has been said, many hiplife lyrics dwell on positive topics. Some warn against promiscuity. For example, "Wobedesen" by Queens Block (*Freedom Song,* 2005) tells men they should respect women; the Kumasi-based Mighazi and Sabato's 2004 video and CD release "Sugar Daddy" warns young girls to beware of elderly men who lure them into sex; and the Timber and Virux groups rap about the AIDS epidemic in "Kasa Kron" (2002). Other songs comment on current events and the concerns of youth, such as Reggie Rockstone's "Do the Do" on the problem of obtaining a foreign visa, Buk Bak's "Tankasse" (*Goldcoast,* 2004), which supports Ghanaian town council campaigns to clean up urban filth, and Don King's 2003 song "Kotofa," which supports the government's campaign for self-discipline. There are also a few political hiplife songs, such as the Native Funk Lords' "Vote for Me Make I Chop President," made during the 2000 elections, "Freedom of Speech," released in 2004 by A Pluz, and Sidney's humorous 2003 song "Scent No" on personal hygiene, which mentions that even "honorables" (parliamentarians) have smelly socks.

Whereas the verbal language of hiplife was quickly indigenized by local artists, the musical and rhythmic backing was not. Gradually, however, this has begun to change, and now there is also a growing interest by some hiplifers in employing resources from old-time highlife. Sometimes the hiplife raps are over short samples of highlife songs. Reggie Rockstone's "Keep Your Eyes on the Road" (1999) was based on Alhaji K. Frempong's "Kyenkyen Bi Adi Ma'wu," Lord Kenya's "Baby Nayaku" sampled Smart Nkansah's Sunsum Band, while Kontihene's "Medofo Paa Beko'" uses a chorus from the old hit "M'Adanfo Pa Beka" by Ani Johnson's Parrots band. Other short samples of highlife include Akyeame's "Ano Bebre" from a song by the old Uhuru dance band of the 1970s, Akasonoma's song "Ososbrokyie," which samples the highlife singer Paa Bobo, and Tic Tac's sampling of two of Pat Thomas's songs ("Menka Bio" and "Santrofe Anome") on his *Masem* album.

In other cases, the hiplife artist raps over a whole highlife recording: like Adane Best's 2004 rap version of "Marfio," which was originally made by Blemabii Ga Cultural Group in the mid-1970s, or Omanhene's remake of the West African highlife hit "Joromi" by the Nigerian highlife star Victor Uwaifo. Hiplifers also sometimes collaborate with the original highlife artists who composed the tune, and together they make a collage of the two styles. Ex Doe did this with Paa Bobo, while Omanhene Pozo's *Ayede Volume One* contains the song "Medofo Adaada Me," which he remade with the female highlife singer Ewurama Badu. He also did a remake of "Kyenkyen Bi Adi Ma'wu" with Alhaji K. Frempong and "Yellow Sisi" with Kofi Sammy. There are some hiplife artists who cross over between the two genres, sometimes singing in highlife style, sometimes in ragga or rap style. Examples include Nana Kwame/Quame, Daasebre Gyamena,[19] Papa Shee, Nana Fynn, the late Terry Bonchaka, and Slim Busterr.

Traditional rhythms and instruments are also sometimes used by hiplifers, such as Adane Best, Omanhene Pozo, Akatakye, Obour, and Okonfo Kwade. Some specific instances are the use of Ga kpanlogo rhythms by Castro, Buk Bak, and Lord Kenya, and the use of Akan rhythms by Bones Nkasei.[20] A few groups employ traditional instruments, like Okonfo Kwade, who includes the northern Ghanaian koliko/kologo lute for his *Boys Boys* CD.[21] As the manager of the Hush Hush Studio, Jeff Quaye ("J. Que") is actually insisting on the use of local rhythms and live percussion for his hiplife artists Batman Samini and Wutah, for what he calls jama hiplife, which uses the Ga word for an animated dance. Going the other way around, the neo-traditional Hewale group collaborated with some hiplifers to produce their *Bakuye* album in 2003, which combined traditional drums, xylophones, and rhythms with raps in Ga and Twi.

Hiplife generates considerable income for the artists and those involved in its recording, production, and marketing. Besides Hush Hush, other studios that record hiplife include the Combined House of Music, Lisarf, Goodies Records, Megastar, and Big Ben (all based in Accra) and Quantum Leap Studio in Kumasi. The top engineers for this music at the moment are Max "Babyface" Morris Twumasi, Zapp Mallett, Saage, Panji Anoff, Jeff Quaye, and Roland "Roro" Ackah. Important radio disc jockeys for hiplife are Bola Ray and Sammy B (both Joy FM) and Ashley (Peace FM). There are also numerous companies that produce and promote hiplife: Frimprince, Soul Records, Agiecoat, Precise Music, Slip Music, Kampsite

Records, Creative Storm Records, and Kaakyire Music. Some also produce music videos of hiplife artists like Slim Busterr, Mad Fish, FBS, Mighazi and Sabato, VIP, and Okonfuo. Reggie Rockstone and Kwade won the Ghana Music Awards best hiplife video in 2003 and 2005. Promoters of hiplife shows and competitions include Club Beer, Star Beer, Nescafe, Coca-Cola, Air Afrique, TV3, the Media Whizz Kids, and Universal Entertainment. The connection between hiplife and commercial companies is also evidenced by the use of hiplife artists to advertise their products on television and billboards.[22]

Since 2005 a distinct split has developed in the hiplife scene. There are the younger hiplifers, such as Batman Samini, Wuta, Tic Tac, Praye, K. K. Fosu, Kwaw Kesse, Ayegbe Edem, Kwabena Kwabena, and Kofi "B" (Boakye Yiadom, Wanlov the Kubolor, and Ofori Amponsah), who sing in ragga and highlife style or incorporate local jama rhythms and employ instrumentalists. They are also increasingly performing live shows, and some are calling this sung style of hiplife "contemporary highlife." Those emulating them have been appearing in a new batch of television programs that encourage live performance, such as Music Music, Mentor House, Cover Version, Bands Alive, and Stars of the Future. This interest by the youth in live performance is also reflected in the appearance of new Accra venues and programs like Hypnotic, Chelsea Place, Bless the Mike, Guitars in the Park, and New Music Ghana, which promote live music, freestyle hiplife, and hip hop and poetry readings.

Some of the pioneering hiplife artists, such as Lord Kenya and Reggie Rockstone, have criticized the jama hiplife style. In 2006 Rockstone came out publicly against it, stating that this type of indigenized hiplife was too parochial for the international market.[23] Consequently, and despite being one of the first hiplifers to rap in Akan, he reverted to rapping in English. Despite these comments, by 2009 Rockstone had become involved with the Cultural Caravan series of countywide hiplife shows organized by the French embassy's Alliance Française and Panji Anoff's Pidgin Studio. The shows included a live band, traditional drummers, the koliko/kologo lute player King Ayisoba, and live performances by the hiplifers Kwaw Kesse, Kubolor, and Rockstone himself, who performed in Twi.

Besides the new contemporary highlife and jama forms of hiplife, there are other brands of hiplife on the scene. One is ragga-influenced hiplife that goes back to the 1990s; under the name raggalife it is currently being developed by Mad Fish (Raymond Frimpong) and Yoggi Doggi. Another is a crunk version of hiplife that has recently surfaced and which, like its American progenitor, downplays the lyrical and emphasizes bass and drums. This dance party form of hiplife is being popularized by 4x4, the KNUST All Stars, the Mobile Phone Boys, and General Shapiro. On the other hand, there is the underground or Ghana or GH rap of Asem, 50 Cedis, O. J. Black, Okyeame Kwame, Kwabena Kwabena, Sarkodie, Ali M, and Hardcore that sticks more to the American hip hop mode and so is often sung in pidgin English and uses improvised freestyling. They also consider the lyrics of both jama and crunk hiplife to be too lighthearted, and so the GH rappers dwell on more thoughtful and socially conscious lyrics.

Finally, there is a convergence between Ghanaian hiplife and American contemporary R&B (also called contemporary urban) that goes back to Ded Buddy and Nana Quame in the 1990s. More and more artists are using this sung mode; some of the current ones who switch between or combine hiplife and R&B include the crooner Fianco Bossman "Chase," Nii (Jospeh Nii Otu Ankrah), Samini (also reggae), DJ Black (Kwadwo Ampofo), Nana Kwabena, K. K. Fosu, Kofi Nti, DJ Ashmen, and Richie (Richard Mensah), who runs Lynx Entertainment. At the same time, a new crop of artists have moved more into a new Afro-pop style that combines R&B with highlife more than hiplife. These include Becca (Rebecca Akosua Acheampong), Jane Awindor "Efysa," the Liberian-born Jane Logan, "Chemphe" Henry Agyekum, who calls his highlife/R&B fusion "urbanlife," and Chico Dawuni, who is, incidentally, the younger brother of Ghana's famous reggae star Rocky Dawuni.

So there are two important processes that seem to be going in hiplife at the moment: the growing use of traditional musical resources, and a trend toward live rather than mimed performance. This latter trend is linked to both the rise of sung highlife modes, such as contemporary highlife, raggalife, and R&B urbanlife, as well as the freestyling of GH rappers. Despite various protestations of some orthodox hiplifers and the GH rappers, jama and contemporary highlife forms of hiplife are currently the dominant modes of this music, and it is precisely these forms that are going furthest in incorporating local rhythms and traditional instruments.

Local Gospel

A very important development in Ghanaian popular dance music since the 1980s is local gospel music that is largely based on the rhythms, melodies, and instrumental resources of highlife dance music.[24] Local gospel is released on recordings by the numerous African separatist churches (spiritual, apostolic, charismatic, and born-again Pentecostal), and these churches employ gospel bands to perform "praises" and "choruses" as part of regular church worship.

Although this gospel explosion dates from the late 1970s, the idea of dancing in Ghanaian churches goes further back. European Christian missionaries forbad the use of dance in worship as sinful (it was associated with the evil flesh), but by the early twentieth century a number of African separatist churches had begun to integrate the traditional African belief in sacred dance. In short, African Christians began to worship God on their feet as well as on their knees in prayer. An example from the 1920s was the Church of the Twelve Apostles, which utilized percussion and dance.[25] By the 1950s there were, according to Acquah (1958: 148), seventeen of these African denominations in southern Ghana, and they endorsed dance and, in some cases, popular music idioms. For instance, in the late 1940s some local church choirs and singing bands began using the instruments of dance bands, brass bands, and guitar bands.[26]

However, the proliferation of local gospel popular dance music (and of the local African churches in general)[27] really began during the late 1970s, although intimations of this go back to the early 1970s when the late Reverend Andersson formed a gospel band and some Cape Coast school students launched their Joyful Way Singers. Around this time well-known guitar band composers also began releasing gospel-highlifes, such as Love Nortey of the Happy Stars and Kumasi-based Kofi Abraham and his Sekyedumasi Gospel Band.

By the 1980s local gospel music was in full swing, and some of the most important pioneering artists and bands were Mary Ghansah, the Tagoe Sisters, Ola Williams, Jonathon Javes Addo, Stella Dugan, Reverend Yaw Agyeman Baidoo (YABS), the Winneba Youth Choir, and the Genesis Gospel Singers of the Kristo Asafo Mission.

I witnessed this boom in gospel music from my own Bokoor Recording Studio, which I set up at Ofankor near Accra in 1982. At first, most of the recording artists were from the secular side: highlife bands, reggae groups, and Afro-rock outfits, with gospel bands being in the minority. However, by the late 1980s the situation had reversed, with most of the bands being church-based. Nevertheless, they were playing the same highlife dance music played by the very same musicians, although of course the lyrics were of a religious nature. Another difference I noticed from my studio work in the 1980s was the growing number of women who came as gospel singers.

Besides the proliferation of local churches and the fact that they had broken the European taboo of dancing in church, another trigger for the current local gospel explosion was the increasing difficulty of running live commercial bands during the 1970s/80s military regimes, which collapsed the commercial music industry and placed ultra-high taxes on "luxury" musical instruments. This encouraged two very different musical developments in the 1980s. The first, already discussed, was the replacement of live performers by the techno-pop alternatives of burger highlife and hiplife. The other was a move toward the local churches, which, unlike secular bands, were charitable bodies that did not have to pay import duties or entertainment taxes (a prepaid tax on the gate fees of commercial dances). As a result, many popular musicians began to move under the wing of the churches, which provided instruments and salaries. Furthermore, the new churches, particularly the Pentecostal ones, were of a quasicommercial business orientation. With their "prosperity" message and Christian businessmen's fellowships, they filled an entrepreneurship vacuum in the early revolutionary and anti-elitist period of Flight Lieutenant Rawlings's government that was inimical to commercial big business. However, the music recording, promotion, and distribution business was able to flourish within the realm of the untaxed churches.

By 1990 music had become such a big business that local gospel represented well over half of the local music airplay, and the PNDC military government of the time, just emerging from a quasi-Marxist-Socialist "cultural revolution," actually instructed the state radio to reduce the amount of gospel music air-play time by half.[28] Despite these state sanctions, gospel music continued to expand, so that from the 1990s a whole host of new local gospel artists and stars came onto the scene: Diana Akiwumi Hopeson, the Soul Winners, Reverend Michael Bonsu, Suzzy and Matt, Cindy Thompson, Helena Rhabbles, Yaw Sarpong, Joe Beecham, Amy Newman, Josh Laryea, and Uncle Fifi.

Women singers played a prominent role in this gospel upsurge, and they have come to dominate the genre. Whereas previously a family would always forbid a daughter to become a popular stage artist (being associated with drink and loose living), they could hardly forbid her to sing in church choirs, even if backed by popular dance music ensembles. Notable current female gospel stars include Mary Agyepong, Sandra Oduro, Jane and Bernice, Ama Boahemma, Esther Smith, Princess Ifeoma (a Nigerian who has performed in Ghana), Hannah Marfo, and Lady Prempeh. Of 133 new gospel artists who emerged around 2002, 71 were women.[29]

Presently, gospel cassettes and CDs form 60 percent of the commercial market.[30] This has created a huge industry involving the growth of gospel producers. Many of the local churches have gone into recording production and distribution since the 1990s. These include JaBenz (Jane and Bernice), Daughters Productions (Daughters of Glorious Jesus), Ester Smith Productions, Joyful Way Incorporated, Uncle Fifi Productions, Reverend Michael Osei Bonsu's KMP Company, and His Majesty gospel music shop in Accra and Kumasi, as well as the German-based producer Bishop Bediako.

Local churches have also established recording studios, one of the first being the Jesus Above All Studio, set up in the late 1980s in East Legon, Accra. This was followed in Accra and Kumasi by the Catholic Bookshop Studio, the Gentiles Revival Ministry Studio, the Christian Music Studio (CMS), the Spirit Digital Studio, the Jehova Nissi Studio, and the Bible School Studio.

Besides recording music, some churches and gospel artists have also moved into film and video production. For example, in 2002 the Kristo Asafo Mission church produced the film *No Easy Target,* directed by Veronica Quarshie and starring the actor "Solo" Soloman Sampah.[31] Many gospel artists also make TV video clips. The Tagoe Sisters won the Friends World Award in 1998 for their video "Anka Metete," and they and Joe Beecham won the Ghana Music Awards of 2003 for best videos. In 2005 Edmund Akwasi Boateng released his successful video "Ntie Atesem Hunu," and Lord "Cosky" Amofa made an impact with the video accompanying the song "Atenbuo" (on his *Hwehwe Onyame* album) about a preacher trying to dissuade a man from using alcohol, cigarettes, and cocaine.[32]

To cater to these developments in the gospel industry, a number of gospel awards have been created. The long-established Entertainment Critics and Reviewers Association of Ghana began giving out ECRAG Awards to gospel artists at the National Theatre in the early 1990s, and in 1994 the National Christian Awards Committee initiated a Gospel Awards Night at which twenty-four bands participated. That very same year the first All-Female Gospel Night was organized by the OXCY promotion company. In 2004 an annual Gospel Music Awards was launched, coordinated by Ms. Demay Ackah Yensu. Local gospel has become so prevalent that it has moved out of the churches into commercial venues. For instance, in Accra the Orion and Palladium cinemas and old Apollo Theatre dance-spots have been taken over by huge all-night church crusades and filled with gospel music. A number of gospel show organizers and masters of ceremonies have also emerged, like Revend Paa Joe Markei, Michael Crabbe, DJ Alfred Larbi, and Paa K. Holbrook-Smith.

As a result of the growth of the commercial gospel music industry and the enormous numbers of gospel musicians in Ghana, unions have been set up to cater to their needs. The first was the Gospel Band Union set up in 1989 by S. Agyeman Duah-Bruku, followed by the short-lived Gospel Pioneers Association and then the Ghana Presbyterian Singing Band Union, established by E. Odei Ntow. During the 1990s a special gospel section was created within the Ghana Musicians Union (MUSIGA). Indeed, the current MUSIGA president is the leading gospel singer Diana Akiwumi Hopeson. Furthermore, in 2005, under the umbrella of MUSIGA, a United Gospel Musicians Association (UGMA) of the Greater Accra Region was formed by Ken Appiah and Andy Frimpong Manso. Its first meetings of seventy-nine artists were held on the premises of the newly created religious FM station in Ghana, Channel R.

Gospel has become so commercially viable in Ghana over the last twenty-five years or so that a number of leading popular artists have moved into this religious genre. Some have moved fully into gospel, such as the Tagoe Sisters and Leslie Tex.[33] Others, finding it difficult to operate within the commercial secular area, have occasionally operated within the patronage of the church. In the 1980s, F. Kenya and his concert party began playing gospel music, while in 1988 Nana Ampadu, leader of the famous African Brothers band, became a musical evangelist. In the 1990s the guitar band musicians T. O. Jazz and Anthony Scorpion were both employed by churches to train gospel groups, and the Ozimzim dance band was revived as a gospel band in 1994 by Apostle Abraham Owusu of the Gentiles Revival Ministry. Some other well-known old-time Ghanaian highlife artists who have experimented with or included gospel material in their repertoires include Kofi Ani Johnson, Jewel Ackah, A. B. Crentsil, J. A. Adofo, Safohene Djeni, Papa Yankson, K. K. Kabobo, C. K Mann, Jesse Jones, A. K. Yebuah, and Kofi Sammy, who in 2000 formed his Okukuseku Practical Angels Band. Some younger musicians have also moved into the gospel music field. In the 1990s Carlos Sakyi released "Thank You Jesus" with female gospel singer Naana Frimpong.[34] The burger highlife musician Daddy Lumba made several gospel releases with his Lumba Productions company, and ex-NAKOREX member Akosua Agyepong moved into gospel. More recently, the hiplife artists Azigiza Junior became born again and under the name Togbe Afrika began releasing gospel songs like "Dela Jesus."[35] Two female hiplife singers also moved into gospel: Jyoti Chander (also known as Joe T) of the 1990s Nananom group, and Aberewa Nana.

The local Ghanaian churches and their new gospel dance music have become a haven for live local pop bands, a ritual arena for collective popular dance sessions, and a productive space for female singers. As exemplified by the impact of African American gospel on the later commercial music of soul and other secular American pop styles, local gospel-highlife is also likely to have a significant effect on the future of Ghanaian commercial music development.

Tourism and the Rise of Commercial Folkloric and Neo-Traditional Bands

Over the last thirty years there has been a marked increase in tourists coming to Ghana, which has positively impacted the traditional music of Ghana in terms of its commercialization onstage and in the recording studio. The foreign exchange of visitors and world music fans has provided revenue for Ghanaian traditional performing artists to move fully or partly away from the noncommercial traditional sector into the commercial one linked to tourism.

Taking performance out of the traditional and mainly rural context and putting it on stage, film, and record is part of the process of "folklorization." This was initially linked to the national development policy that began after independence in 1957, when Nkrumah initiated nationwide festivals, established the Arts Council and national dance ensembles, and introduced the teaching of traditional African music in schools and universities.

Following the overthrow of Nkrumah in 1966, this state-sponsored national folkloric policy was continued. Under the NLC and Busia regimes, the playwright Saka Acquaye became director of the Arts Council (1968–71), which initiated the Anansekrom matinee cultural program for young people. The Arts Council also continued organizing folk music competitions during the Colonel Acheampong/ Akuffo military governments of 1971–79, including the Anansekrom traditional instrumental and folk music competition of May 1975. Then, during the early J. J. Rawlings PNDC military government with its quasi-Marxist rhetoric, a "cultural revolution" was launched, which involved decentralizing the Arts Council into nine (later ten) regional Centers for National Culture, organizing "Sankofa" children's folk music contests, and establishing the biannual National Festivals of Arts and Culture (NAFAC).

As already noted, it was during the military governments of Acheampong, Akuffo, and the early Rawlings period that things became increasingly difficult in Ghana, which resulted in some traditional as well as popular artists leaving Ghana. For instance, Yacob Tetteh Addy and his two brothers, Mustapha Tettey Addy and

Obo Addy, who had formed the Ga kpanlogo drumming group Obuade in 1968, all left in the 1970s to base themselves in Europe and the United States.[36] Many other leading performers also settled abroad to perform and teach traditional Ghanaian drumming and dancing, such as C. K. Ganyoh, Gideon Foli, Godwin Agbeli, George Dzikunu, and Ben Baddo.

Nevertheless, traditional music in the indigenous context of providing ceremonial and recreational music continued unabated during the 1970s/80s. This sector (unlike the commercial popular music one) was not adversely affected by the collapse of the music economy as it was performed within a communal rather than cash-nexus context and, with its instruments and costumes being made of local natural resources, it did not depend on imports.

The second wave of folklorization was a commercial, rather than state-sponsored, one. It began in the late 1980s after the Rawlings PNDC government implemented an IMF-initiated Structural Adjustment Policy when the economy was liberalized and tourism dramatically increased. Between 1992 and 2002, the number of tourists entering the country doubled each year. In 2004, 650,000 foreign tourists visited Ghana, where they generated $800 million, making tourism the third largest foreign exchange earner for the country after gold and timber.[37] Many of these tourists and world music fans were coming to Ghana for its traditional and folkloric groups, who perform at local festivals and ceremonies and onstage at hotels, beach resorts, and international venues such as the National Theatre, Dubois Center, and Alliance Française. Some of these cultural tourists also come to study local music and dance, not only at the University of Ghana's School of Performing Arts but also at the numerous private cultural centers and NGOs that sprang up. The earliest was the African Academy of Music and Arts (AMAA) at Kokorobite, set up in 1988 by the Ghanaian master drummer Mustapha Tettey Addy. Another is the Dagbe Drum School at Kopeyia in Volta Region, established by the late Godwin Agbeli on returning from the United States. Others are the cultural center of the Kukye Kukye Bamboo Orchestra at Masomogor village near the Kakum Nature Reserve, the Dagara Arts Center at Medie set up in 2003 by Bernard Woma of the National Dance Ensemble, the German/Ghanaian Kasapaa cultural village at Nyanyano, and Koo Nimo's Adadan Cultural Resource Centre in Kumasi.

There are also dozens of local private cultural groups that double as performance ensembles and teaching units for foreign visitors, such as the Hewale Sounds' neo-traditional group, which combines the instruments of different Ghanaian ethnic groups and was linked with Professor Nketia's International Center for African Music and Dance at the University of Ghana. Others are Emmanuel Gomado's Odehe Dance Company, Nii Tettey Tetteh's Kusun Ensemble, Kusum Gboo, the Ayekoo Drumming group, Daniel Korenteng's Dzembii, and the Suade Cultural Group.

Many cultural and folkloric groups and artists who perform at hotels and beach resorts also record. Hewale is a case in point; another is that of Osei Korankye, who has been reviving, teaching, and recording the almost defunct *seprewa* harp at the University of Ghana. From the Ga area have come artists and groups making records that combine local percussion with highlife guitar, such as the Sensational Wulomei (*Sani Maye Eko,* 2000) and Ebaahi Soundz, who had released five albums by 2005.[38] From northern Ghana have come the African Showboys, a group of brothers who have been performing Frafra music onstage since the 1980s and who released their first album, *Brother Bold,* in 2005. There is also the internationally recognized performer and teacher of the Dagari *gyil* pentatonic xylophone, the late Kakraba Lobi, who released several CDs in the early 2000s. Finally, there has been a resurgence in sales of folk guitarists like Koo Nimo, Kwabena Nyama, T. O. Jazz, and others who have been releasing the old palmwine version of highlife in recent years.

This chapter has traced the development of Ghanaian popular music from the collapse of the commercial entertainment sector that began in the late 1970s. The response by the younger generation of popular musicians to the resulting vacuum has been twofold. Some moved to the hi-tech options of the spinners, burger highlife, and hiplife, which did away with the expensive personnel and instrumentation of the large ensembles of old-time highlife and concert party bands. Other youth turned to the gospel bands of the local churches. These two options currently dominate Ghanaian local music air-play and commercial recordings.

Burger highlife and hiplife musicians with their drumulators, synthesizers, and beat boxes have become popular not only with local Ghanaian youth but also with the estimated 3 million Ghanaians living abroad. This has created financial opportunities for them abroad as well as at home. However, this internationalism has had one drawback. These hi-tech artists returning home with foreign exchange and cosmopolitan videos have created the impression that their lip-synched styles are recognized worldwide, whereas their music is mainly popular with Ghanaians living abroad. This, I believe, has created a feedback to Ghana that strengthened the use by many young artists of studio-band "machine" music rather than live performance.

But neither burger highlife nor hiplife has significantly crossed over into the lucrative world music market, whose fans prefer what they consider to be the more authentically African live music of Yousou N'Dour, Angelique Kidjo, Salif Ketia, Ali Farka Toure, and others. The only two Ghanaian songs to go fully international since the 1980s are the Pan African Orchestra's "Opus One"[39] and Paul Simon's use of the modified "Yaa Amponsah" highlife song for his late 1980s song "Spirit Voices" (on *The Rhythms of the Saints*).

A double marketing psychology has been recognized by some world music stars, such as Youssou N'Dour, who makes two mixes of his songs: a live feel one for the world music market with a battery of percussionists and full horn section, and a hi-tech one using drum machines and synthesizers for local consumption.

This realization of a double market has taken many years to reach the Ghanaian burger highlife and hiplife musicians, who had believed that as their music was popular abroad (with Ghanaians), it was already international. Furthermore, Ghanaian youth have not had the stimulus of their own homegrown internationally recognized role models equivalent to Youssou N'Dour, who regularly does live performances with Western superstars.

Many Ghanaian burger highlife and hiplife musicians remain convinced that they can become global stars by using drumulators, vocoders, studio engineers, and mimed shows. However, this is beginning to change with the rise of live performance being featured on TV shows, at nightspots, and through the role of various local organizations and foreign embassies, such as the Alliance Française's Cultural Caravan or the German Goethe Institute's "Made in Germany" live burger highlife shows that took place in Accra and Kumasi in 2007 and 2008.

The other major option open to the youth is local gospel, based on the dance rhythms of highlife and other popular music. Through this, the local churches have reclaimed the cathartic release of communal dance found in traditional African worship. As a result dance sessions are found just as much in the churches as they are in the secular dance clubs. Furthermore, gospel has provided Ghanaian women with an important route into contemporary popular dance music, and female gospel singers now outnumber the men. On the other hand, hiplife rappers are nearly all men. So today there is in Ghana a musical gender split between feminized gospel-highlife and macho hiplife.

New imported music styles have also come into the picture, such as reggae, which became increasingly Ghanaianized from the 1980s, and local jazz that caters largely to middle-class Ghanaians and those returning from abroad. Then there is the introduction to Ghana of internationally successful African world music records, augmented by visits to Ghana from stars of this genre like Salif Keita, Youssou N'Dour, Amadou and Mariam, Femi and Seun Kuti, Papa Wemba, Angelique Kidjo, Meiway, Magic System, Manu Dibango, Brenda Fassie, and Yvonne Chaka Chaka. Moreover, Cuban/Puerto Rican salsa dance has become fashionable since the late 1990s with Ghanaian youth who patronize such venues as the Ringway Hotel Costa Rica Club. As a result, some highlife and gospel artists, like C. K. Mann and the Tagoe Sisters, have made salsa-based recordings.

Some of the older highlife big bands have survived or been reorganized, and new ones have been formed. A new generation has also appeared of smaller highlife and Afro-fusion bands and artists, and they are putting on live shows and releasing records for the numerous world music and cultural tourists visiting Ghana. Some examples include Rex Omar, Nat Amanzeba Brew, Takashie, Local Dimension, Nana Tuffour, Felix Owusu, Atongo Zimba, Bawasaba, Paulina Oduro, and Aka Blay's Abiza band. The potential importance of local popular music as a foreign exchange earner through world music sales and tourism has been recognized by the Ghanaian government, which recently reduced the huge import duties on musical equipment and integrated the music sector into its Poverty Reduction Strategy.

Finally, I have noted the recent boom in folklorized forms of traditional music linked to the massive increase in cultural tourism since the late 1980s. Neo-traditional groups and cultural tourism centers have surfaced within the private sector to cater to foreign visitors who want to watch and learn traditional performances. This in turn has encouraged some members of the younger generation to learn and develop the performance skills of their elders.

So despite all the setbacks, Ghanaian popular music has a bright future. Ghana still has an intact traditional performance sector and a newer folkloric one. It has many church-trained instrumentalists, a host of female singers, a layer of world music–influenced highlife and Afro-fusion musicians, a return to live performance modes, an influx of cultural tourists, and a growing interest in indigenous jama rhythms and contemporary highlife by hiplife artists.

A most recent ingredient is what I call the "Ghanaian Sahelian" factor. Well-known popular music artists from Ghana's northern upper regions were less than a handful in the 1970s (Onipa Nua, Amoa Azangeo, and Christie Azuma) and 1990s (Atongo Zimba, Captain Yaba, the African Show Boys, Lady Talata, and Aaron Bebe Sukura). But in the past decade, and with the opening of numerous music NGOs, promotions, and recording studios in Ghana's Northern, Upper East, and West Regions, there has come a flood of new sahelian artists that include King Ayisoba, Lord Wumpini, Kawastone (Muhammed Abdul-Rashid), Sheriff Ghale (Yamusah Mohammad), Abu "Policeman" Sidiq, and the lady artists Sherifatu Gunu, Zina Bizey, Mama Rams, and Sirina Issah.

It is this rich mix of the northern and southern, internal and external, old and new, secular and sacred, male and female that will contribute to the future development of Ghanaian popular music.

NOTES

1. For more details on this early Africanization process, see Collins (2005).

2. For more details on this Africanized form of imported vaudeville and black minstrelsy, see Barber, Collins, and Ricard (1997).

3. The most important 1970s Ghanaian Afro-rock/beat bands were Osibisa, Hedzolleh, Basa-Basa, the Magic/Psychedelic Aliens, Boombaya, Zonglo Biiz, A Band Named Bediako, Big Beats, and Sawaaba Sounds.

4. In 1979, when I was on the executive committee of the Musicians' Union of Ghana, we estimated that one-quarter of all 4,000 registered members were out of the country.

5. "Spinners" were relatively cheap-to-operate outfits employing as few as three people.

6. For highlife themes up to the 1970s, see Brempong (1984), Yankah (1984), Van der Geest and Asante-Darko (1982), and Agovi (1989). In the John Collins/BAPMAF 1930s–1960s shellac record archives collection, only about 15 percent are on the theme of love.

7. The demo tape that got the band on its first European tour was recorded at my Accra Bokoor Studio in 1983.

8. The exceptions were visits by the British rock musicians Mick Fleetwood and Brian Eno.

9. Prior to this, matted hair was associated in Ghana with some forms of traditional religious cults or the unkempt appearance of mentally disturbed people.

10. PANAFEST is a Ghanaian government-initiated pan-African cultural festival based primarily at Cape Coast and Elmina, the site of two important European slaving castles.

11. Like Hedzolleh, Basa Basa was a resident band at Faisal Helwani's Napoleon Club in Accra in the early 1970s.

12. In 2004 Captain Yaba released *Yaba Funk* on the British Retro Afric label.

13. Nii Noi Nortey played in the 1980s with UK-based Dade Krama and Misty and Roots. Kofi Ghanaba passed away in December 2008.

14. For readers' comments on "protest gangsterism" and "stop the wars," see *Graphic Showbiz*, January 13–19, 2000, and *Showbiz* August 26, 2004.

15. See *Graphic Showbiz* editorial and article by William Asiedu (January 13–19, 2000).

16. See "Degrading to Women-hood," *Mirror*, December 16, 2000.

17. *Ghana Times*, December 12, 2002, quoting Gloria Ofori Boadu.

18. MUSIGA received 1,000 letters objecting to hiplife lyrics (*Graphic Showbiz*, April 18–24, 2002).

19. Daasebre himself does not rap, but he includes the local rapper Lord Kenya in his 2001 "Kokooko" release.

20. Bones Nkasei's 2005 song "Ekomamu" uses Akan *adowa* and *abindidwom* rhythms.

21. The late Terry Bonchaka also used this instrument.

22. Reggie Rockstone was the spokesman for Guinness beer, Tic Tac has promoted Ashfoam beds, and Castro has represented Coca-Cola.

23. Rockstone made these assertions in lectures to students in 2006. Nana King also has reservations about whether hiplife in local languages can be marketed internationally. See *Graphic Showbiz*, July 20–26, 2006.

24. Gospel also draws from reggae and other popular idioms.

25. The Church of the Twelve Apostles was set up in Ghana by followers of the Côte d'Ivoire–based Liberian prophet William Wade Harris.

26. See AACC (1958: 70) and Collins (2004) for more information on the separatist Ghanaian churches.

27. By 1991, 1,600 religious organizations were registered with the National Commission on Culture's Religious Affairs Department; 800 were Christian (*Ghana Broadcasting Corporation News*, December 29, 1991). Some estimates put the current number of local churches as high as 4,000.

28. See *Christian Messenger*, July/August 1990.

29. See the *Graphic Showbiz* article on gospel music by Francis Doku, March 4–10, 2004.

30. Musicians Union of Ghana estimates; also see Nii Addokwei Moffatt in *Graphic Showbiz*, January 13–19, 2004.

31. Earlier, this church ran seven gospel bands and a concert party.

32. See the article by Jacqueline Bondze in the *Chronicle*, May 13, 2005.

33. The Tagoe Sisters were initially reggae and highlife session singers with Ras Koby, Felix Bell, Gemann, and Sidiku Buari. Leslie Tex of the Action Faith Ministry was originally a pop singer with Szaabu Soundz, run by Bob Pinodo and myself.

34. Sakyi had worked on Talal Fatal's 1980s album *Forgive and Forget*.

35. See an article by George Maxwell Hayford in *Celebrity News*, December 14, 2004.

36. Mustapha Tettey Addy released his *Kpanlogo Party* album in 1972 and then a string of recordings in Germany (Welt Wunder label) with his Royal Obonu Drums.

37. It has been estimated that 10 percent of the foreign exchange that international tourists actually spend in Ghana is on recreation and entertainment. See Jacob Oti-Awere's article in *Graphic Showbiz*, December 7–13, 2001.

38. Ebaahi Soundz was originally a youth group called Ebaahi Gbiko that worked with the English rock drummer Mick Fleetwood in 1980 on his film *The Visitor*.

39. Nana Danso Abiam's Pan African Orchestra performed at the British WOMAD festival, and in 1996 it released the world music chart hit "Opus One" on Peter Gabriel's Real World label.

Popular Music and Young Male Audiences in Contemporary Malawi

JOCHEN SEEBODE

In this chapter I examine the contemporary and neo-traditional music traditions in Malawi that came into vogue shortly after the rule of long-term president H. K. Banda (1964–1994), with special emphasis on their themes as expressed in the lyrics.[1] I begin by discussing recent developments in the dissemination of music via the Malawian mass media, and then look at the work of several of Malawi's major artists in the genres of electric guitar band music, gospel, reggae, and rap. Saleta Phiri, who continued a guitar-based tradition similar to that of Zimbabwe, sings about a broad variety of contemporary topics, including love, intergenerational conflicts, and awareness of HIV/AIDS.[2] Reggae artist Lucius Banda, who sings of hope and resistance for the poor and downtrodden, rapper Pop Dogg, who, from the diaspora wholly appropriates unadulterated American gansta rap, and gospel hip hop group Masavage could hardly present more of a contrast with each other, and I compare some of their attitudes and stances. I conclude with two examples to show how critical potential, as expressed in the music of many reggae musicians, can be transformed into concrete social and political action by the artists themselves or by parts of the audience.

Malawian Media

The end of the rule of President Hastings Kamuzu Banda in 1994 marked a major turning point in the history of Malawi.

> Under the dictatorship of "Life President" Hastings Banda, who gave the country its name, male visitors to Malawi were forbidden to have long hair, women had to wear skirts below the knee, and flared trousers were illegal. When elections were held in 1994, however, Banda was promptly booted out, and Malawi is now a free and vibrant nation. (Lwanda 2006: 211)

The introduction of video in 1994 and the pluralization and privatization of national and regional radio broadcasting stations starting in 1999 made locally produced and global commercial pop music available to a broader Malawian audience. Although the introduction of regular service by Malawi's national television started late, from 2000 onward (N. Patel 2000; Media Institute of Southern Africa 2004: 29–31), external TV stations like Channel O from South Africa (a pan-African music channel) or MTV from the United States have been available earlier, mostly in tourist areas around Lake Malawi or in the cities. After Malawi's political change, the state-run Malawi Broadcasting Corporation (MBC), which operates the national radio network, introduced a second station (MBC 2). Mostly in cities like Lilongwe or Blantyre, some private local and regional radio stations have been launched since 1998/99 and tried to extend their services nationwide (e.g. 102.5 Capital Radio, FM Power 101, Transworld Radio, or Blantyre FM). Religious stations include Radio Maria, Calvary Family Church Radio, and Radio Islam in the town of Limbe.[3]

Of late, at least for the Malawian elite, internet radio has started to play an important role in the global dissemination of Malawian popular music including rap, reggae, gospel, and church music (mostly hymns sung by choirs). For example, there are Radio Yako, "Malawi's first internet radio" (http://www.radioyako.com/) and KwachaFM (www.kwachafm.com) operating from the United States, UK, South Africa, and Malawi. The latter promotes urban music coming from Malawi and the surrounding African regions. Although there is still a "digital gap" (Trieselmann 2007) between much of the northern hemisphere and Africa, the internet is used for the dissemination of Malawian music and dance videos, which have created an aesthetics of their own (see Seebode 2007, 2010).[4]

Digital media releases like CDs and DVDs and the internet play only a marginal role in the dissemination of music in Malawi so far. However, many of the prominent musicians and bands (e.g. Lucius Banda, Black Missionaries, Mlaka Maliro, and Ethel Kamwendo-Banda) have started to release their latest albums on CD or DVD. Outside of cities like Lilongwe, Blantyre, and Mzuzu, digital media are available in tourist areas along the lakeside and only sparsely in the hinterland, where few people own the equipment.

Presently, the main dissemination channels for popular music are the radio, audio and video cassettes, and concert parties where Malawian and international bands perform. Besides activities of international institutions like the French Cultural Centre in Blantyre, the annual Lake of Stars festival at Lake Malawi has drawn international performers and audiences for years.

Most of the foreign and much of the Malawian produced music is available in the market as illegally copied cassette tapes (bootlegs). Although institutions like the Copyright Society of Malawi (Cosoma) try to fight against audio and video piracy, it is hardly possible to control the informal network of audio and video cassette distributors, including street hawkers in cities and towns, dealers in local markets, and private importers in rural areas.

The mushrooming video shows and international TV channels, which are mostly consumed as public showings, and to a limited extent also the internet, present various music videos where the latest fashion trends and—most important—dance styles and other modes of kinetic movement related to the musical style can be consumed. Usually, as with concert parties, young people visit the movie shows in groups, making comments about the performance watched on the screen and even imitating the most characteristic kinetic movements.

Kinship ties and a history of labor migration within the southern African region have created a strong tradition of cultural exchange in Malawi. Although the political oppression of the Banda regime forced many Malawian intellectuals and artists to leave the country, this tradition could never be interrupted. It led to a brain drain and to the formation of diasporic communities in neighboring African countries as well as in Europe and the United States. Some of the most prominent examples were the musician Wambali Mkandawire and the authors Jack Mapanje and Tiyambe Zeleza.

The higher technical standard of recording facilities abroad attracted many Malawian musicians to record their albums outside the country—even more when after 1994 the level of censorship in Malawi decreased and international contacts became easier and less controlled by a repressive regime. Of late, many of the Malawian musicians and bands (e.g., Overtone Chimombo, Lucius Banda, and the Black Missionaries) have produced their recent releases in South Africa. Members of the Malawian diaspora have always played an important role for the political, economic, and cultural development in their home country from the times of the struggle for colonial independence until the present. The Malawian repertoire of popular music has always entailed a dynamic process of adaptation, modification, and transformation.

Youth and New Musical Styles

After Malawi's transition to a multiparty state in 1994, access to fast spreading technology enabling electronic reproduction (through audio and video cassettes) and the loosening of control and censorship measures led to an increase in aesthetic options and the development of a variety of musical styles. These styles are often associated with young people, who publicly represent them through clothing, hairdressing, language, slang, and gestures. Young bodies, therefore, are "the site on which a youth culture, which is also a counterculture, is expressed. . . . If we consider that countercultural manifestations are above all a language that makes self-expression possible, then the body can be seen as the main tool of young people, the only resource at their disposal in the public space" (Diouf 2003: 10). Globalization and the increased medialization of the world are important factors that have accelerated processes of musical style formation.

The fans of contemporary and neo-traditional Malawian music are mostly male adolescents and young men. After the breakdown of institutionalized political youth organizations of the former ruling party (MCP), adolescents have searched for new role models and strategies to master their lives successfully. Former strategies and options structuring their lives no longer worked in the new Malawi. Nearly everything one could rely on during the Banda regime seemed to have collapsed, with no convincing alternatives at hand. For many of the adolescent and young adult audience, the latest styles of popular music with their main characteristics of telling the "real situation" and of mobilizing and representing emotions directly offered a fertile ground for processes of collective and individual identity formation.[5] Listening collectively to music—be it live performances, tapes, or on the radio—creates a common ground for social cohesion.

Although the public image of young people in Malawi during the Banda era up to the present has been ambivalent, they have viewed themselves as structurally subordinated by the cultural principle of seniority, which was deeply inscribed in Banda's party ideology.[6] Even if they were politically and socially successful, young people always remained in a subordinated status. During the period of transition (1992–1994) that finally resulted in the multiparty system, male youths, especially from intellectual milieus, such as students of the University of Malawi, actively supported the political opposition movement, fighting for a liberalization of political rights. However, some also agitated as an angry mob trying to suppress other Malawians who fought for freedom of expression, especially when male hegemonic privileges were questioned.[7]

During the first governance period of the first democratically elected president, Bakili Muluzi (1994–1999), it seemed unclear how the social and political situation in Malawi would develop, although the economic crisis was already clear. The political and cultural opening of the new Malawi granted adolescents and youths access to various cultural resources, but most of them remained excluded from economic or political resources. For the majority, not much seemed to have changed in Malawi by the political change. Furthermore, with the economic crisis taking dramatic dimensions, increasing inflation and corruption, a decreasing security situation, and the high death toll of the HIV/AIDS pandemic, a better future for them in Malawi seems very far away. This has not changed much under Presidents Muluzi and Bingu wa Mutharika. From the Malawian adults' point of view youths were—and often still are—perceived as a potential danger to the new dominating order.

Keeping the marginal social status of Malawian adolescents and youths in mind, some of the most pressing questions concerning popular music are about the essential topics on the artist's agenda and how the audience relates to them, whether contemporary musical styles express a critique of, or resistance to, the dominating order (and if so, which styles), and whether discourses in music lead to social or political action.

Saleta Phiri and AB Sounds: Bars and Beer Halls, the Ordinary Simple Life, AIDS, and the Political Change in Malawi

Guitar player and singer Saleta Phiri has created his own distinct style using his electric guitar in ways that refer to guitar music from Zimbabwe, which had become internationally famous since the 1980s with the first wave of world music through artists like Oliver Mtukudzi, Thomas Mapfumo, and John Chibadura.[8] Phiri's songs, performed with a throaty voice, are mostly sung in Chichewa with a strong Lomwe accent. Together with his band, the AB Sounds, Phiri, who plays his guitar in a poignant, percussive way, produces a catching and hypnotizing rough sound, which is enriched by a jazz-like walking bass and supported and driven forward by the drums using fast hi-hat strokes in combination with a syncopated bass drum. The group is rounded out by keyboards, which are in the background, providing simple fill-ins.

Often the recording quality of his albums, which have been recorded and distributed mainly by the Portuguese-Shopping-Centre (a studio and store) in Blantyre, is not very good. The simple cover art, typically printed on cheap paper using a monochrome or two-color print technique, supports the image of the raw aesthetics of his music. In most cases there is no information about the instrumentation, names of the band members, or any other details of the recording sessions.

Phiri's lyrics are often structured dialogically: the middle part of many songs includes a kind of conversation with two voices turning indirectly to the audience. In a respectful polite way the compositions tell about conflictive aspects and relations of ordinary people's lives. As with Malawi's contemporary reggae star Lucius Banda (see below), the topics are morally framed. But while Banda is putting Malawian local social conflicts in a wider global context, in most cases Phiri's focus remains on a local or national level.[9] Phiri's songs range from dealing with societal pressures to settling down and getting married ("Oraruwa"), to changing relations between generations ("Malodza") to a central issue in the arts in general in Malawi: HIV/AIDS.[10]

In "Malodza" [Miracles] from the album *Oraruwa*, Phiri describes the lack of respect of the young for the old. Drawing on everyday scenes, he finally turns his astonishment about the violation of the principles of gender hierarchy and seniority into an interpretation claiming this is a miracle that has to be acknowledged and finally coped with communally. Changing power relations between parents and their offspring are also described in the songs "Munyaradzi," from the perspective of a father talking to his son, and "Amina," from the perspective of a mother talking to her daughter.[11] Violations of culturally accepted norms, for example, the refusal to care for old and sick parents, however, are disapproved and wailed about without constructive advice for the audience on what to do about them.

One of many songs taking up the topic of HIV/AIDS is "Ili mu Ufa" [It's in the flour], the title track of one of his albums. The composition was ordered by the former government of Bakili Muluzi during his first period of governance (1994–1999). The song relates the spreading of HIV/AIDS to maize flour, the basic ingredient of Malawian staple food *nsima*.[12] The lyrics follow a call and response scheme, repeating the main statement ("It's in the flour") again and again in the refrain. In between, a second voice in a kind of a talking-blues style comes in elaborating the issue. By relating the usually shamefully discussed issue of HIV/AIDS with the beloved Malawian national meal, Phiri opens up a discursive level that includes practically all Malawians, no matter of what age, sex, status, beliefs, or ethnic affiliation. Phiri claims that AIDS is everywhere and that it is incurable. Because AIDS is omnipresent in Malawi, the disease is associated with the main ingredient of the basic food nsima. To keep on ignoring the disease is hardly possible because you cannot abstain from eating. However, the act of eating (which means here symbolically the sexual act; see Moto 2004) has to be framed morally. The sexual act demands marriage or at least another form of legitimated partnership relation and monogamous behavior.

Here, HIV infection and sexual morality are inseparable. For Phiri, the main reason for the spread of the deadly virus in Malawi is adultery. The use of condoms seems an unsafe strategy to avoid infection. Phiri demands abstention from extramarital relations and to keep strict moral rules based on the principle of matrimonial trust as the only strategy to avoid a further spreading of the virus. He also points out social practices that are related not to sexuality but to poverty, including the common use of razor blades and contaminated injection needles and drain tubes in doctors' offices. But Phiri does not elaborate on reasons for poverty, nor does he give advice on how to avoid "dangerous" practices. He urges his listeners to reject ignorant people who deny the existence of the disease and to refrain from stigmatizing HIV-positive fellow Malawians. He calls upon the audience to care for the infected and closes with practical advice, mentioning social practices by which the virus cannot be transmitted.

In some of his songs Phiri remembers the postcolonial past, focusing on the political change of 1994 and its impact. In the lyrics of songs like "Angwazi" [an honorary title used to address H. K. Banda during the time of his reign] and "Chitenje" [A cloth], both from the album *Palibe Chinsinsi* [There is no secret], the history of the Banda era becomes visible either by panegyrics or by a woman's plea to her husband to buy her a "party cloth."[13]

In "Zasintha" [Things have changed], from the aforementioned album *Ili mu Ufa*, Phiri wails about the exploitation of musicians by political parties and complains about the superficial quality of the political change. After the pessimistic insight, "things have changed . . . but only for those respectable people in the high seats," Phiri asks the government (i.e., the then ruling party, UDF) for help and financial support.[14]

Gospel, Reggae, and Rap

The most important styles in contemporary recorded Malawian music for young audiences are gospel, reggae, and rap. Also often heard in Malawi are soul and country western music from the United States and many kinds of so-called black music and pop music, mostly from South Africa (e.g., Yvonne Chaka Chaka), East Africa (mainly from Tanzania), and Central Africa (mostly of Congolese origin). Popular American country western artists include Jim Reeves, Kenny Rogers, and Dolly Parton.[15] One successful Malawian band operating from South Africa mixing elements of disco music, kwaito, techno, and rap is called Bubu Lazzy (formerly called X Boyz Lazzy).[16]

Some locally produced gospel music might be mistaken by outsiders as pop (i.e., secular) music because of the formal structure (especially its beat) and lyrics (seemingly secular everyday stories). However, a profound knowledge of the spiritual background of the artists and their sponsors as well as the reference of the lyrics to positions of Christian religious organizations is enough for Malawians to categorize it as gospel (see Chirambo 2002).

Many male youths prefer reggae and rap and incorporate into their everyday life related style attributes, such as clothing, hairdressing and other forms of body decoration, language, and gestures. After decades of strict censorship and dress codes, these style attributes distinguish them from others in a significant way, stressing their difference to the mainstream and creating social cohesion.[17] The consumption of music videos and the practice of specific dancing styles also play an important role for reggae and rap enthusiasts.

Malawian youth enjoy Jamaican-produced roots rock reggae (e.g., Bob Marley, Peter Tosh, Burning Spear, and Culture) and lover's reggae (e.g., Eric Donaldson and Black Uhuru) as well as (re)adapted forms, such as that from South Africa (e.g., Lucky Dube and Senzo). More recent styles like dancehall, ragga, and ragamuffin, which cross over with styles of rap music (e.g. Shaggy or Shabba Ranks), are available on the market (Fenn 2004). Following earlier examples of bands like the Roots or Makasu Band, more and more Malawian artists, such as Ben Michael or Brite Nkhata, have started to integrate formal elements of reggae into their musical repertoire using Malawian languages (mostly Chichewa) for their lyrics.

Well-known Malawian reggae artists include the Black Missionaries featuring the late Evison Matafale, Sally Nyundo, and the most prominent, Lucius Banda (see Chirambo 2002). With the help of the Catholic Church, Lucius and his brother Paul Banda became two of the most successful popular musicians and producers in contemporary Malawi. Other Malawian reggae stars who sometimes mix reggae with gospel and other styles are Overtone Chimombo, Emanuel Manda, and clients of the "Balaka school" of Paul and Lucius Banda like Charles Sinetre, Billy Kaunda, Coss Chiwalo, and Master Tongole. The beat and the lyrics of Malawian reggae are aesthetically and semantically very close to church music and gospel, and sometimes Malawian reggae and gospel music intermingle to such an extent that the audience does not separate the two styles in their own classification schemes.

Lucius Banda

In his 1990s releases, reggae artist Lucius Banda and his band commented on the political situation in Malawi and compared it with other political situations of crisis on the African continent and beyond. In "Down Babylon" from his album bearing the same title (1995a), Banda sings in English about "the most malicious dictators of the world," putting Kamuzu Banda and his party (MCP) in the tradition of Hitler, Mussolini, Botha, and Amin.

> "Down Babylon"
>
> This song is against a man who was called a Messiah,
> And killed thousands of people whose remains and bones are still being
>   discovered
> In the rivers of Malawi today.
> A man who took over twenty billion Kwacha from poor people
> And let it be frozen in major banks of the world.
> It is against a man who killed wives and children for the wrongs of their
>   fathers.
> . . .
> This song is against a certain political party found in Malawi
> From the 60s to early 90s.
> A party that killed and tortured people,
> A party that had power more than God,
> A party that could have its way and never be wrong,
> A party that was never wrong.
> . . .
> Down Babylon, down Babylon 'cause Babylon is falling apart.[18]

During his early live performances (in the 1990s and the first years of the new millennium), Lucius Banda took on the role of a follower of the Rastafarian movement who came here to party with the audience. The relation to his audience is made clear by Chirambo (2002: 113):

> "Rastas" is a term he uses for the youth. The youth form the largest group of Lucius Banda's fans. Most of them are unemployed and live in townships under harsh conditions, surviving by vending cheap merchandise along the streets, or as ushers for buses, among other odd jobs. They are a genuinely frustrated group in Malawi.[19]

His sometimes explicitly critical lyrics, his camouflage outfit, and his title "the Soldier" help Lucius Banda to create an image of a people's hero fighting for freedom and justice. Thus he sings in "Mzimu wa Soldier" [Chichewa: Soldier's Spirit] from his album *Yahwe* (1999).

"Mzimu wa Soldier"

Ndimali Soldier wa amphawi	I was a soldier for the poor
Abwenzi anga sanali achuma	My friends were not rich
Anali olema ndi amphawi	They were the lame and the poor
Amndene, olira mchipatala	Those in prison, the crying in hospitals
Ndi amayiamasiye	And widowed women[20]

Reggae, as a polarizing musical style, promotes a "we-and-them" attitude. The singers use a binary opposition scheme to frame the message of the lyrics that sympathize openly with the poor and the downtrodden, accusing the ruling class. The solidarity with the poor and the suppressed, the biblical metaphors used, and the "talk about love"[21] is very attractive for Malawian youths. However, in his early releases he was also skeptical about Kamuzu Banda's successor, Bakili Muluzi, and his party (UDF). In "Njira Zawo" [Their ways] from his album *Ceasefire* (1995) Banda criticizes the regime in Chichewa.

"Njira Zawo"

Dzana ndi dzulo takhalira kuphedwa,	Yesterday, and the other day, we were being killed,
Lero tikhalira kunamizidwa.	Today we are cheated.
Nanga titani poti anthu ndi omwewo,	What can we do since it is the same people.
Angosintha njira zotizunzira.	They've only changed ways of torturing us.
Ali ndi njira zawo.	They've their own ways.
Akamalankhula pakamwa chabe,	When they are talking, it is just words,
Amakhala ngati ngachilungano.	They sound as if they're honest.
Koma mkhale nawo zaka zingapo,	But live with them for some years,
Mudzadzwia anthu awa ndi amodzimodzi,	You'll see it is the same people,
Angosiyana dzina.	They only differ in names.
Ali ndi njira zawo.	They've their own ways.[22]

Recent releases show Lucius Banda as keeper of the history of Malawi's political change. Thus on his album *Survivors* (2006) he composed a song in honor of Chakufwa Chihana after he died in June 2006.[23] Chihana was a political figure in Malawi, dubbed the founder of democracy. During H. K. Banda's dictatorial regime he went into exile after being imprisoned for six years. In 1992, with the winds of political change blowing in the wake of the pastoral letter authored by Catholic bishops, he was the first to come back from the diaspora and challenge Banda's regime openly.[24] He was immediately imprisoned, only to be released in June 1993 when President Banda agreed to a referendum and democratic elections. Chihana formed the Alliance for Democracy Party (AFORD).

"Chihana Wapita" [Chihana is Gone]

Chihana wapita
Munali chikumbu chandale muno,
Amuna olimba mtima,
Ankafunitsitsa kuti aMalawi,tidzikhalirana limodzi.
Tidzawakumbutsa ana athu zambiri yamatipate,
Kuti Chihana ndimzake Bakili anatipezeramatipate.
Chorus:
Ooooh! Chihana wapita,
Simbi yamoto yapita lero,
Yapita kuthupi zintchito yayi,
Yatiphunzitsa kulimba Mtima
Oooh! Chakufwa kulibe,
Munganya uja waluta nadi
Tidzakumbuka zabwino zanu
Chinana awuse mumtendere.

There were political problems here,
A man of courage,
He desperately wanted that Malawians should live together.
We shall remind our children about the history of multiparty politics,
That Chihana and his colleague Bakili,
Brought us multi-party.
Chorus:
Ooooh! Chihana is gone,
The burning iron rod is gone today,
He is physically gone save his works,
You have taught us courage
Oooh! Chakufwa is no more,
Munganya is gone indeed,[25]
We shall remember your good works,
Chihana, rest in peace.[26]

However, after the millennium change, Lucius Banda's musical style changed from reggae to pop music, which fused elements of Congolese, South African, and gospel music. He increasingly started to release songs that carried neither serious political messages nor rebellious attitudes toward the powerful. Instead, he focused on celebrating a hedonist urban lifestyle and was occupied with love songs, drawing a rather apolitical and idealistic picture of his home country. One example is "Malawi Okongala" [Beautiful Malawi] from the album *Survivor*).[27] Not only did his semantic message change but so did his musical style and personal presentation during live performances or in his music videos or DVDs. He switched from roots rock reggae to a fusion of various danceable pop styles impacted by elements of African and global pop music. However, this was not a complete rupture with former political demands.

Rap in Malawi

In the early 1990s, Taps Bandawe, whose recordings had to be imported from South Africa, became the first Malawian rap artist who was broadcast in the country. American rap artists still dominate the Malawian market in the new millennium. A small local scene of rap musicians has developed, but it seems slow-growing and fragile (Fenn 2004 and in this volume). Very well liked, especially among teenagers, in contemporary Malawi is U.S.-produced west coast, gangsta, and other commercial rap (e.g., 2pac, Snoop Doggy Dogg, Dr. Dre, Coolio, Jay-Z, Nas, 50 Cent, and Puff Daddy/P. Diddy). The hammering beat, the offensive hard language, the deep African American slang, the macho and outlaw attitudes, and the underdog status of the artists on display on cassette covers is highly attractive to them. Language and fashion styles also on display in the music videos are selectively imitated, taken on, incorporated, mixed, and reconstructed anew. Music videos often contrast this underdog image with a luxurious ambience (including luxury houses, cars, jewelry). Many of the male adolescent rap enthusiasts wear the accoutrements associated with American hip hop: basketball T-shirts, Nike shoes, baseball caps, and baggy jeans.[28]

In contrast to reggae lyrics, which speak in a collective "we" form, the statements made in rap are centered around "I." This corresponds with the choreography of the dance styles (e.g., local adaptions of break dancing). The use of offensive and obscene language, as for example "The Original Shit Niggaz of Mzuzu," show by the choice of their group name that they intend to provoke and confront the etiquette of official hegemonic culture.[29] But it is also a statement of distinction from norms of the adult culture.

Gangsta Rap: Pop Dogg

Recently, Malawian born, Dublin-based MC Pop Dogg has given an extremely graphic example of the image of the urban bad guy cultivated in gangsta rap. He expresses his individual frustration, his aggressiveness, and virility in the song "They Don't Know" predating his album *Spit Real.*

"They Don't Know"

Pop Dogg is the name
Misdemeanour is the game
I'm meaner with a cane
Like Katrina hurricane
I'm causing turbulence/with my land grenade
Better call the ambulance/and Dublin Fire Brigade
I'm willing/to leave you with scars/and blood spilling
The more I'm killing/the more blood in jars/I'm filling
Don't get my game twisted/I teach a murder lesson

I've got my name blacklisted/in every garda station
I'm like a Bazooka/I dismantle wherever the fuck I'm heading
Got a blow job from a hooker/the day before my wedding
You fucking infants in diapers/and cardigans
Why claiming to be snipers/you ain't go no handguns
I'm scheming/like I'm demented/for the time being
You be screaming/and tormented/on the crime scene
Call me a Taliban I give such a gun /tactical/speech
I mangle and strangle haters and leave them with one/testicle/each[30]

While "They Don't Know" shows little connection with his country of birth, Pop Dogg's "Knock Out" on the same album skillfully plays with Chichewa and English, using them poetically to allude to mythological cultural heroes Bwampini and Zimbalangondo, former autocratic ruler H. K. Banda (Angwazi), ruthless war fighters (kamikaze), and other images from the popular culture sphere, such as action movie star Jean-Claude Van Damme, vampires, and paparazzi.[31] The images used in the lyrics correlate with musical elements used to create the soundtrack for his music video in which the exclusively male musicians of the band are presented as an aggressive group symbolically conquering the urban concrete jungle of Dublin by occupying public spaces with fight dances (alluding to capoeira dancing styles), claiming the street by strolling around with grim faces, or just by publicly hanging out. The song samples the basic riff of "Eye of the Tiger" by the rock band Survivor, which served as the title track for the 1982 *Rocky III* movie in which actor Sylvester Stallone played the character of Rocky Balboa, a socially and economically marginalized boxer of Italian American descent in the USA (Philadelphia) who fought a lonely fight for self-respect, social recognition, and his family.[32] The only means used in this fight were the physical strength of his body and his tremendous will to succeed. The display of an aggressive virility and heroic allusions are obvious in the song.

"Knock Out"

Anthu akufuna awonere nkhondo,
Yabwampini ndizimbalangondo,
Pop Dogg! Yei yeiiii!
Hahahahahahaha! Knock out
Chorus:
Konse mumapita!
Ine ndimaona
Zonse mumachita!
Ine ndimaona
Kukhomo kosatseka
Ine ndimagona
Haha! What's my name?
Popdogg! (repeat 2x)

Ndine m'kulu wogona kukhomo,kosatseka,
Ndisiye ndekha usandipute ndine ndekha chiyendayekha

People want to watch a battle,
Between Bwampini and Zimbalangondo!
Popdogg! Yei yeiiii!
Hahahahahahaha! Knock out!

Chorus:
Where ever you go!
I know
What ever you do!
I know!
Sleeping with the door unclosed[33]
That I also do
Haha! What's my name?
Popdogg! (repeat 2x)
I leave the door open when sleeping
Leave me alone, I live alone[34]

Pop Dogg's poetic usage of language includes complex rhyming schemes (e.g., alliteration of words within sentences) and code-switching between Chichewa and English. His combination of images, symbols, and allusions creates the scenario of a heavy fight in which only the strong and fearless may succeed.

Gospel Hip Hop: Masavage

Secular rappers in Malawi promoting images of hedonistic bad guys living in a hostile violent capitalist world are challenged by religious bands employing the very same aesthetics to spread Christian moral values and messages, such as The Strategy, DJ Lick (Alick Maere), Nyasa Guruz, and Masavage. In 2005/2006 Masavage recorded a song entitled "Malawi Akulira" [Malawi is crying]. It may serve as an example for Malawian gospel hip hop assembling some of this genre's current popular artists in one tune, including "Dynamike" (Mike Munthali), a producer of urban Malawian music, and female rapper Anne Matumbi.

Similar to Pop Dogg, the all-star band employs code switching between Chichewa and American English. Sparsely backed by minimalist keyboard samples, each artist raps through his or her part in a distinguished style. The lyrics put AIDS on the agenda, alluding to biblical values. Artists' solo parts are framed by a collectively sung refrain (call-and-response scheme) that refers aesthetically to South African vocal styles as far as the collective sound of the deep voices is concerned. The band has also produced a music video, in which a Malawian city (either Blantyre or Lilongwe) serves as urban background for the musicians' performances.[35] Masavage also claims street credibility, but in contrast to Pop Dogg's scenario, the group refers to local men's dances (*malipenga*) and to the male working sphere, such as a car workshop, where young mechanics in their working gear join the rapper's vocal performance. In opposition to Pop Dogg, the protagonists are not only shown walking in the streets, but on several occasions they overlook the city from a high rooftop.

The aim of these musicians is to create cleaner images of this musical scene that do not have anything to do with sex, drugs, guns, violence, or crime. They represent themselves as responsible Malawian citizens spreading Christian values.

"Malawi Is Crying"

Malawi akulira
Mphoto yatchimo mbale wangawendiimfa,
Kupewa tchimo sungakwanitse,
Ndimzeru zathu zathupi,
Taona tikulira ndimatenda a edziwa,
Satana asanatipweteke,
Tipewe, tipewe,
Nthenda nditchimo lomwe,
Timuponde pondelele,
Satana timuponde
Timuponde pondelele
Ayesu atsogolere

Chorus:
Tiye ponda! a!a!a!
Ponda! a!a!a!
Ponda, satana timuponde ponde-pondeponde-ponde
Omama! Omama!
Malawi akulira!
Omama! Omama!
Mtundu onse ukutha!
Omama! Omama!
Africa akulira,
Omama! Omama!
Ana onse akufa.

(Rapping by Incyt):
Eee! Ya you know what?
Zisiye zimenezo! Edzi ilibe mzake
You sleep around, you acquire it and please *sindifuna kumva*
Abstain from sex because life is super

. . .

(Rapping by Lex):
Pawayilesi pakanema,
Tsiku nditsiku nkhani yake ndiyamuliliwa edzi,
Mabungwe ndiboma akuyesetsa kutiathane nako kachilombo ka HIV,

Ena apeza mwayi kumanena kutimankhwala awapeza,
Koma makhwala akulu ndikupewa,
Kudziletsa kutsata malamulo a Mulungu.

(Repeat chorus)

. . .

(Rapping by Kinton):
Tigwade pansi tipemphere,
Tikapanda titha ofunika tipewe,
Mwana wachichepele akonda bwanjichisembwele,
Gwada pansi tipemphere lekachiwerewere

. . .

(Rapping by DR Docsy):
Likakhala dzuwa ndikupewa,
Chiphadzuwa ndikupewa,
Mtimawo kuuleza,
Kuopa dzuwa lomaliza kuphedwa,
Kusiya kuunikira atsogoleri amawa.

(Rapping by Dynamike):
Think about that:
What do you have, what do you lose?
What do you gain?
Exercise your periodic control and pain.
You don't wanna do that.
You don't wanna move back.
You wanna might contract.
The word is abstain!

(Rapping by Barry):
Amzanga,
Tatsegulani maso anu. Khalani pansi muganizire zamoyo wanu. Tonse ngati
anthu tinachokera patali. Kondomu chani. Bwanji makani. Pewani. Moyo
ngokoma zedi. Pewani. Kondomu muyitaye uko! Pewani. Moyo ngokoma zedi.
Pewani.
Kondomu muyitaye uko!

(English translation)

Malawi is crying
A result of sin, my friend is death,
You can't succeed not to sin,
By the will of the body alone,
See we are crying because of AIDS,
Before Satan vanquishes us,
Abstain, abstain,
Disease is synonymous with sin,
Let's stamp him down.

Let's stamp Satan down,
Stamp him down, down,
Jesus, lead the way.

Chorus:
Let us stamp! A! a! a!
Stamp! A! a! a!
Stamp, stamp Satan down! Stamp-stamp-stamp-stamp,
Omama! Omama!
Malawi is crying,
Omama! Omama!
The population is dying,
Omama! Omama!
Africa is crying,
Omama! Omama!
All the children are dying.

(Rapping by Incyt):
Eee! Ya you know what?
Leave that alone! AIDS has no equal,
You sleep around, you acquire it, and please I don't want to hear that.

Abstain from sex because life is super. . . .
On radio and television,
Every day the issue is the AIDS pandemic,
NGOs and government are trying hard to win the battle against HIV,
Some unscrupulous are saying we have discovered a cure,
But the main cure is prevention,
Abstinence and following God's laws.

(Repeat chorus)
. . .
Kneel down and pray,
Otherwise we shall all die, it is necessary to abstain,
Why is a young person obsessed with sex?
Kneel down and pray, stop being promiscuous.

. . .
From the sun, you can protect yourself,
From beautiful women, protect yourself,
Hold your desires,
In case the beautiful women can kill you,
Preventing you from guiding the next generation of leaders.
Think about that:
What do you have, what do you lose?
What do you gain?
Exercise your periodic control and pain.
You don't wanna do that.

You don't wanna move back.
You wanna might contract.
The word is abstain!

(Rapping by Barry):
My friends,
Open your eyes. Sit down; take time to reflect about your life. As people, we all
    have come from afar. What is a condom? Why are you stubborn? Abstain.
    Life is so sweet. Abstain. Throw away the condom! Abstain. Life is so sweet.
Abstain.
Throw away the condom!

The precious issue of HIV/AIDS and the surrounding discourses of morality in which the state, churches, donor community, media, schools, universities, families, and the general public take different positions is a highly contested terrain—leaving aside individual social practices. For many Malawians, the Church is one of the main sources of morality. Christian ideology in Malawi encourages abstinence and being faithful as the only means of avoiding HIV/AIDS. Condoms are deemed unreliable, giving people a false sense of security and encouraging promiscuity, which is considered sinful before God. Other officially propagated moral advice by Malawian authorities (e.g., as a governmental strategy for the Malawian young to fight the HIV/AIDS pandemic) and the international donor community may conflict with this opinion.

In general, international influence at a cultural level is viewed by many rather conservative moralists as a corrosive factor of the moral fabric of the society. However, the Malawian government subscribes to the donor community line of thought by propagating an "ABC" strategy (Abstain–Be faithful–Condomize). Christian churches in Malawi subscribe only to the first two preventive strategies. They preach that if you are single, you should abstain from sex. If married, you ought to be faithful. From this perspective, the use of condoms implies having outside sexual relations. The message in the song, therefore, is in conflict with the officially propagated government-donor driven preventive message and most possibly also with common sexual practices of many youths and adults in Malawis.

Some Comparisons

Although the examples above show that there is Chichewa rap in Malawi, the integration of local Malawian languages is rudimentarily developed compared with neighboring countries, such as Tanzania (see Perullo in this volume). Cassette tapes with local rap are not easily found in Malawi apart from a small number of urban areas where one can also find live rap performances. There the skills of the artists rapping over instrumental samples or rapping cover versions of well known hits are presented live before the audience in a kind of a competition mode (see Fenn in this volume).[36] However, as indicated above, a slowly growing Malawian rap and hip hop scene has emerged that is promoted through the developing media. Reasons for the slow growth include the absence of "structures which anchor the vision of the genre in the country" and the small number of "hip youths" available in Malawi, as DJ Lomwe of FM 101 Power radio station put it in an interview.[37]

While the locally produced gospel music is widespread among an audience that includes both genders, reggae and rap are the domain of mainly male youths. Reggae fans propagate collective values, which confront the social and political practice of the powerful: the collective identity of the powerless and oppressed youths ("we") appears in strict opposition to the homogeneous concept of the powerful oppressors ("them").

Among the younger rap fans, individualistic concepts of an American lifestyle (including luxury goods and attributes of urban African American culture) are appropriated and displayed via the adolescent body. Since most rap enthusiasts are male, the figure of the black gangsta is a primary role model. It fuels the imagination with the image of a marginalized underdog who, against all odds, has made it: a black cultural hero who has conquered a white consumer's paradise.

While most of the adults agree with (or at least do not oppose) representations of local gospel musicians, rap and reggae have more potential for conflict. "Deep" reggae fans' display of dreadlocks, their supposed propagation of marihuana use, and the rebellious attitude evoked by a symbolic profession of belief in the Rastafarian movement open up a space for controversial discussion and negotiation of norms and values. Positions in this debate are heterogeneous. Not only most adults but also most young men are not willing to accept the ideological background of Rastafarianism in full consequence. Only in urban and tourist areas along the lakeside, where beach resorts have created a space different from common Malawian social reality, has a Rastafarian scene evolved which expresses itself publicly with a closed set of stylistic elements.[38] Of late, Rastafarian scenes in certain urban regions (e.g., parts of Lilongwe and Blantyre) have spread.

Rap music—especially gangsta rap—creates the deepest controversy between generations. The spectacle of stylistic representation and the values propagated through them makes this style highly attractive to boys. The violation of commonly accepted social and cultural norms through offensive language, the use of fashion symbols from the consumer's world of the capitalist West, and the play with the figure of the individualistic aggressive gangster or young urban offender evokes fear among the adults.

Conclusion: Male Youths, Popular Music, and Resistance

Different images of male adolescents and young men are connected with distinct musical styles: from the figures of the dread soldier fighting against political oppression and violence (reggae) to the urban gangster who appears as a clever

hero (rap). But have these images of male youths in transition had any effect on social reality, or are they only symbolic possibilities of critique and resistance?[39]

I conclude with two examples that show how the capacities of resistance of contemporary music have been transformed into social action. In 2001 the suspicious
death of Malawian reggae artist Evison Matafale in police custody led to political
demonstrations. Emotions and political statements by the participants were expressed by singing Matafale's antigovernment songs. Some of these demonstrations were organized and dominated by dreadlocked members of the Malawian
Rastafarian community. They ended with street riots and clashes with the police
in Blantyre and Zomba. "The Prophet" (as Matafale was nicknamed), in his songs
"satirised the tendency in current Malawian politics towards nepotism, corruption and patronage" (Mapanje 2002: 180). He also wrote protest letters to the then
ruling president Bakili Muluzi. Therefore, many Malawians related the musician's
death to similar experiences during Banda's days when the notorious Young Pioneers used to deal with critical voices by silently executing them. Other clashes
with the police followed in Zomba after a great number of people had attended
Matafale's funeral: "Then a peaceful student demonstration at Chancellor College,
which followed the singer's death, turned into riots. One student was shot dead
and several injured" (Mapanje 2002: 180). During these demonstrations and riots
that were now dominated by university students, protest songs were shouted with
lyrics like "this is our country but the police and Muluzi have destroyed it," using
the melody of a 1915 anti-colonial song, or "Policemen, prepare to pay the bill for
the blood you spill."[40]

This example demonstrates the potential of certain styles of popular music to
mobilize youths to express their protest as a group—at least temporarily—even
if there might only be a diffuse consciousness about concrete common demands
functioning simply as a general expression of malcontents with the general political situation.

The final example is about the institutionalization of protest by a self-proclaimed
representative of the youth. Malawian reggae artist Lucius Banda has recently changed
his position as a critic from the outside to one from the inside: he has been elected
to parliament as a member of the United Democratic Front, which was Malawi's
ruling party until 2004. The ambivalence of this step is obvious. On the one hand, it
can be interpreted as an attempt to move critique and protest into the mainstream
political institutions. On the other hand, this different political location implies the
danger of becoming corrupted or absorbed by administrative duties.

After the musician-cum-politician made a motion in parliament in 2005 pro-
posing procedures to impeach President Bingu wa Mutharika, who had cultivated
a deep conflict with former president Bakili Muluzi, Banda was accused of fraud
(faking his school certificates to qualify as a candidate in 2004). The Zomba Magis-
trate Court sentenced him to twenty-one months in prison in August 2006. Three
months later, after Banda had begun serving his sentence in Zomba Maximum

Prison, the verdict was overturned by the High Court in Blantyre, and he could walk free. Shortly afterwards he launched his album *Survivors,* and in December 2006 he performed in Zomba Prison for his former inmates.

His composition "Johnny" (on the *Survivors* album) tells the story of his imprisonment from his own subjective viewpoint, thereby relating his individual fight against Malawian authorities to the collective struggle of Malawians and other peoples for freedom and against oppression. He employs Christian aesthetics and rhetoric, but also alludes to political dimensions of Martin Luther King's famous speeches in the early 1960s.

Johnny

(spoken) Preamble:
I would like to dedicate this song to all the oppressed people, the downtrodden, the poor people of Malawi. One thing I would like to say, tough times do not last, but tough people do last. How hard it might be, how difficult it might be. We will sing free at last, free at last, thank God we are free at last!
Mwana wanga John tsimzina,
Andimanga unyolo kumanja,
Andiponya ku bode wa kuZomba ine,
Kawauze mayi ako, kuti dadi amangidwa.
Ndakulakwila chiyani,
Fukolanga lokondeka,
Ndinakometsela mbili yako ine,
Lero undibwenzera,
Unyolo wakundende.

Chorus:
Udzasowa anthu,
Udzafuna anthu,
Dziko lapansi m'lozungulira, m'lozungulira.
Sindiwopa munthu,
Ozumza thupi,
Ndidziwa Ambuye adzandiyankha, adzandiyankha.

Johnny
John my son close your eyes,
They have imprisoned my wrists,
They have thrown me at the back of a pickup on my way to Zomba,
Tell your mum that dad has been imprisoned.
What wrong have I done to you,
My beloved country!
I worked hard to create a good name for you,
Today my payment is
Handcuffs on my way to prison!

Chorus:
Nobody will be there for you,
When you will need them.
You never know what will happen tomorrow,
I am not afraid of people
Who torture the body.
I know God will hear me, God will hear me.

Like the song "Chihana wapita" (see above), this composition narrates recent political history and links it with ideas of struggle for political freedom. It shows that in 2006 Lucius Banda had not yet completely given up his role as a critical observer of Malawi politics. However, he has lost the status of a self-proclaimed representative of subordinated Malawian youths, since he himself has become an established member of the Malawian elite. Compared with his earlier releases (from 1994 to the millennium change), the musician's political attitude to "fight for the poor and oppressed" has vanished and rather turned into a platitude and farce. For example, he still uses the nickname "Soldier," and he refers to his "rebellious period" by wearing expensive camouflage uniforms onstage.

The subsequent release of *JC 51 Maximum* in the beginning of 2007 provides a blend of rumba, reggae, gospel, and kwaito music with Malawian flavors. Although the album title refers to his former cell in Zomba Prison, Banda claims that in his lyrics he has "shied away from politics" and turned to "love songs."[41]

Whether this is just another round in the Malawian game of "chameleon politics" (Englund 2002) with no relevant outcome for the youth who used to form the backbone of Lucius Banda's success as a musician or whether the artist keeps on criticizing the powerful from within while he himself has become one of them remains an interesting field for further investigation.

NOTES

1. Gerhard Kubik (1987: 1–3; 1991: 203–204) has criticized both the terms "neo-traditional" and "popular" with regard to music, arguing that there are only "African music traditions" with different life spans and with different historical impacts. Following Mensah (1970), Kubik (1987: 2) distinguishes among "passive," "moribund," and "active music traditions." For encyclopedic short overviews of postcolonial Malawian popular music, see Lwanda (2006) and Bender (2000: 239–43). For early popular music in Malawi, see Chirambo (2006), Kubik (1981, 1987, 1989), Malamusi (2004), Nurse (1964), Strumpf (1992, 1998), and Strumpf and Phwandaphwanda (1993). Lwanda (2006: 215–18) contains a selected discography of various neo-traditional and contemporary Malawian musicians. His Pamtondo Records internet site (http://www.pamtondo.com) advertises CDs and music videos of distinct Malawian music traditions. For studies of more recent music, see Chimombo and Chimombo (1996), Chirambo (2002), Lwanda (2003), Gilman and Fenn (2006), and Fenn (2004).

The analysis of popular music in Malawi in this contribution is focusing mainly on the two governance periods of Bakili Muluzi (1994–2004). The use of the ethnographic present in the text refers to this time period unless passages are indicated otherwise.

2. Phiri's death was recognized by a presidential honor (James Chavula, "Government Praised for Honouring Matafale, Saleta," *Nation*, July 9, 2010, http://www.nationmw.net, search "Saleta Phiri").

3. Radio Maria was established in Italy by priests and laypeople broadcasting religious and social programs 24 hours a day from Mangochi. The primary language for broadcasting is Chichewa/Chinyanja although there are also few other programs in Yao.

4. For information on the African rap scene, including Malawian artists, see africanhiphop.com. Malawian artists can be found on youtube.com, myspace.com, and malawithewarmheart.com.

5. See, for example, the rap song "Hali Halisi" [Swahili: The Real Situation] by Tanzanian artist Mr. 2 alias Too Proud (Joseph Mbilinyi) from his album *Niite Mr. 2* (1998), which was a musical hit all over Malawi, Tanzania, and beyond by the end of the 1990s.

6. The Banda regime tried to control them, restrictively trying to integrate them into the framework of the dominant ideology. In the perspective of many ordinary citizens, they were feared as Malawian Young Pioneers (MYP) who played the role of omnipresent and omnipotent watchdogs of the oppressive apparatus of Banda's MCP, terrorizing and denunciating the people. However, some of the MYP activities (e.g., agricultural or educational programs) were quite welcomed, especially in rural areas.

7. For example, some male students terrorized a university lecturer, I. Phiri, who published a study about sexual harassment of female students by their male counterparts on the campus of the University of Malawi/Chancellor College in Zomba (Phiri 1997).

8. See Kwaramba (1997) for an analysis of Thomas Mapfumo's Chimurenga music in Zimbabwe.

9. Phiri and other popular musicians, such as the late Evison Matafale, have been honored with national awards by President Bingu wa Mutharika (*Nation*, July 9, 2010).

10. In "Oraruwa" Phiri takes the perspective of the opposite sex, a common device in popular music of Malawi and the whole southern African region, according to Lwanda (2003). Michael Lamuel Mwale, one of my main field assistants in Malawi, invented the neologism "movious" (translating "Oraruwa") to characterize a person who "is unsettled and ending up having sex with anyone." Examples of recordings concerned with HIV/AIDS include the album *Tiimbire Yesu* by the Katawa Singers (1993), where they claim that "life is now more dangerous" [*kunja kuno kwaopsya*] because of AIDS (Lwanda 2002: 155), the poem "Ndekha wa mantha" of Malawian Philly Bongoley Lutaaya (who died of HIV/AIDS), which has been transformed into a song on Lucius Banda's album *Down Babylon* (1995), the album *Ndichiritsen* [Heal me] (1997) of the deceased composer, guitarist, and singer Paul Chaphuka, the songs of Ethel Kamwendo and the Ravers Band and Elizabeth Kachale, or in rap songs of Masavage. AIDS is also a very important issue in men's dances (Seebode 2003, 2009).

11. Both songs are included in the album *Ambewe* [Mr. Mbwene].

12. *Nsima* is a stiff porridge made from a base of maize or cassava flour combined with soup made from vegetables (*ndivo*), sometimes enriched with meat or fish.

13. This is a piece of cloth with H. K. Banda's portrait printed on it, which women had to wear in public on certain occasions. I could not determine the date of recording of this album, but it is possibly earlier than Phiri's album *Ili Mu Ufa*.

14. *Zasintha* [Things have changed] was one of the main slogans used by multiparty activists or sympathizers to describe the situation during and after Malawi's transition period (1993/94) to a formally democratic multiparty system. Overtone Chimombo comments

on the process of political change in his album bearing the same title, but in his songs he draws a more optimistic picture of the transition process and its impact.

15. An example of Malawian adaptation of U.S. country western music is the album *Akoma Akagonera: Chichewa Country and Western* by the band Padangokhala (which consists of Allan and Pierson Ntata), 1998, recorded in Studio K., Blantyre, Malawi.

16. See their albums *Bubu* (1997), *Mission On* (1998), and *Dollar Yashupa.*

17. For censorship of traditional and popular music in pre- and postcolonial Malawi, see Chirambo (2006).

18. The lyrics, originally sung in English, are from Chirambo (2002: 106–107). Apart from the refrain, the words are spoken in a kind of a talking-blues style, with a dark, slow shouting voice that evokes images of a church sermon. They are backed by a mid-tempo gospel-like reggae beat. For a variation on this song ("Down Babylon II"), see Lucius Banda's album *Ceasefire* (1995).

19. Although I agree with Chirambo's general interpretation, he implicitly equates male adolescents and young men with youth in general, which introduces a male-oriented bias into his interpretations.

20. Transcription and translation from Chirambo (2002: 105).

21. This is a translated quotation from several informal interviews with mainly female Malawian adolescents during my fieldwork in Malawi (1998–2000).

22. Transcription and translation from Chirambo (2002: 115).

23. Music videos of "Chihana Wapita" and other Lucius Banda songs mentioned in this chapter may be found on YouTube.

24. For a discussion of the role the churches in Malawi played during the period of transition (1992–94) and after see the contributions in Nzunda and Ross (1995), Ross (1997) and Phiri and Ross (1998). For a historical analysis of post-colonial "confrontations between state and church in Malawi," see Schoffeleers (1999).

25. Chakufwa Chihana was also fondly called "Munganya," which in Chitumbuka means "friend." According to Vincent Jumbe (personal communication, January 2008), Chihana used the term when referring to his political friends, and with the passage of time the word became associated with him, hence his nickname.

26. The Chichewa transcriptions and English translations for "Chihana Wapita," "Knock Out," "Malawi Is Crying," and "Johnny" are by Vincent C. Jumbe. I thank him for this and for further discussions about interpretation, which made me aware of the depth of metaphors in the song texts.

27. Many people know this song as "Kuchekuche." Kuchekuche is a Malawian beer sold in 0.5 liter bottles. Because other Malawian beer bottles used to hold only 0.33 liters, this signifies affluence and prosperity. However, according to Vincent Jumbe (personal communication, January 2008), in Chichewa slang, *kuchekuche* also means "party all night long, until dawn."

28. Many adolescents call these oversized baggy jeans "Yo!-trousers" (abbreviation for "young urban offenders"). Some of the Malawian rap fans refer explicitly to their dress style as "OG" gear (abbreviation for "original gangsta"). See also Fenn (2004).

29. I witnessed an early live performance of this group in Mzuzu, 1998, where the rappers underlined the image of the bad guys onstage by the choice of their dress, including leather jackets and dark sunglasses.

30. Lyrics quoted from http://www.popdogg.com (accessed 04/20/2007), which has since been deleted. For recent information about Pop Dogg, see http://www.myspace.com /popdogg and http://www.reverbnation.com/popdogg.

31. The battle of Bwampini and Zimbalangondo alludes to the ancient classical Homeric epic battle between Chaldeans and Trojans for Helen. In Malawi, there is a Chichewa book based on the Homeric epics. Bwampini and Zimbalangondo are the major characters in the book, which was used as a literature text in secondary schools. Angwazi was one of the praise names of H. K. Banda, referring to him as the "savior" (Posner 1995), the all-powerful "lion," and the "conqueror" (Gilman 2004), glorifying his heroic fight for Malawi's decolonization.

32. Stallone's other famous character, Rambo, was also very popular with young men throughout Africa and beyond.

33. This is a Chichewa common saying that refers to a courageous person. That is, if you are able to sleep while the main door into the house is open at night, then you are considered fearless.

34. The chiyendayekha is a big monkey who lives and walks alone, unlike smaller monkeys. Morally, the animal typifies individualistic tendencies, as opposed to official cultural values. However, in "Knock Out," moral values are symbolically subverted and the communitarian ethos is challenged by individualism.

35. Both of the video performances are on youtube.com.

36. This cultural tradition of competition is well known also for dances (e.g., *malipenga*) in Malawi (see Kerr 1998; Seebode 1999, 2003, 2009).

37. See http://hiphoparchive.org, October 1, 2008. However, it is doubtful whether, as DJ Lomwe says, "marketing strategies of music in Malawi are basically tilted against the progress of the genre." In my opinion, it is rather the low degree of urbanization in Malawi that seems to be a major factor preventing this urban style from growing faster than any conspiracy of the Malawian music industry.

38. These groups in Nkhata Bay, Monkey Bay, or elsewhere around Lake Malawi, for example, consist mainly of older youths (in their mid-twenties and above) working in the tourist business, selling such items as carvings, fashion, or regalia of the Rastafarian movement. In many cases, the public display of Rastafarian aesthetics dominates over serious attempts to take on most ideological aspects of the Rastafarian movement. The target group for their economic activities consists mostly of international low budget travelers.

39. For a recent analysis of popular music's critical potential within the public sphere during the rule of H. K. Banda and beyond, see Lwanda (2009).

40. See BBC News from December 14 and 29, 2001, various articles in the Malawian daily *Nation* from November and December of the same year, and Amnesty International Report 2002.

41. See BBC News from August 31, 2006, articles in *The Nation* from November 4, 2006, November 27, 2006, December 12, 2006, and January 16, 2007. Lucius Banda's 2006 and 2007 releases are also available on CD/DVD. In 2007, state lawyers have asked the Supreme Court to order a retrial or uphold Banda's conviction of 2006 (*Nation*, March 13, 2007).

PART 6.
DRUMMING
(MALI)

Urban Drumming
Traditional Jembe Celebration Music in a West African City (Bamako)

RAINER POLAK

Jembe music today represents a global cultural good. Over the past half a century, thousands of professional players have proved innovative and successful in urban and transnational music markets. Contrary to common categorizations of African drum and dance performance genres as essentially rural and pre-modern ("neo-traditional" at best), jembe music has been urbanized and become part of the urban popular culture in West African cities, such as Bamako, capital of the Republic of Mali. Drummers have contributed substantially to make urban space, social relations and culture what it is in Bamako today.

The jembe drum originates from the Manden [French: *Manding*], a mostly rural region in southwestern Mali and northeastern Guinea (Charry 1996, 2000: 193–241). There, people have traditionally performed jembe music to animate local dance events on social, agricultural, and religious occasions. Since the early 1960s, the drum has entered the programs of state-sponsored folkloric ensembles in Guinea and Mali. It has also been part of the popular celebration culture in the greater region's cities. The metropolitan centers of present-day jembe playing, Abidjan, Dakar, Conakry, Bobo Dioulasso, and Bamako, all are outside the instrument's older core area of distribution (with Bamako just at the border; see map 12.1).

The jembe has been culturally appropriated in Europe and North America since the 1980s (Zanetti 1996). More recently, Japan, Australia, Brazil, South Africa, and many other countries have followed this trend. The new contexts of jembe music outside West Africa include stage shows, music education (both for children and adults), and use as a vehicle for social cohesion, such as drum circles, workshops for at-risk youth, and corporate team building. The urbanization, nationalization, and globalization of jembe music have been mutually conditioning and reinforcing one another (Polak 2000). Channels of feedback between local and global contexts include emigration of jembe players and export of instruments from West Africa, cultural tourism to West Africa, and the mass-mediatization of jembe music in CDs, DVDs, teaching handbooks, and online resources.

This chapter offers a case study of musical urbanization examining the repertory of jembe pieces commonly performed in Bamako. In this city, jembe drumming has been the most popular style of celebration music since the 1960s. Male players have professionalized and commodified formerly communal musical work and today form a large occupational group. This chapter interprets the history, structure, and popularity of their repertory in the context of the urban audience.

I draw on about eighteen months of field research in Mali, which I carried out in several stages throughout the 1990s. The ethnographic present tense throughout this chapter refers to that decade. The focus was on a group of twenty-five professional musicians based in Badialan, a residential area west of Bamako's city center. For a comparative perspective on urban drumming, I also paid visits to villages and small towns in the rural regions to Bamako's south (Manden) and north (Bèlèdugu). I collected data with a broad range of methods:

- participant observation and experience as a part-time professional drummer, performing about 120 life cycle celebrations in Bamako;
- biographical interviews with a dozen urban drummers of all generations;
- analysis of audio and video field recordings; and
- a statistical survey of the more than 400 performances carried out by the focus group of twenty-five professionals during a twelve-month period in 1997–98.

The Urban Population

Bamako was founded in the seventeenth century and had fewer than 1,000 inhabitants when the French seized power in 1883. Typical for a (post)colonial metropolis, it was growing fast in the twentieth century. Much of the growth resulted from immigration. Bamako had 1 million inhabitants in the late 1990s and 1.8 million in 2009.[1] The Malian capital thus ranks among the fastest growing cities in the world today. Bamako has always been marked by its population's heterogeneity in regional origins, ethnic identities, and professional specializations. This qualifies it as a city according to views from urban sociology, anthropology, and history.[2]

In precolonial times, areas of the town were associated with ethnic, social, or professional identities. Bamako's founding Niare lineage was of Soninke origin, eventually assimilating to Bamana [French: Bambara] language and culture and giving its name to the city's Niarela quarter. Other neighborhoods were named for traders of sahelian origin (Dravela, Tauatila) and Bozo river fishing people (Bozola). During early colonial rule, Bamana and Maninka [French: Malinké] peasants from surrounding areas and colonial soldiers, railway workers, and civil servants from various regions of French West Africa came to live in Bamako. The population's majority identified as Bamana, the group that used to occupy most of the capital's territory and immediate surroundings. After World War II, however, the urban population's ethnic composition began to reflect that of the colonial and then national territory.[3] Ethnic identities were still ascribed to residential districts built around the colonial center in the 1920s. However, new districts no longer bore ethnically specific names or showed ethnic biases from the 1950s onwards. Today, neighborhoods rarely reproduce ethnic, social, and professional differences (Westen 1995: 63–84). Most of the population lives in highly diversified *quartiers populaires*. Interethnic marriage is frequent (Antoine and Djiré 1998: 125).

Urban Celebration Culture

Life cycle transition rites emerged as the major social occasions of jembe drum and dance celebrations in Bamako since 1945. About 90 percent of jembe celebration performances were held in the context of weddings, according to our survey of 1997–98. Weddings in the city serve to set up and reinforce social relations (Brand 2001: 67). The public exchange of gifts, consumption of food and drinks, the performance of song and praise (the griot's domain), and jembe drum and dance performances provide modes of interaction that create and display social capital. Women in Bamako think of their participation in celebrations as a duty that also serves their own interests in sociability, recreation, and gaining social and economic security through reciprocal relationships.

Life cycle celebrations usually take place in the streets of residential areas, just in front of the compound where the organizing family lives. Broad rectangular streets became characteristic of the colonially planned residential areas in Bamako from the 1920s onwards. The authorities designed the streets to ease traffic and control public space. The residents, however, found the streets ideal for drum and dance events. With jembe celebration culture, the female population temporarily takes over a part of the urban public space (see fig. 12.1). Traffic has to take a detour.

The festive gatherings of some one, two, or three hundred people are open to the public. Yet a cultural constraint keeps males from taking part in roles other than professional performer. These urban celebrations frame a largely female domain.

The participants come together through various channels of the organizing family's networks. Most of the guests are female relatives. Others come as neighbors, common club members, occupational colleagues, and friends. The music, dancing, and colorful and joyful crowd also attract party crashers: mostly kids from the neighborhood. Each celebration forms a singular gathering of a complex network of people of heterogeneous ethnic and social backgrounds.

Within a circle formed by the participants, drummers and female singers make a front side. Members of the circle take turns dancing in the central ground. Groups of dancers sedately circle the ground in a single file (fig. 12.2). Periods of group dance continually alternate with swift successions of short (10–30 sec), energetic face-to-face encounters, individually or in pairs, with the lead drummer (fig. 12.3).

Drummers, singers, and dancers do not perform as fixed ensembles, but find one another spontaneously. The drum ensemble and most singers come as hired professional specialists with commercial interests. By contrast, everybody is welcome to take on the role of dancer: organizers, invitees, occupational specialists (fig. 12.4), and incidental attendees. Jembe drum and dance performance is participatory; it aims at involving people in expressive social interaction (Polak 2007; see also Knight 1984). Taking turns at dancing has at least two functions. First, it shows the participant's personal involvement in the public celebration, thus socially realizing and supporting its underlying ritual occasion. Second, it presents the dancer's identity to the public.

When people dance, they identify with the performed piece. The repertory of jembe pieces is a reservoir of musical metaphors (Fernandez 1974; Waterman 1990: 213ff.; Coplan 2008). Each piece is associated with various meanings that its performance can embody. In the city, pieces can connote a particularly broad range of attributes: ethnic identities, regional origins, and social, professional, and age groups, among others. Some pieces also relate to the individual's role in the social occasion, for instance, the role of the bride's *denbaw* (honorary mothers), those few elder female relatives of the jubilee who organize and finance the event.[4] The *denbaw* present themselves to the public by wearing the *denbajalan* [honorary mother's headband], which usually are monogrammed with the owner's name or initials (see figs. 12.3 and 12.8), and dancing the *denbafòli* [honorary mother's rhythm]. *Denbafòli* is the most often and extensively played drumming piece at Bamako celebrations.

Musical Repertory and Performance

Performing jembe music is to improvise with widely known musical materials and models. The musicians' working repertory consists of a certain number of recognizable pieces, each identifiable by a set of musical phrases played in specific multipart relationships by the two to six ensemble members.[5] The musical structures of the pieces are open to change. Sometimes several pieces merge into a larger suite. Sometimes, new ones emerge. Conflict occurs between competing individuals, as well as between generations, about how one should play a piece. The degree of awareness of how to play a certain piece is different between apprentices and experienced musicians. Nobody knows all pieces, after all. A young jembe player once explained to me: "Before you can learn to play all pieces, a new one will appear," thus frustrating wishes for a systematic survey or authoritative control of the repertory. Despite all these disclaimers, the repertory in Bamako forms a body of musical units, which is well known among performers and audiences across the city. These units serve as a cultural resource for making music and dance together without reading or rehearsal. The repertory thus preconditions performance; performance interprets and re-creates the repertory at the same time.[6] Playing jembe music amounts to "performance-composition" or "situational re-composition," as Meki Nzewi (1997) coined the term.

Drumming at a celebration means to reproduce pieces on demand. Jembe drummers think of their music making as work (Polak 2004; see figs. 12.5 and 12.6). Each piece agrees with certain songs and dance patterns that it accompanies, coordinates, and focuses. Drummers intend to make people stand up and dance. They pick pieces with regard to who, among the attendees, might dance. Performing repertory is intentional action, purposely addressing a specific portion of the audience. "Whereas jelis [griots] play pieces honoring specific persons, drummers play pieces honoring groups of people" (Charry 2000: 12). Only in the urban context of professional celebration music have drummers adopted the griot's custom of approaching and praising individuals (figs. 12.2 and 12.7).

The job of the drummers in this situation is threefold. First, they create a joyful excited atmosphere and groove: a dense, repetitive, polyphonic texture of melorhythmic drumming patterns, which are performed with much swing, drive, and feeling, and synchronized in intricate multi-part relationships. Second, they embody and present a specific piece of the multimodal celebration performance repertoire, such as a certain drum ensemble piece that corresponds to certain dance movements and songs. Each piece usually reminds a portion of the audience of aspects of their backgrounds and identities, which, together with the groove, incites them to dance. The first dunun part is of particular importance for identifying and characterizing the piece of repertoire performed. Third, the drummers not only translate into sound and accompany the dancer's movements, they also interact with her. The lead jembe player, in particular, engages in a sort of multimedia dialogue with the dancer.

Views may differ about which piece is to come with which song and dance when, and why, and what it means. The repertory is not a static system of fixed items but a ground for social interaction that is open to change. For instance, songs that were formerly set in the drumming piece called *menjani* in the 1960s and 1970s have been accompanied with *suku*, which is more popular today. Jembe pieces are neither fixed in time nor unambiguous in the present. Their musical structures, cultural meanings, and social significance are continually reenacted and renegotiated in performance. For instance, a certain set of drumming phrases identified as a spirit possession piece (*jinafòli*) in the 1970s was appropriated by professional drummers for a profane children's song and dance (*sumale*); despite the protest of

possession cult leaders, the formerly exclusive piece entered the standard repertory of mundane wedding celebration music.

The repertory's metaphoric aspect is central to the popular appeal of drum and
dance celebrations. In the following two sections, I interpret two trends of change:
ethnic diversification, on the one hand, and integration of a common urban core
repertory, on the other.

Diversification

Sagele is a large village some 70 km south of Bamako. In and around Sagele,
three pieces (*furasifòli, kisa/wurukutu,* and *madan*) are played at almost every
celebration. Beyond these pieces, the common repertory has no more than a dozen
pieces. One will rarely hear more than five or six of them at a typical village celebration.

The urban repertory is more diverse.[7] Like in the village, three pieces are performed at almost every celebration (*dansa, marakadòn/denbafòli,* and *suku*). However, there are some twenty-five commonly performed pieces (see table 12.1) and
an additional twenty-five pieces that are more specialized. At a typical Bamako
wedding, one can be sure to hear at least ten to fifteen pieces. These combine more
flexibly and change more swiftly than is the case in village celebration music.

Until the 1950s, many families living in Bamako still invited music ensembles
from their regions of origin when they had a celebration. The dozen or so professional resident jembe players then had mainly their own regional pieces in their
personal repertories and played primarily for those families who came from the
same regions. Celebration culture in the city used to differ according to people's
ethnic identities and regional origins. The community of participants and the musical repertory at each celebration was more homogeneous than today: "In those
times, all were on their own. For whatever ethnic group you played, you played
their pieces. To play all pieces at a single wedding, this was not done" (Yamadu
Bani Dunbia, Bamako, January 8, 1998).

In the 1960s, urban jembe drummers began to adopt and adapt dozens of pieces
from diverse regions, ethnic groups, and social contexts in Mali as well as a few
from neighboring countries. Many of these pieces had not been jembe pieces originally. For instance, Soninke musicians from northwestern Mali first performed the
piece *marakadòn* on hourglass drums (*donka*). In Khaso, a region in west central
Mali, they played *dansa, garankedòn,* and *sanja* on the griot's cyclindrical drums
(*jelidunun* or *khasonkadunun*). Thus, of the six most important pieces in today's
Bamako repertoire, only two (*suku* and *kirin*) were jembe pieces before they came
to the city.

The larger part of today's Bamako jembe repertory came into being in only one
or two decades. The process of regional musical appropriation ended in the 1970s
when the more important ethnic, regional, and social status groups each showed
up in the urban repertoire with at least one specific piece. The local Bamana group's

Table 12.1. Drumming pieces realized at more than 20 percent of celebrations in Bamako in 1997–98

Piece	Frequency (%)	Piece	Frequency (%)	Piece	Frequency (%)
dansa	97	bònjalan	43	maninkamòri	30
marakadòn	96	didadi	43	menjani	24
suku	94	dununba	42	fulafòli	23
kirin	82	baya yuguba	39	bara	22
garankedòn	62	sunun	39	numufòli	22
sanja	62	tansole	39	sogoninkun	22
sumalen	54	tisanba	39	sungurunbanin	21
madan	50	bolon	38		
tasaba	45	sabarifòli	34		

Source: Author's survey, Bamako 1997–98.
Note: Out of 434 performances surveyed, I here make use of only those statistical data that I could corroborate through personal observation and/or audio recordings (N=120).

pieces, such as *tisanba* and *tansole,* from Bamako and surrounding areas were among the last to be adopted. Longer than other groups, Bamana resisted the rising popularity of urban jembe playing and supported their own celebration music genres and musicians, such as *bònkolo* drummers and *ngusunbala* xylophone players.[8] Yet the jembe became irresistible in the city.

Urban youth culture has been the second most important source of innovation in the Bamako jembe repertoire. Every year or two a new dance is all the rage with children and youth. They demand that the drummers contribute their share. In the 1970s and 1980s, jembe players have translated Afro-American pop music styles, such as funk, disco, reggae, and rap, into drumming pieces. They transposed pieces of the Senegalese sabar drum orchestra, which in Bamako specializes in urban youth entertainment, into their style and repertoire.[9] Since the mid-1990s, they have adopted rhythms from televised pop songs from Kinshasa, Abidjan, Paris, and Bamako. In 1997, for instance, drummers all over the city played *tasaba* and *baya yougouba,* jembe pieces that had originated two or three years earlier from pop songs by Les Youtous and Aisha Koné, respectively, from Abidjan. In the same year, Bamako singer Yoro "Bruce" Diallo's latest hit, "Muchacha Fernando," was about to be reinterpreted as a jembe piece. It did not work very well and stayed *en vogue* only about half a year or so. Bamako drummers could not agree on how to translate the pop song's beat and feeling. Not every innovation turns out musically satisfying to the audience.

Typically, two or three contemporary creations are among the ten or fifteen most popular jembe pieces at a time. Opposing views exist about their status. Traditionally minded persons—most older drummers, for instance—deny such vogue pieces the cultural and social significance that marks the older repertory of "real" or "normal" pieces, as they say. However, many of these critics in their younger days have themselves contributed to creating and popularizing vogue pieces. Even today, they would rather not express such views in the face of an audience at a celebration. Their evaluation depends on the situational context and personal interests.

Many vogue pieces more or less rapidly go out of fashion one or two years after their success. Some, however, have made it into the more stable repertory of standards. These have lost their exclusive association with youth. Adult women, too, dance them today (see figs. 12.8–12.10).

The diversified urban repertory offered a large part of the female urban population both an opportunity and a reason to take part in a common framework of celebration, cutting across differences of origin, status, and age. In the urban context, many newly adopted pieces took on the character of metaphors of their regional, ethnic, or social contexts of origin. In several cases, pieces took on ethnonyms as complementary or even primary names. For instance, in the Wasulun region, some 150 km south of Bamako, there is a piece named *kirin,* after the instrument (a calabash beaten with sticks) on which they play it. When the piece became popular in Bamako as part of the jembe music repertoire, the urbanites started to call it *wasulunka* [lit. Wasulun-person], as they call the people of this region.[10] Other pieces took on professional status group's names, such as *jelidòn* [griot's dance] for *sanja*. Still others became associated with an age group, such as *sabarifòli* [sabar playing] with the youth. Participants now could identify with an ethnic, status, or age group by following the call to dance to "their" piece.

In the village, pieces of the local repertoire usually do not express ethnic or professional identities. Even a piece such as *sabarifòli* from Senegal, which came to the Manden region south of Bamako only some decades ago, appears as local and "Maninka" as any other piece. In an interview, Namakan Keita (born about 1964), farmer and village drummer from Sagele, defended *sabari*:

> RP: Do not *sunun* and *sabari* come from elsewhere, from other people?
> NK: *Sabari* has been played here for quite some time, more than 20 years.
> RP: But originally it was a piece of the Wolof people from Senegal.
> NK: Yes, maybe, but we play it here for a long time.
> RP: People say that *sunun* is a piece from Kaarta, from the north of Mali.

NK: *Ah, bon?* [French term in the original, with skeptical or ironic distance in tone]
RP: Yes, that is what I heard.
NK: According to my calculation, this is a piece of ours. I have found it here. It
   has been played here since I was born. Thus, one can say that it is a local
   piece. (Sagele, June 21, 1997)

In Bamako, just as in Sagele, people feel that their pieces form a local repertory. However, urban musicians and audiences more than rural ones understand
that their pieces originally came from elsewhere some time ago. For instance, in
Bamako they know *sunun* as a piece originating from Kaarta, thus addressing the
people from this region (Kagooro) and related Bamana groups. *Sabari* is a piece
of the local youth in Bamako, but at the same time, everybody knows it is a piece
from Senegal. Drummers continually play it when people they identify as having Senegalese backgrounds are present in the audience. Some call it *wolofofòli*
[piece of the Wolof], associating it with Senegal's largest ethnic group. Urban repertoire can evoke both origin-related and local-oriented urban meanings at the
same time.

In a word, repertory is more complex and polysemous in the city than in the village. Diversification came along with ethnic connotations of pieces. The continued
attachment of ethnicity to musical pieces does *not* point to a lack of urbanism,
as Claude Meillassoux (1968) assumed in his seminal study of Bamako. In contrast to the then commonsense notion of African urbanization as equal to "detrib-
alization," performing ethnicity was functional to setting up new forms of social
relationships among people of diverging backgrounds in the city (J. Mitchell 1956,
1987).

While jembe pieces and dances became metaphors of ethnic identities, their
performance created a context attended by an increasingly mixed audience. The
heterogeneous urban population now joined in a common local framework of
celebration, thus surpassing the older segregation of expressive culture according
to ethnic and regional origins. Differentiation—not abandonment—of ethnicities
marked the first stage of urbanization of the repertoire, allowing celebration culture
to transcend the diverse origins of urbanites.

The Urban Core Repertory

The diversification of the Bamako repertory took place largely in the 1960s
and 70s. Somewhat later, in the 1970s and 80s, a core repertory of common popular appeal emerged. This further added to the integrative quality of drum and
dance performance at urban celebrations.

As noted above, in both village and urban contexts there are three primary
drumming pieces played at almost all drum and dance celebrations. In the village
music of Sagele this core repertory (*furasifòli*, *kisa/wurukutu* and *madan*) makes
for over 80 percent of the playing time.[11] In Bamako, the three core pieces (*dansa*,
marakadòn/denbafòli, and *suku*) add up to 40 percent of all playing time. This pref-

erence is still remarkable in view of some 50 to 60 existing pieces, of which an average of 12 to 15 is performed at a typical wedding.

The urban core pieces are independent of the ethnic identities of the organizers, audiences, and musicians. By contrast, pieces such as *sunun* (associated with Bamana), *fulafòli* (with Fulani/Peul), and *menjani* (with Maninka peoples) do correlate with, for instance, the organizer's ethnic identity (table 12.2).

The core pieces, like most others, continue to have connotations of ethnic and regional origins. At the same time, they show associations with social roles, status groups, and age groups. For instance, *marakadòn* is associated, first, with the Soninke ethnic group, called Maraka by Bamana speakers. Second, *marakadòn* relates to groups of long-distance traders also called Maraka in Bamana, even if they do not necessarily speak or identify as Soninke. Third, the piece refers to the region of Kayes in western Mali, from where most Soninke/Maraka originate, in general. Yet, fourth, the piece also addresses the so-called honorary mothers (*denbaw*) who organize and finance the celebration. It even bears *denbafòli* [honorary mother's piece] as a second name. By extension, the piece also speaks to all mothers with grown-up children and to all older women in general.

Dansa is associated with the Khasonka ethnic group and the Khaso region in western Mali. Specifically, it reminds people of social occasions of agricultural contexts, such as harvesting. *Dansa* also relates to the social group of griots (*jeli*), whose urban associations first made the piece popular in the 60s.[12] *Suku*, from a Bamako perspective, belongs to the Maninka people and the Manden region south of Bamako. Young, unmarried women love to dance it, because it refers to its older social context of excision and circumcision rites, that is, to a significant experience in the recent formation of their identities.[13]

The core repertoire can evoke a multitude of social references and cultural associations, and thus can address several segments of the audience at the same time. The core pieces also stand out as they can move flexibly to and from other pieces within the same stretch of playing. *Dansa* and *maraka,* in particular, have annexed and absorbed various other rhythms that today are no longer played as individual pieces in their own right. Such fusions and the resulting increase in programmatic flexibility have further contributed to the core pieces' wealth of meanings. Finally, they are of inherent musical appeal. In the words of jembe drummers, the core pieces' popularity is based on their being suitable for many different dances and songs, and on their ability simply to please everybody:

> *Marakadòn* is well ordered, everyone can dance to it. People like it. And all songs can be set to it. Otherwise, the Maraka [people] themselves sing their songs in their own language. It was the Bamana who adopted *marakadòn* and made it so popular. (Drisa Kone, Bamako, March 14, 1998)
>
> Besides, the jembe players themselves, too, love *marakadòn*. Even if they probably also consider people's expectations: When you tell some jembe players to play something, they will start out immediately with *marakadòn*. (Madu Jakite, Bamako, March 10, 1998)

Table 12.2. Frequency of pieces played in relation to the ethnic identity of the organizing family, out of 120 events

		Bamana (%)	Fulani (%)	Maninka (%)
	dansa	91	100	100
Urban core pieces	*marakadòn/denbafòli*	97	91	100
	suku	91	95	94
	sunun	49	23	29
Urban ethnic pieces	*fulafòli*	17	36	12
	menjani	14	23	59

Source: Author's survey, Bamako, 1997–98.

A Musical Tradition Urbanizes

Until the 1950s, jembe music was one among many traditional celebration music genres carried on in Bamako. It had been a rural practice before. During the 60s and 70s, jembe players urbanized socioeconomically, by professionalizing and commodifying the service of music performance, as well as musically. Musical change concerned form, style, and, as examined in this chapter, repertory.

First, reinterpreting drumming pieces as metaphors of the diverse ethnic and regional origins of migrants served to broaden and integrate the heterogeneous urban audience into a homogeneous framework of celebration culture. Second, a local core repertory emerged. These innovations have allowed for the lasting functionality and popularity of jembe music in the city. Today Bamako jembe players talk of their style as *yanfòli* [local drumming], *bamakòfòli* [Bamako drumming], *dugukònòfòli* [inner-city drumming], or *dugubafòli* [big city drumming]. These expressions suggest the urban professionals think of their style as different from rural styles both locally and in a categorical sense. In their view, theirs is an urban form of music.

Some Bamako professionals and I once performed at a wedding on the urban outskirts. The celebration's participants were of homogeneous ethnic identity (Songhay). It soon became clear that the celebration could not succeed because most of the people present did not know how to dance to our Bamako celebration music. The organizing family only recently had migrated from northern Mali to the city. Most guests were visitors from the countryside. During a short break, a member of the organizing team made an excuse for the celebration being so sluggish: "We are all Songhay. We do not know jembe dancing well." (November 30, 1997) But she obviously, nevertheless, found it proper for a wedding in Bamako to have a jembe ensemble playing. From the immigrant's perspective, jembe dance and drumming represents the customary way to celebrate a Bamako wedding.

The audience's preference for jembe celebration music in Bamako cuts across boundaries of social class and ethnic identity. According to our survey from 1997–98, the largest three ethnic groups among the urban population (Bamana, Maninka, and Fulani) each comprise close to 25 percent of the total number of organizers of jembe celebrations in Bamako.[14] By contrast, the jembe is an important part of the rural celebration culture among only one of these groups (Maninka). In addition, people of about a dozen more ethnic identities from Mali and some from neighboring countries are engaging jembe players in Bamako. Some organizers call both a Bamako based jembe ensemble and a more ethnically specific ensemble on the same occasion. There are two customs of putting the two parties together into the program. First, they sometimes perform by turns. Second, they often perform simultaneously in separate spaces. In this case, the ethnically specific ensembles perform somewhere inside, within the walls of a compound or inside a house, while the jembe performance takes place in the street. An experienced jembe player comments: "Well, you may be of whatever descent, if you find it absolutely necessary, you do your business inside, your affairs, you go and sort them out inside the house. Yet what the Bamako people like, you take it and settle it in the streets. That is a matter of agreement" (Jeli Madi Kuyate, Bamako, February 5, 1998).

In cases of two music ensembles performing the same celebration, one can observe a difference of preferences with regard to the participants' age. As a rule, the majority of younger and medium aged attendees prefer to dance to the jembe, whereas the ethnic ensemble attracts an older audience.

Urban Tradition and Popular Culture

In the 1950s and 60s, Africanist urban anthropology focused on migrants adapting to modernity. Researchers assumed that modern forms of popular culture were an index to urbanization. Conversely, they took what they supposed to be traditional culture as an expression of remaining relationships to rural society, thus of the lack of urbanization. From a European perspective, Bamako then was not a true (modern) city yet. Research misrepresented Bamako's residential areas as large villages. Dance and drum celebrations were among the most colorful clichés in that image.[15]

In his book *Mande Music,* ethnomusicologist Eric Charry (2000: 24, fn. 12) used the concepts of the traditional and the modern to "distinguish sensibilities associated with old musical instruments, genres and styles from more recent ones." Charry placed jembe celebration music on the traditional side, in contrast to guitar, harp, lute, and xylophone players who all can perform in both traditional and modern styles and contexts. People in Bamako, indeed, would rarely think of jembe celebrations as a modern affair. Addressed as *fòli* (percussive celebration music), people distinguish it from *musique,* which is a loanword from French applied mainly to "modern" pop music. *Jenbefòli,* in contrast to *musique,* is not put on stage in the concert context (as it is in Western countries), but rather only in the folkloristic context of state sponsored dance shows meant to represent "traditional" culture. Radio and TV rarely broadcast jembe music. Charry thus seems right in placing jembe celebration culture on the traditional side of this duality; participants in Bamako weddings think of their practice as a local tradition. The problem is that this implicitly equates the traditional with the rural, that is, jembe celebration music as "a village tradition (which can be carried on in urban areas)" (Charry 2000: 194; parentheses in the original). This does not suffice to understand its transformation in the twentieth century. As shown in this chapter, jembe music has not been merely continued, but reinvented in Bamako. About two-thirds of the Bamako repertory, for instance, comes from other music traditions and has been markedly recomposed or rearranged in jembe music performance. This repertory combines aspects of difference, on the one hand, and commonality, on the other, allowing its users (audiences and dance performers) to both culturally distinguish themselves and affirm a common local culture at the same time. In response to the urban audience, resident jembe players have contributed creatively to making urban culture what it is.

Since the 1980s, urban music in Africa has been addressed mostly through the concept of popular culture (or arts). Karin Barber outlined the field in an influential review article:

> Popular art can be taken to mean the large class of new unofficial art forms which are syncretic, concerned with social change, and associated with the masses. The centers of activity in this field are the cities, in their pivotal positions between the rural hinterland on the one hand and the metropolitan countries on the other. (Barber 1987: 23)

Popular culture studies have helped include into academic study the many urban styles of African music, which traditional perspectives of anthropology and ethnomusicology had ignored (Fabian 1978; Coplan 2008; Waterman 1990). It is thus worth discussion whether this concept would also support understanding jembe celebration music as an urban tradition.

Jembe celebration music in Bamako conforms to Barber's (1987) characterization of popular arts in many respects. It forms a vital framework of public interaction and communication, but is not sponsored or disseminated through official channels, spaces, and institutions; it is unofficial art. Responding to social change, it is open to fast musical change. It is syncretic in that it draws on diverse cultural sources, and creatively merges elements of these into a new form.[16] It is lively in the cities where it appeals to large parts of the population across social, ethnic, religious, and other boundaries. It falls perfectly into what, again according to Barber (1987), is a typical economic context of popular art forms in Africa. Individualism, self-employment, competition, and market relationships entail artisan-like, work-oriented attitudes to performance and stimulate personal and generation-specific stylistic differentiation and innovation. Urban jembe celebration music is open to novices. No institutionalized constraints, such as formal apprenticeship, keep young entrants off the labor market. The audience's demand, through the commercialization of the drummers' work, plays an influential role in the production and style of the music (Polak 2005).

On the other side, jembe celebration music differs in important aspects from what is seen as typical of popular arts in Africa. First, it is not mass distributed. Second, while popular culture has been characterized as being relatively free from the normative (e.g. stylistic) constraints supposedly typical of official or traditional culture (Fabian 1978, 1998), jembe music is not. Although there is more space for creativity in urban than in rural jembe playing, it would be wrong to say that urban jembe playing is low in artistic norms. The music labor market filters innovations. Urban professional jembe players experience the market as a restrictive and stylistically homogenizing institution (Polak 2004). Third, urban jembe music is not radically syncretic. The syncretic confluence of indigenous and foreign cultural elements is held to underlie the qualitative novelty attributed to popular musics in Africa (Waterman 1990). The "foreign" is often identified with "Western" cultural items. Jembe players indeed innovate, but continuity and references to pasts and origins are still important to their performance. They indigenize and fuse elements from different cultural sources, but the foreign elements they select do not often come from outside Africa. The urbanization of jembe music rather lives by intra-African cultural confluence (cf. Hampton 1980).

Many African music studies—whether they use the concept of "popular" or not—associate the urban with the modern, cosmopolitan, and the rural with the traditional. The striving for modernization and the cultural appropriation of "Western" elements indeed mark much musical change in urban Africa. The popular culture concept has helped to focus and understand this "absorbing a shock from outside" (Diawara 1997). However, urbanization and modernization are not identical (Coquery-Vidrovitch 1991). The recent history of jembe music shows that traditional arts make a massive and distinct contribution to urban popular culture in West Africa.

ACKNOWLEDGMENTS

I am grateful to the German Research Council (Deutsche Forschungsgemeinschaft, or DFG) for financing the core body of research underlying this chapter in the context of the graduate studies program "Cross-Cultural Relationships in Africa" (1996–99) at Bayreuth University. The present chapter was published in an

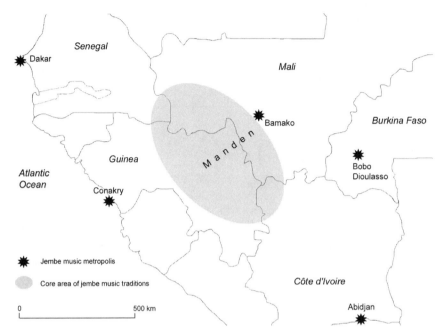

Map 12.1. Urban centers and rural core area of jembe music traditions.

earlier form as "City Rhythms: The Urbanization of Local Drum/Dance Celebration Music in Bamako," in *Experts in Mandé*, ed. Jan Jansen (Leiden: Nederlandse Vereniging van Afrika Studies, 2003). I wish to thank Andreas Meyer and Jan Jansen for many valuable comments and corrections that helped to shape the present text. Finally, I would like to thank Madu Jakite, professional drummer from Bamako, who contributed to collecting statistical data, which underlies many of the chapter's arguments. I dedicate this paper to the memory of Musa Kamara (ca. 1964–2008), mason, dunun player (see figs. 12.2 and 12.7), and the most good-humored person I ever met.

NOTES

1. See M. Gosselin (1953), Villien-Rossi (1966), Meillassoux (1968), Vaa (1990), Sanogo (1993), Westen (1995), Miseli (1998), and Brand (2001) for more detailed demographic data. See INSTAT (2009) for the latest census figures published by the Institut National de la Statistique of the Republic of Mali.

2. See Wirth (1938), J. Mitchell (1966, 1987), and Coquery-Vidrovitch (1991).

3. See Meillassoux (1963, 1968), Villien-Rossi (1966), Diakité (1993), and Sanogo (1993).

4. A note on orthography: Bamana (*bamanankan*) is the vernacular language of Bamako. Bamana terms are spelled according to the dictionary of Bailleul (1996) and set in italics.

Figure 12.1. Bamako wedding celebration. Photo by Rainer Polak, 2007.

Figure 12.2. Dunun player Musa Kamara focuses the head of a group dance; the dunun is a cyclindrical drum accompanying the jembe. Photo by Rainer Polak, 2007.

Figure 12.3. Denba Mme Diallo and age-mate come in for a synchronized duet dance encounter with the lead jembe player, Sedu Balo (right). Photo by Rainer Polak, 2007.

Figure 12.4. Professional singer and animator Mamanin Kante—with microphone, standard equipment at urban weddings—takes a run-up for a solo dance performance. Photo by Rainer Polak, 2007.

Figures 12.5 and 12.6. Jembe players Modibo Kuyate (left) and Sedu Balo at work, performing with women from the audience. Photo by Rainer Polak, 2007.

Figure 12.7. Dunun player Musa Kamara (ca. 1964–2009) earns two 1,000 Franc CFA bills for having called the denba to dance. Photo by Rainer Polak, 2007.

Figure 12.8. Married women, including the celebration's organizer (denba Mme Diallo), enjoy themselves performing a youth dance. Photo by Rainer Polak, 2007.

Figure 12.9. Teenagers enjoy themselves at a self-organized jembe-dance celebration. Photo by Rainer Polak, 1997.

Figure 12.10. Teenagers perform jembe music and dance at a wedding. Photo by Rainer Polak, 1997.

5. The first cylindrical accompanying drum (*dunun*) has a particularly distinctive quality in defining a piece. It also serves as a timeline and phrasing referent. Dancers will often sing it aloud when it is important to unambiguously relate the dance pattern to the musical phrase. The sequence of patterns played by the lead jembe drummer also contributes to identifying each piece. See Polak (2004: 111–48; 2010) for musical analysis and transcriptions.

6. Faulkner and Becker (2009) describe this interactive, processual nature of repertory in the case of jazz.

7. See Reyes-Schramm (1982) on the diversity of repertoire as a marker of the urban in the case of New York City.

8. The *bònkolo* is a wooden, single-headed drum comparable in shape and playing technique (with one bare hand and one light pliable stick) to the Senegalese sabar. The *ngusunbala* is a huge equi-pentatonic xylophone of three and a half octaves.

9. On the original contexts of sabar music in The Gambia and Senegal, see Knight (1974) and Tang (2007).

10. Further ethnonyms used as names of drumming pieces in Bamako are *marakadòn* (Soninke people from the region of Kayes), *manenkamòri* (Maninka of the region of Kankan in Guinea), *fulafòli* (Fulani from the region of Macina in the Niger Delta), *bamanafòli* (Bamana from the Bèlèdugu region), *senufofòli* (Senufo from the region of Sikasso), *minyanka-fòli* (Minyanka from the region of Koutiala), and *bòbòfòli* (Bobo from the region of San).

11. *Furasifòli* is associated with circumcision or excision and is called *suku* in Bamako and other parts of Manden. *Kisa* is associated with agrarian occasions as, for instance, harvesting. *Wurukutu* is a second (uptempo) part to *kisa* and is associated with fast and athletic dancing of youths. *Madan* is known throughout the Manden as well as in Bamako under the same name. It formerly was associated with male dancing on the occasion of political events such as the assumption of power of kings or chiefs.

12. See Meillassoux (1968: 107ff.) and Charry (2000: 268) for more details on the famous Ambiance griot association and its popular wedding celebration music performances.

13. Despite strong internationally sponsored campaigns to eradicate female gender mutilation, as female excision is termed in Western feminist and human rights discourses, it is still practiced, legal, and affirmed by many individuals and groups in Mali. There is also a pro-excision discourse in Mali, arguing that the anti-excision campaigns represent a recent form of Western cultural colonialism (C. Gosselin 2000).

14. While anthropological and historical research has shown the constructedness and fluidity of ethnic identities, jembe musicians and their audiences usually are quite clear about their own ethnic identities and the ethnic affiliations of the jembe pieces that are performed.

15. See M. Gosselin (1953), Villien-Rossi (1966: 253), and Meillassoux (1968: 143–47). For similar views of different West African cities, see Little (1965). For reviews of Africanist urban anthropology, see Hannerz (1980: chap. 4) and Coquery-Vidrovitch (1991).

16. Compare Arnoldi (1987, 1995) on the importance of creativity and innovation to traditional arts in rural Mali.

Music for an African Twenty-First Century

ERIC CHARRY

With such an enormous reputation and legacy as the home of a global diaspora that has so powerfully impacted the lives of so many of the planet's inhabitants, one might expect that Africa's artists would have larger worldwide recognition. But this is not the case. Perhaps doomed by its role as the motherland, the birthplace of humanity and source of inspiration for those outside the continent, Africans have not had an easy time getting their share, except in the low-profile margins of world music and drumming. This irony is not lost on Africa's latest generation. With full, although often sporadic and low-speed, access to real and virtual world cultural currents, young Africans, like the generations who preceded them, want full participation in global culture and not just as a new market of consumers for foreign products. Senegalese world music icon Youssou N'Dour summed up some of this frustration in the midst of Live 8, a 2005 concert in the UK aimed at the Group of 8 (G8) nation leaders about to meet in Scotland: "The cancellation [of debt] is ok, more aid is ok, but open your market for Africa!"[1]

This book is about some of the vital musical currents that young Africans are now creating or continuing to carry on. The several generations before them established a presence and appreciation for African music outside the continent. The generations of the 1990s and 2000s have new challenges, including the onslaught of music from the United States.

While the African continent has nurtured thousands of musical traditions with their own unique repertories, from the very localized to the larger supra-regional, it has also absorbed influences from outside the continent and thoroughly integrated them for many generations. (For a quick sense of the breadth of musical traditions, just multiply the number of African countries-over 50—by the number of local languages in each country—often several dozen—and estimate that each group of language speakers would have at least a few distinct musical genres.) Rap and the larger hip hop culture of which it is a part are but the latest in a long line of foreign imports. A list could include Arab styles of solo chanting spread by Muslims beginning in the seventh century, European styles of sacred (Christian) and secular vocal and instrumental melody and harmony taking root in the nineteenth century, Latin American and Caribbean song, dance, and rhythms beginning in the early twentieth century, and American jazz, rhythm and blues, and rock from the 1950s onward. These imports carry with them the larger musical systems in which they are embedded. All of these influences have been transformed to such an extent that their varied manifestations should rightfully be considered African music or perhaps an African tributary of a global current. Hip hop is currently undergoing a similar process and provides an extraordinary window into processes of musical and cultural change.

In the half-century since the first African musical artist gained international fame in the northern hemisphere (South African Miriam Makeba), only a handful of Africans have broken through the barrier that surrounds the continent when it comes to high profile musical exports. Both Makeba and South African Hugh Masekela breached the Top 40 of the U.S. pop song charts in the 1960s, a feat that has only been accomplished one more time, by Cameroonian Manu Dibango with his "Soul Makossa" in the early 1970s. Masekela's 1968 "Grazing in the Grass" hit number one, an achievement yet to be duplicated by an African.[2] Africans appearing on the rhythm and blues charts have not had a much greater presence. U.S. album chart rankings are not that different, although the London-based Ghanaian-Nigerian-Caribbean group Osibisa did break into both the pop and R&B album charts with their 1971 self-titled LP. Although American chart rankings are not the only barometer of widespread recognition and success for African artists, the United States does have the largest and most visible music market in the world as well as the second largest population of peoples of African descent outside Africa (after Brazil). Africans have had a greater presence in European markets, although still mostly marginal—that is, unless one considers the newfound success of children of African immigrants, such as rappers Serigne Mbaye (Disiz la Peste) and Abd al Malik, and the first French rapper to achieve widespread commercial success, MC Solaar.[3]

The 1980s generation demonstrated the viability of African artists to participate in the arena of international pop music, although on a very modest scale. They also showed how Africans can creatively integrate European, American, and Caribbean musics into their own cultures and produce an original and unique synthesis that speaks to their contemporaries while maintaining a profound grasp of the ironies and paradoxes in such an endeavor. This was the era of the world music market that inspired a new U.S. Grammy category in 1991 (World Music) and then a split into two in 2003 (Contemporary and Traditional).[4] It was an international generation of artists who initially achieved acclaim in their own and neighboring countries, including Youssou N'Dour and Baaba Maal (Senegal), Salif Keita, Ali Farka Toure, Oumou Sangare, and Toumani Diabate (Mali), Mory Kante (Guinea), King Sunny Ade and Fela Kuti (Nigeria), Thomas Mapfumo (Zimbabwe), Ladysmith Black Mambazo (South Africa), and Angelique Kidjo (Benin). Now, more than two decades later, this generation, mostly in their fifties and sixties (or deceased), remain the gold standard both within and outside Africa, representing the aspirations of Africans who grew up in the decades immediately before and after political independence.

But what of the young African generations of the 1990s and 2000s? The major story, as it is everywhere else in the world, is hip hop. But there are other stories. Jamaican reggae and its compatriot ragga (a kin to American rap dating from the 1980s) continue to inspire Africans. African gospel music, sometimes similar but not identical to its African American relative, and sometimes based on local styles, such as highlife, is thriving. Jembe drumming, first introduced to audiences around the world in the 1950s and 1960s by tours of Guinean national ballets, took off in the 1990s as African drummers fanned out around the world, performing and teaching, stimulating interest and opportunities back home. These drummers might stand as a model for how youth can continue and uphold the legacy of long-standing traditions and still successfully adapt and flourish in the modern world. And then there are the inheritors of the spirit of the 1980s generation, those who continue to mine their local traditions and shape them for contemporary audiences. In this chapter I take up some of the compelling concerns confronting Africans as they participate in these music cultures.

A Globalization/Authenticity Nexus in Hip Hop

Perhaps the most controversial and urgent concern among the young African hip hop generation is how to embrace, shape, and use hip hop so that it can function as an authentic expression of their identity. This concern is not unique to Africa. Few places in the world today are untouched by hip hop culture, and youth are challenged everywhere with making it—the music, dance, fashion, ways of speaking, living, and relating to authority—their own. In Africa, though, there are the added factors of being the ancestral homeland of not only those who created hip hop, but, also of part of their cultural legacy. The role of that African legacy within African American culture remains a subject of much debate, captured in the opposition or continuing dialogue between roots (inherited from Africa) and routes (developed in diaspora). The return trip home of that legacy filtered through centuries of African American experience in the form of hip hop was nothing short of explosive.

Two terms can help capture overarching interrelated phenomena which are at play in the dispersion and reception of hip hop culture around the world: globalization and authenticity. Both terms are highly charged and overworked. Globalization as a historical process (as opposed to an ideology) can refer to the ever-increasing flow of people, goods, and ideas around the world and the varied impacts. These flows and circulations are neither random nor even-handed, but can be heavily weighted and can move in diverse directions covering diverse territories. "The possible trajectories of cultural globalization," Zeleza (2006: 23) has noted, "can range from hegemonization to homogenization to heterogenization to hy-

bridization." Globalization, including the dispersion of hip hop in Africa, can sometimes lead to a deepening of interest in, and even revitalization of, local culture,
just as it can lead to blind hero worship based on some of the most negative stereotypes around.[5] Original engagements with the way things work on the ground presented in this book provide compelling studies of some of these varied responses.[6]

Hip hop going global can provoke two axes or overlapping fields of responses
from those who embrace it outside the United States. One axis sees hip hop as
an expression primarily of contemporary African American urban youth culture,
which serves as a model. By adopting ways of speaking, rapping, moving, and
dressing of African American hip hop artists, participants consider themselves
close or true to the source. The other axis sees hip hop as a malleable, indeed universal form whose core lies in its ability to enable youth to speak to local concerns.
Here participants downplay the necessity of racial identification in favor of being
true to oneself, that is, representing one's own locality, concerns, and culture.[7]

White Australian hip hoppers provide a strong statement of support for the latter axis, "derived not from color or race, but from truthfulness to oneself ... [thus]
it is okay to be white and into Hip Hop as long as you don't misrepresent who you
are" (Maxwell 2003: 161, quoted in Harrison 2008: 1794).[8] Pennycook (2007: 98)
refers to this idea as "the global spread of a culture of being true to the local." The
internal tensions in the two-pronged "global spread of authenticity" (98) offered
by hip hop, then, offer participants a spectrum of options in how they can relate to
both its African American culture of origin and their own local cultures. However,
there are some stakes involved, as Harrison (2008: 1791) notes regarding scholarly
writing, of "failing to acknowledge black American contributions to national and
global culture ... [or] celebrating multiculturalism with a blind eye to power relations." Both axes must be in play.[9]

Ranges of Authenticities

Authenticity and identity remain hot-button issues these days. The meanings of these terms can be quite fluid and easily challenged and critiqued, but they
still can be effective fields for analysis, especially given that people use them in
everyday conversation and writing.[10] In the introductory chapter to this volume
I quoted a usage of authenticity by DJ Sidney, who said that Afrika Bambaataa's
presence "helped give [his TV] show authenticity." Below I quote Manthia Diawara,
who referred to a perception that Bamako youth enamored with rock and roll in
the 1960s "were mimicking the culture of the colonizer, which shut the door to authentic self-actualization." Sidney's usage points to authenticity as being close to
the source of a tradition. Diawara's usage points to being true to one's self by being
true to one's culture. These three areas—point of origin, individuality, and group
(cultural, social, ethnic) identity—are the major flash points.

The key questions, at least from an ethnomusicological perspective, are not
whether something is authentic or not or how authentic it is. These will always be

up for debate based in large part on personal taste and agenda. (An artist can easily strike one listener as being real or sincere and another as being fake; and both listeners can be right.) But, rather, what are the criteria of authenticity used by the artist and audience, what codes are they drawing on to establish an authentic presence, and, on a more basic level, why is it so important to establish one's authenticity in the first place?

McLeod's (1999) systematic investigation of the importance of authenticity and how it is invoked in American hip hop can help establish a solid foundation against which related efforts outside the United States can be contextualized. He examined hip hop magazines (over a six-month period), internet discussion groups (three-month period), song lyrics (six-year period), and press releases (six-month period), and collected more than 800 authenticity claims, or "symbols of authenticity discourse," which he defined as any appearance of the words *true, real,* or *authentic* (or their various derivatives) in relation to the genre. Based on this body of data he formulated six distinct but interrelated categories ("semantic dimensions of meaning") of authenticity that are drawn upon by hip hop artists, fans, and critics. He then conducted twenty-three interviews with a wide range of hip hop artists to test the validity of his categories. McLeod found that invocations of authenticity (perhaps the most common being "keeping it real") "are performed often, resonate deeply, and are widely shared by members of the hip-hop community . . . to maintain that culture's identity" (137–38).[11]

McLeod's six dimensions were each exemplified by two opposing terms or concepts. In each of his following pairings, the first was considered "real" (authentic) and the second was considered "fake" (inauthentic) with regard to hip hop.

1. Social-psychological: staying true to yourself versus following mass trends
2. Racial: black versus white
3. Political-economic: underground versus commercial
4. Gender-sexual: hard versus soft
5. Social-locational: the street versus the suburbs
6. Cultural: old school (a culture with a history) versus mainstream (a contemporary commodity offered up on the radio or TV) (McLeod 1999: 139)

McLeod richly illustrated each of his dimensions. For example, what Wu-Tang Clan member Method Man told McLeod (1999: 140) fits squarely into the social-psychological construct: "I make music that represents me. Who I am. I'm not gonna calculate my music to entertain the masses. I gotta keep it real for me." A line from Tupac Shakur's "I Ain't Mad at Cha" provided an example of the social-locational (it could also function in the economic dimension): "I moved up out of the ghetto, so I ain't real now?" (143). And so on. As hip hop was increasingly gaining mainstream acceptance in the mid- and late 1990s, when McLeod was collecting his data, those closest to the culture invested heavily in asserting and guarding their authenticity.[12]

Ten years later, Harrison (2008: 1784) reviewed how academics in the social sciences wrote about hip hop authenticity and race. The two prongs are present here. In the 1990s one group of scholars emphasized that hip hop was a fundamentally, if not exclusively, black genre. In contrast, other scholars emphasized "hip hop's ability to cross social borders and engage a range of racial/ethnic subjects" forming a bond among urban youth and becoming the voice of a generation, "facilitating pan-ethnic coalitions rooted in culture and politics rather than color," where attitude more than race determines legitimacy (1790).[13]

The creative career of Afrika Bambaataa illustrates some of the subtleties of race and hip hop's origins, which may not be fully appreciated both outside and within the United States. Bambaataa's credentials as a former gang member turned peacekeeper and DJ in the 1970s are impeccable. His musical taste as a DJ was eclectic, drawing heavily on his desire to challenge his African American Bronx NY audience, playing, for example, white rock and European electronica. His classic "Planet Rock" was the result of a close collaboration with producer Arthur Baker and musician John Robie (both of whom are white).[14] This was hip hop before the days of sampling. Marley Marl, who interned with Baker, is widely credited with inventing sample-based hip hop in the mid-1980s. Hank Shocklee, architect of Public Enemy's sound, which exemplified the sample-based genre, was not shy about crediting the engineers (who are white and Asian American) on their classic album *It Takes a Nation of Millions* as "geniuses when it comes to sound and making stuff sound amazing. To me, those guys were just as important to creating the sound of Public Enemy as we were in terms of producing it and making all the beats. They knew how to get anything I needed done" (Shocklee in Buskin 2010).[15] While Shocklee may be generous in his assessment of the relative value of creative input, still, black artists, especially those who were iconic of blackness in the genre, were not averse to collaborating with whites in creating, shaping, and realizing their sound (not their lyrics or vocal flow, to be sure). And, as noted in the introductory chapter, Bambaataa was the one who encouraged his admirers in France not to imitate African American culture, but rather to make hip hop locally meaningful, to rap in their own language. While the cultural environment and aesthetics of rap are firmly rooted in African American communities, both that environment and those aesthetics were partly shaped in conversation within a broader American cultural context, not as insular as some might imply and not always as a resistance movement.

African Authenticity

Authenticity as a concept and practice had official sanction in postcolonial Africa and was crucial in the formation of independent nations. Joseph-Désiré Mobuto, who became president of the Democratic Republic of the Congo in a coup in 1965, formulated a policy of *authenticité* that included eliminating the colonial names of cities and streets, establishing fashion codes that favored African dress, and greeting foreign heads of state with drumming (Adelman 1975). (He changed his country's name to the Republic of Zaire in 1971 and his own name in 1972 to Mobutu Sese Seko, the shortened form of a much longer name.) Similar fashion codes were put in place in the 1960s in newly independent socialist countries such as Tanzania (Perullo, this volume) and Mali (Manthia Diawara 2005: 248).[16]

Sekou Toure, first president of the Republic of Guinea, was a pioneer in establishing regional and national music and dance groups that mined local culture to forge a new national identity. Toure saw African culture as "truly flourish[ing] . . . in the villages amongst the common people, whose mentalities and social behaviour are the authentic foundation of African humanism" (Toure in 1963 cited in Dave 2009: 458). This notion of village authenticity was drawn upon and expanded by creative urban artists, both those who came up in those village traditions and those who received colonial-era training in European music, choreography, and staging technique. Toure's efforts, replicated by many African governments, were part of a larger movement in Africa to shed foreign influences in favor of a more authentic African identity. That authenticity could be constructed anew, does not negate, devalue, or ridicule the concept, but rather enriches it. The same goes for identity.[17]

Having struggled to form their own national identities in the wake of political independence, it must have come as a shock to that generation to see a new form of colonization taking over their grandchildren, but this time from the diaspora. The opening minutes of an excellent documentary about Kenyan hip hop lays out the problem. After showing film footage of colonial era Kenya, anticolonial resistance, and then independence celebrations in the 1960s, the narrator says:

> Today, Kenya tackles a new breed of colonization. . . . Its chameleon-like quality has allowed it to integrate with cultures around the world. . . . It is hip hop and it has arrived without warning. . . . In the vein of colonialism it's dictating the choice of attire [shot of a young Kenyan male wearing a do-rag and Allen Iverson NBA basketball shirt], language, and lifestyle in general. Unlike the colonists, its presence is welcomed and widely embraced by the majority. (*Hip Hop Colony*, Wanguhu 2007)

Discussions of authenticity are complicated by expanded notions of home. For example, Ghanaian hiplife founder Reggie Rockstone spent much of his early life in London and New York (Shipley, this volume). Nana King was raised in Los Angeles, where he performed with Tupac Shakur, and returned to Ghana where he raps in English (Collins, this volume). Positive Black Soul co-founder Amadou Barry (aka Doug E. Tee) spent much of his early life in France. And Bamboo (Simon Kimani) of the Kenyan group K-South grew up in Los Angeles before being sent to a Kenyan boarding school because he fell in with the wrong crowd.[18]

Identities in African hip hop, either implicitly assumed or explicitly claimed, can be rooted in age group, gender, place (a particular neighborhood, quartier, or city), nationality, ethnicity (expressed by language choice), global citizenship (being a cosmopolitan), or race, which can range from being African (or Nubian or Azanian) to black (a member of a large diaspora). Other kinds of traditional identities, such as those of lineage and social class, appear to be less relevant for recent generations of African youth, although neighborhood can stand in for economic class. Taking on stage names, which totally obscure the identifying powers of family names, can be seen as a sign of refuting traditional associations.

If one mark of authenticity in American commercial rap is membership in a marginalized African American youth underclass (McLeod's "black" and "street"), then how can African youth striving to go beyond imitation, who reject glorification of sex, narcotics, crime, violence, and materialism, establish their credentials? One way is to claim their Africanness (more specific than "black"), something like an ancestral birthright. Another is to claim the moral and educational high ground in accordance with African values in which they were brought up. This latter stance is fraught with paradoxes.

From the very beginning of rap's development, with Afrika Bambaataa and his Zulu Nation, Africa was privileged, although not necessarily verbalized, as the source and homeland of African Americans and their culture. Afrika Bambaataa (born Kevin Donovan) named himself after the early twentieth century Zulu chief Bhambatha, who fought South African colonial forces. The combination of visiting Africa in his teens (as a result of winning an essay-writing contest) and being inspired by the Hollywood film *Shaka Zulu,* led him to choose his name and form the peacekeeping cultural organization Zulu Nation. In the early 1990s Afrocentrism, in the form of dress, proclaiming African roots, and referring to oneself as African, became more public in U.S. rap. Some kind of connection with Africa, therefore, no matter how symbolic, seemed important for some African American hip hop artists.[19]

Schulz (this volume) notes that some Malian rappers draw on their blackness, that is, membership in the larger diasporic community, which allies them with African Americans, and also their Africanness, which gives them an authenticity that their African American brothers and sisters do not have. Furthermore, they claim that their role as conservative moral forces is deeply rooted in African culture, thereby giving them an African authenticity that is beyond that of American rappers.[20] But this kind of diasporic and moral authenticity, Schulz notes, is countered by some of their compatriots who, seeing their attachment to foreign cultural values and distance from local traditional music, dismiss rappers' claims to authenticity.

Drawing on blackness can have a more expansive meaning in South Africa and North Africa. In Cape Town, where hip hop first took root in South Africa, rappers whose genealogies connect them to places outside Africa as well as within (those called colored in the apartheid system) draw on a variety of symbols in embracing a black consciousness. Battersby (2003) has identified four in particular that show up in lyrics, record label and album names, and album artwork. African American culture is one obvious symbol, which aligns with aspects of their Cape Town community's experience, such as a history of servitude and struggle for civil rights and a direct line of musical influence beginning in the late nineteenth century brought in by African American minstrel troupes, jubilee singers, and later jazz musicians. "Ghetto" symbolizes a shared sense of exclusion and oppression. "Azania," initially used in East Africa and perhaps derived from Arabic or Persian meaning "land of the blacks," refers to an ancient African unity symbolizing both resistance and continental pride. And the very local "District Six" refers to a Cape Town area that was the scene of forced removal in 1966 to make room for whites.[21]

In North Africa, Angela Williams (2010: 68, 84–86) notes three themes in identity construction in Egyptian hip hop: nationalism, pan-Arabism, and connective marginality (a reference to Osumare 2007). The first two localize the genre, in the sense of being true to one's culture. The third makes the connection to hip hop's African American roots, specifically by using an African American English dialect and by referring to themselves as "niggas" or "sand niggas." MC Brownfingaz from Marrakesh, Morocco, defends his use of the term: "I feel like I have a right to use it, because I'm African. I ain't white. . . . [Nigga] carries a lot of other senses apart from being black, because it ain't all about being black, it's about being an underdog" (in *I Love Hip Hop in Morocco,* Asen and Needleman 2007).

The descriptors "underground," "socially conscious," and "educate" are inextricably linked to authenticity in African hip hop. What goes for Kenya is representative across the continent:

> The underground Hip-Hop group of Kalamashaka [and others] . . . hold the view that their own kind of music is the authentic Hip-Hop . . . other than entertainment, the main focus . . . is to inform, educate, and enlighten the public. . . . Because of the "socially conscious" message they seek to propagate . . . [they] consider themselves revolutionaries. They aspire to embrace the classical meaning of Hip-Hop (Wetaba 2009: 175).

Baker (2002: 56), who analyzed Dakar's rap scene in 2001, found a similar common thread of three hip hop values in her conversations and interviews: educate your audience, tell your truth, and start a message. A socially conscious African hip hop, just like the American variety, may have taken some time to develop. South African hip hop pioneers Emile YX and Shamiel X told Lee Watkins (this volume) that writers can be inclined to misrepresent initial stages of hip hop in South Africa as being part of the anti-apartheid struggle; in the 1990s and 2000s, however, there has been a strong sense of an underground, which contrasts with the commercial industry.[22]

Another claim for authenticity concerns rappers referring to themselves as griots, likening themselves to oral historians, journalists, or the moral conscience of their society. Tang (this volume) discusses the subtleties and paradoxes of this position, distinguishing between African griots engaging in a hereditary profession that has been part of their lineage for generations and those who appropriate some of their roles, picking and choosing without having the traditional authority to do so. Key paradoxes include the attachment of griots to the ruling class and their tarnished reputation as opportunistic praise singers, both of which run counter to a rebel hip hop sensibility. As Tang shows, some Senegalese rappers are well aware of these problems, which either escape the sensibilities of those outside Africa or are simply ignored.

In Tanzania, an ironic understanding of authenticity took root early on when some insisted on rapping in English and staying true to the American form. The group Kwanza Unit had an "underground" aesthetic, taking an "anti-populist, purist vision, catering more toward what they saw as the ideals of the genre. They considered themselves underground, as opposed to those who wanted to commercialize and rap in local languages" (Perullo 2007: 261). Here is a case of some Tanzanian youth claiming authenticity to hip hop by staying as close as possible to the American source, while others who tried to personalize the genre to make it speak to their own situations were viewed as commercializing and diluting the genre. Similarly, as Fenn (this volume) notes, imported musics held greater cosmopolitan appeal and carried higher status in Malawi.

Striking a balance between local authenticity and global citizenship is an important concern for many African youth. Ghanaian hiplife pioneers Reggie Rockstone and Rab Bakari consciously crafted their music for multiple audiences, including Ghanaians at home and non-Ghanaians abroad. While explaining the importance of having a Kenyan term to name a style (called *genge*), rapper Nonini (and a second unidentified rapper) were clear about their intentions.

> [speaking in Sheng, quotation marks indicate English:] Kenyan music is called "Kenyan" or "local. Local??!!" It's not some illicit brew. . . . Just a "local artist." Damn it, that name sucks. "Who? This is just another local artist. . . . local music." We do not want that tag. "So we want a name for our music. We are trying to build a name for our music." (*Hip Hop Colony*, Wanguhu 2007)

Granting a name to their music distinguishes it as a unique form of expression and not just a tributary or backwater.[23]

Language Choice

A fundamental paradox confronting African rap artists concerns language choice. The more they shape the genre to reflect and express their own experience, the more they rely on African languages and the less their chances of being understood by an international audience. Language choice is not a simple matter of colonial, yet international European versus authentic, yet local African. For example, Reed (this volume) notes that French is so common and internalized in Côte d'Ivoire that it has lost much of its colonial associations. But more fundamentally, English or French are the only languages that can be used to communicate across the continent.

The balance between local and wider communication can shift over time. As Collins (this volume) notes, on the one hand, some rappers see the new very popular jama style in Ghana (using local languages) as too parochial for an international audience, stimulating a return to English. On the other hand, Perullo and Fenn (2003: 49) note that Mr. II, a pioneer of rapping in Swahili, "realized that Western audiences desire to hear African languages, like Swahili in African music. He explained that most Tanzanian artists realize this as well and switched from English to Swahili in an effort to sell their music internationally."

Perullo and Fenn (2003: 20) have noted that Tanzanian emcees use English to rap about life's pleasures and their own prowess and use Swahili to move away from this kind of celebratory rap to focus on social problems pertinent to Tanzania.[24] But they caution about hard and fast dichotomies, pitting English against Swahili or Chichewa (in Malawi). As with French in many ex-colonies, English has been used in Africa for a long time, and so it is not that foreign. Both English and African languages are viable choices, but with different shades of meaning.

The cases of Tanzania and Malawi illustrate some of the subtle strands that can distinguish neighboring countries from each other. German and then British colonial policy encouraged the widespread use of Swahili in Tanganyika, fearing a threat of Africans learning the colonial language. As a result, Swahili dominates throughout Tanzania (and some neighboring regions). English, dominant in politics and economics, is understood by a minority. The affluent youth who first picked up rap used English. A group like Kwanza Unit had a niche audience: affluent East African youth familiar with American and European cultures. In the mid- and late 1990s, when independent radio played more foreign than local music, rapping in English was more beneficial and it was better produced. From mid-1999 Swahili rap with improved production values swelled the market and became popular for building a national hip hop culture. Mr. II's 1998 album *Niite Mr. II* was the first highly successful album of Swahili rap since Saleh J's pioneering effort in 1992 (Perullo and Fenn 2003: 26–33).

Contrasting with neighboring Tanzania, in Malawi English is the language of educational instruction and Chichewa symbolizes historical (pre-1994) dominance of one region in Malawian politics and economics (Perullo and Fenn 2003: 35). As in Tanzania, rapping in English in Malawi involves boasting and lighter messages; Chichewa is more apt for conveying more significant and positive social messages. In other countries English and French may indeed be flexible enough to serve both purposes. In Egyptian rap, English, which more typically signifies prestige and elitism, has been turned around to "express resistance against the English-speaking world" (A. Williams 2010: 68–70).

In Francophone countries, the option of using three languages—the colonial language (French), the mother tongue of rap (English), and an African mother tongue—is always there. In Positive Black Soul's "New York/Paris/Dakar," a song that clearly engages this tripartite heritage, the three languages come rapid fire one after the other:

> I came all the way from Senegal speakin' Wolof
> *Xam nga fii ma jogee baby mingi tuddu Jollof*
> [You know where I come from, baby, it's a place called Djollof]
> *Alors, d'accord encore on partage la même passion*
> [So yeah, it's true we share the same passion]
> *Le même micro et là ma foule la même nation.*
> [The same micro, and here my posse, the same nation.][25]
> (Positive Black Soul, "New York/Paris/Dakar")

Faada Freddy, of the Senegalese rap group Daara J, understands the problem and also the importance of getting a message across.

> Lee Kasumba (Radio YFM, South Africa): There's a big debate about the whole language issue. You guys rhyme in . . . Wolof and you also rhyme in French and English. When you go to different countries . . . does language ever become an issue, or how do you get your message across?
>
> Faada Freddy: Yeah, the thing is we have to stick to our native language because it's beautiful, Wolof, it's beautiful. If you use Swahili or, you know, another African language . . . you stick to it and . . . show it out. Because it's important to show the real value of the African image that it's beautiful. . . . But at the same time we need to get understood. So, therefore, we tryin' to make a junction of our culture, our native language, but at the same time we tryin' to deal with other languages. This makes ourselves, you know, understood, and makes the people get the message, you know, which is very important. Because, I think, above all, hip hop is a matter of message, you know . . . the most important thing for us is to show the new image of this young African generation, which is a very ambitious generation, and a very strong generation . . . to give a prop that Africa is not that land of misery that everybody is imagining. (africanhiphop.com, episode 1, January 2005, 54:00)

The significance of a message is pervasive throughout Africa.[26]

Not only is language choice a fundamental decision, but so is the dialect. As Kidula (this volume) notes, it was not until Kenyans began rapping in Sheng, an urban slang mixing Swahili, English, and whatever local African language is predominant, that they gained an audience. Sheng belongs to Kenyan youth, although it has spread to Swahili speakers in neighboring countries. Not only did English alienate singers from the Kenyan conditions they claimed to represent, notes Kidula, but Sheng had the advantage of being flexible enough so that it could represent not just a country or city but even a neighborhood. Such was the case with Kalamashaka's "Tafsiri Hii," which moved rap to a national level in Kenya in 1999. Nigerian rap emerged in the mid-1990s, embedded in pidgin English, which ensured a wide audience that cut across class and ethnic boundaries (Shonekan, this volume). Shipley (this volume) notes that Reggie Rockstone could switch not only between Twi and pidgin (a Ghanaian hybrid with English), but also between Ghanaian and African American English dialects. This fluency and ease of code-switching appealed to the lifestyles of the urban community of young Accra hiplifers. Rockstone's seamless rapping alternating between English and Twi (translated with English subtitles) at the opening of the documentary *Living the Hiplife* (Shipley 2007) is one of the more expert demonstrations of the kind of linguistic sophistication that rap outside the United States can achieve.[27]

The Messages

The messages of much African rap, especially its social consciousness and global vision, are one of its most significant distinguishing features, certainly compared to its American counterpart. In a continent that hosts more than its share of the world's economically poorest nations, young Africans are aware of the catastrophic ills that can plague society. Despite the almost insuperable shadow cast by American rap around the world, the messages conveyed in African rap have assumed a degree of importance that has helped it survive the onslaught from its wealthier progenitor.

HIV/AIDS awareness, unemployment, government corruption, lack of opportunity, the sometimes marginal position of women, and the erosion of moral values are common topics in African rap. African emcees often see themselves, and are seen by their peers, as educators (Fenn and Schulz, this volume). In Ghana, the National Theater Festival took advantage of rap's potential and prescribed educational themes for its participants, such as abstinence and AIDS awareness, discouraging themes of love and violence (Shipley, this volume).

The political potential of African rap, that is, its ability to raise awareness of social issues and impact change, has been surveyed extensively by Künzler (2007, 2011b). Documentary films are often drawn to the political advocacy aspect of African hip hop. For example, *Democracy in Dakar* is set around the 2007 presidential election in Senegal and the role of rap artists in mobilizing youth. Whether this is more a function of the interests of documentary filmmakers or perhaps that emcees in some countries are more politicized than in other countries, hip hop in Senegal has drawn youth into the arena of social and political critique in a big way. The role of rap artists such as Balti and El General (Hamada Ben Amor) has been widely recognized as being integral to the recent revolution in Tunisia (Curry 2011). And the international nongovernmental children's rights organization Plan enlisted the seventeen-member rap collective AURA (Artistes Unis pour le Rap Africain) to produce an album, video, and a touring musical comedy. Launched in 2006, their Poto-Poto campaign for awareness about young people's problems in Africa features some of the most well known hip hop artists from ten, mostly Francophone African countries.[28]

While African rap may provide strong critiques of contemporary social situations, it also provides messages of optimism, as noted above in the interview with Faada Freddy, who hopes to convey the beauty of Africa. The very name Positive Black Soul reflects this: "Our objective is to make the maximum number of people outside of Africa understand that we don't live in trees. To show the positive side of the black soul" (Didier Awadi in Winders 2006: 159). Nationalism appears frequently as a point of pride. Whereas American rappers often refer to the specific neighborhood or housing project where they grew up (see McLeod's "street" above), Africans would more typically take pride in their country and their more general identity as Africans.[29] Some notable exceptions include the Kenyan hit "Tafsiri Hii," which references the Dandora neighborhood of Nairobi, the Malawian group C.O.B. Connection (named after their neighborhood), who have a strong ethos of representing where they come from, and the Ghanaian group VIP, who similarly represent Nima, one of the poorest sections of Accra (see Kidula, Fenn, and Shipley, this volume).[30]

Reggae as a genre has connotations regarding its messages that distinguish it from rap, making it useful and effective in certain political and social circumstances. In Malawi and Côte d'Ivoire, as Seebode and Reed show in this volume, reggae has been used to symbolize a collective resistance to oppression (a "we" ethos). This contrasts with the more individual, self-centered ethos of rap. Malawian and Ivoirian reggae singers, such as Lucius Banda and Tiken Jah Fakoly, consciously used the genre to make explicit political and social critiques of the goings-on in their countries.

Seebode (this volume) poses the question about whether rap artists have any effect on social reality. This can be hard to gauge, although rap and hip hop may indeed be the primary means of mobilizing youth. To what ends—whether there are specific plans and platforms—is an open question. African governments and nongovernmental organizations alike, that is, symbols of authority, have used hip hop to send out positive messages and to mobilize youth, and youth actively participate in these efforts, suggesting that it can function in diverse ways, with anti-authoritarian rebellion being just one among many options.[31]

Gospel music, including gospel rap, so popular in Anglophone countries, by definition, thrives on its positive messages. As Kidula (this volume) notes for Kenyans, rap has become the space for political and social lobbying while gospel is for moralizing, although its artists may also provide social critique.

Profanity and Gun Culture

While profanity in rap lyrics is much less widespread in Africa than in the United States, it still can be a major cause for concern. There appears to be a significant difference between rap in Francophone countries, many of which are predominantly Muslim and may see less public profanity (e.g., Senegal, Mali), and Anglophone countries, which have large Christian populations (e.g., Ghana, Nigeria, Kenya). Another factor may be having a socialist political past, as in Tanzania where there is a history of government intervention and censorship.

Probably the biggest factor regulating profanity is the continued strength and importance of family ties. Nehabi, a female MC from South Africa, explains:

> There are certain things that I won't say, you know, that are going to embarrass my family. You know, I mean, I think that's a huge thing in terms of Africa, like, you don't, your family plays a bigger role. . . . So I think that's why you have a lot less men going out there and, you know, speaking about women in derogatory ways in their music in terms of what's going on in hip hop in Africa in comparison to everywhere else, you know. Because you answer to your family more directly here than anywhere else. (*Counting Headz,* Magubane and Offer 2006)

When there is vulgarity, or perhaps just a youthful aggressiveness, African adults point to its foreignness. The South African parents of a teenaged female aspiring rapper are probably representative of many African parents and their children:

> Father: There is this music that have started, I don't know where it comes from.
> Mother: It's so vulgar, sure.
> Father: It's as if somebody's looking at you and, you know, telling you where to get off. So really, if that is a new trend, or an introduced culture. It's not our culture. (*Mix,* Dzuguda 2004)

Shipley (this volume) has similarly quoted a member of the Ghanaian National Commission on Culture complaining that rap is not a Ghanaian tradition and that it "encourages kids to ignore . . . proper Ghanaian values of respect." Collins (this volume) notes that the International Federation of Women Lawyers in Ghana threatened lawsuits against radio stations for playing recordings with misogynist hiplife lyrics. But, as Collins observes, such lyrics also function to mark the younger generation and distance them from older people. Seebode (this volume) makes a similar point about marking off generational differences, quoting the violent and graphic sexual lyrics of Malawian born, Dublin-based MC Pop Dogg. Shonekan (this volume) quotes a Nigerian poet and professor who objects to the loss of one's identity in favor of the "borrowed clichéd mask of the other."

Senegalese rappers are adamant that vulgarity, especially public disrespect of women, is not part of their culture.[32] Senegal is a devoutly Muslim country, where Sufi sects predominate, allowing, even encouraging, music and dance. In Tanzania, roughly 35 percent Muslim and 30 percent Christian on the mainland and predominantly Muslim on the island of Zanzibar, rappers shy away from vulgarity and radio DJs do not accept it for airplay (Perullo 2005: 96; 2007: 264–65; Lemelle 2006: 240–41). Perullo and Fenn (2003: 27, 47) suggest that the strong socialist legacy may be responsible for a priority put on socially productive lyrics with educational value. I would add that this may not be the only reason stopping youth looking to rebel in a liberalizing environment from assimilating American images of sex and violence. Such imagery just may not be relevant to young males in African Muslim societies.

Along with profanity, gun culture is also less relevant or fascinating for many young Africans. They have other problems to worry about, as expressed by the emcee JJC.

> The only thing I would say that is different from the Nigerian artists and the American artists is the language and the gun culture. We don't have that much of a gun culture. We don't like it. We want to live. We want to survive, we got too much drama already. We don't need no more Kill you Kill you. No, let's enjoy life, let's talk about how creative you can use words. Your language and other languages, and how well you can twist up and make it as best 8- or 16- bar or 36-bars. It's how clever you are. People out there are reading dictionaries and learning words so that they can be the best lyricists. That's what is African, that's what's happening right now. (JJC in *Afrolution,* Birch et al. 2005)

Canadian-based K'Naan simply notes that violence is a part of everyday life in his native Somalia, and so it is neither special nor glorifiable, but rather uncool and a sign of misfortune (Pennycook and Mitchell 2009: 31).[33]

Africanizing the Music

While rapping about African concerns in African languages seems like an obvious step for a uniquely African hip hop to emerge, drawing on local music can be a more difficult undertaking; it also took longer to take root. One reason may be that African hip hop crews are less connected with local musical culture and therefore unprepared to make the synthesis. A number of solutions have arisen.

One strategy is to invite guest artists to add local flavor, a favorite device in Senegal and Mali. Another strategy is to program a keyboard to sound like an African instrument. A third strategy is to sample African recordings, either providing the main musical foundation for a piece or as added color. Didier Awadi's first solo album, *Parole d'honneur—Kaddu Gor* (2002), uses all three devices. The introduction to "Patrimoine" has a keyboard programmed to sound like a kora (21-string harp), "Neye Leer" is based on a kora pattern played by guest Kawding Cissokho, and "Mandjou 2002" is based on a sample of the late 1970s hit "Mandjou" by the Malian group Les Ambassadeurs (featuring Salif Keita). Awadi's first album with Positive Black Soul, *Salaam* (1996), similarly uses the kora and various Senegalese percussion instruments, although they typically remain subservient to the drum set and synthesizers.[34]

Collins (this volume) provides examples of these strategies for Ghanaian hiplife: rapping over short samples of highlife songs, rapping over whole highlife songs, remaking highlife songs with rap, collaborating with highlife artists, and using

Ghanaian drum rhythms or instruments. The ready acceptance of highlife as a distinctly Ghanaian genre of music bodes well for the acceptance of hiplife as a Ghanaian genre. As Collins indicates, highlife is a generic term for various mid-twentieth-century styles with foreign origins. Shipley (this volume) points to Akyeame's 1999 song "Masan Aba" (or "Mesan Aba"), which was perhaps the first originally produced hiplife song to combine elements of highlife, Twi language rap, local humor, storytelling, and hip hop.[35]

African Convergences/Revitalizing Local Traditions

As a move toward claiming the African origins of rap, some point to African traditions that are similar in some way. Africans appear to acknowledge that rap did not directly emerge from these traditions, but rather suggest that convergences indicate that rap is indeed African-based, finally returning home. Almost any place in Africa can claim some relation to rap, given the pervasiveness of oratory and percussion traditions, many of which are uncanny in their resemblances. The title track of Daara J's 2003 album *Boomerang* explicitly makes the claim: "Rap music was born in Africa, grown in America and it went around the world to come back to Africa like a boomerang" (Tang, this volume). Although sometimes specifics might be given, at other times the claims are quite generic, as in the following from an aspiring South African female emcee.

> It's got African origins, you know. Like break dancing, you can see it used to be like fight dancing for African tribes. You can trace some of the moves to that, you know. Even rapping, like African poetry the way it was said, the drums, everything, man, it reflects Africa. (*Mix*, Dzuguda 2004)

In Senegal, the poetic form taasu performed by women bears great similarities with rap, and rappers cite this as an ancestor, although perhaps not literally. Tang's interview with Didier Awadi (this volume) reveals that he is aware enough of both the similarities, to claim the connection, and the differences, to understand that a direct link may just be a purely rhetorical gesture. In Mali, the Bamana musical form called baara, in which young people direct criticism at authority, can be cited to establish a historical continuity with rap (Schulz, this volume). In Tanzania, young and old alike point to ngoma (local drum and dance traditions) as bearing similarities, if only in spirit rather than actual sound (Perullo, this volume). In some Kenyan rap, self-praise and ways of introducing oneself may have a direct connection with Luo lyrical and epic practice (Kidula, this volume; Nyairo and Ogude 2005). In Ghana, generations-old royal palace traditions can serve as a rhetorical source. As rapper Sidney has noted, "When you put beats behind this thing, this is pure rap, pure rap!" (*Living the Hiplife*, Shipley 2007).[36]

A more subtle connection concerns how rap functions socially in Africa. In Mali, when rappers insert personal addresses into their performances, they are establishing a continuity with the past by cultivating social bonds. Hip hop has also encouraged the gathering together of individuals there somewhat along lines of traditional youth- or gender-based associations. In this African equivalent of posses, rappers are associated with male youth associations (Schulz, this volume). In Tanzania, rappers are associated with neighborhood camps, with up to 1,000 of them in Dar es Salaam, which provide a sense of identity based on class, education, and ideology. These camps have precedents in the organization of groups centered around dansi and taraab bands of earlier decades (Perullo, this volume).

Globalization, in the form of sending American rap around the world, can indeed stimulate renewed interest in homegrown oral traditions. Reggie Rockstone recognizes his own limitations and appreciates the work of the next generation: "These cats today, they're deep. I mean they really go into the traditional proverbs, the deep indigenous culture from the villages" (in Shipley, this volume). Obrafour has been cited as rapping in "pure . . . Twi filled with . . . proverbs . . . bring[ing] in the authentic Ghanaian culture" (unidentified rapper in Shipley, this volume). Obour was brought up in a chief's palace in Ghana and draws on the wisdom of his elders to such a degree that an elder in his home village asked him to explain one of the proverbs he heard on Obour's rap on the radio. The National Theater Festival in Ghana has recognized this potential in integrating rap into its competitions.

K'Naan has used hip hop to help revive oral traditions in his native Somalia. This not only connects the two disparate traditions, but then makes a case that rap is a continuation of those traditions (Pennycook and Mitchell 2009: 33–35). This appears to be a natural process around the world, as when, for example, Japanese rapper Hime draws on the ancient poetry form *tanka* (Condry 2006: 178–179). On the other hand, although some older people may recognize convergences with a local tradition, young rappers may not even be aware of it, as Keeler (2009: 3) has noted in Burma. Connections to the past in many cases may be more symbolic than substantial.[37]

In Uganda, American-style break dancing has been used to empower at-risk youth and heal war-torn areas. It has been especially effective there because it does not have ethnic associations, and therefore everyone can participate without fear. Ugandan youth can recognize its African convergences, and in different localities they can put their own styles into it, in effect revitalizing local dance traditions, but within a safe context (*Bouncing Cats,* Elderkin 2010).[38]

Imitation, Assimilation, Transformation

Appropriating, integrating, and transforming a foreign art form into a locally meaningful genre is nothing new for Africans, and African hip hop provides a rich laboratory in which to view processes of change. Africans across the continent have done this for centuries. As Perullo (this volume) notes, several Tanzanian genres of music began as imitations of foreign styles, with the pattern being imitation, localizing the sounds, words, and meanings, and finally innovating. Such was the case beginning in the late nineteenth century with the Egyptian import now known as taarab, in the 1920s with the form of ballroom dance music now known as dansi, and with kwaya (choir), a Tanzanian variety of the European Christian choral music that was taught at missionary facilities.

In the 1950s, Cuban music enjoyed great popularity around the world, especially in Africa, where it was generically called rumba. In the Belgian Congo (later Zaire), it was embraced to such a degree that on the eve of political independence, African Jazz, one of the two top bands in the country, had a major hit with their song "Independence Chachacha." Giving new lead roles to the guitar, Congolese rumba became an African staple. In the immediate postcolonial era in Guinea, state-patronized orchestras combined Cuban and local musics, gradually developing their own signature sounds, again led by guitarists.[39]

Sponsorship of musical groups by new African states swept across the continent in the 1960s. Efforts were especially keen in socialist or socialist-leaning nations, such as Guinea and Mali, which appreciated the impact of forging national identities through the arts. The key factors here are that the order was government initiated, singing in African languages was a priority, and popular dance musics were supported. By contrast, rap in Africa in the 1980s was initially an antiauthoritarian youth initiative.

In the 1970s some Ghanaians looked to African American culture as a way of distinguishing themselves from the generation who grew up under colonial rule. Some adopted foreign styles of dress, hairdressing, and music (Shipley, this volume). The situation was similar in Mali. In a discussion of the work of Malian photographer Malick Sidibé, the Guinean-born, Malian-raised, French-educated, American-based university professor Manthia Diawara reflects on the impact of rock on his circle of close friends in late 1960s Bamako:

> Malick Sidibé's photographs . . . of the 1960s . . . show exactly how the young people in Bamako had embraced rock and roll as a liberation movement, adopted the consumer habits of an international youth culture, and developed a rebellious attitude toward all forms of established authority. . . . To both the independence leaders and the military regime in Bamako, the youth . . . were mimicking the culture of the colonizer, which shut the door to authentic self-actualization. . . . The youth in Bamako did not want to be restricted in their freedom, and therefore used it to express the themes and aesthetics of Pan-Africanism, the black diaspora, and rock and roll. (Manthia Diawara 2005: 243, 248–49, 250)

Just exchange 1990s for 1960s and hip hop for rock and roll in the above quotation, and some of the similarities between these generations become eerily evident. It may be helpful to further delineate three generations of musical transformations: the immediate postcolonial generation of the 1960s to mid-1970s; the world music generation of the later 1970s and 1980s; and the hip hop generation of the 1990s and 2000s. Fully assessing the commonalities and differences among these generations will be an important yet difficult task. Younger observers may not fully appreciate the heroism and creativity of the earlier generations; older observers may have a difficult time seeing through some of the surface features of imitation to appreciate the transformations of the younger generations.

The Africanizing process, still in progress to be sure, is demanding. In Senegal, the style called mbalax was all the rage in the 1980s, closely associated with Youssou N'Dour, who had a hero status. Positive Black Soul eventually learned to integrate rap with mbalax.

> In the beginning it was no Mbalax at all. It was anti Mbalax. . . . Because of Mbalax, rap couldn't happen in Senegal. So we had to break Mbalax. . . . But some years after, we understood that we needed that energy and the colour and the instruments. . . . We started putting it together in 1989. But it was very tough for us. . . . They would say, "No man. No rap today. It's impossible!" . . . Because they didn't want to hear the Rap. They would say we were just playing Americans and we are a little bit crazy. (Didier Awadi interviewed by Meghelli, in Spady, Alim, and Meghelli 2007: 651)

Globalization, the Internet, and Mass Media

While the internet has given Africans the opportunity to post their music onto what may seem like a level playing field of dispersion, there is no guarantee that their postings will find much of an audience. African hip hop has had very little impact in the United States, for example, outside of highly targeted expatriate communities, such as Kenyans (Kidula, this volume). On a trip to Senegal, Akon (2005: 116) simply noted that "hip hop in the United States pretty much ignores Africa." In an interview about 2005, Arrested Development's Speech, who projected one of the more Afrocentric images in rap of the previous decade, seemed to be unaware of what Africa already offered up beyond imitation.

> Hip hop in Africa could be so much more [than the commercialized American variety]. The rhythm should be sick! Sick! They should be doing time signatures that we can't even comprehend because that's what they know. They should be doing chants that we can't even comprehend. Rhyming styles that we can't even start to think of. (Speech in *Afrolution,* Birch et al. 2005)

Traffic on africanhiphop.com, probably the most visible African hip hop site, barely registers in the blogosphere.[40] And African rappers are rarely invited to collaborate with their American counterparts.[41]

While Africans have tried to globally disseminate their music via the internet, reaching a small audience, the continent has undergone a mass media blitz that has made American music, including rap, even more readily available. It may seem all the more remarkable, therefore, that in the face of such mass media exposure, young people are willing and able to create music cultures that remain relevant to their own lived experiences. But perhaps it is not so unusual in Africa. When emcees from Ouaga All Starz rap the following, the first in French (by Dhudn'J), the second in one of Burkina Faso's local tongues (by David le Combattant), one gets a sense that harnessing a colonial legacy and a modern mass media blitz and reshaping and making them locally meaningful is part and parcel of African life.

> *T'étonne pas qu'en pays de l'Oncle Sam*
> [Don't be amazed that in the land of Uncle Sam]
> *On parle au'jourd'hui du pays de Tom Sank*
> [I speak today of the land of Tom Sank] (Thomas Sankara, Burkina
>   revolutionary hero)
> *La langue française, je l'appris à l'école*
> [The French language, I learned it in school]
> *Et c'est sur Trace TV que j'ai connu Akon*
> [and through 'Trace TV' I discovered Akon]
> . . .
> Hip hop hurts more than a slap in your face
> Hold the mic with devotion
> It belongs to you, it's your entire life
> It is the channel that allows you to valorize your culture
> ("Ouaga All Starz" by Ouaga All Starz in Fangafrika [CD and DVD], Stay
>   Calm! Productions 2008)

But the internet has also allowed Africans to appropriate and sample music that has no tangible diasporic connection. Lee Watkins (this volume) has noticed this from South Africa, causing him to question the effectiveness of considering what is happening there as diasporic, as opposed to global. Hip hop communities around the world may be more connected by poverty, marginalization, or the sheer aesthetic pleasure of a shared youth music than by racial solidarity.[42] The term *black*, in a new South African context (and in many parts of the world), can symbolize a racially inclusive consciousness, as is the case in Cape Town. The community-based Bush Radio there, for example, saw itself and its target community, much of which was categorized as colored under the apartheid regime, as black, reflecting this consciousness (Bosch 2003: 121–28).[43] If black, for some, represents a state of mind, then there may indeed be a thin line between a diasporic and a global community.

Young Elites

Throughout Africa (with Nigeria perhaps providing an exception) rap was initially a genre of the educated elite—those who had better access to foreign goods and ideas and a desire for them. Once rap gained a foothold, it was eventually picked up by expanding spheres of youth. This process was quite the opposite of its American origins, where it developed in economically depressed communities with little media attention, discovered by downtown New York trendy circles, and then commercially disseminated.[44]

As can be seen in the chapters here on Mali, Tanzania, Kenya, and Ghana, it was the youth who looked to France, the United Kingdom, and the United States for current trends in music and fashion, bypassing their own local and national cultures. They were attracted to hip hop and shaped it to their own needs.[45] They represented a new generation, as Faada Freddy noted, an ambitious generation. His group, Daara J, exemplifies some of this generation's aspirations and personal backgrounds.

> "Rap is all about the message. We say things like the ghetto isn't really that great. That the ghetto can be changed." Not that Daara J come from the ghetto, exactly. All three have middle-class backgrounds. Their parents are accountants and teachers [and] they'd expected their children to do the same. ("We had to convince them that you could be a rapper and still abide by your African roots.") Faada Freddy studied accountancy for a while, played guitar, piano, and the thunderous sabar drums on the side. (Faada Freddy quoted in Cornwell 2004)[46]

Access to a piano in Africa, certainly not as easy as it is in Europe and North America, sets Faada Freddy apart from the vast majority of his peers.

It was no coincidence that in South Africa rap first took root in Cape Town. Caught in an apartheid system between overprivileged whites and underprivileged blacks, the mixed-race population of Cape Town had limited but relatively more economic and political access than black communities. Therefore,

> hip-hop was a relatively accessible cultural form (as Ready D [of Prophets of da City] freely admits). Coloured people on the Cape Flats may have had to fight over limited numbers of hip-hop tapes sent by friends and relatives from overseas, but they undoubtedly had more stereos and more connections outside South Africa than their black counterparts (Neate 2003: 173).

Shipley (this volume) points out the irony of young Ghanaians looking to the United States for legitimization of their own African culture, perhaps more of an issue for urban elites than rural Ghanaians.[47] In Mali, there is a tension between the social critique of rappers and the privileges that they enjoy because of their family and economic background. Young people's dependence on their parents is often a precondition of their criticism of parental control and other intergenerational conflict, suggesting a middle-class sensibility (Schulz, this volume).

The foreign ties of many of Africa's most prominent rappers is uncanny. Positive Black Soul's co-founders had exceptional backgrounds for Senegalese: Amadou Barry grew up in France, and Didier Awadi's father was a church organist—a sure sign in a Muslim country of having strong ties to European culture (RFI Musique 2008).[48] Reggie Rockstone was born in England, moved back and forth to the United States, and attended one of the most elite boarding schools in Ghana.

Also uncanny is the similarity to the process by which Christian church music was integrated into African life. It was primarily an elite group of individuals educated in European art and church music who introduced church music to the masses (Omojola forthcoming; Kidula forthcoming).

Gender Preferences

Female performers are a minority presence in African rap. Female rappers and hip hop crews can be found throughout Africa, but they are viewed, and they view themselves, as exceptional, having to fight against strong odds. Every country, it seems, has a pioneering female group, dating from the later 1990s or 2000s, along with a few female rappers who have attained some prominence. Senegal's first major female group is the three-member ALIF, who have issued a single CD since their founding in 1997. South Africa's Cape Town–based Godessa (L. Watkins, this volume) has issued a single CD since their founding in 2000; they play a major role in a documentary about female rappers in South Africa (*Counting Headz*, Magubane and Offer 2006) and member EJ von Lyrik has recently released two solo CDs. Ghana's first major female group, Triple M, started out as a gospel trio in the mid-1990s before turning to hiplife and releasing two albums (Jabbaar-Gyambrah 2007: 232–45). Tanzanian camps have female members, and there are some female emcees (Perullo, this volume).[49]

However, Kenyan Michael Wanguhu, director of the documentary *Hip Hop Colony*, which featured female MC Nazizi, notes a recent change, especially in the industry as a whole.[50]

> There's a lot of females who are holding it down right now in a lot of places in that whole industry in Kenya. . . . As far as TV shows, things are really changing right now. They're getting a voice. It's a new platform for them. . . . The radio shows, the hosts, and all of that, the majority of them are women. . . . They are running things. (Wanguhu in Arnold 2006: 315)

The phenomenon of females having more access to the industry as organizers rather than emcees, as Godessa-member Shame says (L. Watkins, this volume), may be widespread. In Ghana, for example, female radio and TV personality Blakofe helped popularize hiplife through her show *GoldBlast*, in which she featured Ghanaian artists (*Living the Hiplife*, Shipley 2007).

Where are women in African music performance? As Polak (this volume) notes, in Mali they are heavily invested in the dance-drumming events that dominate Bamako, as the primary participants (dancers) and organizers. In these roles they are the major stimulants not only for the maintenance of symbols of ethnic identity via

dance rhythms but also for change and innovation in repertories. This phenomenon is widespread, certainly in western Africa where Mande jembe and Wolof
sabar drumming are present.

Outside of drumming-related dance, Malian females prefer the music and messages of national female pop singers and generally are disinterested in the male
world of rap (Schulz 2002a, this volume). Some of those messages, as in some of
the songs of Wassoulou vocal star Oumou Sangare, assertively speak to the rights
and dignity of women (Durán 1999). Preferences for pop over rap is probably the
case throughout much of Africa, although as hip hop culture becomes more and
more pervasive, younger generations of women may be more apt to embrace it.
One strategy used by Malians (and all over Africa) has been collaborations between rappers and female pop stars. Mokobe, a French rapper with Malian origins,
has collaborated with Oumou Sangare when he was a member of the French rap
group 113 ("Voix du Mali"), Mokobe on his own has collaborated with Senegalese
vocalist Viviane ("Safari"), and Malian rap group Tata Pound has collaborated with
vocalist Nabintou Diakite ("N'Dia").[51]

In South Africa, kwaito has proven to be not only the most popular musical
genre among youth in the post-apartheid era (1994–) when the genre emerged
in full force, but one that is a major arena for women, both as performers and
consumers. Initially consisting of imported electronic dance music (called house)
from the United States, it was slowed down, taking on added musical layers and
vocals in South African languages such as Zulu and Sesotho. The first commercially successful kwaito group, Boom Shaka, consisted of two males (one, an ex-
member of Prophets of Da City) and two females. Vocalist Brenda Fassie, who
gained star status in the 1980s in a genre called bubblegum, dominated the South
African music industry through its kwaito years until her death in 2004. About
2005 a major kwaito album could outsell a major South African hip hop album in
the order of 10 to 1 (300,000 copies compared with 20,000–30,000 copies).

Although the two genres are sometimes conflated, many make a sharp distinction between the hedonistic sexually charged world of kwaito and hip hop, in particular the more socially conscious variety. This difference has caused concern at
Cape Town-based Bush Radio in their move to play kwaito (Bosch 2003: 208–32).
But there is more to the story. Kwaito lyrics are in precolonial Bantu languages
and therefore have a strikingly local, specifically black township linguistic identity.
Kwaito is also primarily produced by black-owned record labels. South African
rap has typically been delivered in English or Dutch-based Afrikaans (although in
vernacular dialects) and is viewed more as part of an international current. As Lee
Watkins (this volume) has noted, recent rap in local tongues such as Xhosa has had
an uphill battle in terms of broader acceptance. The ascendance of commercial hip
hop may contribute to a blurring of genre boundaries. And one might put a more
positive interpretation on the overt sexuality (and occasional vulgarity) of kwaito:
as Impey (2001: 44, 47) has suggested, by acting out the part of being sex objects,
kwaito women are carving out a commanding presence in the music industry and

may actually be parodying and ultimately subverting that role. Or as Gqola (2004: 144) writes: "So successful was Brenda [Fassie] at her self-representation as a complex sexual being that even for her detractors it was unheard of to have her characterised as a sexual object."[52]

Gospel and other music associated with Christian worship is also a major outlet for African women. While hardly on the radar outside Africa, local gospel music outsells rap, at least in Ghana and Kenya (Collins, Kidula, this volume), and probably in most Anglophone countries with a predominant Christian population. Gospel music in Ghana and Kenya draws women, both as consumers and as singers, in which they dominate the genre; churches have become a "productive space" for female singers (Collins, this volume). The explosive growth of Christianity not just in Africa (especially as African Independent Churches) but around the world shows no sign of letting up (Jenkins 2007).[53]

Drumming and Folkloric Troupes

Hand or stick drumming and its associated dancing are still vital activities in many parts of Africa, especially for youth who are constantly transforming them. Many African youth are able to incorporate both local music and dance traditions and foreign cultural currents into their lives, forging new cultural styles.

The circuitous global routes that the highly specialized jembe drum has traveled is extraordinary, making more inroads around the world than any other kind of African music, rap included. Rooted in the soil of the old Mande world along the Niger River that traverses Guinea and Mali, the jembe was brought to the capital cities of Bamako and Conakry where newly established national ballets in the 1950s and 1960s turned it into an important symbol of local identity. It toured the world in the hands of village-trained ballet drummers, planting seeds that have sprouted schools and new uses wherever it landed. In an unlikely twist, it has penetrated and in some cases even replaced drumming traditions within Africa itself, hopping across the continent as far afield as South Africa, an uncommon occurrence where musical instruments are strong symbols of ethnic identity.[54]

This global takeover has been known in the northern hemisphere for a few decades, with drum circles, jembe schools, and factory-produced instruments marking the musical landscape. Drummers from the western African heartland remained the ultimate authorities, but new generations of teachers and performers not born in Africa began taking on these roles. Perhaps the most dramatic example of an Africa-wide takeover was televised to a huge audience around the world at the South African FIFA World Cup Kick-Off Celebration concert (June 10, 2010). A massive crowd of jembe drummers and dancers opened the event, which also featured a jembe group with female drummers.[55]

Ubiquitous in the capital cities of Mali and Guinea, and in increasing numbers of cities across Africa, jembes are the most omnipresent symbol of African drumming in the world. As Polak (this volume) warns, though, jembe drumming and dancing are not static rural forms. Drummers and dancers are keenly aware of the origins of their repertory and yet have adapted to the times, both urbanizing and modernizing, two processes he suggests should be kept distinct for analytical purposes. Bamako jembe players are finding new ways to embrace new immigrants in the capital city, and they are adept at appropriating new rhythms and dances and bringing them fully into their repertory and performance practice.[56] This welcoming sensibility and the jembe-based celebrations that permeate the city give character to and help define the identity of Bamako. As a very public outdoor music, jembe-based celebrations attract crowds and have mass appeal. It is in this sense, Polak proposes, that the genre is an urban popular music.

Jembe drumming provides a fascinating foil for rap—they are going through somewhat similar processes of globalizing, although taking very different paths. One is a centuries-old tradition that has taken root abroad in the past several decades. Completing the circle, success abroad and study tours to Africa stimulate young people to carry on the tradition back home. (Similar processes are at work elsewhere, as Collins notes in Ghana where folkloric and neo-traditional groups are having a renaissance, inviting foreign tourists for study, resulting in a stimulation of the local economy.) Intimately wrapped up in notions of ethnic identity, the jembe has adapted, and it is used as a vehicle for urban, regional, national, continental, and global unity, losing increasing degrees of its specific associations along the way.

Rap, on the other hand, is a recent tradition, also originally associated with a specific place and culture, but rooted in aesthetics that developed in the Americas by peoples whose ancestors left Africa centuries ago through forced human trafficking. Rap made its way back to Africa in a highly mass-mediated form with thickly transformed sonic and social values, hardly recognizable to many. Yet young Africans did indeed find relevance and potential, just like their parents and grandparents had done with other musical styles coming in from the diaspora.

An Africa-wide ability to embrace and transform is the fuel for the artistic expression that continues to animate the continent. It is an abundant and constantly renewable creative resource. The deep-time circuits and vast global dispersion of African expressive aesthetics make them one of the most fascinating, far-reaching, and powerful cultural forces around.

NOTES

1. N'Dour continued: "It's about dignity. . . . Africa definitely have this image about poverty, about war, about AIDS. But this is not the only image of Africa. Africa wanna move forward. Africa have something smiling, something positive. Open your market for new Africa!" (*Live 8*, Eden Project/WOMAD 2005).

2. For chart rankings, see allmusic.com or the extensive series of books by Joel Whitburn (www.recordresearch.com). Makeba, Masekela, and Dibango have all published autobiographies. Senegalese American Akon has risen to the top of the American pop and

R&B charts, but his years growing up in the United States have enabled him to pass as a bona fide American R&B artist. For his relationship with Senegal, where he is considered a hero, see Akon (2005) and Laura Checkoway, "The Kon Artist," *Vibe* (April 2007): 90–95. Chamillionaire (Hakeem Seriki) and Wale (Olubowale Victor Akintimehin), both U.S.-born children of immigrants from Nigeria, have recently had commercial success in the rap market. In interviews posted to YouTube, they have discussed their Nigerian heritage, although neither had been there as of about 2008 (search "Chamillionaire Nigeria" and "Wale Nigeria" on YouTube).

    3. Youssou N'Dour and Neneh Cherry's duet "Seven Seconds," which breached the Billboard Hot 100 chart at 98, did hit number one in eight markets around the world and number 3 in the UK, and it was named best song by MTV Europe in 1994; *The Guide (Wommat)*, the album on which it appeared, sold one million copies worldwide (Williamson 2000).

    4. In a major restructuring, these two categories were folded back into a single world music category beginng in 2012 (http://www.grammy.org/recording-academy/announcement /category-list).

    5. For example, Speech (Todd Thomas) from Arrested Development has noted, "Some of the African hip hop I've seen, they're more emulating what we do, and it saddens me because Africa has so much more. And I don't want them to come with the bling bling and some nice cars and women dancing and booty shorts and that's what hip hop is. It's not" (*Afrolution*, Birch et al. 2005). Also, Positive Black Soul from the early 2000s: "[Many] African crews will dress like, behave like, talk like, and try to sound like the African American rap artists. . . . Who are we kidding . . . you know that that CD is not worth jack." (quoted in Lemelle [2006: 240] from the now defunct www.nubianunderground.com).

    6. Zeleza (2003) provides an extensive overview of writing on globalization with reference to Africa (see especially the first chapter); Ntarangwi (2009: 1–43) devotes two chapters to globalization and hip hop in East Africa; and Pennycook (2007) provides a critical look at dichotomies in globalization theories from the perspective of how English has been reshaped through hip hop around the world. The automatic link between globalization and hip hop can readily be appreciated by looking at the titles (or subtitles) of almost any book that covers the genre outside of the United States (Toop's 1991 *Rap Attack 2: African Rap to Global Hip Hop* is a misnomer—it only covers the United States): *Global Noise* (Mitchell 2001), *Hip Hop and the Globalization of Black Popular Culture* (Basu and Lemelle 2006), *Tha Global Cipha* (Spady, Alim, and Meghelli 2006), *Hip-Hop Japan: Rap and the Paths of Cultural Globalization* (Condry 2006), *The Africanist Aesthetic in Global Hip-Hop* (Osumare 2007), *Global Englishes and Transcultural Flows* (Pennycook 2007), *Globale Spuren eines lokalen Kulturphänomens* [Global Traces of a Local Cultural Phenomenon] (Bock, Meier, and Süss 2007), *Stationen einer globalen Musikkultur* [Milestones of a Global Music Culture] (Stemmler and Skrandies 2007), *Global Linguistic Flows* (Alim, Ibrahim, and Pennycook 2009), *East African Hip Hop: Youth Culture and Globalization* (Ntarangwi 2009), and *The Languages of Global Hip Hop* (Terkourafi 2010a). The many books about hip hop in France (including Durand 2002, which covers the Francophone world) are exceptions, probably because the genre was so thoroughly integrated into French youth culture so early on.

    7. My formulation here was inspired by Harrison's (2008: 1791) excellent survey of academic literature, especially his reference to Bennett (1999). See Bennett (2001: 88–103) for a concise statement of some of these and other issues in hip hop going global.

8. Also see Wood (2009: 183–184) on the black British hip hop group London Posse, who drew "specifically upon their own experiences. . . . The acknowledgement of the originality of their contribution to Hip Hop culture by American artists such as Chuck D. helped reject criticisms that Hip Hop was an essentially African American form and foregrounded Hip Hop as a hybrid and highly malleable genre that could be widely adopted and adapted in multiple sites and locations."

9. This issue of acknowledging the innovators has long marked the jazz world, as Monson (2007: 70–71) has noted: "The idea of the modern artist was a double-edged sword. . . . [It] provided a rhetoric through which white musicians could insist that the music be understood as colorblind and dismiss those who emphasized its black heritage as reverse racists. . . . The music tends to be cast as either universal or ethnically particular, colorblind or fundamentally black, with many jumping from one side to the other depending on the contextual situation."

10. Authenticity may be the single most discussed issue in hip hop. For some of the basic viewpoints from the past two decades, see Forman and Neal (2012: 69–223), "No Time for Fake Niggas: Hip-Hop Culture and the Authenticity Debates." Recent takes include Terkourafi (2010b: 6-13) for a global perspective, Peterson (2005) and MacNeil and Mak (2007) for interdisciplinary approaches to notions of authenticity, and Weisethaunet and Lindberg (2010) for authenticity in rock. Zeleza (2006) offers a relevant wide-ranging discussion of African identity and language; for broader musings on identity, see the fall 2006 issue of *Daedalus* ("On Identity"). Brubaker and Cooper's (2000: 11) observation that the virtually automatic and obligatory "standard qualifiers indicating that identity is multiple, unstable, in flux, contingent, fragmented, constructed, negotiated, and so on . . . risk becoming mere place-holders, gestures" is still on target over a decade later and can apply to many other terms used in academic discourse. Readers may sense an indiscriminate, or perhaps elastic use of two other terms throughout my two chapters—*youth* and *generation*—although I hope that the context will provide appropriate clarification. Warikoo's (2011) comparative ethnographic study of the relationship between hip hop–inflected youth culture and academic achievement in a very targeted age group (fourteen- to seventeen-year-olds), population (children of Indian, Indo-Caribbean, and Afro-Caribbean immigrants), and setting (a high school in New York and in London) provides a rich model for the benefits of keeping an unusually tight focus. For a concise overview of issues in the study of youth culture, see Wulff (1995); for a more expansive history and critique, see Huq (2006).

11. McLeod was especially concerned with such invocations being related to the threat of assimilation into mainstream culture.

12. The music, specifically the use of electronic samples, has also been a subject of intense debate about authenticity (see Marshall 2006).

13. Harrison (2008: 1785–86) effectively questions a number of assumptions that lay beneath the surface: Where along a historical continuum do references to authentic hip hop point, and how dynamic are conceptions of points of origin? Who are the models of authenticity—artists (who are predominantly black) or anyone who is part of a more multiracial hip hop nation? Furthermore, does "artist" refer mainly to MCs (predominantly black) or does the term include DJs, break dancers, and graffiti writers, who are more multiracial? And there can be slippage with the term *black*, ranging from a specifically African American to an African diasporic identity, at times effacing cultural differ-

ence (e.g., American, Jamaican, British, Ghanaian). See Harrison (2009: 83–119) for a related discussion of race and authenticity in San Francisco underground hip hop. The multicultural origins of New York hip hop culture can be appreciated in the coverage given in one of the first books on the subject (Hager 1984). Also see Rivera (2003) and Flores (2000) on Puerto Rican involvement, especially the extended quotation from Charlie Chase: "It's a street thing. I liked it because it came from the street and I'm from the street. I'm a product of the environment" (Flores 2000: 128–29).

14. For more on the collaboration between Afrika Bambaataa and Arthur Baker, see Buskin (2008) and interviews with both, carried out in the late 1990s by Frank Broughton, http://www.djhistory.com/interviews/afrika-bambaataa, and Broughton and Bill Brewster, http://www.djhistory.com/interviews/arthur-baker.

15. Engineer Nick Sansano, on the other hand, credits Shocklee's Bomb Squad with broadening his perspective and giving him a valuable education in aesthetics (B. Jackson 2000). These examples could be oversimplified as white technological know-how in the service of implementing black ideas. However, this stereotype devalues the collaborative give-and-take in creative processes and ignores traditions of experimenting with technology that cut across racial lines. See Veal (2000: 2-3, 36-42), for example, for a wideranging discussion of technological experimentation in relation to Jamaican dub.

16. See Allman (2004) for various studies of the role of dress in the formation of African identities.

17. An ironic example of appropriating authenticity is the 1979 album *Dans l'authenticité* [In authenticity] by vocalist Salif Keita and guitarist Manfila Kante, leaders of the Malian orchestra Les Ambassadeurs. Keita sings some of the older pieces in the repertory of the griot (or jeli) with just acoustic guitar accompaniment by Kante. Irony exists on two levels here: Keita comes from the Malian noble non-artisan class and does not belong to the griot's lineage—he is breaking long-standing social taboos by taking up their repertory; and the acoustic guitar, clearly a foreign import, was integrated into the griot's tradition deeply enough so that it is considered part of that tradition. See Charry (2000) and Counsel (2006) for more on the efforts of Sekou Toure.

18. See http://www.africanloft.com/bamboo-kenyan-hip-hop-artist-on-africanloft/ and http://www.facebook.com/pages/Bamboo/236269744559?v=info.

19. For Bambaataa's African connection, see Hager (1984: 6–7) and http://www.djhistory.com/interviews/afrika-bambaataa. See Decker (1993) and Boyd (1997: 49) for discussions of Afrocentricity in rap from the late 1980s and early 1990s, including Public Enemy, Sister Souljah, Queen Latifah, X-Clan, and Arrested Development, and Wamba (1999: 280-82) for a backlash by members of NWA. Early engagements with Africa include "Bite It" (1984) by Drum (Sugarhill Records' house band), which has a simulated African bell pattern at the end and claims to have "real Swahili" rapping (www.discogs.com /viewimages?release=99070), "A.F.R.I.C.A." by Stetsasonic (*On Fire*, 1986), and "Africa (Goin' Back Home)" by Doug E. Fresh (*The World's Greatest Entertainer*, 1988). The name Zulu Nation can present a dilemma in Africa. While adopting Bambaataa's Zulu Nation philosophy, Ray, of South Africa's Black Noise, explains that "it wouldn't be wise of us to use the name Zulu Nation, because it would be looked upon as choosing a side politically" (in Battersby 2003: 118).

20. Akon's "Senegal" (2006) takes both approaches, referring to Senegal as "the ghetto" (linking it to diasporic ghettos), and educating his listeners about the trials and tribula-

tions of African immigrants. See Wittman (2004) for an analysis of socio-religious conservatism in the Senegalese rap genre called *bul faale* (*boul falé*).

21. See Haupt (2004) for more on Cape Town rappers and black identity. Some of his critiques may be defused by Lee Watkins (this volume).

22. Reggie Rockstone's listing of the three elements for success in Ghanaian rap may speak specifically to Ghanaian sensibilities: "Laughter . . . Sense . . . Dance, you know, flow" (*Living the Hiplife*, Shipley 2007). The very next scenes in Shipley's documentary, however, bring home the importance of educating and a social message. In a twist on keeping it real, Kenyan rapper Prezzo brags about his inherited wealth because that's who he is, and some look to him as a role model (Seiler and JJC 2005, East Africa [11:55]). See Mose (2011) for caution about reifying an underground/mainstream dichotomy.

23. See Wetaba (2009: 168–75) for an analysis of this quotation and the concept of local in Kenyan hip hop. See L. Watkins (2004: 143) for how the South African first generation hip hop group Black Noise constructs authenticity by articulating the "style, intonation, and struggles of the local hip hop community," and Thompson (2011: 253) for an exploration with members of the Tanzanian hip hop group X Plastaz of the "positive, but still highly stereotyped and problematic, image of the Maasai" that they project.

24. Kenyan rapper Big Mike Adewa (of Nanoma) fluently uses Sheng for celebratory self-aggrandizing in *Hip Hop Colony* (Wanguhu 2007). I thank Job Ogutu for his translation.

25. I thank Djibril Bah for this translation.

26. See the documentary by Maga Bo (2007) and *Democracy in Dakar* (Herson, McIlvaine, and Moore 2007, episode 5) for interviews with Senegalese rappers including Xuman (Pee Froiss) and Keyti (Rap'adio, Dakar All Stars) talking about their use of English, French, and Wolof.

27. See Auzanneau and Fayol (2004), Higgins (2009), and A. Williams (2010) for detailed analyses of sophisticated language use by rappers in Senegal, Tanzania, and Egypt, respectively; see Haupt (2001) for the significance of using gamtaal, a Cape Flats dialect of Afrikaans (which itself is a mixture of primarily Dutch and other languages used in South Africa) by Cape Town rap groups; and see Kimminich (2004b) for an analysis of the storytelling aspect of Senegalese rap. On the other hand, Kenyan journalist Ogova Ondego suggests that some urban Nairobi rappers may not have a command of certain languages, such as Kikuyu, and by extension of their traditional culture either (in Samper 2004: 39). See Bradley (2009) for a broad-based analysis of language use in American rap, and A. Patel (2008) for recent scientific inquiry into the relationship between the sonic nature of various spoken languages and musical flow, a promising frontier for assessing some of the differences in rapping styles around the world.

28. See J. Mbaye (2011) and www.plan-childrenmedia.org (search poto-poto).

29. Unusual in its inclusiveness is The Roots' "Do You Want More?" (from their 1994 album of the same title), which has shout-outs ranging from Philadelphia neighborhoods, New York boroughs, other cities, states, regions (West Coast, Down South, Puerto Rico), and foreign cities and countries (London, Tokyo, Germany), to simply "Africa." Shouting out a continent in the context of the previously heard degrees of geographic specificity could be taken as a lack of consciousness about places within that continent just as easily as a show of broad solidarity.

30. The Hama Boys were named after a neighborhood in Algiers (Miliani 2002: 765). National pride can spill over into continental pride, as in "We Are Africans" by UK-based

Nigerian rapper JJC (Abdul Bello), which collectively claims those "with black in your skin," "a lot of melanin," and, by the end of the piece, "mixed race, white." The official You-Tube channel for the video describes it as "Serious, but also fun, tongue-in-cheek," a significant disclaimer given the laundry list of racial traits proudly claimed, including speed, rhythm, and sexual prowess. The Naija remix backs up to national pride, featuring many Nigerian artists. See http://www.youtube.com/user/BigBoyzEnt.

31. For other examples of rap impacting public political discourse in Africa, see Nyairo and Ogude (2005) and Stroeken (2005).

32. See *Democracy in Dakar* (episode 5). For a similar claim from Morocco, see Seiler and JJC (2005, North).

33. See Lemelle (2006: 239) for similar attitudes about guns and violence in Tanzania.

34. Awadi speaks about these strategies of Africanizing hip hop, as do the groups Djanta Kan (Togo) and H2O Assouka (Benin) in the documentary *Fangafrika* (Stay Calm! Productions 2008).

35. See L. Watkins (2004: 134–43) for examples of both Prophets of Da City and Black Noise drawing on South African and especially Cape Town musical traditions. "Right Here in Front of You" features UK-based Ty and BREIS (both with Nigerian roots) rapping over a drum beat of fellow-Nigerian Tony Allen, an important architect of Fela Kuti's sound since the 1960s, on an album of remixes of Allen's beats (Allenko Brotherhood Ensemble, 2001).

36. See Norris (2005) and Gordon (2006), in which members of Daara J claim a direct connection with taasu, and McNee (2000) and Tang (2007) for how taasu functions in a traditional Wolof context. Other examples include Ekiti Yoruba speech-song called *alamo* (Osumare 2007: 33–35), the Yoruba oral poetic form *ewi* and abuse and proverbial songs called *orin ebu* (or *orin owe*) (Omoniyi 2009: 117), and *okwevuga*, a form of reciting heroic deeds among the Banyankore/Banyankole of Uganda (Mushengyezi 2003: 116). The Ghanaian Anlo-Ewe socio-musical drama called *halo* (Avorgbedor 2001) bears a remarkable resemblance to certain aspects of rap. "Attention na SIDA," released in 1987 by Franco, one of Africa's most prolific and beloved vocalist/guitarists, bears some relation to rap in that he lectures about the dangers of AIDS and how to prevent its spread. But the rapping is an anomaly in Franco's repertory, and other than the subject matter, the performance bears little of the hip hop sensibility that would mark the younger generation.

37. Also see Huq (1999: 141) and Prévos (2002: 42–43) for continuities with earlier forms in French rap.

38. I am paraphrasing Abraham "Abramz" Tekya, director of Breakdance Project Uganda. Abdul Kinyenya, a founding member of this organization, is pictured on the front cover of this volume.

39. This Africanization process has been well documented for many nations, such as Tanzania (Askew 2002), Congo/Zaire (Stewart 2000, B. White 2008), Senegal (Shain 2002, 2009, 2012), Guinea and Mali (Charry 2000, Counsel 2006), Ghana (Collins 1992a), Nigeria (C. Waterman 1990, Veal 2000), and Zimbabwe (Turino 2000). The CD *Out of Cuba: Latin American Music Takes Africa by Storm* (Compilations [Other], 2004) collects recordings on the Gramophone and Victor labels issued on the HMV GV series aimed at the African market from 1933-1958.

40. Search "africanhiphop.com" on www.alexa.com (for international usage) and www.compete.com (for U.S. only). Whatever questions there may be regarding the gathering

and interpretation of statistics, the site clearly has relatively low traffic compared with, for example, allhiphop.com. *Billboard* (Kwaku 2000) devoted a brief article to africanhiphop. com in 2000.

41. One such invitation resulted in Sierra Leone rapper Chosan narrating the opening of Kanye West's 2005 video *Diamonds from Sierra Leone*. Chosan's experience with the project, including lack of recognition in the video credits, and his perspective gained from living in the United States provide a strong indictment of the lack of global, let alone diasporic, consciousness of commercial rap in the United States. See http://www.jamati.com /online/music/chosan-speaks-out/ and an extended radio interview at www.blogtalkradio .com (search Chosan). The 2009 BET Hip Hop Awards show featured a special segment with Tanzanian X Plastaz member Gsan rapping in Swahili with the likes of Nigerian American Wale and KRS-One. Subsequently, the segment separated out the Africans, opting to feature single African countries—Ghana in 2010 and Nigeria in 2011 (This is Africa 2011).

42. Osumare (2007: 61–74) suggests four "connective marginalities" that are responsible for the embrace of hip hop around the globe: a shared cultural aesthetic (peoples of African descent in the Americas and elsewhere who share an "Africanist" aesthetic that is typically marginalized in its national context), class (second-class citizenship due to lack of wealth or political power), historical oppression (due to social status), and youth.

43. See Sharma (2010: 1-5) for a similar example of "global race consciousness" from an Indian American (desi) rapper.

44. In the 1980s, American groups whose members came from middle-class backgrounds became more visible. Some (Run-D.M.C., Public Enemy) maintained an urban street sensibility; others (De La Soul, and later Arrested Development) opened out to more middle-class sensibilities. Depictions of ghetto life by the 1990s superstars did little to dispel notions of hip hop's primary field of operation.

45. Malm and Sarkar (1997, "Dar es Salaam") note the relative privilege of Dar es Salaam rappers, but see Lemelle (2006: 236–37), who cautions that middle class in Tanzania and in the United States is not the same, and also quotes members of Kwanza Unit objecting to this middle-class characterization.

46. See Norris (2005) for a similar story about their schooling.

47. Wamba (1999: 11) registers a slightly different kind of irony—emulation of mythical symbols—when his Tanzanian friends requested him to bring back from the US leather medallions with maps of Africa on them: "how ironic it was that the medallions were worn by trendy African American hip-hop fans in a desire to celebrate their African heritage, and would be worn by my African friends back home in an attempt to emulate African Americans celebrating Africa."

48. A documentary on Positive Black Soul shot in London and Dakar (*African Portraits* 1996?) shows both their relatively higher economic and educational status (by their fluency in English, shared by some members of their posse, which would have been at least their third language after Wolof and French).

49. See the discography for the CD recordings by ALIF, Godessa, EJ von Lyrik, and Triple M. Female rappers also occasionally guest on compilations or albums by male rappers. See *Fangafrika* (Stay Calm! Productions 2008) for interviews and performances with ALIF, Priss K (from Côte d'Ivoire), and ZM (Niger). Barz and Liu (2011: 362-83) examined the lives and work of Tafash and Twig, two female emcees in Uganda (the only they

encountered in the capital city Kampala's hip hop scene as of 2008) and recorded them for their CD compilation *Kampala Flow* (2010).

50. See Wetaba (2009: 300–304) for an analysis of the presence of females in Kenyan hip hop. Ntarangwi (2009: 44–66) devotes a chapter to "Hip Hop and Gendered Identities," focusing especially on the Kenyan female rapper Wahu, as well as others from Tanzania and Uganda. Wahu briefly discusses the problems of being a female rapper in Kenya in Seiler and JJC (2005, East Africa [14:25]).

51. Music videos for these three pieces can be found on the internet. An example of this kind of collaboration from North Africa is "Rayah Wayne" by Tunisian rapper Balti (2009) with pop singer Ameni Souissi (Amani Swissi).

52. Additional sources used for the two paragraphs on kwaito include McCloy (n.d.), Sean Cole (2005), Seiler and JJC (2005, South), and Declan Walsh, "Brenda Fassie: Brash and Brilliant Queen of African Pop," *Independent* (May 12, 2004), www.independent.co.uk (search Brenda Fassie). Sales figures in the previous paragraph are from Sony Music Africa executive Paul Thackwray (Seiler and JJC 2005, South [15:50]). See Magubane (2006) for further discussion of kwaito, rap, and Boom Shaka. Skwatta Kamp was the first Johannesburg-based hip hop group to have a domestic gold record (25,000 copies), with their 2003 album *Mkhukhu Funkshen*. In 2004 Johannesburg-based radio station YFM, which claimed a listenership of 1.76 million, had an average playlist of up to 50 percent South African music, 30 percent of which was hip hop, a genre that significantly increased the station's white listenership (Coetzer 2004).

53. See Muller (1999), Kidula (forthcoming), and Omojola (forthcoming) for case studies of music making in African Christian worship and Kalu (2010) for a broad-based study of the continuing rise of African Pentecostalism and related music and dance.

54. See Polak (2000) and Flaig (2010) for more on the globalization of the jembe.

55. The official song and video shows Shakira (featuring Freshly Ground) with jembe drummers behind her (search "Waka Waka" on vevo.com). Mali was disproportionately represented at the concert with Amadou and Mariam (including a jembe soloist), Vieux Farka Toure, and Tiniwaren. The dominance of jembe drumming in the New York Broadway show *Fela*! is just one among many examples of its infiltration into foreign African traditions (in this case Nigerian afrobeat). The drum is now fairly common in Ghana, a clear foreign import, somewhat surprising, given the continued vitality of Ghanaian drumming ensembles.

56. The kind of finely detailed ethnographic studies of the role and origins of pieces that go into an urban (rather than village) repertory, like Polak has carried out in Bamako, are a rarefied field in African music.

BIBLIOGRAPHY AND ONLINE SOURCES

AACC (All-Africa Church Conference)
1958   *The Church in Changing Africa: Report*. New York: International Missionary Council.

Abbas, Basel
2005   "An Analysis of Arabic Hip-Hop." Thesis, SAE London.

Abu-Lughod, Lila
1990   "The Romance of Resistance: Tracing Transformations of Power through Bedouin Women." *American Ethnologist* 17: 41–55.

Acquah, Ione
1958   *Accra Survey*. London: University of London Press.

Adelman, Kenneth Lee
1975   "The Recourse to Authenticity and Négritude in Zaire." *Journal of Modern African Studies* 13 (1): 134–39.

Adelt, Ulrich
2005   "'Ich Bin der Rock'n'Roll-Übermensch': Globalization and Localization in German Music Television." *Popular Music and Society* 28 (3): 279–95.

Africahit.com
2006   "Akon ou l'Afrique moderne." Published Friday, November 24. Accessed April 7, 2007. http://www.africahit.com/news/index.php?mod=article&cat=senegal&article=707.

Agawu, Victor Kofi
2003   "Contesting Difference: A Critique of Africanist Ethnomusicology." In Martin Clayton, Trevor Herbert, and Richard Middleton, eds., *The Cultural Study of Music: A Critical Introduction*, 227–37. London: Routledge.

Agovi, K. E.
1989   "The Political Relevance of Ghanaian Highlife Songs since 1957." *Research in African Literatures* 20 (2): 194–201.

Akindès, Francis
2004   *The Roots of the Military-Political Crises in Côte d'Ivoire*. Research Report no. 128. Uppsala: Nordiska Afrikainstitutet.

Akindes, Simon
2002   "Playing It 'Loud and Straight': Reggae, Zouglou, Mapouka, and Youth Insubordination in Côte d'Ivoire." In Mai Palmberg and Annemette Kirkegaard, eds.,

Playing with Identities in Contemporary Music in Africa, 86–103. Uppsala: Nordiska Afrikainstitutet.

Akon (as told to Knox Robinson)
2005 "Prodigal Son." *Vibe* (November): 108–16.

Alim, H. Samy, Awad Ibrahim, and Alastair Pennycook, eds.
2009 *Global Linguistic Flows: Hip Hop Cultures, Youth Identities, and the Politics of Language.* New York: Routledge.

Allman, Jean, ed.
2004 *Fashioning Africa: Power and the Politics of Dress.* Bloomington: Indiana University Press.

Anderson, Paul
1995 "Ellington, Rap Music, and Cultural Difference." *Musical Quarterly* 79 (1): 172–206.

Androutsopoulos, Jannis, ed.
2003 *HipHop: Globale Kultur—lokale Praktiken.* Bielefeld: Transcript.

Androutsopoulos, Jannis, and Arno Scholz
2003 "Spaghetti Funk: Appropriations of Hip-Hop Culture and Rap Music in Europe." *Popular Music and Society* 26 (4): 463–79.

Antoine, Philippe, and Mamadou Djiré
1998 "Un célibat de crise?" In Philippe Antoine, Dieudonné Ouédraogo, and Victor Piché, eds., *Trois générations de citadins au Sahel: Trente ans d'histoire sociale à Dakar et à Bamako,* 117–46. Paris: L'Harmattan.

Anyidoho, Kofi
1983 "Oral Poetics and Traditions of Verbal Art in Africa." PhD diss., University of Texas, Austin.

Ariefdien, Shaheen, and Nazli Abrahams
2006 "Cape Flats Alchemy: Hip-Hop Arts in South Africa." In Chang (2006: 262–70).

Ariefdien, Shaheen, and Marlon Burgess
2011 "Putting Two Heads Together: A Cross-Generational Conversation About Hip-Hop in South Africa." In Saucier (2011: 219–52).

Arnold, Eric K.
2006 "Put Your Camera Where My Eyes Can See: Hip-Hop Video, Film, and Documentary, a Roundtable Curated by Eric K. Arnold, with Rachel Raimist, Kevin Epps, and Micahel Wanguhu." In Chang (2006: 306–20).

Arnoldi, Mary Jo
1987 "Rethinking Definitions of African Traditional and Popular Arts." *African Studies Review* 30 (3): 79–83.
1995 *Playing with Time: Art and Performance in Central Mali.* Bloomington: Indiana University Press.

Askew, Kelly
2002 *Performing the Nation: Swahili Music and Cultural Politics in Tanzania.* Chicago: University of Chicago Press.

Auzanneau, Michelle
2002 "Rap in Libreville, Gabon: An Urban Sociolinguistic Space." In Durand (2002: 106–25).

Auzanneau, Michelle, and Vincent Fayol
    2004   "Aeusserungsereignis und Sprachvariabilitaet im senegalesischen Rap." In Kimminich (2004a: 205–32).
Avorgbedor, Daniel K.
    2001   "'It's a Great Song!' *Haló* Performance as Literary Production." *Research in African Literatures* 32 (2): 17–43.
Bailleul, Charles
    1996   *Dictionnaire Bambara-Français.* Bamako: Éditions Donniya.
Baker, Esther Marian
    2002   "Handlin' Rhymes: Hip Hop in Dakar, Senegal." MA thesis, University of California at Los Angeles.
Baker, Houston, Jr.
    1993   *Black Studies, Rap, and the Academy.* Chicago: University of Chicago Press.
Bakhtin, Mikhail
    1990   *The Dialogic Imagination: Four Essays.* Trans. Michael Holquist and Caryl Emerson. Austin: University of Texas Press.
Balliger, Robin
    1999   "Politics," in Bruce Horner and Thomas Swiss, eds., *Key Terms in Popular Music and Culture,* 57–70. Maldon: Blackwell..
Banes, Sally
    1981   "To the Beat Y'All: Breaking Is Hard to Do." *Village Voice* (April 10). Reprinted in Sally Banes, *Writing Dancing in the Age of Postmodernism,* 121–25. Middletown, CT: Wesleyan University Press, 1994.
Barber, Karin
    1987   "Popular Arts in Africa." *African Studies Review* 30 (3): 1–78.
    1997   *Readings in African Popular Culture.* Oxford: James Currey, and Bloomington: Indiana University Press.
Barber, Karin, John Collins, and Alain Ricard
    1997   *West African Popular Theatre.* Bloomington: Indiana University Press.
Barrow, Steve, and Peter Dalton
    1997   *Reggae: The Rough Guide.* London: Rough Guides.
Barz, Gregory, and Gerald C. Liu
    2011   "Positive Disturbance: Tafash, Twig, HIV/AIDS, and Hip Hop in Uganda." In Barz and Judah M. Cohen, eds., *The Culture of AIDS in Africa: Hope and Healing in Music and the Arts,* 362–83. New York: Oxford University Press.
Basu, Dipannita, and Sidney J. Lemelle, eds.
    2006   *The Vinyl Ain't Final: Hip Hop and the Globalization of Black Popular Culture.* London: Pluto.
Battersby, Jane
    2003   "'Sometimes It Feels Like I'm Not Black Enough': Recast(e)ing Coloured through South African Hip-Hop as a Postcolonial Text." In Herman Wasserman and Sean Jacobs, eds., *Shifting Selves: Post-Apartheid Essays on Mass Media, Culture and Identity,* 109–29. Cape Town: Kwela Books.
Bauman, Richard
    2004   *A World of Others' Words: Cross-Cultural Perspectives on Intertextuality.* Malden, MA: Blackwell.

Bauman, Richard, and Charles Briggs
  1992 "Genre, Intertextuality and Social Power." *Journal of Linguistic Anthropology* 2 (2): 131–72.
Bazin, Hugues
  1995 *La culture hip-hop.* Paris: Desclées de Brouwer.
Beckman, Janette (photographs), and B. Adler (text)
  1991 *Rap! Portraits and Lyrics of a Generation of Black Rockers.* New York: St. Martin's Press.
Bender, Wolfgang
  2000 *Sweet Mother: Moderne afrikanische Musik.* 2d ed. Wuppertal: Peter Hammer.
Benga, Ndiouga Adrien
  2002 "'The Air of the City Makes Free': Urban Music from the 1950s to the 1990s in Senegal: Variété, Jazz, Mbalax, Rap." In Palmberg and Kirkegaard, eds., *Playing with Identities in Contemporary Music in Africa,* 75–85. Uppsala: Nordiska Afrikainstitutet.
Bennett, Andy
  1999 "Rappin' on the Tyne: White Hip Hop Culture in Northeast England—an Ethnographic Study." *Sociological Review* 47 (1): 1–24. Portions reprinted in Bennett, *Popular Music and Youth Culture: Music, Identity, and Place,* chap. 6 ("Hip-Hop am Main, Rappin' on the Tyne"). New York: Palgrave, 2000.
  2001 *Cultures of Popular Music.* Buckingham, UK: Open University Press.
Berger, Harris M.
  2003 "Introduction: The Politics and Aesthetics of Language Choice and Dialect in Popular Music." In Harris M. Berger and Michael Thomas Carroll, eds., *Global Pop, Local Language,* ix–xxvi. Jackson: University Press of Mississippi.
Berger, Harris, and Giovanna Del Negro
  2004 *Identity and Everyday Life: Essays in the Study of Folklore, Music, and Popular Culture.* Middletown: Wesleyan University Press.
Bernard, James
  1992 "A Newcomer Abroad, Rap Speaks Up." *New York Times* (August 23) Section 2: 1, 22. Additional related material by other authors on 22–23.
Biaya, Tshikala
  2000 "Jeunes et culture de la rue en Afrique urbaine (Addis-Ababa, Dakar et Kinshasa." *Politique Africaine* 80: 21–31.
Blank, Polly de
  2007 "French Rapper Relishes Moral Role." *BBC News,* May 19. http://news.bbc.co.uk /2/hi/europe/6670069.stm.
Bock, Karin, Stefan Meier, and Gunter Süss, eds.
  2007 *Hip Hop Meets Academia: Globale Spuren eines lokalen Kulturphänomens.* Bielefield: Transcript.
Bocquet, José-Louis, and Philippe Pierre-Adolphe
  1997 *Rap ta France.* Paris: Flammarion. Reprinted with different pagination 1999, by Éditions J'ai lu.
Bosch, Tanja Estella
  2003 "Radio, Community, and Identity in South Africa: A Rhizomatic Study of Bush Radio in Cape Town." PhD diss., Ohio University.

Bose, Fritz
    1959   "Western Influences in Modern Asian Music." *Journal of the International Folk Music Council* 11: 47–50.
Bourdieu, Pierre
    1984   *Distinction: A Social Critique of the Judgment of Taste.* Cambridge, MA: Harvard University Press.
Boyd, Todd
    1997   *Am I Black Enough for You? Popular Culture from the 'Hood and Beyond.* Bloomington: Indiana University Press. Portions reprinted in Forman and Neal (2004: 325–40).
Bradley, Adam
    2009   *Book of Rhymes: The Poetics of Hip Hop.* New York: Basic Civitas Books.
Brand, Saskia
    2001   *Mediating Means and Fate: A Socio-Political Analysis of Fertility and Demographic Change in Bamako, Mali.* Leiden: Brill.
Brempong, Owusu
    1984   "Akan Highlife in Ghana: Songs of Cultural Transition." PhD diss., Indiana University.
Brenner, Louis
    n.d.   *Youth as Political Actors in Mali.* Manuscript.
Brooke, James
    1987   "Senegal Hails Vendor Home from 5th Ave." *New York Times* (January 2): A3.
    1988   "Coveted U.S. Visa Elusive Now for Senegalese." *New York Times* (April 13): A15.
Broughton, Simon, Mark Ellingham, and Jon Lusk, eds., with Duncan Clark
    2006   *The Rough Guide to World Music,* vol. 1, *African and the Middle East.* London: Rough Guides.
Broughton, Simon, Mark Ellingham, David Muddyman, and Richard Trillo, eds.
    1994   *World Music: The Rough Guide.* London: Rough Guides.
Broughton, Simon, Mark Ellingham, and Richard Trillo, eds.
    1999   *World Music: The Rough Guide,* vol. 1, *Africa, Europe, and the Middle East.* London: Rough Guides.
Brown, Daniel
    2003   "Ted Josiah, Nairobi, 2003." http://ted_josiah.mondomix.com/en/itw2208.htm.
Brubaker, Rogers, and Frederick Cooper
    2000   "Beyond 'Identity.'" *Theory and Society* 29 (1): 1–47.
Buskin, Richard
    2008   "Afrika Bambaataa and the Soul Sonic Force: 'Planet Rock,' Classic Tracks." *Sound on Sound* (September). http://www.soundonsound.com/sos/nov08/articles/classictracks_1108.htm.
    2010   "Public Enemy 'Black Steel in the Hour of Chaos': Classic Tracks." *Sound on Sound* (January). http://www.soundonsound.com/sos/jan10/articles/classictracks_0110.htm.
Cannon, Steve
    1997   "*Paname City Rapping:* B-Boys in the *Banlieues* and Beyond." In Alec G. Hargreaves and Mark McKinney, eds., *Post-Colonial Cultures in France,* 150–66. London: Routledge.

Capps, Randy, Kristen McCabe, and Michael Fix
   2011   *New Streams: Black African Migration to the United States.* Washington, DC: Migration Policy Institute. www.migrationpolicy.org/pubs/AfricanMigrationUS .pdf.
Cathcart, Jenny
   1989   *Hey You! A Portrait of Youssou N'Dour.* Oxford: Fine Line Books.
Causey, Andrew
   1999   "Fan: The Singasinga Table Lamp and the Toba Batak Art of Conflation." *Journal of American Folklore* 112 (Summer): 424–36.
Cestor, Élisabeth, and Hicham Abkari
   2008   "L'irruption du rap au Maroc: Entretien d'Élisabeth Cestor avec Hicham Abkari," *Africultures* (October 21). http://africultures.com (search Hicham Abkari).
Chang, Jeff
   2005   *Can't Stop, Won't Stop: A History of the Hip-Hop Generation.* New York: St. Martin's Press.
   2006   ed. *Total Chaos: The Art and Aesthetics of Hip-Hop.* New York: Basic Civitas Books.
Charry, Eric
   1996   "A Guide to the Jembe." *Percussive Notes* 34 (2): 66–72.
   1999   "A Note on the Spelling of the Drum Called Jembe." http://echarry.web.wesleyan .edu/jembe-spelling.html.
   2000   *Mande Music: Traditional and Modern Music of the Maninka and Mandinka of Western Africa.* Chicago: University of Chicago Press.
Chartsinfrance.net
   2007   http://www.chartsinfrance.net/Akon/index-20270.html.
Chimombo, Steve, and Moira Chimombo
   1996   *The Culture of Democracy: Language, Literature, the Arts, and Politics in Malawi, 1992–1994.* Zomba: WASI Publications.
Chirambo, Reuben M.
   2002   "'Mzimu wa Soldier': Contemporary Popular Music and Politics in Malawi." In Englund (2002: 103–22).
   2006   "Traditional and Popular Music, Hegemonic Power and Censorship in Malawi." In Michael Drewett and Martin Cloonan, eds., *Popular Music Censorship in Africa,* 109–26. Aldershot: Ashgate.
Clifford, James
   1994   "Diasporas." *Cultural Anthropology* 9 (3): 302–38.
Coetzer, Diane
   2004   "South Africa's Hip-Hopping." *Billboard* (April 17): 57, 60.
   2006   "MTV Expands African Operations." *Billboard* (May 27): 16.
   2008   "Africa Wants its MTV." *Billboard* (August 23): 13.
Cohen, Sara
   1999   "Scenes." In Bruce Horner and Thomas Swiss, eds., *Key Terms in Popular Music and Culture,* 239–50. Malden, MA: Blackwell.
Cole, Catherine M.
   1997   "'This Is Actually a Good Interpretation of Modern Civilisation': Popular Theatre and the Social Imaginary in Ghana, 1946–66." *Africa* 67 (3): 363–88.
   2001   *Ghana's Concert Party Theatre.* Bloomington: Indiana University Press.

Cole, Sean
2005   *South Africa's Kwaito Generation.* Inside Out, WBUR Boston. http://insideout
          .wbur.org/documentaries/kwaito.
Collins, John
1992a   *West African Pop Roots.* Philadelphia: Temple University Press.
1992b   "Some Anti-Hegemonic Aspects of African Popular Music." In Reebee Garofalo,
          ed., *Rockin' the Boat: Mass Music and Mass Movements,* 185–94. Boston: South
          End Press.
1994   *Highlife Time.* Accra: Anansesem Publications.
2004   "Ghanaian Christianity and Popular Entertainment: Full Circle." *History in Af-
          rica* 31: 407–23.
2005   "The Decolonisation of Ghanaian Popular Entertainment." In Toyin Falola and
          Steven Salm, eds., *Urbanization and African Cultures,* 119–37. Durham, NC:
          Carolina Academic Press.
Condry, Ian
2006   *Hip-Hop Japan: Rap and the Paths of Cultural Globalization.* Durham, NC: Duke
          University Press.
Coplan, David B.
2008   *In Township Tonight! South Africa's Black City Music and Theatre.* 2d ed. Chicago:
          University of Chicago Press.
Coquery-Vidrovitch, Catherine
1991   "The Process of Urbanization in Africa." *African Studies Review* 34 (1): 1–98.
Counsel, Graeme
2006   "Mande Popular Music and Cultural Policies in West Africa." PhD diss., Univer-
          sity of Melbourne. Published in 2009 by VDM Verlag.
Cullman, Brian
1991   "World Music's Hope: Can West Africa's Youssou N'Dour Pass the Global Test?"
          Rolling Stone (November 15): 21–23.
Curry, Neil
2011   "Tunisia's Rappers Provide Soundtrack to a Revolution," *CNN* (March 2). http://
          www.cnn.com/2011/WORLD/meast/03/02/tunisia.rappers.balti/.
Daoudi, Bouziane
2000   "Algerian Rappers Sing the Blues." *UNESCO Courier* (July/August): 34–35.
Darby, Derrick, and Tommie Shelby, eds.
2005   *Rhyme 2 Reason.* Chicago: Open Court.
Dave, Nomi
2009   "*Une Nouvelle Révolution Permanente:* The Making of African Modernity in
          Sékou Touré's Guinea." *Forum for Modern Language Studies* 45 (4): 455–71.
Decker, Jeffrey Louis
1993   "The State of Rap: Time and Place in Hip Hop Nationalism." *Social Text* 34:
          53–84.
Diakite, Drissa
1993   "Origines et histoire de Bamako." In Ecole Normale Supérieur de Bamako, ed.,
          Bamako, 9–22. Bordeaux: Centre de Recherches sur les Espaces Tropicaux.
Diawara, Mamadou
1997   "Mande Oral Popular Culture Revisited by the Electronic Media." In Karin Bar-

ber, ed., *Readings in African Popular Culture,* 40–47. Bloomington: Indiana University Press.

Diawara, Manthia

1998   *In Search of Africa.* Cambridge: Harvard University Press.

2005   "The 1960s in Bamako: Malick Sidibe and James Brown." In Harry Elam Jr. and Kendall Jackson, eds., *Black Cultural Traffic: Crossroads in Global Performance and Popular Culture,* 242–64. Ann Arbor: University of Michigan Press.

Dieng, Abdoul Aziz, Yann N. Diarra, Sophie Bachelier, and El Hadj Ndiaye, eds.

1999   *En avant, la musique: Annuaire des métiers de la musique au Sénégal.* Dakar: Enda Tiers Monde.

Diop, Abdoulaye-Bara

1981   *La Société Wolof: Tradition et Changement.* Paris: Karthala.

Diouf, Mamadou

2003   "Engaging Postcolonial Cultures: African Youth and Public Space." *African Studies Review* 46 (2): 1–12.

Dorsch, Hauke

2004   "Griots, Roots, and Identity in the African Diaspora." In Kokot Walktraud, Khachig Tölölyan, and Carolin Alfonso, eds., *Diaspora, Identity, and Religion: New Directions in Theory and Research,* 102–16. London: Routledge.

Drewal, Margaret Thompson

1991   "The State of Research on Performance in Africa." *African Studies Review* 34 (3): 1–64.

Du Bois, W. E. B.

1903   *The Souls of Black Folk.* Chicago: A. C. McClurg.

Duka, John

1984a   "For the Blacks in France, a Farewell to Fraternity." *New York Times* (April 14): 2.

1984b   "In Paris, a Young Black Society." *New York Times* (April 20): A16.

Durán, Lucy

1989   "Key to N'Dour: Roots of the Senegalese Star." *Popular Music* 8 (3): 275–84.

1999   "Stars and Songbirds: Mande Female Singers in Urban Music, Mali, 1980–99." PhD diss., University of London.

Durand, Alain Philippe, ed.

2002   *Black, Blanc, Beur: Rap Music and Hip-Hop Culture in the Francophone World.* Lanham, MD: Scarecrow Press.

Duranti, Alessandro

1994   *From Grammar to Politics: Linguistic Anthropology in a Western Samoan Village.* Berkeley: University of California Press.

During, Simon

1999   "Editor's Introduction," in During, ed., *The Cultural Studies Reader,* 2d ed. London: Routledge, 441–50.

Ebron, Paulla A.

2002   *Performing Africa.* Princeton: Princeton University Press.

Englert, Birgit

2003   "Bongo Flava Still Hidden: 'Underground' Rap from Morogoro, Tanzania." *Stichproben (Wiener Zeitschrift für kritische Afrikastudien)* 5 (3): 73–93.

Englund, Harri, ed.
   2002   *A Democracy of Chameleons: Politics and Culture in the New Malawi.* Uppsala and Blantyre: Nordiska Afrikainstitutet and Christian Literature Association in Malawi (CLAIM/MABUKU).
Eure, Joseph D., and James G. Spady, eds.
   1991   *Nation Conscious Rap.* Brooklyn, NY: PC International Press.
Fabian, Johannes
   1978   "Popular Culture in Africa: Findings and Conjectures." *Africa* 48 (4): 315–34.
   1998   *Moments of Freedom: Anthropology and Popular Culture.* Charlottesville: University of Virginia Press.
Faulkner, Robert R., and Howard S. Becker
   2009   *Do You Know . . . ? The Jazz Repertoire in Action.* Chicago: University of Chicago Press.
Fenn, John
   2004   "Rap and Ragga Musical Cultures, Lifestyles, and Performances in Malawi." PhD diss., Indiana University.
Ferguson, James
   2002   "Of Mimicry and Membership: Africans and the 'New World Society.'" *Cultural Anthropology* 17 (4): 551–69.
Fernandez, James
   1974   "The Mission of Metaphor in Expressive Culture." *Current Anthropology* 15 (2): 119–45.
Finnegan, Ruth
   1989   *The Hidden Musicians: Music-Making in an English Town.* Cambridge: Cambridge University Press.
Flaig, Vera H.
   2010   "The Politics of Representation and Transmission in the Globalization of Guinea's Djembé." PhD diss., University of Michigan, Ann Arbor.
Flores, Juan
   2000   *From Bomba to Hip Hop: Puerto Rican Culture and Latino Identity.* New York: Columbia University Press. Chapter 6 ("Puerto Rocks," 115–39) reprinted in Forman and Neal (2012: 74–91).
Forman, Murray, and Mark Anthony Neal, eds.
   2004   *That's the Joint! The Hip-Hop Studies Reader.* New York: Routledge.
   2012   *That's the Joint! The Hip-Hop Studies Reader.* 2d ed. New York: Routledge.
Frith, Simon
   2004   Introduction to *Popular Music: Critical Concepts in Media and Cultural Studies,* vol. 3: *Popular Music Analysis,* 1–4. New York: Routledge.
Garofalo, Reebee, ed.
   1992   *Rockin' the Boat: Mass Music and Mass Movements.* Boston: South End Press.
George, Nelson
   1998   *Hip Hop America.* New York: Viking.
George, Nelson, Sally Banes, Susan Flinker, and Patty Romanowski
   1985   *Fresh: Hip Hop Don't Stop.* New York: Random House.
Gillham, Angela
   2008   "'Street Ballet' Battle Snaps into Action." *Herald* (February 29).

Gilman, Lisa
    2004 "The Traditionalization of Women's Dancing, Hegemony, and Politics in Malawi." *Journal of Folklore Research* 41 (1): 33–60.
Gilman, Lisa, and John Fenn
    2006 "Dance, Gender, and Popular Music in Malawi: The Case of Rap and Ragga." *Popular Music* 25: 369–81.
Gilroy, Paul
    1991 "Sounds Authentic: Black Music, Ethnicity, and the Challenge of a 'Changing' Same." *Black Music Research Journal* 11 (2): 111–36.
    1993 *The Black Atlantic: Modernity and Double Consciousness.* Cambridge: Harvard University Press.
    2004 "It's a Family Affair." In Forman and Neal (2004: 87–94). Originally published 1992 in Gina Dent, ed., *Black Popular Culture,* 303–16. Seattle: Bay Press.
Githinji, Peter
    2003 "Language Attitudes: Nairobi People and Sheng." MA thesis, Michigan State University.
Gokh-Bi System
    2007 "Sonicbids Electronic Press Kit." http://www.sonicbids.com/GokhBiSystem.
Gordon, Ed
    2006 "Faada Freddy." *News and Notes,* National Public Radio (August 18). http://www .npr.org/templates/story/story.php?storyId=5669709.
Gosselin, Claudie
    2000 "Feminism, Anthropology, and the Politics of Excision in Mali: Global and Local Debates in a Postcolonial World." *Anthropologica* 42 (1): 43–60.
Gosselin, M.
    1953 "Bamako, ville soudanaise moderne." *Afrique et Asie* 21: 31–37.
Gqola, Pumla Dineo
    2004 "When a Good Black Woman Is Your Weekend Special: Brenda Fassie, Sexuality, and Performance." In Natasha Distiller and Melissa Steyn, eds., *Under Construction: 'Race' and Identity in South Africa Today,* 139–48. Sandton, South Africa: Heinemann.
Graham, Ronnie
    1992 *The World of African Music.* London: Pluto Press.
Grass, Randall
    1986 "Fela Anikulapo-Kuti: The Art of an Afrobeat Rebel." *Drama Review* 30 (1): 131–48.
Gross, Joan, David McMurray, and Ted Swedenburg
    2002 "Arab Noise and Ramadan Nights: *Rai,* Rap, and Franco-Maghrebi Identities." In Jonathan Xavier Inda and Renato Rosaldo, eds., *The Anthropology of Globalization: A Reader,* 198–230. Malden, Mass.: Blackwell.
Gupta, Akhil, and James Ferguson
    1992 "Beyond 'Culture': Space, Identity, and the Politics of Difference." *Cultural Anthropology* 7 (1): 6–23.
Haas, Peter J., and Thomas Gesthuizen
    2000 "Ndani ya Bongo: Kiswahili Rap Keeping it Real." In Frank Gunderson and Gregory F. Barz, eds., *Mashindano! Competitive Music Performance in East Africa,* 279–95. Dar es Salaam: Mkuki na Nyota.

Hager, Steven
  1984   *Hip Hop: The Illustrated History of Break Dancing, Rap Music, and Graffiti.* New York: St. Martin's Press.
Hale, Thomas A.
  1998   *Griots and Griottes.* Bloomington: Indiana University Press.
Hampton, Barbara L.
  1980   "A Revised Analytical Approach to Musical Processes in Urban Africa." *African Urban Studies* 6: 1–16.
Hannerz, Ulf
  1980   *Exploring the City. Inquiries toward an Urban Anthropology.* New York: Columbia University Press.
  1987   "The World in Creolization," *Africa* 57 (4): 546–59. Reprinted in Barber (1997: 12–18). Bloomington: Indiana University Press.
Harrison, Anthony Kwame
  2008   "Racial Authenticity in Rap Music and Hip Hop." *Sociology Compass* 2 (6): 1783–1800.
  2009   *Hip Hop Underground: The Integrity and Ethics of Racial Identification.* Philadelphia: Temple University Press.
Haupt, Adam
  1999   "Healing the Hood." *Mail and Guardian* (Johannesburg) (March 5).
  2001   "Black Thing: Hip-Hop Nationalism, 'Race,' and Gender in Prophets of da City and Brasse vannie Kaap." In Zimitri Erasmus, ed., *Coloured by History, Shaped by Place: New Perspectives on Coloured Identities in Cape Town,* 173–91. Colorado Springs: International Academic.
  2004   "Identity and the Politics of Representation in Hip-Hop." In Herman Wasserman and Sean Jacobs, eds., *Shifting Selves: Post-Apartheid Essays on Mass Media, Culture, and Identity,* 199–209. Cape Town: Kwela Books.
Havard, Jean-Francois
  2001   "Ethos 'Bul faale' et nouvelles figures de la reussite au Senegal." *Politique Africaine* 82: 63–77.
Hazard
  2009   "Zimbabwe Legit Persevere Through Two Decades of Hip Hop." Posted February 3. www.worldhiphopmarket.com/blog/?p=510.
Heath, Deborah
  1988   "The Politics of Signifying Practice in Kaolack, Senegal: Hegemony and the Dialectic of Autonomy and Domination." PhD diss., Johns Hopkins University.
Hebdige, Dick
  1979   *Subculture: The Meaning of Style.* London: Methuen.
Helenon, Veronique
  2006   "Africa on Their Mind: Rap, Blackness, and Citizenship in France." In Basu and Lemelle (2006: 151–66).
Hershkovits, David
  1983   "London Rocks, Paris Burns, and the B-Boys Break a Leg." *Sunday News Magazine* (April 3). Reprinted in Raquel Cepeda, ed., *"And It Don't Stop": The Best American Hip-Hop Journalism of the Last 25 Years,* 27–34. New York: Faber and Faber, 2004.

Herskovits, Melville J.
  1966   *The New World Negro: Selected Papers in Afroamerican Studies.* Bloomington: Indiana University Press.
Herson, Ben
  2000   "'Fat Beats, Dope Rhymes, and Thug Lives': Youth, Politics, and Hip-Hop Culture in Dakar." Senior thesis, Hampshire College.
Hesmondalgh, David, and Caspar Melville
  2001   "Urban Breakbeat Culture: Repercussions of Hip-Hop in the United Kingdom." In Mitchell (2001: 86–110).
Higgins, Christina
  2009   "From 'da bomb' to bomba: Global Hip Hop Nation Language in Tanzania." In Alim, Ibrahim, and Pennycook (2009: 95–112).
Hoffman, Barbara G.
  2000   *Griots at War: Conflict, Conciliation, and Caste in Mande.* Bloomington: Indiana University Press.
Hofmeyr, Isabel, Joyce Nyairo, and James Ogude
  2003   "Specificities: 'Who Can Bwogo Me?' Popular Culture in Kenya." *Social Identities* 9 (3): 373–82.
Hogg, Michael A., Deborah J. Terry, and Katherine M. White
  1995   "A Tale of Two Theories: A Critical Comparison of Identity Theory with Social Identity Theory." *Social Psychology Quarterly* 58 (4): 255–69.
Holman, Michael
  1984   *Breaking and the New York City Breakers.* New York: Freundlich.
Honwana, Alcinda, and Filip de Boeck, eds.
  2005   *Makers and Breakers: Children and Youth in Postcolonial Africa.* Oxford: James Currey.
Hughes, Langston
  1993   *Big Sea: An Autobiography.* 2d ed. New York: Hill and Wang.
Huq, Rupa
  1999   "Living in France: The Parallel University of Hexagonal Pop." In Andrew Blake, ed., *Living through Pop,* 131–45. New York: Routledge.
  2001   "*Rap à la française*: Hip-Hop as Youth Culture in Contemporary Post-Colonial France." In Andy Furlong and Irena Guidikova, eds., *Transitions of Youth Citizenship in Europe: Culture, Subculture and Identity,* 41–60. Strasbourg: Council of Europe.
  2006   *Beyond Subculture: Pop, Youth, and Identity in a Postcolonial World.* New York: Routledge.
Hymes, Dell
  1974   "Ways of Speaking." In Richard Bauman and Joel Scherzer, eds., *Explorations in the Ethnography of Speaking,* 433–52. London: Cambridge University Press.
Ikonne, Uchenna
  2009a "Nigerian Rap: The First Decade (1981–1991)." Posted August 14, http://www.africanhiphop.com/africanhiphopradio/naija-nigerian-80s-rap-on-vinyl/.
  2009b "Everybody Wanna Be Like Mike." Posted July 4, http://combandrazor.blogspot.com/2009/07/everybody-wanna-be-like-mike.html.
Impey, Angela
  2001   "Resurrecting the Flesh? Reflections on Women in Kwaito." *Agenda* 49: 44–50.

Inda, Jonathan Xavier, and Renato Rosaldo
2002 "Introduction: A World in Motion." In Jonathan Xavier Inda and Renato Rosaldo, eds., *The Anthropology of Globalization: A Reader*, 1–32. Malden, MA:
Blackwell.

INSTAT (Institut National de la Statistique du Mali)
2009 "District de Bamako." In INSTAT, ed., *Résultats d'enquêtes*. http://instat.gov.ml
/documentation/bamako.pdf.

Ivaska, Andrew
2002 "'Anti-Mini Militants Meet Modern Misses': Urban Style, Gender and the Politics of 'National Culture' in 1960s Dar es Salaam, Tanzania." *Gender and History*
14 (3): 584–607.

Jabbaar-Gyambrah, Tara Aminah
2007 "Hip-Hop, Hip-Life: Global Sistahs." PhD diss., SUNY Buffalo.

Jackson, Blair
2000 "In the Groove with Nick Sansano," *Mix* (November 1). http://mixonline.com
/mag/audio_groove_nick_sansano.

Jackson, John
2005 *Real Black: Adventures in Racial Sincerity*. Chicago: University of Chicago Press.

Jenkins, Philip
2007 *The Next Christendom: The Coming of Global Christianity*. Rev. ed. New York:
Oxford University Press.

Johnson-Odim, Cheryl, and Florence Mba
1997 *For Women and the Nation: Funmilayo Ransome-Kuti of Nigeria*. Urbana: University of Illinois Press.

Joseph, May
1998 "Soul, Transnationalism, and Imaginings of Revolution: Tanzanian Ujamaa and
the Politics of Enjoyment." In Monique Guillory and Richard C. Green, eds.,
Soul: Black Power, Politics, and Pleasure, 126–38. New York: New York University
Press.

Kalu, Ogbu U.
2010 "Holy Praiseco: Negotiating Sacred and Popular Music and Dance in African
Pentecostalism." *Pneuma* 32 (1): 16–40.

Kane, Ousmane Oumar
2011 *The Homeland Is the Arena: Religion, Transnationalism, and the Integration of
Senegalese Immigrants in America*. New York: Oxford University Press.

Kapchan, Deborah, and Pauline Turner Strong
1999 "Theorizing the Hybrid." *Journal of American Folklore* 112 (445): 239–53.

Keeler, Ward
2009 "What's Burmese about Burmese Rap? Why Some Expressive Forms Go Global."
American Ethnologist 36 (1): 2–19.

Kerr, David
1998 *Dance, Media-Entertainment, and Popular Performance in South East Africa*.
Bayreuth: E. Breitinger.

Keyes, Cheryl L.
1996 "At the Crossroads: Rap Music and its African Nexus." *Ethnomusicology* 40 (2):
223–48.
2002 *Rap Music and Street Consciousness*. Urbana: University of Illinois Press.

Kidula, Jean Ngoya

1996 "Cultural Dynamism in Process: The Kenya Music Festival." *Ufahamu* 25 (1/2): 63–68.

2000 "Polishing the Luster of the Stars: Music Professionalism Made Workable in Kenya." *Ethnomusicology* 44 (3): 408–28.

forth. *Music in Kenyan Christianity: Logooli Religious Song.* Bloomington: Indiana University Press.

Kiefer, Julien

2006 "Les jeunes des 'Grins' de the et la campagne electorale à Ouagadougou." *Politique Africaine* 101 (March/April): 63–82.

Kimmelman, Michael

2008 "For Blacks in France, Obama's Rise Is Reason to Rejoice, and to Hope." *New York Times* (June 17): E2.

Kimminich, Eva

2001 "Enragement und Engagement: Beobachtungen und Gedanken zur WortGewalt des franzoesischen und frankophonen Rap." In Kimminich and Claudia Kruells-Hepermann, eds., *Wort und Waffe,* 141–76. Frankfurt: Peter Lang.

2004a ed. *Rap: More than Words.* Frankfurt: Peter Lang.

2004b "(Hi)Story, Rapstory und 'possible worlds': Erzaehlstrategien und Koerperkommunikation im senegalesischen Rap." In Kimminich (2004a: 233–72).

Kioko, A. N., and M. J. Muthwii

2004 "English Variety for Public Domain in Kenya." In Margaret Jepkirui Muthwii and Angelina Nduku Kioko, eds., *New Language Bearings in Africa: A Fresh Quest,* 34–49. Buffalo, NY: Multilingual Matters.

Klein, Gabriele, and Malte Friedrich

2003 *Is This Real? Die Kultur des HipHop.* Frankfurt: Suhrkamp.

Knight, Roderic C.

1974 "Mandinka Drumming." *African Arts* 7 (4): 24–35.

1984 "Music in Africa: The Manding Contexts." In Gerard Béhague, ed., *Performance Practice: Ethnomusicological Perspectives,* 53–90. Westport, CT: Greenwood Press.

1991 "Music out of Africa: Mande Jaliya in Paris." *World of Music* 33 (1): 52–69.

Krims, Adam

2000 *Rap Music and the Poetics of Identity.* Cambridge: Cambridge University Press.

KRS-One

2009 *The Gospel of Hip Hop: First Instrument.* Brooklyn: powerHouse Books.

Kubik, Gerhard

1981 "Neo-Traditional Popular Music in East Africa since 1945." *Popular Music* 1: 83–104.

1987 *Malawian Music: A Framework for Analysis.* Assisted by Moya Aliya Malamusi, Lidiya Malamusi, and Donald Kachamba, and edited by Mitchel Strumpf. Zomba: Centre for Social Research and Department of Fine and Performing Arts, Chancellor College, University of Malawi.

1989 Musiker aus Malawi/Musicians from Malawi. "Opeka nyimbo" Musiker-Komponisten/Musician-composers (in cooperation with Moya Aliya Malamusi). Commentary booklet to LP, Museum Collection Berlin (West), vol 15,

     edited by Artur Simon. Berlin: Staatliche Museen zu Berlin—Preußischer Kulturbesitz. Ethnologisches Museum.
1991   "Muxima Ngola—Veränderungen und Strömungen in den Musikkulturen Angolas im 20. Jahrhundert." In Veit Erlmann, ed., *Populäre Musik in Afrika*, 201–71. Berlin: Staatliche Museen zu Berlin—Preußischer Kulturbesitz. Ethnologisches Museum.
Künzler, Daniel
2007   "The 'Lost Generation': African Hip Hop Movements and the Protest of the Young (Male) Urban." In Mark Herkenrath, ed., *Civil Society: Local and Regional Responses to Global Challenges*, 89–127. Zurich: LIT Verlag.
2011a "South African Rap Music, Counter Discourses, Identity, and Commodification beyond the Prophets of Da City." *Journal of Southern African Studies* 37 (1): 27–43.
2011b "Rapping Against the Lack of Change: Rap Music in Mali and Burkina Faso." In Saucier (2011: 23–49).
Kwaku
1995   "S. Africa's Prophets Move to U.K.; Nation Album Due." *Billboard* (January 7): 38.
2000   "Words and Deeds: African Hip-Hop Getting Web Exposure." *Billboard* (December 23): 23.
Kwaramba, Alice Dadirai
1997   *Popular Music and Society. The Language of Protest in 'Chimurenga' Music: The Case of Thomas Mapfumo in Zimbabwe*. Oslo: Department of Media and Communication, University of Oslo.
Launay, Robert
1982   *Traders without Trade: Responses to Change in Two Dyula Communities*. Cambridge: Cambridge University Press.
1992   *Beyond the Stream: Islam and Society in a West African Town*. Berkeley: University of California Press.
Leach, Andrew
2008   "'One Day It'll All Make Sense': Hip-Hop and Rap Resources for Music Librarians." *Notes* 65 (1): 9–37.
Legrand, Emmanuel, and Michael Paoletta
2005   "MTV Networks Gets Back to its Roots Via Broadband and Launches 100th Channel in Africa." *Billboard* (April 30): 32–33.
Lemelle, Sidney J.
2006   "'Ni Wapi tunakwenda': Hip Hop Culture and the Children of Arusha." In Basu and Lemelle (2006: 230–54).
Leymarie-Ortiz, Isabelle
1979   "The Griots of Senegal and Change." *Africa* (Rome) 34 (3): 183–97.
Lipsitz, George
1994   *Dangerous Crossroads: Popular Music, Postmodernism, and the Poetics of Place*. New York: Verso.
Little, Kenneth
1965   *West African Urbanization: A Study of Voluntary Associations in Social Change*. Cambridge: Cambridge University Press.
Lobeck, Katharina
2002   "Dakarapping." *fROOTS* (August/September): 20–21, 23, 25

Logan, John R. and Glenn Deane
  2003   "Black Diversity in Metropolitan America." Lewis Mumford Center for Com-
          parative Urban and Regional Research, University at Albany, SUNY. http://
          mumford.albany.edu/census/report.html.
Lwanda, John L.C.
  2002   "Tikutha: The Political Culture of the HIV/AIDS Epidemic in Malawi." In H. En-
          glund (2002: 151–65).
  2003   "Mother's Songs: Male Appropriation of Women's Music in Malawi and South-
          ern Africa." *Journal of African Cultural Studies* 16 (2): 119–41.
  2006   "Malawi: Sounds Afroma!" In Broughton, Ellingham, and Lusk (2006:
          211–18).
  2009   "Music Advocacy, the Media, and the Malawi Political Public Sphere, 1958–
          2007." *Journal of African Media Studies* 1 (1): 135–54.
MacNeil, Heather Marie, and Bonnie Mak
  2007   "Constructions of Authenticity." *Library Trends* 56 (1): 26–52.
Madichie, Nnamdi O.
  2011   "Marketing Senegal through Hip-Hop—A Discourse Analysis of Akon's Music
          and Lyrics." *Journal of Place Management and Development* 4 (2): 169–97.
Magaldi, Cristina
  1999   "Adopting Imports: New Images and Alliances in Brazilian Popular Music of the
          1990s." *Popular Music* 18 (3): 309–29.
Magubane, Zine
  2006   "Globalization and Gangster Rap: Hip Hop in the Post-Apartheid City." In Basu
          and Lemelle (2006: 208–29).
Mail and Guardian
  1997   "Lauded Abroad While Banned by SABC." Johannesburg *Mail and Guardian*
          (January 24).
Malamusi, Moya Aliya
  2004   "The Popular Dance of Mbumba in the 1980s." *Ntama: Journal of African Music
          and Popular Culture* (January 4). http://ntama.uni-mainz.de/.
Malik, Abd al
  2009   *Sufi Rapper: The Spiritual Journey of Abd al Malik.* Trans. Jon E. Graham. Ro-
          chester, VT: Inner Traditions. Originally published in French, 2004.
Malm, Krister and Monika Sarstad
  1997   *Rap, Ragga, and Reggae in Nairobi, Dar es Salaam, and Lusaka in 1997.* http://
          www.visarkiv.se/en/mmm/media/africa/index.html.
Maluka, Mustafa
  2007   "Hip-Hop in Algiers: The Microphone That Broke the Silence." In Stemmler and
          Skrandies (2007: 111–20).
Mangesho, Peter
  2003   "Global Cultural Trends: The Case of Hip-Hop Music in Dar es Salaam." MA
          thesis, University of Dar es Salaam.
Mangin, Timothy R.
  2004   "Notes on Jazz in Senegal." In Robert O'Meally, Brent Hayes Edwards, and Farah
          Jasmine Griffin, eds., *Uptown Conversation: The New Jazz Studies*, 224–48. New
          York: Columbia University Press.

forth. "Mbalax: Cosmopolitanism in Senegalese Urban Popular Music and Culture." PhD diss., Columbia University.

Mapanje, J.
2002 "Afterword. The Orality of Dictatorship: In Defence of My Country." In Englund (2002: 178–87).

Marshall, Wayne
2006 "Giving Up Hip-Hop's Firstborn: A Quest for the Real after the Death of Sampling." *Callaloo* 29 (3): 868–92.

Maultsby, Portia K.
1983 "Soul Music: Its Sociological and Political Significance in American Popular Culture." *Journal of Popular Culture* 17 (2): 51–60.
1990 "Africanisms in African American Music." In Joseph E. Holloway, ed., *Africanisms in American Culture*, 185–210. Bloomington: Indiana University Press.

Maxwell, Ian
2003 *Phat Beats, Dope Rhymes: Hip Hop Down Under Comin' Upper.* Middletown, CT: Wesleyan University Press.

Mbaye, Jenny F.
2011 "Hip-Hop Political Productions in West Africa: AURA and its Extraordinary Stories of Poto-Poto Children." In Saucier (2011: 51–68).

Mbaye, Ousmane
1999 "Rap attaque sur l'Afrique: l'explosion sénégalaise." *Rythmes* 6 (3): 2e trimestre. http://www.chanson.ca/action/rhythmes/R18/18premierplan.html (accessed January 9, 2008, no longer available).

McBride, James
2007 "Hip-Hop Planet." *National Geographic* (April): 100–119.

McCloy, Maria
n.d. "Kwaito." *Rage: SA Urban Culture Online.* www.rage.co.za (select Music: SA Music History).

McLaughlin, Noel, and Martin McLoone
2000 "Hybridity and National Musics: The Case of Irish Rock Music." *Popular Music* 19 (2): 181–99.

McLeod, Kembrew
1999 "Authenticity within Hip-Hop and Other Cultures Threatened with Assimilation." *Journal of Communication* 49 (4): 134–50. Reprinted in Forman and Neal (2012: 164–78).

McNee, Lisa
1996 "Selfish Gifts: Senegalese Women's Autobiographical Discourses." PhD diss., Indiana University.
2000 *Selfish Gifts: Senegalese Women's Autobiographical Discourses.* Albany: State University of New York Press.
2002 "Back from Babylon: Popular Musical Cultures of the Diaspora, Youth Culture, and Identity in Francophone West Africa." In Richard A. Young, ed., *Music, Popular Culture, Identities*, 231–47. Amsterdam: Rodopi.

Meadows, Eddie S.
2010 *Blues, Funk, Rhythms and Blues, Soul, Hip Hop, and Rap: A Research and Information Guide.* New York: Routledge.

Media Institute of Southern Africa, ed.

2004   *Southern African Media Directory 2004/05.* Windhoek: Media Institute of Southern Africa. www.misa.org/researchandpublication/annualreport/Annual Report
2004.pdf.

Meghelli, Samir

2004   "Returning to *The Source, En Diaspora*: Historicizing the Emergence of the Hip-
Hop Cultural Movement in France." *Proud Flesh* 3. www.africaknowledgeproject
.org/index.php/proudflesh/article/view/212 (available by subscription only), formerly available at www.africaresource.com/proudflesh/issue3/meghelli.htm.

Meillassoux, Claude

1963   "Histoire et institutions du *kafo* de Bamako, d'après la tradition des Niare." *Cahiers d'Études Africaines* 14: 186–227.

1968   *Urbanization of an African Community: Voluntary Associations in Bamako.* Se-
attle: University of Washington Press.

Mensah, Atta Annan

1959   "Problems Involved in the 'Arrangement' of Folk Music for Radio Ghana." *Journal of the International Folk Music Council* 11: 83–84.

1970   "The Music of Zumaile Village, Zambia." *African Music* 4 (4): 96–102.

Miliani, Hadj

2000   "Savoirs inscrits, saviors prescrits et leur expression symbolique en mileu urbain
en Algérie: Le case u rap." *VEI Enjeu* 123 (December): 149–62.

2002   "Culture planétaire et identités frontalières: À propos du rap en Algérie." *Cahiers
d'Études Africaines* 42 (4): 763–76.

Miller, Daniel

1995   "Consumption as the Vanguard of History: A Polemic by Way of Introduction."
In Miller, ed., *Acknowledging Consumption: A Review of New Studies,* 1–57. New
York: Routledge.

Mills, Elizabeth Shown, and Gary B. Mills

1984   "The Genealogist's Assessment of Alex Haley's Roots." *National Genealogical Society Quarterly* 72: 35–49.

Mills, Gary B., and Elizabeth Shown Mills

1981   "Roots and the New Faction: A Legitimate Tool for Clio?" *Virginia Magazine of
History and Biography* 89: 35–49.

Mitchell, James C.

1956   *Kalela Dance.* Rhodes-Livingston Papers 27. Manchester: Manchester University
Press.

1966   "Theoretical Orientations in African Urban Studies." In Michael Banton, ed., *The
Social Anthropology of Complex Societies,* 37–68. London: Tavistock.

1987   *Cities, Society, and Social Perception: A Central African Perspective.* Oxford: Clar-
endon Press.

Mitchell, Tony, ed.

2001   *Global Noise: Rap and Hip-Hop outside the USA.* Middletown, CT: Wesleyan
University Press.

Mlekani, Cosman

2002   "Sumaye Awataka Wasanii Kuacha Kuigaiga" [Sumaye wants artist to stop copy-
ing]. *Nipashe* (May 29).

Modic, Kate
  1996 "Song, Performance, and Power: The bèn ka di Women's Association in Bamako, Mali." PhD diss., Indiana University.
Monson, Ingrid
  2007 *Freedom Sounds: Civil Rights Call Out to Jazz and Africa*. New York: Oxford University Press.
Morakinyo, Dele
  1990 "The Music Industry in Nigeria over the Years." *Nigerian Music Awards Annual*. Lagos: PMAN and Ideas Communication Ltd.
Mose, Caroline
  2011 "Jua Cali-Justice: Navigating the Mainstream-Underground Dichotomy in Kenyan Hip-Hop Culture." In Saucier (2011: 69–104).
Moto, Francis
  2004 "Towards a Study of the Lexicon of Sex and HIV/AIDS." *Nordic Journal of African Studies* 13 (3): 343–62.
Msimango, Ziphezinhle
  2008 "Any Given Sunday." Johannesburg *Sunday Times* (February 17).
Muller, Carol Ann
  1999 *Rituals of Fertility and the Sacrifice of Desire: Nazarite Women's Performance in South Africa*. Chicago: University of Chicago Press.
Mushengyezi, Aaron
  2003 "Rethinking Indigenous Media: Rituals, 'Talking' Drums, and Orality as Forms of Public Communication in Uganda." *Journal of African Cultural Studies* 16 (1): 107–17.
Ndiaye, Pap
  2008 *La condition noire: Essai sur une minorité française*. Paris: Calmann-Lévy.
Ndoye Mbengue, Mariama
  1982 "Introduction à la littérature orale léboue: Analyse ethno-sociologique et expression littéraire." PhD diss., Université Cheikh Anta Diop, Dakar.
Neate, Patrick
  2003 *Where You're At: Notes from the Frontline of a Hip Hop Planet*. Riverhead Books: New York.
Negus, Keith
  2004 "The Business of Rap: Between the Street and the Executive Suite." In Forman and Neal (2004: 525–40). Originally published 1999 in Negus, *Music Genres and Corporate Cultures*, New York: Routledge.
Nelson, Tara Denice
  1997 "Debating Blackness: The Case of Hip Hop and Ragga in Harare, Zimbabwe." MA thesis, University of Iowa.
Neophytou, Nadia
  2005 "Talking War and Peace." Johannesburg *Mail and Guardian* (October 28).
Newman, Jason
  2008 "'Uncle' Ralph McDaniels, a Hip Hop Pioneer, Still inside the Box." *Village Voice* (July 16). www.villagevoice.com (search Ralph McDaniels).
New York Times
  1985 "Street Peddlers from Senegal Flock to New York." *New York Times* (November 10): 52.

Niang, Abdoulaye
    2006   "Bboys: Hip-Hop Culture in Dakar." In Pam Nilan and Carles Feixa, eds., *Global Youth? Hybrid Identities, Plural Worlds,* 167–85. New York: Routledge.

Njane, M. M.
    2001   "Rap Music Made in Kenya: How Kenyan Is It?" MA project, Kenyatta University Nairobi, Kenya.

Nketia, J. H. Kwabena
    1973   "The Study of African and Afro-American Music." *Black Perspective in Music* 1 (1): 7–15.

Noel, Peter
    2000   "Africans Are Dying, Too: The Forgotten Victims of the Livery Cabbie Murders." *Village Voice* (April 19–25). www.villagevoice.com/2000-04-18/news/africans-are-dying-too/.

Norris, Michelle
    2005   "Interview with Daara J." *All Things Considered,* National Public Radio (May 20). www.npr.org/templates/story/story.php?storyId=4660446.

Nouripour, Omid
    1998   "A List of Senerap-Records (1998)." *Ntama: Journal of African Music and Popular Culture.* www.uni-hildesheim.de/ntama/. (select African Hip Hop)

Ntarangwi, Mwenda
    2009   *East African Hip Hop: Youth Culture and Globalization.* Urbana: University of Illinois Press.

Nurse, George T.
    1964   "Popular Songs and National Identity in Malawi." *African Music* 3 (3): 101–106.

Nwagwu, Cordelia
    1997   "The Environment of Crises in the Nigerian Education System." *Comparative Education* 33 (1): 87–95.

Nyairo, Joyce, and James Ogude
    2003   "Popular Music and the Negotiation of Contemporary Kenyan Identity: The Example of Nairobi City Ensemble." *Social Identities* 9 (3): 383–400.
    2005   "Popular Music, Popular Politics: Unbwogable and the Idioms of Freedom in Kenyan Popular Music." *African Affairs* 104 (415): 225–49.

Nyakiti, Charles Orawo
    2002   "Music Creativity among the Traditional Luo." Paper presented at Kenyatta University music symposium on the theme "Africa as the Cradle for a Holistic and Integrated Approach to Music," November 20–23.

Nzewi, Meki E.
    1997   *African Music: Theoretical Content and Creative Continuum. The Culture-Exponent's Definitions.* Oldershausen: Institut für Didaktik populärer Musik.

Nzunda, Matembo S., and Kenneth R. Ross, eds.
    1995   *Church, Law, and Political Transition in Malawi, 1992–1994.* Gweru: Mambo Press.

Obeng, Samuel
    1999   "Requests in Akan Discourse." *Anthropological Linguistics* 41 (2): 230–51.

Ojukwu, Emeka O.
    1989   *Because I Am Involved.* Ibadan: Spectrum.

Okege, Oladipo
1992 *Contemporary Social Problems: Historical Outline of Nigeria*. Ibadan: Dare Standard Press.
Okpewho, Isidore, ed.
1990 *The Oral Performance in Africa*. Ibadan: Spectrum Books.
Olaniyan, Tejumola
2004 *Arrest the Music! Fela and His Rebel Art and Politics*. Bloomington: Indiana University Press.
Omojola, Bode
forth. *Yoruba Music in the Twentieth Century*. Rochester, NY: University of Rochester Press.
Omoniyi, Tope
2009 "'So I Choose to Do Am Naija Style': Hip Hop, Language, and Postcolonial Identities." In Alim, Ibrahim, and Pennycook (2009: 113–35).
Osumare, Halifu
2005 "Global Hip Hop and the African Diaspora." In Harry Elam Jr. and Kendall Jackson, eds., *Black Cultural Traffic: Crossroads in Global Performance and Popular Culture*, 266–88. Ann Arbor: University of Michigan Press.
2007 *The Africanist Aesthetic in Global Hip-Hop: Power Moves*. New York: Palgrave Macmillan.
Oumano, Elena
1999 "Words and Deeds: Senegal's PBS Forges African Hip-Hop." *Billboard* (September 4): 30–31.
Panzacchi, Cornelia
1994 "Livelihoods of Traditional Griots in Modern Senegal." *Africa* 64 (2): 190–210.
1996 *Mbalax Mi: Musikszene Senegal*. Wuppertal: Hammer.
Patel, Aniruddh
2008 *Music, Language, and the Brain*. New York: Oxford University Press.
Patel, Nandini
2000 "Media in the Democratic and Electoral Process." In Martin Ott, Kings M. Phiri, and Nandini Patel, eds., *Malawi's Second Democratic Elections: Process, Problems, and Prospects*, 158–85. Blantyre: Christian Literature Association in Malawi (CLAIM).
Peigne-Giuly, Annick
1996 "Quand Sidney surfait sur le smurf à la télé." *Liberation* (April 23): 34.
Pennycook, Alastair
2007 *Global Englishes and Transcultural Flows*. New York: Routledge.
Pennycook, Alastair, and Tony Mitchell
2009 "Hip Hop as Dusty Foot Philosophy: Engaging Locality." In Alim, Ibrahim, and Pennycook (2009: 25–42).
Perry, Donna A.
1997 "Rural Ideologies and Urban Imaginings: Wolof Immigrants in New York City." *Africa Today* 44 (2): 229–59.
Perullo, Alex
2003 "'The Life That I Live': Popular Music, Urban Practices, and Agency in Dar es Salaam, Tanzania." PhD diss., Indiana University.

2005 "Hooligans and Heroes: Youth Identity and Rap Music in Dar es Salaam, Tanzania." *Africa Today* 51 (4): 74–101.

2007 "'Here's a Little Something Local': An Early History of Hip Hop in Dar es Salaam, Tanzania, 1984–1997." In Andrew Burton, James Brennan, and Yusuf Lawi, eds., *Dar es Salaam: The History of an Emerging East African Metropolis,* 250–72. Dar es Salaam, Tanzania: Mkuki wa Nyota.

2011 *Live from Dar es Salaam: Popular Music and Tanzania's Music Economy.* Bloomington: Indiana University Press.

Perullo, Alex, and John Fenn
2003 "Language Ideologies, Choices, and Practices in Eastern African Hip Hop." In Harris M. Berger and Michael Thomas Carrol, eds., *Global Popular Music: The Politics and Aesthetics of Language Choice,* 19–51. Jackson: University Press of Mississippi.

Peterson, Richard A.
2005 "In Search of Authenticity." *Journal of Management Studies* 42 (5): 1083–98.

Phiri, Isabel Apawo
1997 "Marching, Suspended, and Stoned: Christian Women in Malawi 1995." In Kenneth R. Ross, ed., *God, People and Power in Malawi: Democratization in Theological Perspective,* 63–105. Blantyre: Christian Literature Association in Malawi (CLAIM).

Phiri, Kings M., and Kenneth R. Ross, eds.
1998 *Democratization in Malawi: A Stocktaking.* Blantyre: Christian Literature Association in Malawi (CLAIM).

Pierre, Jemima
2002 "Race across the Atlantic: Mapping Racialization in Africa and the African Diaspora." PhD diss., University of Texas, Austin.

Polak, Rainer
2000 "A Musical Instrument Travels around the World: *Jenbe* Playing in Bamako, in West Africa, and Beyond." *World of Music* 42 (3): 7–46. Reprinted 2005 in Jennifer Post, ed., *Ethnomusicology: A Contemporary Reader,* 161–86. New York: Routledge Press.

2004 *Festmusik als Arbeit, Trommeln als Beruf: Jenbe-Spieler in einer westafrikanischen Großstadt.* Berlin: Reimer.

2005 "The Commercialization of Celebration Music in Bamako." In Jan Jansen and Stephen Wooten, eds., *Wari Matters: Ethnographic Explorations of Money in the Mande World,* 135–61. Münster: Lit Verlag.

2007 "Performing Audience: On the Social Constitution of Focused Interaction at Celebrations in Mali." *Anthropos* 102 (1): 3–18.

2010 "Rhythmic Feel as Meter: Non-Isochronous Beat Subdivision in Jembe Music from Mali." *Music Theory Online* 16 (4). http://mtosmt.org/.

Pollard, Lawrence
2004 "Rap Returns Home to Africa." *BBC News,* September 2. http://news.bbc.co.uk/go/pr/fr/-/2/hi/africa/3622406.stm.

Posner, Daniel N.
1995 "Malawi's New Dawn." *Journal of Democracy* 6 (1): 131–45.

Potter, Russell
1995   *Spectacular Vernaculars: Hip-Hop and the Politics of Postmodernism.* Albany: State University of New York Press.

Prévos, André
1996   "The Evolution of French Rap Music and Hip Hop Culture in the 1980s and 1990s." *French Review* 69 (5): 713–25.
2001   "Postcolonial Popular Music in France: Rap Music and Hip-Hop Culture in the 1980s and 1990s." In Mitchell (2001: 39–56).
2002   "Two Decades of Rap in France: Emergence, Developments, Prospects." In Durand (2002: 1–21).

Rebensdorf, Alicia
1996   "'Representing the Real: Exploring Appropriations of Hip-Hop Culture in the Internet and Nairobi." Senior thesis, Lewis and Clark College.

Reed, Daniel B.
2001   "Pop Goes the Sacred: Dan Mask Performance and Popular Culture in Postcolonial Côte d'Ivoire." *Africa Today* 48 (4): 67–87.
2003   *Dan Ge Performance: Masks and Music in Contemporary Côte d'Ivoire.* Bloomington: Indiana University Press.
2005   "The *Ge* Is in the Church and Our Parents Are 'Playing Muslim': Performance, Identity, and Resistance among the Dan in Postcolonial Côte d'Ivoire." *Ethnomusicology* 49 (3): 347–67.

Regis, Marlon
2005   "Reasoning with Daara J: 'Bling My Soul.'" August 16. http://www.jahworks.org /music/interview/daara_j.htm.

Remes, Pieter
1998   "'Karibu Geto Langu/Welcome in My Ghetto': Urban Youth, Popular Culture, and Language in 1990s Tanzania." PhD diss., Northwestern University.
1999   "Global Popular Musics and Changing Awareness of Urban Tanzanian Youth." *Yearbook of Traditional Music* 24: 1–26

Reuster-Jahn, Uta
2007   "Let's Go Party! Discourse and Self-Portrayal in the *Bongo Fleva* Song 'Mikasi.'" *Swahili Forum* 14: 225–44.

Reyes-Schramm, Adelaida
1982   "Explorations in Urban Ethnomusicology: Hard Lessons from the Spectacularly Ordinary." *Yearbook for Traditional Music* 14: 1–14.

RFI Musique
1999   "Biography: Positive Black Soul." *Radio France Internationale,* July. http://www .rfimusique.com/siteen/biographie/biographie_6210.asp.
2003   "Biography: Daara J." *Radio France Internationale,* February. http://www.rfimusique .com/siteen/biographie/biographie_7778.asp.
2008   "Biography: Didier Awadi." *Radio France Internationale,* January. http://www .rfimusique.com/musique/siteen/biographie/biographie_8004.asp.

Rice, Timothy
1994   *May It Fill Your Soul: Experiencing Bulgarian Music.* Chicago: University of Chicago Press.

Rivera, Raquel Z.
   2003   *New York Ricans from the Hip Hop Zone*. New York: Palgrave Macmillan.
Robertson, Robert
   1992   *Globalization: Social Theory and Global Culture*. London: Sage.
Rose, Tricia
   1994   *Black Noise: Rap Music and Black Culture in Contemporary America*. Middletown, CT: Wesleyan University Press/University Press of New England.
Ross, Kenneth R., ed.
   1997   *God, People, and Power in Malawi: Democratization in Theological Perspective*. Blantyre: Christian Literature Association in Malawi (CLAIM).
Rycroft, D. K.
   1977   "Evidence of Stylistic Continuity in Zulu Town Music." In Klaus Wachsmann, ed., *Essays for a Humanist: An Offering to Klaus Wachsmann*, 216–60. Spring Valley, NY: Town House Press.
Saakana, Amon Saba
   1995   "Culture, Concept, Aesthetics: The Phenomenon of the African Musical Universe in Western Musical Culture." *African American Review* 29 (2): 329–40.
Saavedra Casco, Arturo J.
   2006   "The Language of the Young People: Rap, Urban Culture, and Protest in Tanzania." *Journal of Asian and African Studies* 41: 229–48.
Samper, David A.
   2002   "Talking Sheng: The Role of Hybrid Language in the Construction of Identity and Youth Culture in Nairobi, Kenya." PhD diss., University of Pennsylvania.
   2004   "'Africa Is Still Our Mama': Kenyan Rappers, Youth Identity, and the Revitalization of Traditional Values." *African Identities* 2 (1): 37–51.
Sanogo, Bakary
   1993   "La population de Bamako." In Ecole Normale Supérieur de Bamako, ed., *Bamako*, 53–78. Bordeaux: Centre de Recherches sur les Espaces Tropicaux.
Saucier, P. Khalil, ed.
   2011   *Native Tongues: The African Hip-Hop Reader*. Trenton, NJ: Africa World Press.
Schoffeleers, Matthew
   1999   *In Search of Truth and Justice: Confrontations between Church and State in Malawi, 1960–1994*. Blantyre: Christian Literature Association in Malawi (CLAIM).
Schulz, Dorothea
   1999   "In Pursuit of Publicity: Talk Radio and the Imagination of a Moral Public in Mali." *Africa Spectrum* 99 (2): 161–85.
   2001a *Perpetuating the Politics of Praise: Jeli Praise Singers, Radios, and Political Mediation in Mali*. Köln: Rüdiger Köppe.
   2001b "Music Videos and the Effeminate Vices of Urban Culture in Mali." *Africa* 71 (3): 325–71.
   2002a "'The World Is Made by Talk': Female Youth Culture, Pop Music Consumption, and Mass-Mediated Forms of Sociality in Urban Mali." *Cahiers d'Études Africaines* 168, 42 (2): 797–830.
   2002b "Reklame in Mali: Popsängerinnen und die Vermittlung von Bildern der kosmopolitischauthentischen malischen Frau." In Tobias Wendl, ed., *Reklamekunst in*

Afrika, 154–60. Munich: Prestel (Catalogue to the exhibit "Advertisement Art in Africa," Iwalewa African Studies Centre, University of Bayreuth).

2004 "'God Is Our Resort': Islamic Revival, Mass-Mediated Religiosity, and the Moral Negotiation of Gender Relations in Urban Mali." Habilitation thesis, Free University, Berlin.

2005 "Love Potions and Money Machines: Commercial Occultism, and the Reworking of Social Relations in Urban Mali." In Stephen Wooten, ed., *Wari Matters: Ethnographic Explorations of Money in the Mande World,* 93–115. Münster and Hamburg: Lit Verlag.

Schumacher, Thomas
1995 "'This Is a Sampling Sport': Digital Sampling, Rap Music, and the Law in Cultural Production." *Media, Culture, and Society* 17 (2): 253–73.

Seebode, Jochen
1999 *Malipenga, Samba, Rap, und Reggae—Anmerkungen zu Jugendkulturen in Nordmalawi.* Sozialanthropologische Arbeitspapiere der Freien Universität Berlin, Institut für Ethnologie, SAAP, no. 81.

2003 "Tanzwettkämpfe, Transformationsprozesse, und Identität: Tanzstile junger Männer in Nordmalawi." In Ute Luig and Jochen Seebode, eds., *Ethnologie der Jugend: Soziale Praxis, moralische Diskurse, und inszenierte Körperlichkeit,* 199–239. Münster, Hamburg and London: LIT Verlag.

2007 "Malawis Populärmusik, männliche Jugendliche, und die Medien." *Journal-Ethnologie.de* 5: Digitale Welten. http://www.journal-ethnologie.de.

2009 "Jugend, Musik, und Tanz in Post-Banda-Malawi (1994–2004): Männliche Jugendliche in Chitipa und Karonga." PhD diss., Freie Universität Berlin.

2010 "Klang-Bewegungs-Räume: Musikvideos, Rapmusik, und die Inszenierung jugendlicher Männlichkeiten in Post-Banda-Malawi." In Dorothea E. Schulz and Jochen Seebode, eds., *Prisma und Spiegel: Ethnologie zwischen postkolonialer Kritik und Deutung der eigenen Gesellschaft,* 276–94. Hamburg: Argument Verlag.

Seiler, Bobby and JJC (Abdul Rasheed Bello)
2005 *Afropop: The Rise and Rise of African Hip Hop.* Four parts. Produced by Bobby Seiler, narrated by JJC. Broadcast on *BBC World Service: The Music Feature,* March 7, 14, 21, 28. Rebroadcast on BBC Radio 1Xtra (November). Each part at http://www.bbc.co.uk/1xtra/tx/documentaries/afropop_west.shtml (substitute east, south, north).

Sessay, Doreen
2001 "Freizeitverhalten von Jugendlichen in Bamako." Research Project Report, Institute for Ethnology, Free University, Berlin.

Shain, Richard M.
2002 "Roots in Reverse: *Cubanismo* in Twentieth-Century Senegalese Music." *International Journal of African Historical Studies* 35 (1): 83–101.

2009 "The Re(Public) of Salsa: Afro-Cuban Music in *Fin-de-Siècle* Dakar." *Africa* 79 (2): 186–206.

2012 "Trovador of the Black Atlantic: Laba Sosseh and the Africanization of Afro-Cuban Music." In Bob W. White, ed., *Music and Globalization: Critical Encounters,* 135–156. Bloomington: Indiana University Press.

Sharma, Nitasha Tamar
 2010   *Hip Hop Desis: South Asian Americans, Blackness, and a Global Race Consciousness.* Durham, NC: Duke University Press.
Shipley, Jesse Weaver
 forth. *The Entrepreneur's Aesthetic: Circulation and Celebrity in Ghanaian Hiplife.* Durham, NC: Duke University Press.
Shitandi, Wilson
 2002   "Kenyan Popular Music: Bridging the Gap between the New and the Old." Paper presented at Kenyatta University Music Symposium on the theme "Africa as the Cradle for a Holistic and Integrated Approach to Music," November 20–23, 2002.
Silverstein, Paul
 2002   "'Why Are We Waiting to Start the Fire'? French Gangsta Rap and the Critique of Capitalism." In Durand (2002: 45–67).
Sinclair, David
 1992   "Rapping the World." *Billboard* (November 28): R16, R22.
Singer, Milton
 1972   *When a Great Tradition Modernizes: An Anthropological Approach to Indian Civilization.* New York: Praeger.
Smitherman, Geneva
 1997   "'The Chain Remain the Same': Communicative Practices in the Hip Hop Nation." *Journal of Black Studies* 28 (1): 3–25.
Sosibo, Kwanele
 2006   "100% Zulu Boy." Johannesburg *Mail and Guardian* (October 13).
Spady, James G., H. Sammy Alim, and Samir Meghelli
 2006   *Tha Global Cipha: Hip Hop Culture and Consciousness.* Philadelphia: Black History Museum Press.
Stapleton, Chris, and Chris May
 1987   *African All-Stars: The Pop Music of a Continent.* London: Quartet. Reprinted 1990, *African Rock: The Pop Music of a Continent.* New York: Dutton.
Stemmler, Susanne, and Timo Skrandies
 2007   *Hip-Hop und Rap in romanischen Sprachwelten: Stationen einer globalen Musikkultur.* Frankfurt am Main: Peter Lang.
Stewart, Gary
 2000   *Rumba on the River: A History of the Popular Music of the Two Congos.* New York: Verso.
Stoller, Paul
 1994   "Ethnographies as Texts/Ethnographers as Griots." *American Ethnologist* 21 (2): 353–66.
 2002   *Money Has No Smell: The Africanization of New York City.* Chicago: University of Chicago Press.
Stolzoff, Norman
 2000   *Wake the Town and Tell the People: Dancehall Culture in Jamaica.* Durham: Duke University Press.
Straw, Will
 1991   "Systems of Articulation, Logics of Change: Communities and Scenes in Popular Music." *Cultural Studies* 5 (3): 368–88.

Stroeken, Koen
2005 "Immunizing Strategies: Hip-Hop and Critique in Tanzania." *Africa* 75 (4): 488–509.
Strumpf, Mitchel
1992 ed. A companion booklet to *Daniel Kachamba Memorial Cassette*. With commentary from Gerhard Kubik and text transcription and translation from Gerhard Kubik and Donald Kachamba. Zomba.
1998 "Obituary. It is very sad to report the sudden death of Mr. Black Paseli, noted early Malawian popular musician." *WASI: The Magazine for the Arts* 9 (3): 28.
Strumpf, Mitchel, and Kondwani Phwandaphwanda, eds.
1993 *Readings in Malawian Music: A Collection of Previously Published Articles on Malawian Music*. Zomba: Zomba Music Society.
Sturmer, Martin
1998 *The Media History of Tanzania*. Salzburg: Afro-Asiatiches Institut.
Sure, Kembo
2004 "Establishing a National Standard and English Language Curriculum Change in Kenya." In Margaret Jepkirui Muthwii and Angelina Nduku Kioko, eds., *New Language Bearings in Africa: A Fresh Quest*, 101–15. Buffalo, NY: Multilingual Matters.
Suriano, Maria
2006 "Utajiju! It Is Up to You! Bongo Flavour 'in da house': Muziki wa Kizazi Kipya, Youth Culture and Globalisation in Tanzania." *Proceedings of the Jubilee Symposium on Kiswahili na Utandawazi-Swahili and Globalisation*, 173–93. Institute of Kiswahili Research, University of Dar es Salaam.
2007 "'Mimi Ni Msanii, Kioo Cha Jamii': Urban Youth Culture in Tanzania as Seen through Bongo Fleva and Hip-Hop." *Swahili Forum* 14: 207–23.
Takyi, Baffour K.
2009 "Africans Abroad: Comparative Perspectives on America's Postcolonial West Africans." In Isidore Okpewho and Nkiru Nzegwu, eds., *The New African Diaspora*, 236–54. Bloomington: Indiana University Press.
Tamari, Tal
1991 "The Development of Caste Systems in West Africa." *Journal of African History* 32: 221–50.
Tang, Patricia
2005 "Senegal." In Shepherd et al., eds., *The Continuum Encyclopedia of Popular Music of the World*, vol. 6, *Africa and Middle East*, 173–77. London: Continuum.
2006 "Telling Histories: Memory, Childhood, and the Construction of Modern Griot Identity." In Susan Boynton and Roe-Min Kok, eds., *Musical Childhoods and the Cultures of Youth*, 105–20. Middletown, CT: Wesleyan University Press.
2007 *Masters of the Sabar: Wolof Griot Percussionists of Senegal*. Philadelphia: Temple University Press.
Tannenbaum, Rob
2006 "Playboy Interview: Kanye West." *Playboy* (March): 49–54, 132–33.
Taylor, Timothy
1997 *Global Pop: World Music, World Markets*. New York: Routledge.

Tenaille, Frank
   2002 *Music Is the Weapon of the Future: Fifty Years of African Popular Music.* Chicago:
         Lawrence Hill Books.
Terkourafi, Marina
   2010a ed. *The Languages of Global Hip Hop.* New York: Continuum.
   2010b "Introduction: A Fresh Look at Some Old Questions." In Terkourafi (2010a: 1–18).
Terrell, Tom
   1999 "The Second Wave: 1980–1983." In Alan Light, ed., *The Vibe History of Hip Hop,*
         43–51. New York: Three Rivers Press.
   2007 "World Music at Global Rhythm Features Daara J." March 23. www.globalrhythm
         .net/WorldMusicFeatures/DaaraJ.cfm.
Thibaudat, Jean-Pierre
   1982 "Une Semaine en Rap: Africa Bambaataa, Roi Zoulou du Bronx." *Liberation* (Oc-
         tober 26): 20–21.
This Is Africa
   2011 "Nigerian Kings and Queens: Pros and Con of Separate African BET Cypher
         Vidz." October 26. www.thisisafrica.me.
Thompson, Katrina Daly
   2008 "Keeping It Real: Reality and Representation in Maasai Hi-Hop." *Journal of Afri-
         can Cultural Studies* 20 (1): 33–44.
   2011 "Bongo Flava, Hip-Hop and 'Local Maasai Flavors': Interviews with X Plastaz."
         In Saucier (2011: 253–97).
Tolsi, Niren
   2006 "Survival of the Lyrics (Skwatta Kamp)." Johannesburg *Mail and Guardian* (No-
         vember 17).
Toop, David
   1984 *The Rap Attack: African Jive to New York Hip Hop.* London: Pluto Press.
   1991 *Rap Attack 2: African Rap to Global Hip Hop.* Rev. ed. London: Pluto Press.
   2005 "Rap." www.grovemusic.com.
Tracey, Hugh
   1954 "The State of Folk Music in Bantu Africa: A Brief Survey." *Journal of the Inter-
         national Folk Music Council* 6: 32–36.
Trieselmann, Werner
   2007 "Die Überwindung des digitalen Grabens: Ein medienethnologischer Ansatz für
         marginalisierte Kids in Rio de Janeiro." *Journal-Ethnologie.de* 5: Digitale Welten.
         http://www.journal-ethnologie.de.
Turino, Thomas
   2000 *Nationalists, Cosmopolitans, and Popular Music in Zimbabwe.* Chicago: Univer-
         sity of Chicago Press.
Turner, Victor
   1969 *The Ritual Process: Structure and Anti-structure.* Chicago: Aldine.
Vaa, Mariken
   1990 "Paths to the City: Migration Histories of Poor Women in Bamako." In Jonathan
         Baker, ed., *Small Town Africa: Studies in Rural-Urban Interaction,* 173–81. Up-
         psala: Scandinavian Institute of African Studies.

Valk, Peter de
 1996 *African Industry in Decline: The Case of Textiles in Tanzania in the 1980s.* New
        York: St. Martin's Press.
Van der Geest, Sjaak, and Nimrod K. Asante-Darko
 1982 "The Political Meaning of Highlife Songs in Ghana." *African Studies Review* 25
        (1): 27–35.
Veal, Michael E.
 2000 *Fela: The Life and Times of an African Icon.* Philadelphia: Temple University
        Press.
 2007 *Dub: Soundscapes and Shattered Songs in Jamaican Reggae.* Middletown, CT:
        Wesleyan University Press.
Vick, Karl
 2000 "Reggae Artists Voiced Nation's Discontent." *Washington Post* (January 30).
Villien-Rossi, M.-L.
 1966 "Bamako, capitale du Mali." *Bulletin de l'Institut Fondamental d'Afrique Noire,*
        série B 1–2: 249–380.
Wade, Peter
 1998 "Music, Blackness, and National Identity: Three Moments in Colombian His-
        tory." *Popular Music* 17 (1): 1–19.
 1999 "Working Culture: Making Cultural Identities in Cali, Colombia." *Current An-
        thropology* 40 (4): 449–71.
Wallis, Roger, and Krister Malm
 1984 *Big Sounds from Small Peoples: The Music Industry in Small Countries.* New York:
        Pendragon Press.
 1987 "The International Music Industry and Transcultural Communication." In James
        Lull, ed., *Popular Music and Communication,* 112–37. Newbury Park, CA: Sage.
Wamba, Philippe
 1999 *Kinship: A Family's Journey in Africa and America.* New York: Dutton.
Warikoo, Natasha K.
 2011 *Balancing Acts: Youth Culture in the Global City.* Berkeley and Los Angeles: Uni-
        versity of California Press.
Warner, Remi
 2011 "Colouring the Cape Problem Space: A Hip-Hop Identity of Passions." In Saucier
        (2011: 105–44).
Waterman, Christopher A.
 1990 *Jùjú: A Social History and Ethnography of an African Popular Music.* Chicago:
        University of Chicago Press.
 1998 "Chop and Quench." *African Arts* 31 (1): 1–5.
Waterman, Richard
 1963 "On Flogging a Dead Horse: Lessons Learned from the Africanisms Contro-
        versy." *Ethnomusicology* 7 (2): 83–87.
Watkins, Lee
 2004 "Rappin' the Cape: Style and Memory, Power in Community." In Sheila White-
        ley, Andy Bennett, and Stan Hawkins, eds., *Music, Space, and Place: Popular
        Music and Cultural Identity,* 124–46. Burlington, VT: Ashgate.

Watkins, S. Craig
    2005   *Hip Hop Matters: Politics, Pop Culture, and the Struggle for the Soul of a Movement.* Boston: Beacon Press.

Weisethaunet, Hans, and Ulf Lindberg
    2010   "Authenticity Revisited: The Rock Critic and the Changing Real." *Popular Music and Society* 33 (4): 465–85.

Weiss, Brad
    2002   "Thug Realism: Inhabiting Fantasy in Urban Tanzania." *Cultural Anthropology* 17 (1): 93–124.

Westen, August C. M. van
    1995   "Unsettled: Low-Income Housing and Mobility in Bamako, Mali." PhD diss., Utrecht University.

Wetaba, Aggrey Nganyi R.
    2009   *Kenyan Hip-Hop as a Site of Negotiating Urban Youth Identities in Nairobi.* Göttingen: Sierke Verlag.

White, Bob W.
    2008   *Rumba Rules: The Politics of Dance Music in Mobutu's Zaire.* Durham, NC: Duke University Press.

White, Hylton
    2001   "Tempora et Mores: Family Values and the Possessions of a Post-Apartheid Countryside." *Journal of Religion in Africa* 31 (4): 457–79.

Williams, Angela
    2010   "'We Ain't Terrorists, but We Droppin' Bombs': Language Use and Localization in Egyptian Hip Hop." In Terkourafi (2010a: 67–95).

Williams, Raymond
    1977   *Marxism and Literature.* Oxford: Oxford University Press.

Williamson, Nigel
    2000   "Youssou N'Dour Cuts a Pop 'Joko': Sony Album Marks Senegalese Artist's Return to Mainstream." *Billboard* (January 15): 16, 20.

Winders, James A.
    2006   *Paris Africain: Rhythms of the African Diaspora.* New York: Palgrave Macmillan.

Wirth, Louis
    1938   "Urbanism as a Way of Life." *American Journal of Sociology* 44: 1–24.

Wittmann, Frank
    2004   "Sexismus, Islamismus, and Ghettoromantik: Die Dakaer HipHop-Bewegung Bul faale im Kontext der globalen Postmoderne." In Kimminich (2004a: 181–204).

Wood, Andy
    2009   "'Original London Style': London Posse and the Birth of British Hip Hop." *Atlantic Studies* 6 (2): 175–90.

Wright, Donald R.
    1981   "Uprooting Kunta Kinte: On the Perils of Relying on Encyclopedic Informants." *History in Africa* 8: 205–17.

Wulff, Helena
    1995   "Introducing Youth Culture in its Own Right: The State of the Art and New Possibilities." In Vered Amit-Talai and Wulff, eds., *Youth Cultures: A Cross-Cultural Perspective,* 1–18. London and New York: Routledge.

Yankah, Kwesi

1984 "The Akan Highlife Song: A Medium for Cultural Reflection or Deflection?" *Research in African Literatures* 15 (4): 568–82.

1995 *Speaking for the Chief: Okyeame and the Politics of Akan Royal Oratory.* Bloomington: Indiana University Press

Young, Robert

1995 *Colonial Desire: Hybridity in Theory, Culture, and Race.* London: Routledge.

Zahan, Dominique

1963 *La Dialectique du Verbe chez les Bambara.* Paris: Mouton.

Zanetti, Vincent

1996 "De la place du village aux scènes internationales: l'évolution du jembe et de son répertoire." *Cahiers de musiques traditionnelles* 9: 167–88.

Zekri, Bernard

1982 "Une semaine en rap: Mister Freeze et Misses Blue." *Liberation* (October 28): 21.

1994 "Quand un journal visite l'histoire: 15 ans de rap séparent ces deux photos." *Actuel* 48 (December): 86–88.

Zeleza, Paul Tiyambe

2003 *Rethinking Africa's "Globalization,"* vol. 1, *The Intellectual Challenges.* Trenton, NJ: Africa World Press.

2006 "The Inventions of African Identities and Languages: The Discursive and Developmental Implications." In Olaoba F. Arasanyin and Michael A. Pemberton, eds., *Selected Proceedings of the 36th Annual Conference on African Linguistics,* 14–26. Somerville, MA: Cascadilla Proceedings Project. www.lingref.com, document #1402.

DISCOGRAPHY

113 [France]
  2003   *Dans l'urgence.* Small SMA 5075846-6.
Abdul-Kareem, Eedris [Nigeria]
  2004   *Jaga-Jaga.* Kennis Music. Lagos, Nigeria.
Abidjan City Breakers [Côte d'Ivoire]
  1986   *Abidjan City Breakers.* www.africanhiphop.com/radio_archive/trial1.html
Adzee, Zaki [Nigeria]
  1998   *Kakaki.* Ivory Music. Lagos, Nigeria.
Akon (US/Senegal)
  2006   "Smack That," "Senegal." Universal.
Akyeame [Ghana]
  1999   *Nkonson Konson.*
Allenko Brotherhood Ensemble [UK]
  2001   *The Allenko Brotherhood Ensemble.* Comet 022. Reissued 2002, Shanachie 66031.
         "Right Here in Front of You" reissued on *The Rough Guide to African Rap*, 2004.
Alif [Senegal]
  2004   *Dakamarap.* Out Here Records OH001.
Anikulapo Kuti, Fela [Nigeria]
  1979   *International Thief Thief.* Kalakuta. Lagos, Nigeria.
Awadi, Didier [Senegal]
  2002   *Parole d'honneur—Kaddu Gor.* Cassette.
  2004   *Un autre monde est possible.*
  2006   *Sunugaal.* Super D/Phantom Sound and Visi.
DJ Azigiza Junior [Ghana]
  1998   *Woye Bia.*
Baba Fryo featuring Cashman Davies [Nigeria]
  1998   *Denge Partz.*
Balti [Tunisia]
  2009   *L'album avant l'albombe.* Raw Poetix.
  2010   *Le journal.* Raw Poetix.
Bantustan [South Africa]
  2007   *Banturap.* Grahamstown (self-produced).
Big Idea [South Africa]
  2006   *Hot Box.* Durban: Ruffinary Records. Produced by Nathan Redpath.
Bil de Sam [Guinea]
  2000   *Exil.* Mi Cora Son/Mélodie.

Bisso Na Bisso [France/Congo-Brazzaville]

    1999   *Racines . . .* V2, VVR1005632.

Black Noise [South Africa]

    1992   *Pumpin Loose Da Juice.* One World Records/Tusk.

    1995   *Rebirth.*

    1998   *Hiphop Won't Stop.* Making Music.

    2001   *Circles of Fire.*

    2003   *Rotational High.*

Black Reverendz [Nigeria]

    1998   *Black Reverendz.* Sol Records Limited. Lagos, Nigeria.

Blackky [Nigeria]

    1999   *Return of the Blackman.* Ivory Music. Ikeja, Lagos, Nigeria.

Bonchaka, Terry [Ghana]

    2004   *Bonchaka Project 2004: Zoozey.* PSI Records.

Cashless Society [South Africa]

    2000   *Blaze the Breaks.* Johannesburg: Fondle 'Em Records.

Chagrin d'Amour [France]

    1981   "Chacun fait (ce qu'il lui plait)." Single.

Compilations (Africa)

    2002   *Africa Raps.* [Senegal, Mali, The Gambia]. Trikont, US-294.

    2003   *African Consciences.* Emma/Universal 066 734-2.

    2004   *The Rough Guide to African Rap.* Rough Guides/World Music Network RGNET1126 CD.

    2005   *Afrolution, vol. 1: The Original African Hip Hop Collection.* Afrolution 002.

    2007   *Urban Africa Club: Hip Hop, Dancehall* and Kwaito. Out Here Records.

    2008   *Fangafrika.* Staycalm! Productions.

    2008   *Many Lessons: Hip Hop, Islam, West Africa.* Piranha.

    2010   *Retour vers le futur, Part 1: Ghetto fab soldats, Vol. 2.* Pr4prod.

Compilations (Algeria)

    1999   *Algerap.* Virgin.

    2000   *Wahrap: La nouvelle generation rap d'Oran.* Atoll Music.

Compilations (France)

    1990   *Rapattitude.* Virgin France.

    1992   *Rapattitude 2.* Labelle Noir.

    1998   *Le Flow: The Definitive French Hip Hop Compilation.* Delabel/Virgin 72438 459602 6.

    2000   *Le Flow: The French Hip Hop Avant garde.* Delabel/Ultra Records UL1057-2.

Compilations (Ghana)

    2008   *Black Stars: Ghana's Hiplife Generation.* Out Here Records OH008.

Compilations (Kenya)

    1998   *Kenyan: The First Chapter.* Produced by Tedd Josiah. Audio Vault.

    1999   *Kenyan: The Second Chapter.* Produced by Tedd Josiah. Audio Vault.

    2002   *Rough Guide to the Music of Kenya.* Patterson D. and Werner Graebner (comps). World Music network.

    2002   *Ogopa 1: Kenya Club Classics.*

    2003   *Ogopa 02: Strictly for the Hanye in You.*

Compilations (Nigeria)

2006 *Lagos Stori Plenti: Urban Sounds from Nigeria*. Out Here Records OH005.

Compilations (Other)

1990 *Hip Hop Artists against Apartheid: Ndodemnyama* (Free South Africa). Warlock, WAR-067.

1993 *Planet Rap: A Sample of the World*. (MC Solaar, Prophets of the City). Tommy Boy.

1994 *Stolen Moments: Red Hot + Cool*. GRP Records.

2004 *Global Hip Hop*. Manteca MANTCD048.

2004 *Out of Cuba: Latin American Music Takes Africa by Storm*. Compilation and text by Janet Topp Fargion. Topic Records/British Library Sound Archive TSCD 927.

2006 *The Celluloid Collection*. Collision/Grooveattack, CCT 3007–2.

Compilations (Senegal)

1997 *Senerap: Freestyle, Vol. 1*.

1998 *Senerap: Freestyle, Vol. 2*.

1999 *Streets of Dakar: Generation Boul Falé*. Stern's Africa STCD 1084.

2000 *Da Hop: Le son de Dakar*. Jololi/Delabel.

2004 *African Underground: Vol. 1, Hip-Hop Senegal*. Nomadic Wax/Notable.

2007 *African Underground: The Depths of Dakar*. Nomadic Wax/African Underground/ Notable.

Compilations (South Africa)

2000 *Kwaito: South African Hip Hop*. Stern's/Earthwork Records STEW 42CD.

2007 *Planetary Assault*. Pioneer Unit PIONEERCD001.

2007 *Jarring Effects Label Selection of Cape Town Beats*. Jarring Effects, FX065.

Compilations (Tanzania)

2004 *Bongo Flava: Swahili Rap from Tanzania*. Out Here Records OH003.

n.d. *Volumes. 1–3: Hot Bongo Hits, Ujumbe na Ladha (MJ Records)*. GMC, Cassette.

Compilations (Uganda)

2010 *Kampala Flow: East African Hip Hop from Uganda*. LimePulpRecords.com.

Daara J [Senegal]

1997 *Daara J*. Declic, 8429482. Recorded in Paris and London.

1999 *Xalima*. Declic.

2003 *Boomerang*. Wrasse, WRASS 105. Distributed in the UK by Universal.

2010 *School of Life*. Wrasse WRASS262.

Daddy Showkey [Nigeria]

2004 *Ghetto Soldier*. Felin Records, Lagos.

Dakar All Stars [Senegal]

2005 *Dakar All Stars*. Africa Productions.

Dee Nasty [France]

1984 *Panam' city rappin*.

Diop, Aby Ngana [Senegal]

1994 *Liital*. Studio 2000. Cassette.

Disiz la Peste (aka Serigne Mbaye) [France]

2000 *La Poisson rouge*. Nouvelle Donne/Barclay/Universal 549 407-2.

2003 *Jeu de société*. Barclay.

2004 *Itinéraire d'un enfant bronzé*. Barclay/Universal, 982 472 4.

2005 *Les Histoires Extraordinaires d'un Jeune de Banlieue.* Barclay/Universal, 983149–5.

2009 *The End.* Naïve NV 818311.

Dizzy K Falola [Nigeria]

1982 *Excuse Me Baby* (includes "Saturday Night Raps"). On www.africanhiphop.com/radio_archive/2008-show1.html.

Doug E. Fresh and the Get Fresh Crew [USA]

1988 *The World's Greatest Entertainer.* Reality F-9658.

E-sir [Kenya]

2003 *Nimefika.* Produced by Ogopa Djs.

EJ von Lyrik [South Africa]

2008 *Method in the Madness.* High Voltage.

2010 *The Human Condition.* High Voltage.

Emileyx and Jamayka Poston [South Africa and Angola]

2003 *Conquering Lions.* Cape Town. Produced by Lungelo Lubelwana.

Ex-Doe [Ghana]

1999 *Maba.*

Fab Five Freddy [USA]

1982 "Change the Beat." "A" side by Fab Five Freddy; "B" side by Beside. 12-inch 33 ⅓ rpm single. Celluloid, 156.

Fakoly, Tiken Jah [Côte d'Ivoire]

1996 *Mangercratie.* (Contains "Mangercratie," "Le Descendant.") Abidjan: JAT Music.

2000 *Le Caméléon* (contains "Promesses de Caméléon," "Le Pays Va Mal"). Abidjan: JAT Music (rereleased by Barclay/Universal, 2008).

2002 *Françafrique.* Barclay/Universal 589613-2.

Faye, Mbaye Dieye [Senegal]

1995 *Oupoukay.* With Sing Sing Rhythms. Saprom. Cassette.

2002 *Songa Ma.* Major Productions, Xippi. Cassette.

Fnaire [Morocco]

2007? Yed el Henna.

Franco and OK Jazz [Congo-Kinshasa]

1987 *Attention na SIDA.* Sonodisc, CDS 6856.

GidiGidi and Majimaji [Kenya]

2000 *Ismarwa.* Produced by Ted Josiah, reissued by A'mish Records 2002.

2002 *Unbwogable.* Single, marketed by A&M Records.

GidiGidi and Wicky Moshi [Kenya]

2002 *Atoti.* Single. Produced by Ted Josiah.

Godessa [South Africa]

2004 *Spillage.* High Voltage.

Guru [USA]

1993 *Jazzmatazz.* Chrysalis.

H-Kayne [Morocco]

2005 HK-1426. Platinum Music.

2009 *H-Kaynology.*

Jal, Emmanuel, and Abdel Gadir Salim [Sudan]

2005 *Ceasefire.* Riverboat/World Music Network TUGCD 1038.

Junior and Pretty [Nigeria]
    1998   *Kings of Pidgin Rap: No Pain, No Gain.* Produced by Mighty Mouse.
JJC and 419 [Nigeria/UK]
    2003   *Atide.* Backbone.
Kalamashaka [Kenya]
    1999   *Tafsiri Hii.* Single first marketed by Ted Josiah.
K'Naan [Somalia/Canada]
    2005   *The Dusty Foot Philosopher.* Universal.
    2007   *The Dusty Foot on the Road.* Wrasse.
    2009   *Troubador.* Universal.
Kontihene [Ghana]
    2001   *Nyankonton.*
Maal, Baba [Senegal]
    1994   *Firin' in Fouta.* Mango 162-539 944-2.
Mac Mooger [Tanzania]
    1995   *The Mac Mooger.*
Malik, Abd al [France]
    2004   *Le face à face des coeurs.* Atmosphériques 981 378-9.
    2006   *Gibraltar.* Atmosphériques 983790-2.
    2007   *Tout feu tout slam.* EMI/Mixed Repertoire.
    2008   *Dante.* Polydor 5312873.
Mbaye, Serigne (see Disiz la Peste)
Mbaye, Thio [Senegal]
    1993   *Rimbax.* Harry Son/Syllart. Cassette.
    2000   *Ndaali.* Studio 2000. Cassette.
MBS [Algeria]
    1999   *Le Micro Brise le Silence.* Universal/Island, 546-26-2.
MC Solaar [France]
    1991   *Qui sème le vent récolte le tempo.* Polydor.
    1994   *Prose combat.* Cohiba/Polydor
    1997   *Paradisiaque.* Polydor.
    1998   *MC Solaar.* Polydor.
    1998   *Le Tour de la question.* Sentinel Ouest.
    2001   *Cinquième As: Fifth Ace.* Sentinel Ouest.
    2003   *Mach 6.* Sentinel Ouest.
    2007   *Chapitre 7.* Sentinel Ouest.
McLaren, Malcolm [UK]
    1983   *Duck Rock.* Produced by Trevor Horn. Charisma/Island.
Mokobe [France]
    2007   *Mon Afrique.* Sony BMG, 88697109792.
Morobe, Ishmael [South Africa]
    2000   *Roba Letheka.* Distributed in South Africa by EMI.
Murray, David
    1997   *Fo Deuk Revue.* [with guests PBS] Justin Time Records JUST 94-2.
Ndiaye Guewel, Papa [Senegal]
    1997   *Papa Ndiaye Guewel.* Studio Xippi. Cassette.

N'Dour, Youssou [Senegal]
  1994   *The Guide (Wommat)*. Chaos/Columbia 476508-2.
Obrafour [Ghana]
  1999   *Pae Mu Ka.*
Ogada, Ayub [Kenya]
  1993   *En Mana Kwoyo.* Real World Records.
Pee Froiss [Senegal]
  1996   *Wala Wala Bok.* Cassette.
  1997   *Affaire Bou Graw.* Cassette.
  1999   *Ah Simm.* Cassette.
  2001   *F.R.O.I.S.S.* Cassette.
  2003   *Konkerants.* Night and Day.
Plantashun Boiz [Nigeria]
  2004   *The Beginning of Body and Soul.* Chuma Sound Center. Nigeria: Dove Music.
Positive Black Soul [Senegal]
  1993   Cassette produced by French Cultural Center.
  1996   *Salaam.* Mango/Island, 162-531 029-2.
  2000   *Run Cool.* Palm Tree/Africa Fete/East West France/Warner, 8573 86845 2.
  2002   *New York/Paris/Dakar.* Africa Fete Diffusion, AFD 005; Universal-Island,
         3 448969232525. Recorded in Dakar and New York.
Prophets of Da City [South Africa]
  1990   *Our World.* Ku Shu Shu Records, KVL 5107.
  1992   *Boomstyle.* Ghetto Ruff.
  1993   *Age of Truth.* Ghetto Ruff. Distributed in South Africa by Tusk Records.
  1994   *Phunk Phlow.* Ghetto Ruff.
  1995   *Universal Souljaz.* Rough Trade, RTD 141.3403.2.
  1997   *Ghetto Code.* Ghetto Ruff, POCCD 005.
Rap'adio [Senegal]
  1998   *Ku Weet Xam Sa Bop.* Cassette.
  2001   *Soldaaru Mbed.* Cassette.
Rockstone, Reggie [Ghana]
  1997   *MaKaa MaKa!!* [*Ma Ka Ma Ka*] Kassa Records.
  1999   *Me Na Me Kae.* Kassa Records.
Rufftone [Kenya]
  2002   *Mwikulu.* Produced by R-Kay.
Saba Saba [Uganda]
  2008   *Tujja Babbya: The Hardway.* Tujjababy Productions.
Saleh J [Tanzania]
  1991   "Ice Ice Baby." Single.
  1994   *Swahili Rap.* Cassette.
Seck, Bada [Senegal]
  1997   *Génération Boul Falé.* Studio 2000. Cassette.
Sharpa, Ben [South Africa]
  2008   *B. Sharpa.* Pioneer Unit, PIONEERCD002.
Skwatta Kamp [South Africa]
  2003   *Mkhukhu Funkshen.* Gallo.

Soji [Nigeria]

1998   *Wake Up*. Kennis Music. Ikeja, Lagos, Nigeria.

Teteula, Tony [Nigeria]

2003   *Nigerian Gbedu Mix. Uwa Wu Paw-Paw*. Lagos, Nigeria.

Thiopet, Pape, and Lamine Day Bonde [Senegal]

2002   *Bouko Rathieuti*. Studio 2000. Cassette.

Tic Tac [Ghana]

2000   *Philomena*. Cassette.

Touré, Lamine and Group Saloum [Senegal]

2005   *Lamine Touré and Group Saloum*. Nomadic Wax.

Triple M [Ghana]

2003   Koti.

2005   *3–1=3M (Mempe)*.

Trybesmen [Nigeria]

1999   *L.A.G. Style: The Debut Album*. Trybe Records. Exec Producers S. O. Dabiri.

VIP [Ghana]

2006   *Ahomka Womu*. Goodie Music Production.

Wilson, Daniel [Nigeria]

1995   *No Exhibit*. Ivory Music. Lagos, Nigeria.

Zimbabwe Legit [Zimbabwe/USA]

1992   *Zimbabwe Legit*. EP. Hollywood Basic HB-61284.

Zulu Boy [South Africa]

2006   *Masihambisane*. Distributed in South Africa by Native Rhythms.

TANZANIA (PERULLO)

This discography covers the years 1995–2006 and focuses on hip hop, R&B, and other albums released in Dar es Salaam.

AY

2004   *Hisia Zangu*. FKW 204. Cassette.

Afande Sele

2004   *Darubuni Kali*. GMC Wasanii (GR-4, 056). CD.

Balozi

2002   *Ubalozini*. GMC. Cassette.

Balzi Dolasoul

2000   *Balozi Wenu*. GMC. Cassette.

Bambo and Fresh P.

n.d.   *Watanzania Halisi*. FKW (060) Cassette.

Banana

n.d.   *Banana*. GMC Wasanii Promoters Ltd., Smooth Vibes. CD.

Bantu Pound

1995   *Gangstarz*. FM Music Bank. Cassette.

Big Dog Pose

n.d.   *Kamili*. FKW. Cassette.

Bizman

2005   *Ningekuwa Kwetu*.GMC Wasanii Promoters Ltd. CD.

Bushoke
    2005   *Barua.* GMC Wasanii Promoters Ltd. (GR-4, 084). CD.
Bwana Misosi
    n.d.   *Nitoke Vipi?* GMC Wasanii Promoters Ltd. CD.
Caz-T
    n.d.   *Bantu Pound.* GMC (306). Cassette.
CJ Massive
    2003   *Tribute to Cool James.* GMC. Cassette.
Da Unique Sisterz
    2001   *Kimya Kingi.* GMC (GMC 300). Cassette.
Darda King
    2006   *Nimekubalika 2006.* Mfalme (B000ELJ2NQ). CD.
Daz Baba
    2005   *Elimu Dunia.* GMC Wasanii. CD.
Dudubaya
    n.d.   *Amri Kumi za Mungu.* FKW (FK Mitha, Kings Brothers, Wananchi Stores). Cassette.
Ferooz
    2005   *Safari.* GMC Wasanii. CD.
Gangwe Mobb
    2002   *Simulizi la Ufasaha.*GMC Wasanii Promoters Ltd., Maasai Entertainment Inc. CD.
    2003   *Nje/ Ndani.* GMC Wasanii. Cassette.
Inspekta Haroun
    n.d.   *Pamba Nyepesi.* GMC Wasanii. Cassette.
Jay Moe
    2002   *Ulimwengu Ndio Mama.* GMC. Cassette.
Jaymoe
    2005   *Mawazo ya Jaymoe.* GMC Promoters Ltd. (GR-4 054). Cassette.
Jimmy Jamal
    2005   *Sayari.* FKW (F. K. Mitha and Sons, Kings Brothers, Wananchi Stores). Cassette.
Joni Woka and Lion
    n.d.   *Nani Alaumiwe?* GMC. CD.
Joslin
    2005   *Perfume.* GMC Wasanii RP-060621. Cassette.
Juma Nature
    2005   *Ubin-Adam Kazi.* GMC Wasanii Promoters Ltd. P. Funk and Bongo Records. CD.
    2006   *Zote History.* GMC Wasanii Promoters Ltd. and Bongo Records. CD.
Kikosi cha Mizinga
    2005   *Kufa au Kupona.* None. CD.
King Crazy GK
    n.d.   *Nitakufaje?* GMC Wasanii Promoters Ltd. (GR-4, 31), East Coast Team. CD.
Lady Jay Dee
    2005   *Moto.* GMC (Smooth Vibes). CD
MB Dog
    2006   *Si Uliniambia.* GMC Wasanii RP-060413. Cassette.

Mbilinyi, Joseph (a.k.a. II Proud, Mr. II, and Sugu)
    1995   II Proud: *Ni Mimi.*
    1996   Mr. II: *Ndani ya Bongo.* FM Music Bank.
    1998   Mr. II: *Niite Mr. II.* FM Music Bank.
    2002   Sugu: *Itikadi.* GMC Wasanii Promoters Ltd., Kwetu Entertainment. CD.
    n.d.   Sugu: *Ujio wa Umri [Coming of Age].* GMC Wasanii/ Deiwaka Productions. Cassette.
Mike Tee
    n.d.   *Mnyalu Inc.: Sintobadilika.* GMC Wasanii. Cassette.
Mike Tee and Mac D
    n.d.   *Kama Mjawako.* GMC. Cassette.
Mr. Blu
    n.d.   *Lil Sama aka Mr. Blu.* FKW. Cassette.
Mr. Ebbo
    2005   *Kazi Gani.* GMC Wasanii Promoters Ltd. (GR-4, 195), Mr. Ebbo, Motika Records. CD.
Mwana Fa
    2002   *Binamu.* GMC Wasanii. Cassette.
O Ten
    2003   *Mimi.* GMC Wasanii Promoters Ltd. (GR-5, 345), East Coast Team. CD.
Prince Dully Sykes
    n.d.   *Historia ya Kweli.* GMC. Cassette.
Professor Jay
    2006   *J.O.S.E.P.H.* GMC Wasanii Promoters Ltd. (GR-5, 365). CD.
Ray C
    n.d.   *Na Wewe Milele.* GMC Wasanii Promoters Ltd. (GR-4, 063), Smooth Vibes. CD.
Rudala, Bob
    2005   *Mimi Nimekuchagua Wewe.* GMC Wasanii Promoters Ltd. (GB-4, 136), Smooth Vibes. CD.
Saleh J
    1996   *Swahili Rap no. 1.* Self-release. Cassette.
Various Artists
    n.d.   *Volumes. 1–3: Hot Bongo Hits, Ujumbe na Ladha (MJ Records).* GMC. Cassette.
Various Artists
    2006   *Bongo Flava: Swahili Rap from Tanzania.* Out Here Records (B0006FX8GC). CD.
Wachuja Nafaka
    2002   *Mzee wa Busara.* GMC. Cassette.
Wagosi wa Kaya
    n.d.   *Ripoti Kamili.* GMC (MJ Productions). Cassette.
    n.d.   *Nyeti.* GMC Wasanii (GR-5, 413). Cassette.
Wanaume (TMK)
    2002   *Kutoka Kiumeni.* GMC Wasanii (GR-4 222). Cassette.
X Plastaz
    2004   *Maasai Hip Hop.* Out Here Records OH002. CD.
Zay B
    2006   *Kufa na Kuzikana.* GMC. CD.

MALAWI (SEEBODE)

Alleluya Band
  2005? *The Best of Alleluya Band*. Recorded in Balaka, Malawi, at IY Sudios.
Banda, Lucius
  1994   *Song of a Poor Man*. Recorded in Balaka, Malawi, IY Production.
  1995a *Down Babylon*. Recorded in Balaka, Malawi, IY Production.
  1995b *Ceasefire*. Recorded in Balaka, Malawi, IY Production.
  1998   *Take Over*. Manufactured by Audio Digital, Lilongwe, Malawi.
  1999a *Yahwe*. Recorded in Balaka, Malawi, IY Production.
  1999b *Unity*. Recorded in Balaka, Malawi, IY Production. Black Missionaries (feat. Evison Matafale).
  n.d.   *Kuimba 4*.
Bubu Lazzy (formerly: X Boyz Lazzy)
  1998   *Mission On*. Recorded in South Africa at Andy Studios.
  n.d.   *Dollar Yashupa*. Recorded in South Africa at 106 Studio.
Chaphuka, Paul
  1997   *Ndichiritseni*. Recorded in Balaka, Malawi, IY Production.
Chimombo, Overtone
  n.d.   *Zasintha*. Recorded in Studio K, Blantyre, Malawi. 1998 *Chuma*. Recorded at 106 Studios, Chigumula, Blantyre, Malawi.
Chiwalo, Coss
  1999? *Amandikonda*. Recorded in Balaka, Malawi, at IY Studios.
Kachale, Eliza
  n.d.   *Nthawi Yafika*. Recorded in Balaka, Malawi, at IY Studios.
Kachamba, Daniel
  1992   *Daniel Kachamba Memorial Cassette*. Historical recordings 1967–1983 and companion booklet edited by Mitch Strumpf.
Kaliati, Elias and Kenneth ang' a Ning'
  n.d.   *Wankulu Ndani M'banja*. (Typical Traditional Songs.)
Kamwendo, Ethel and the Ravers Band
  1998? *Ahkwaka*.
  n.d.   *Chikondi*. Katawa Singers, featuring Thomas Auden Perfect.
  n.d.   *Wedding Special, vol. 1*.
Kaunda, Billy
  1998? *Mwapindulanji*? Recorded in Balaka, Malawi, at IY Studios.
  1999   *Alibe Mau*.
  2005? *Muyime Kaye*.
Manda, Emmanuel
  1998   *Jani-Passi*. Recorded at Studio K, Blantyre, Malawi.
Maliro, Mlaka
  2006? *The Collection*. CD.
Master Tongole
  1999? *Mazunzo*. Recorded in Balaka, Malawi, at IY Studios.
Mhango, Reverend Chimwemwe
  1998? *Titemwanenge*.

Mhango, Chimwemwe, and Benjamin
  n.d.   *Chiharo*. Manufactured and distributed by Baptist Media Centre, Blantyre, Malawi (on behalf of the artists).
Micheal, Ben
  1998   *Tilire* [Let's All Cry].
Mkandawire, Wambali
  1988   *Tizamtamanda*. Cape Town, South Africa, Krakatoa Music Works.
  1991a   *Kavuluvulu* [Whirlwind]. Glasgow, UK, Jump Productions.
  1991b   *Kumtengo*. Glasgow, UK, Jump Productions.
  1999   *Ntchemo*. Recorded at Joe's Garage, Johannesburg and Cape Town (Krakatoa MusicWorks), South Africa.
Moffat, Grace Chinga
  2005?   *Thandizo Langa*.
Museum Collection Berlin (West) (edited by Artur Simon)
  1989   *Music of Malawi*. Vinyl double LP and companion booklet with a commentary by G. Kubik in cooperation with M. A. Malamusi. Musiksammlung der Staatlichen Museen zu Berlin, Stiftung Preussischer Kulturbesitz, vol. 15. Berlin.
Namoko, Allan, and Chimvu River Jazz Band
  1997   *Zonse Ndi Moyo* [Sounds of Malawi]. Marketed and distributed by Clifton Bazaar, Limbe, Malawi.
Nkhata, Brite, and Makasu
  1998   *Muroyi*. Recorded in High Density Studios. High Density Records.
Padangokhala (Allan and Pierson Ntata).
  1998   *Akoma Akagonera*. Chichewa Country and Western. Recorded in Studio K, Blantyre, Malawi.
Paseli Brothers Band
  1989   *Early Recordings* (plus interview with B.P. by Mitchell Strumpf on side B).
Phiri, Saleta, and AB Sounds.
  1997?   *Palibe Chiusisi*.
  1997?   *Ambewe* (Vol. 2).
  1997?   *Ili Mu Ufa* (Vol. 3).
  1997?   *Oraruwa* (Vol. 4).
Sapitwa
  n.d.   *Malawi's Top Soukous-, Manganje-, und Tchopa-Band. Sapitwa presents Patrick Tembo (Papa) and Tepu Ndiche (Tepu Tepu)*. Recorded in Studio K, Blantyre, Malawi.
Sinetre, Charles
  1995   *Dalitsani Dziko*. Recorded in Balaka, Malawi, at IY Studios.
Tiyamike Band
  1997   *Chilungamo*. Recorded in Balaka, Malawi, at IY Studios.
Various Malawian Artists
  1997   *Pamtondo. The Last Pound? Electric and Acoustic Music from Malawi, the Warm Heart of Africa*. Produced by John Lwanda. Glasgow: Pamtondo.
X Boyz Lazzy
  1997   *Bubu*. Recorded in South Africa at Andy Studios.

VIDEOGRAPHY

Absa, Moussa Sene, dir.
2007   *Terranga Blues.* Music by Daara J.
Ahearn, Charlie, dir., prod.
1982   *Wild Style.* Grandmaster Flash, Fab 5 Freddy, Rock Steady Crew.
2005   *Bongo Barbershop.*
African Portraits, Public Broadcasting Service
1996?   *Positive Black Soul.* www.youtube.com/watch?v=yKzcwxa2JVE.
Asen, Josh, and Jennifer Needleman, dirs., prods.
2007   *I Love Hip Hop in Morocco.* Rizz Productions. ilovehiphopinmorocco.com.
Birch, Trenton, Dennis Tapfuma, and Trevor Henen
2005   DVD accompanying *Afrolution,* vol. 1, *The Original African Hip Hop Collection.*
Afrolution 002. Urban Africa Club. Out Here Records.
Black Noise
2004   *Hip Hop! How To. #1.* With DJ Thee Angelo and Emile Jansen. Bowline Music.
Bouchareb, Rachid, dir.
2001   *Little Senegal.*
Bowey, John R., dir., prod.
1990   *African Wave: South African Music and Its Influences,* vol. 2, *Prophets of the City.*
Released on VHS 1998 and DVD 2004 by Princeton, NJ: Films for the Humani-
ties and Sciences.
Cepeda, Raquel, dir.
2007   *Bling: Blood Diamonds and Hip Hop.* VH1. Issued on DVD as *Bling: A Planet
Rock.*
Dzuguda, Rudzani, dir.
2004   *Mix.* Produced by Bridget Pickering. Dzuguda Productions for SABC1. Film Resource Unit. www.dzugudapro.co.za.
Eden Project/WOMAD
2005   *Live 8: Africa Calling.* Recorded live at Eden Project, Cornwall, England, July 2,
2005. Rhino.
Elderkin, Nabil, dir.
2010   *Bouncing Cats.* Red Bull Media House.
Fredericks, John, dir.
2007   *Mr. Devious.* 4 Wall Films; Rainbow Circle Films.
Hacke, Gabriel, and Anna Roch, dirs.
2004   *Bongo Flava: HipHop-Kultur in Tansania.* http://www.bongoflava.de.
Herson, Ben, Magee McIlvaine, and Chris Moore, dirs., prods.

2007 *African Underground: Democracy in Dakar.* Nomadic Wax/Sol Productions. nomadicwax.com/democracyindakar.

n.d. *African Underground: Democracy in Paris.* Nomadic Wax/Sol Productions. nomadicwax.com/film/democracy-in-paris/.

Ivanga, Imunga, dir.

2003 *Dôlé* [Money]. California Newsreel.

Jacobs-Fantauzzi, Eli, dir.

2010 *Homegrown: Hiplife in Ghana.* Clenched Fist Productions. http://www .hiplifemovie.com/.

Lenoir, Jérémie, dir.

2007 *Doto Silence.* dotosilence.com.

Lion, Jean Jacques, dir.

2001 *Hip Hop Senegal.* Médiathèque des trois mondes.

Macklin, Scott, and Angelica Macklin, dirs.

2008 *Masizakhe: Building Each Other.* Open Hand Reel. www.openhandreel.com.

Maga Bo, dir.

2007 *Documentary Interview with Xuman and Keyti.* Filmed in Dakar, Senegal. http:// vimeo.com/1935925?ab.

Magubane, Vusi, and Erin Offer, dirs.

2006 *Counting Headz: South Afrika's Sistaz in Hip-Hop.* Chopshop Multimedia. www .myspace.com/countingheadz.

Malapa, Benny, dir.

2005 *Ouaga Hip Hop: Festival International de la culture hip-hop Burkina Faso (Octobre 2003).* Insomnia World Sales.

Mazurek, Brett, dir.

2009 *Diamonds in the Rough: A Ugandan Hip Hop Revolution.* H2ONewsreel/Third World Newsreel.

Meulenberg, Martin, prod., Ben Hewett and Thomas Gesthuizen, local prods.

2000 *Hali Halisi: Rap as an Alternative Medium in Tanzania.* Scherpenzeel Media Foundation and Madunia Foundation. On www.youtube.com.

Ready D and Shaheen Ariefdien

2003 *Cape Town 2003: Ready D and Shaheen Ariefdien: Can't Stop the Prophets.* Red Bull Music Academy. www.redbullmusicacademy.com (search Shaheen).

Robin, Alexis, dir.

2011 *Le IV Festival International Malabo Hip Hop.* Institut culturel d'expression française. http://vimeo.com/22931762

Roizès, Philippe, dir.

1999 *Je rap donc je suis.* La Sept ARTE and Compagnie Panoptique Cie des Phares et Balieses. On www.youtube.com.

Said, Abdulkadir Ahmed, dir., co-prod., and Bridget Thompson, co-prod.

2003 *Rhythms from Africa: Scratch, Mix and —?* Tomas Films; Acacia Entertainment; Film Resource Unit. Johannesburg: Film Resource Unit.

2003 *Rhythms from Africa: Gold, Tears, and Music.* Tomas Films; Acacia Entertainment; Johannesburg. Film Resource Unit.

2003 *Taarab, an Ocean of Melodies.* Johannesburg: Film Resource Unit (distributor).

Shipley, Jesse Weaver, dir., prod.
    2007   *Living the Hiplife.* Third World Newsreel. www.livingthehiplife.org.
Stay Calm! Productions
    2008   *Fangafrika: la voix des sans-voix.* DVD, CD, and booklet. Stay Calm! Productions (Stephane Rinaldi, Guillaume Mouillé, Vincent Plassard, Laurent Goudet, Pascal Goudet, and Renaud Lioult). fangafrika.com.
Thybaud, Denis, dir., Pascal Houzelot, prod., Oxmo Puccino, writer
    2005   *Dans tes rêves.* (Featuring Disiz la Peste.) Mosca Films; Studio Canal; France 2 Cinema avec la participation de Canal Plus.
Valente, Oliver A. dir.
    2007   *What Is Bongo Flava?* On www.youtube.com.
Wanguhu, Michael, dir., prod.
    2007   *Hip Hop Colony: The African Hip Hop Explosion.* Emerge Media/Image Entertainment.
Williams, Weaam, dir., prod.
    2006   *Hip Hop Revolution.* Shamanic Organic Production. http://www.shamanic.co.za/01main.htm.

WEBOGRAPHY

Please see the book's website (www.iupress.indiana.edu/a/hiphop) for up-to-date links to sources referenced in this volume and to recordings of some of the artists covered here.

ERIC CHARRY is Associate Professor of Music at Wesleyan University. He has published extensively on music in Africa, including *Mande Music: Traditional and Modern Music of the Maninka and Mandinka of Western Africa* (2000). He wrote the introduction to Babatunde Olatunji's autobiography (*The Beat of My Drum*, 2005) and is completing a manuscript on the emergence of an avant-garde in jazz in the 1950s and 1960s.

JOHN COLLINS has been active in the Ghanaian/West African music scene since 1969 as a guitarist, band leader, music union activist, journalist, and writer. He taught music at the University of Ghana until 2005. He is manager of Bokoor Recording Studio, chairman of the BAPMAF Highlife—Music Institute and archives, a patron of the Ghana Musicians Union (MUSIGA), and a leader of the Local Dimension highlife band.

JOHN FENN is Assistant Professor in the Arts and Administration Program at the University of Oregon's School of Architecture and the Allied Arts. He has conducted field research on popular music and youth identity in Malawi, folk arts and material culture in southern Indiana and the Pacific Northwest, and the cultural history of African American communities in Eugene and Springfield, Oregon. His current research projects include work with boutique effects pedals, as well as ethnographic work in Beijing with experimental musicians as part of the ChinaVine project (http://chinavine.org).

JEAN NGOYA KIDULA is Associate Professor of Ethnomusicology at the University of Georgia at Athens. Her publications include articles on Kenyan ritual and religious folk and popular music and on music in the African academy. She has written about gospel music in North America and Africa and is a co-author of *Music in the Life of the African Church* (2008). Her book *Music in Kenyan Christianity: Logooli Religious Song* is forthcoming with Indiana University Press.

ALEX PERULLO is Associate Professor of Ethnomusicology and African Studies at Bryant University. His research interests include popular music, youth and urban society, and intellectual property rights in eastern and central Africa. He has published articles in *Africa Today, Popular Music and Society, Ethnomusicology,* and several edited volumes. His book *Live from Dar es Salaam: Popular Music and Tanzania's Music Economy* (Indiana University Press, 2011) examines the formation of one of the most prosperous music economies in Africa.

RAINER POLAK is Senior Research Fellow (principal investigator) at Cologne University of Music and Dance. He is author of *Festmusik als Arbeit, Trommeln als Beruf: Jenbe-Spieler in einer westafrikanischen Großstadt* (2004), which received the 2003–2004 academic award of the German Association for African Studies. He has published in *The World of Music, Anthropos,* and *Music Theory Online,* is anthologized in *Ethnomusicology: A Contemporary Reader* (2006), and will contribute to forthcoming editions of the *Continuum Encyclopedia of Popular Music of the World (EPMOW)* and *New Grove Dictionary of Musical Instruments.* Polak's approach to West African percussion ensemble music includes perspectives from social and cultural anthropology as well as from empirical musicology and music theory. He also performs and teaches jembe music.

DANIEL B. REED is Associate Professor of Folklore and Ethnomusicology at Indiana University. He is author of *Dan Ge Performance: Masks and Music in Contemporary Côte d'Ivoire* (Indiana University Press, 2004), which won the Amaury Talbot Prize from the Royal Anthropological Institute for best book in African anthropology. He has also published articles in journals such as *Ethnomusicology* and *Africa Today* and is co-author, with Gloria Gibson, of the CD-ROM *Music and Culture of West Africa: The Straus Expedition* (Indiana University Press, 2002).

DOROTHEA E. SCHULZ is Professor in the Department of Cultural and Social Anthropology at the University of Cologne, Germany. Her new book, *Muslims and New Media in West Africa* (Indiana University Press, 2011) deals with Islamic revivalist movements in Mali that rely on media technologies to promote a relatively new conception of publicly enacted religiosity. She has also published widely on media practices and public culture in sahelian West Africa, gender studies, and the anthropology of the state. Her new research project deals with Muslims in Uganda. It investigates Muslim practices of coming to terms with death in a situation of continued ecological and social disaster and irruption.

JOCHEN SEEBODE is Research Associate and Lecturer at the Institute of Anthropology of Free University Berlin. His fields of interest include anthropology of religion, political anthropology, anthropology of youth, and popular culture. His publications include a monograph about ritual, power, and spirit possession in Asante (South Ghana) and various articles about dance, music, and youth in Ghana and Malawi.

JESSE WEAVER SHIPLEY is Assistant Professor of Anthropology and coordinator of Africana studies at Haverford College. He has written on music, performance, popular culture, football, theater, and politics in Ghana, South Africa, and the United States. He is author of *The Entrepreneur's Aesthetic: Circulation and Celebrity in Ghanaian Hiplife Music* (Duke University Press, forthcoming). His documentary film *Living the Hiplife* (Third World Newsreel 2007) has been featured at numerous film festivals around the world.

STEPHANIE SHONEKAN is Assistant Professor of Ethnomusicology and Black Studies at the University of Missouri. She is author of *The Life of Camilla Williams: African American Classical Singer and Opera Diva* (Edwin Mellen Press, 2011). Her creative and scholarly work focuses on the revolutionary and musical influence of Funmilayo Ransome-Kuti on her legendary son, Fela Anikulapo Kuti. Her short film *Lioness of Lisabi*, which is loosely based on the life of Ransome-Kuti, was awarded first prize by the Children's Jury of the Chicago International Children's Film Festival.

PATRICIA TANG is Associate Professor in Music and Theater at the Massachusetts Institute of Technology. She is author of *Masters of the Sabar: Wolof Griot Percussionists of Senegal* (2007). She is the founder and co-director of Rambax, MIT's Senegalese drum ensemble, and has performed extensively with Senegalese mbalax band Nder et le Setsima Group (violin) and with the Afro-mbalax band Lamine Touré and Group Saloum (violin and keyboards).

LEE WATKINS teaches ethnomusicology at Rhodes University in South Africa. He has been conducting research on rap music and hip hop in South Africa since the 1990s and has undertaken research on rap music and hip hop in China. His research interests include the study of music in relation to migration and diaspora studies, asymmetrical relations, the musical aesthetics of marginal expressive cultures, and music developmental studies. He has several publications on rap music in South Africa and on migrant Filipino musicians in Hong Kong.

Most people and musical genres are listed under their country entries; authors are listed individually. Page numbers in *italics* refer to illustrations.

producers, 195; recording studios, 16; Temeke (TMK), 203; Upanga, 199
democracy, 31, 32, 66; multiparty, 15. *See also individual country names*
Denmark, 214
dialogue, 185; call and response, 157, 239; between dancer and drummer, 265; of genres, 53, 185; in a globalized world, 71; hiplife and rap, 50; lyric structure, 238; national, 36; with peers, 122; between roots and routes, 285
diaspora, 4, 39, 40–41, 43–44, 47, 53, 147; aesthetic, 133–36, 138, 139, 143; Africa as motherland, 82, 283; black, 30–32, 33, 71, 131, 290, 301, 310n13; boomerang phenomenon, 82, 299; colonization from, 289; connections through naming, 48; and global, 70–72, 283, 303; and hybridity, 149–50; and identity, 55n14, 290; Kenyan, 177, 181–84; and Malawi, 234, 235, 242; musical connections, 160–64, 171; and musical memory, 183; rap as diasporic genre, 57, 82, 131, 308; reggae and, 95, 174; roots and routes, 57, 63, 71, 149, 285; and South Africa, 73
Diawara, Manthia, 133–34, 136, 286, 301
Dibango, Manu, 154, 230, 284
Diouf, Mamadou, 236
disco, 12, 13, 43, 213, 240; and jembe, 267
DJs (deejays), in Ghana, 31, 35, 50, 212, 221; in Kenya, 177, 179; in Malawi, 114; in Nigeria, 148; scratching, 21n13, 34, 174; turntabling, 65
dreadlocks, 37, 48, 142, 152, 214–15, 232n9, 251, 252
drum(s): African, 53, 54n13, 56n23, 80, 82, 84, 85, 191, 196, 298, 299, 307–308; greeting heads of state with, 289; Western, 87, 100, 181, 192, 193, 194, 298. *See also* African musical instruments (bònkolo, calabash, dondo, donka, dundun, dunun, gome, kirin, sabar); jembe; Tanzania: ngoma
drum machines, 12–13, 48, 49, 192, 193, 213, 229
Du Bois, W. E. B., 150

Dublin, 244, 245, 297
Dunham, Katherine, 90n7
During, Simon, 197

East Africa, 205, 207n12, 240, 291, 293; consumers, 178, 183, 293; music awards, 177, 182; musical forms, 187; sound, 195; urban culture, 202
education, 300; about African roots, 89–90; and entertainment, 114–15, 116, 119, 121–22; hip hop skills, teaching of, 60, 64, 65; in Kenya, 181, 184; in Nigeria, 151, 167n5; NGOs and, 117, 122; rap, use of for, 44, 59, 114–19, 121–22, 131, 177, 290, 291, 297, 312n22
educator(s): dismissing rapper's role as, 130; emcees as, 115, 118, 139, 295
Egypt, 187, 291, 293, 301
electronic synthesizer, 12, 31, 44, 48, 54n6, 213, 229, 298; simulating a kora, 87, 298
English: Anglophone, 14, 24n35, 39, 149, 296, 307; fluency in, 14, 33; in Francophone Africa, 107n5; as language of instruction, 112, 293; mixed with Swahili, 175–77; opening the market, 183; as purist, 292; reverting to rapping in, 222, 293; status of, 33–34, 54n11, 66, 293, 294; targeting an audience, 87
Equatorial Guinea, 1
ethnicity, 290, 300, 307, 308; in Côte d'Ivoire, 94, 97–98, 99; diversification, 266–69; fluidity of, 281n14; in France, 8–9; in Ghana, 44, 55n23; in Kenya, 172, 173, 176–77, 180, 184, 185; in Mali, 261–81, 305–306; in Nigeria, 150; private and public, 272; in Senegal, 90n1; in South Africa, 64, 65–66; in Tanzania, 189, 190, 196. *See also* African languages and peoples; pidgin; race

family: connections, 37, 134; dynamics, 138, 140, 156, 165; embarrassment, 45, 297; ensembles, 80, 172; ethnic identity, 271; genealogy, 81; griot, 84, 90n7, 96; heritage, 183; name, 19, 290; networks, 263, 266; privilege, 304; rap group as,

166; African American artists in, 166; American magazines, 153; cinema, 152; emulation of American rappers, 153–55; external influences, 150; favorite American artists, 153; freedom of speech, 159; Ghanaian highlife in, 212; highlife, 155, 156, 166; Igbo highlife, 153; Jimmy Cliff in, 214; juju, 155, 165, 166; lack of opportunity, 151, 158; Music Association, 166; music in a depressed economy, 165–66; oil boom, 152, 153; poor conditions, 151–52; radio, 147, 148, 150, 152, 153; respect for parents, 155–56; television, 147, 150, 152–53. *See also* African languages and peoples (Egba, Igbo, Yoruba); afrobeat; humor; Lagos; lyrics
Nigerians, 23n26; Abdul-Kareem, Eedris, 148, 154, 157; Ade, Sunny, 165, 284; Adzee, Zaki, 154; Allen, Tony, 313n35; Art-Alade, Oludare, 150; Asikpo, Rick, 13; Baba Fryo, 147, 152, 153, 160, 161; Black Reverendz, 154, 157; Blackface, 148, 159; Blackky, 147; Boulaye, Patti, 153; Chimezie, Bright, 153; Coque, Oliver de, 153; Daddy Showkey, 147, 152, 158; Ekundayo, Ronnie, 12; Eldee, 150–51, 153, 157; Emphasis, 13; Falola, Dizzy K, 12; Freestyle, 153–54, 157; I. C. Rock, 13; Joe Black, 152, 153; Junior, 13; Junior and Pretty, 147, 148, 152, 155, 157–60, 161–62, 163–64; Kuti, Fela, 13, 30, 55n15, 108n13, 155, 156–59, 161, 165, 166n5, 218, 284; Kuti, Femi, 167n6, 230; Kuti, Seun, 19, 230; Lagbaja, 157, 167n6; Lanre D., 165; Mams and Hart, 12; Mbaga, Prince Nico, 156; Mouth MC, 13; Okotie, Chris, 153; Oragbon, Godwin, 166n1; Osundare, Niyi, 154–55; Prince 2000, 152, 153; Ras Kimono, 147, 215; The Remedies, 154, 157; Soji, 153; Stonecold, 154; StylePlus, 153; Terry, 13; Tetuila, Tony, 153, 154; Timi Gawi, 12–13; Trybesmen, 147, 148, 157, 164, 165; 2Face, 148, 153; Weird MC, 148; Wilson, Daniel, 147. *See also* JJC (Abdul Bello); United Kingdom (people): Unsung Heroes

nigga, 154, 244, 291
nongovernmental organizations (NGOs), x, 17, 18, 24, 68, 113, 117, 122, 228, 231, 249, 295, 296
Ntarangwi, Mwenda, 190
Nubian, 88, 290
Nzewi, Meki, 265

Okpewho, Isidore, 161
oratory, 45, 47, 161–64, 173; African American, 91n16; alliteration, 42, 246; griot skills, 80–83; in Mali, 136–38; oral history, 79, 81, 96, 185, 291; public speaking, 41, 49; Reggie Rockstone's style, 42; verse recitation, 178. *See also* African American(s): dialect and African rap; flow; griot; indirect; intertextuality; metaphor; poetry; praise; protest; proverbs; rhythm; storytelling
Osibisa, 54n4, 216, 284
Osumare, Halifu, 314n42. *See also* connective marginalities

pan-African, 31, 40, 46, 174, 179, 182, 301; and Positive Black Soul, 83; reggae as, 95
pan-Arabism, 291
pan-ethnic, 288
Paris, 4–9, 134, 267; City Breakers, 6, 12, 14
patronage, 46–47; state, 213
Pennycook, Alastair, 286
Perullo, Alex, 23n32, 292, 293, 297
pidgin, 13, 29; communication across ethnic lines, 161, 294; in Ghana, 35, 37, 40, 47, 51, 218, 222, 295; in Kenya, 180; in Nigeria, 147, 149, 163–64
Planet Hip Hop Festival, 62
poetry, 3, 19, 49, 171, 174, 178–79; hunter's, 129–30. *See also* Senegal: taasu
politics: contesting power through music, 92, 103–104, 107n7, 108n17, 254; and French language, 98; in hiplife, 48, 220; in Kenya, 174–77; Lucius Banda as politician, 252–54; in Malawi, 125n12, 239, 241–43; in Mali, 136; political action, 234, 237, 295, 296; and rap, 24n43, 172; in Senegal, 83; in South Africa, 57, 73. *See also* consciousness; democracy;

ture in Mali, 142, 143; and dance drumming, 307; dependency, 134, 135–36, 140–41, 304; generational conflict, 45–46, 130, 137–38, 219–20, 238, 244, 251, 301; hip hop as voice for, 110, 172, 177, 220, 288; identification with ragga, 110, 116; identification with reggae, 95–96, 116; identity, 111, 114, 121, 141, 148, 150–52, 175–76, 186n11, 199, 205, 206, 251, 270, 290; identity politics, 115–18, 123; international culture, 301; jembe dance preferences, 272; and jembe innovation, 267–68; marginal status, 4, 131, 143, 237; messages, 116–20; protest culture, 133–36, 138, 140, 143; rap mobilizing, 295, 296; speaking out in public, 41, 49, 185. *See also* African languages and peoples: Sheng

Zimbabwe, 22n23, 25n44; guitar-based traditions in, 234; Mapfumo, Thomas, 284; world music artists, 238; Zimbabwe Legit (Akim Ndlovu, Dumisani "Dumi Right" Ndlovu), 22n23, 23n33
zouk, 187, 195
Zulu Nation, 6, 290, 311n19